DRAWING ON ANGER

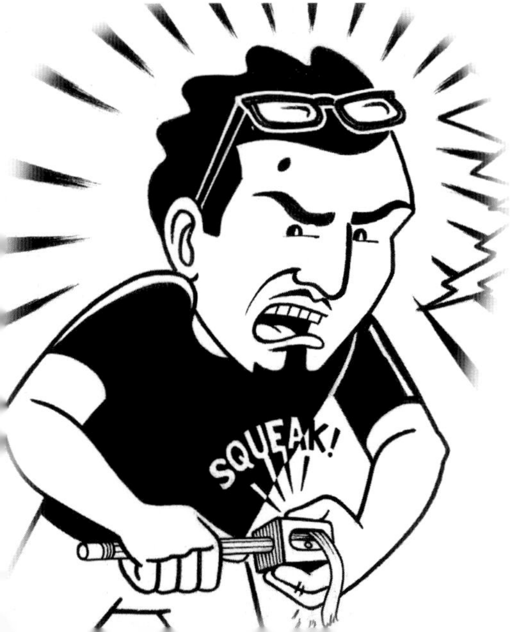
SQUEAK!

DRAWING ON ANGER
Portraits of U.S. Hypocrisy

ERIC J. GARCÍA

Mad Creek Books, an imprint of
The Ohio State University Press
Columbus

Mad Creek Books, an imprint of The Ohio State University Press.

Library of Congress Cataloging-in-Publication Data
Names: García, Eric J., 1977– author.
Title: Drawing on anger : portraits of U.S. hypocrisy / Eric J. García.
Other titles: Latinographix: The Ohio State Latinx comics series.
Description: Columbus : Mad Creek Books, an imprint of The Ohio State University Press, [2018] | Series: Latinographix: The Ohio State Latinx comics series | Includes bibliographical references and index.
Identifiers: LCCN 2018005533 | ISBN 9780814254905 (pbk. ; alk. paper) | ISBN 081425490X (pbk. ; alk. paper)
Subjects: LCSH: United States—Politics and government—21st century—Comic books, strips, etc. | United States—History—21st century—Comic books, strips, etc. | United States—Foreign relations—21st century—Comic books, strips, etc. | Domestic relations—United States—21st century—Comic books, strips, etc.
Classification: LCC PN6727.G3785 D73 2018 | DDC 320.973/0207—dc23
LC record available at https://lccn.loc.gov/2018005533

Cover design by Lindsay Starr
Text design by Eric J. García and Juliet Williams
Type set in Helvetica
Printed by Pacom. PRINTED IN THE REPUBLIC OF KOREA.

∞ The paper used in this publication meets the minimum requirements of the American National Standard for Information Sciences—Permanence of Paper for Printed Library Materials. ANSI Z39.48-1992.

Dedicated to my mom and dad, whose morals shaped my understanding of Justice.
Without their love and support I would not be here.

Thanks to my siblings for blazing the trails and leading the way.

Thanks to all the people who pushed to me to make this book,
especially for their help in editing and correcting my misspelled wurds.

Foreword

by Dr. Frederick Luis Aldama
Arts and Hummanities Distinguished Professor of
English at The Ohio State University

Political Cartooning at Its Unified Best

Unlike those halcyon days of youth, these days, I barely have time for the Funnies. You know, those cartoons that fill the backs of newspapers and on Sundays even get their own multipage inserts. When I do get my hands on a local daily like SF's *Chronicle* or Columbus's *Dispatch,* I scour for those likely to appear Latino penned strips such as by Héctor Cantú and Carlos Castellanos, Baldo. Their Latino-specific cultural settings and punch lines make me smile—even chortle out loud.

But my encounter with print news and their Funnies is less and less. I've found a more satisfying steady diet of Funnies on the Internet. Perhaps Funnies is a misnomer for what I gravitate toward. Yes, they are cartoons. And, yes, some are funny. But mostly they bite hard, opening eyes to our world increasingly shaped by sociopolitical misdeeds. Even Lalo Alcaraz's playful anthropomorphic strips (*Migra Mouse, La Cucaracha,* and *Pocho*) have a sobering kickback.

Eric J. García has been inking cartoons for over a decade. Those that make up *Drawing on Anger* are precisely the kind of one-panel cartoons that I seek out to experience discomfort more than comfort. García's geometric eye for art and sharp ear for dialogue and commentary clear the space for us to perceive, think, and feel anew about the world we inhabit. His skilled strokes of pen and brush along with surgically precise insertion of words and concepts demand that we absorb his panels as a gestaltic whole. And, taken as a unified whole, they transcend the specifics of time and place— sociopolitical referents—in ways that make meaningful today those injustices of yesterday.

García seeks to disturb and discomfort. That is, when he chooses to distill then reconstruct specific building blocks that make up reality, he uses the shaping devices of art and writing in ways that aim to destabilize his viewer-readers. In this way, García's genealogy is less Shultz with his comforting *Peanuts* and more that of the sociopolitical-charged discomfort constructed in the work of French Honoré Daumier. He shares less common ground with Mexican Gabriel Vargas Bernal's *La familia Burrón* and Quino's *Mafalda* than with printmaker, lithographer, and cartoonist José Guadalupe Posada.

Certainly, readers young and old giggle with *Peanuts, La familia Burrón,* and *Mafalda*. Perhaps counterintuitively I also add here Mexican cartoonist Rius. If we look closely at *Los supermachos* and *Los agachados,* for instance, we see that while he offers sociopolitical critiques leveled at the class (caste?) system in Mexico, he does so by focusing on specific portrayals of Mexican cultural traditions. This focus on a shared Mexican cultural heritage allows his work to pass from one generation to the next much more easily than is the case with cartoons that focus on the politics that take place in a definite moment and particular place.

Whether we're talking about a *Peanuts* or a *Baldo,* a *Mafalda* or a *Los supermachos,* these cartoons play it safe in the way they envelop human emotion and behavior within reconstructed cultural traditions. They don't venture into the oft-capricious and violent realm of politics. In this sense, García (and his forefathers) have odds stacked against them: how to distill and then reconstruct an artifact (cartoon) from material reality that is so tied to time and place. He chooses to distill and then reconstruct, for instance, the specifics of the Bush cabinet's acts of genocide in Iraq and to torture innocents, policy that led to femicide along the Mexico-U.S. border, the U.S. complicity in the disappearance and murder of 43 Mexican students, and the passing of inhumane anti-immigration and anti-abortion laws among others. His art creates new networks of meaning between the conquest of the Americas and today's U.S. global imperialism.

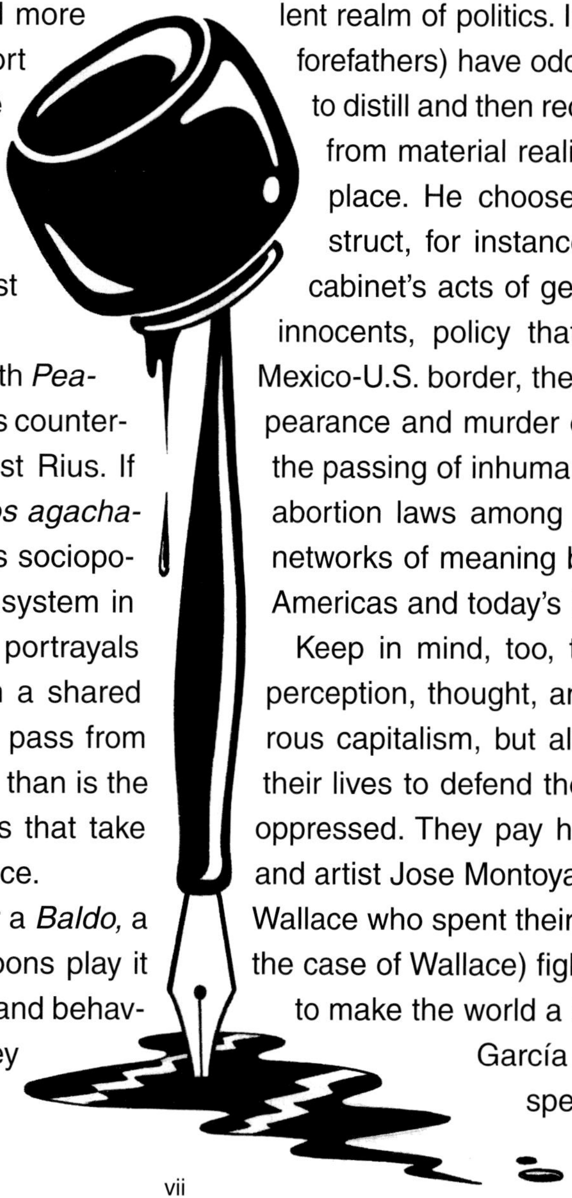

Keep in mind, too, that García makes new our perception, thought, and feeling not only to barbarous capitalism, but also of those that have given their lives to defend the rights of the exploited and oppressed. They pay homage to those like activist and artist Jose Montoya and Black Panther Herman Wallace who spent their lives (and gave their lives in the case of Wallace) fighting with and for the people to make the world a better place.

García chooses to reconstruct very specific sociopolitically charged events that many of my students today likely are too young to recall and that because of the tendency of memory erosion many of us older folks might not recall either. With art that takes as its point of departure a specific historical, social, or political event, the usual order of things is that it has a short shelf life. Political cartoons tend to have a quick expiration date. Once the topical referent is out of mind, the meaning is lost. Yet, there is no such corrosion taking place within García's cartoons. They powerfully discomfort today as much as they did yesterday.

García pulls this off in his unity of the visual with the verbal. There is an organic, global cohesion between the geometric devices used to give shape to the visual elements and the written devices used to voice political issues. As a unified whole, the drawing and the writing leave no doubt about his intentions. We are never kept wondering about what he wants to convey. García's unity of affect achieves holistically and with piercing clarity its goals.

To further clarify the remarkable nature of García's adept ability at creating a unified, gestaltic whole experience in the reader-viewer, let me turn briefly to those cartoons that appear in *The New Yorker*. The dialogue and/or caption are additive, and not a necessary element in the making of the whole. One of my colleagues is constantly trying to win the weekly contest of adding a caption or inventing a dialogue to the art. That is, one can separate the drawing from what you want the drawing to mean or say. This is not possible with García's work, which is through and through a unified, organic whole.

Drawing on Anger is a powerful reminder that in the hands of a wordsmith and visual virtuoso like García it is the careful way he constructs a relationship between the object (cartoon) and the subject (us) that creates discomfort that transcends time and place. García's achievement: his close observation of reality only to break it down and give it new shape through visual and verbal artistic means. This means the skilled deforming and reforming of bodily shapes and facial traits in willfully directed ways that lead to clear-sighted truths about the captains of capitalism that are destroying our world day by day. Paradoxically, then, it is García's deft ability to deform and reform the building blocks of reality that give us a truer representation than say a photograph of the most murderous politicians such as Bush Jr., Cheney, Alberto González, and others.

With *Drawing on Anger,* we see political cartooning at its best. His clean, clear-cut geometrizing of the reconstruction of those sociopolitical building blocks of reality is without fault. His look into political events and ideas is incisive. Together, the clear and distinct drawing and the clear and distinct text form an inseparable organic whole that outlive their immediate circumstances and political referents. In this they offer a springboard to progressive political action that's agile and sturdy enough to stand the test of time.

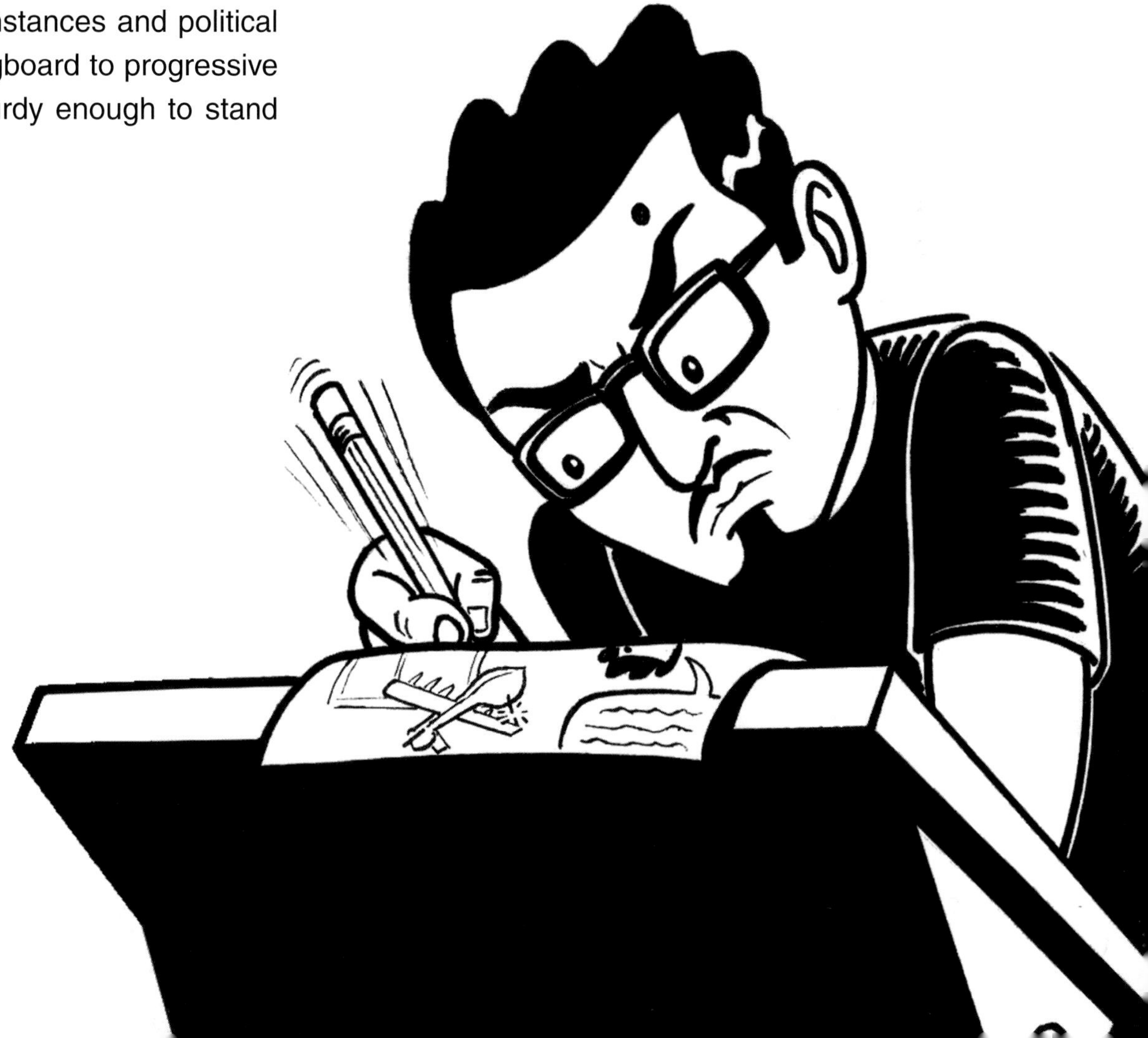

Preface

by Dr. Eloy J. García
Civil Rights Lawyer and Activist

Eric García is a highly respected political cartoon artist seen by many as the Chicano equivalent to the great revolutionary political cartoonists Naji al-Ali or Khalil Bendib. Like al-Ali and Bendib, García's nationally recognized cartoons have struck a unified chord of resistance and defiance to injustice and imperialism. Eric García's cartoons give voice to the often voiceless occupied Chicano community of the United States. García's cartoons are often considered "too hot" for national syndication, but not hateful or debasing in the recent tragic Charlie Hebdo tradition. García's cartoons bite, not out of hatred, but because of their honesty and critical take on reality outside the purviews of the censored press. Taking on all the difficult subjects that most U.S. citizens choose conveniently to ignore, García's cartoons lampoon and highlight current events in relation to: U.S. racism, police brutality, ethnic identity, torture, imperialism, the War on Terrorism, and injustice in general.

Born and raised in Albuquerque's South Valley, García earned his Bachelor's in Fine Arts from the University of New Mexico and Master's of Fine Arts from the School of the Art Institute (SAIC) of Chicago. García has shown in numerous national and international Latin American exhibitions and has continually received many awards, fellowships, and residencies. Known for mixing history and culture with contemporary themes, Eric J. García always tries to create art that is much more than just aesthetics.

Historically political cartoonists have used the image of Uncle Sam as the male representation and Lady Liberty as the female symbol of the United States. Eric García's political cartoons revive these well known historical caricatures to critique and satirize current events as viewed through the eyes of a Chicano artist. García's cartoons openly question the lofty ideals that the United States touts in its public discourse and the sad hypocritical reality. García's cartoons continually portray the "macho" Uncle Sam with his sleeves rolled up and acting as an arrogant and boisterous bully who is intent on getting his way. In García's cartoons, Lady Liberty plays the faithful wife and conscience of Uncle Sam. She represents the "ideal" image of the country, a representation of democracy, freedom, and justice—the conscience of the hot-headed Uncle Sam. Lady Liberty constantly calls out Uncle Sam on his errant ways, prodding and chastising his continuous destructive behavior. This contradictory relationship plays out in many of the cartoons with a supporting cast of other characters.

In García's drawings, we continually see the image of the "Fat Cats" representing the moneyed interest and/or transnational corporations. These "Fat Cats" are usually accomplices of Uncle Sam depicted smoking cigars, sporting black ties and top hats as they count the money or savor their profits. The blindfolded Lady Justice of Greco/Roman mythology—sword and scale in hand—appears as the representative of fair and equal treatment under the law. Unfortunately, she is usually being mistreated by Uncle Sam, and rescued by Lady Liberty. Police and the Justice officials are also given a historical representation that goes as far back as the sixteenth century as a symbol of general disdain: the Pig. The "Pigs" are usually portrayed as harassing, beating up, or misapplying justice—an interesting interpretation of how a young Chicano artist views authority on the streets of Albuquerque or Chicago. The Republicans and Democrats are symbolized by the traditional fat elephant and beleaguered donkey respectively. Local and national political figures are also caricatured, including Arizona and New Mexico governors to George W. Bush, Barrack Obama, and their cabinet officials, all of which are also routinely skewered. García also takes heartfelt time to recognize prominent individuals who have lived exemplary lives in the service of others, believing that these honorable individuals did not receive the public acknowledgment they deserve for a lifetime of service.

The following cartoons are just a sampling of the thousands done by García, arranged in a chronological order from 2004 to 2016. Paging through the cartoons, one absorbs a different critical Chicano perspective of uncensored world events. García offers an honest, humorous perspective that dares to speak the truth to power. His contribution in spurring discussion and critical thought is significant, and something much needed in today's complicated world.

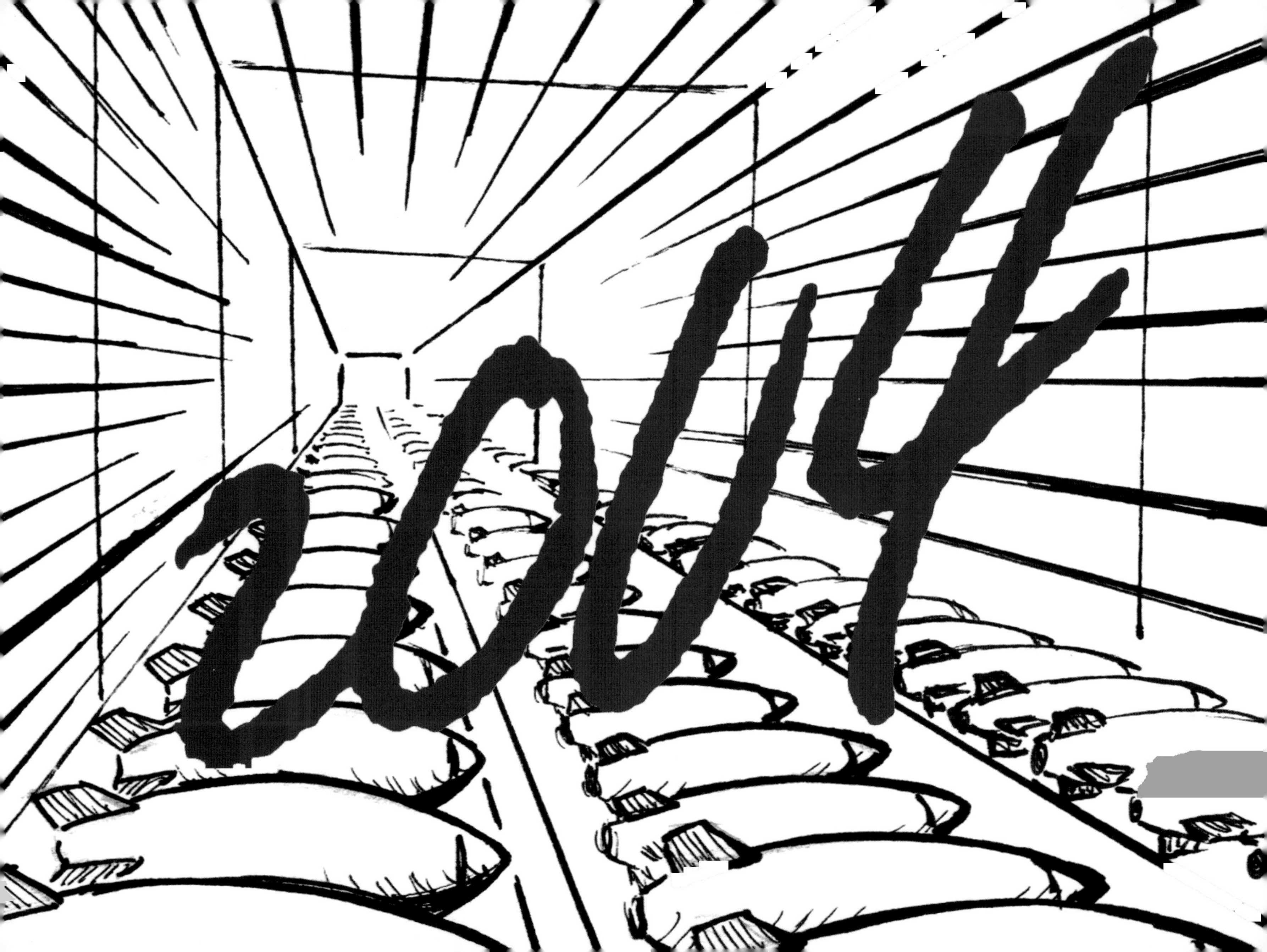
2014

2004

Latinos made strides that year, gaining powerful positions within the ranks of the empire of the United States. George W. Bush was controversially reelected, and along with his cabinet of cronies, they continued their reign of terror across the Middle East. Secretary of Defense Donald Rumsfeld justified torture techniques, and the abuse at the U.S. military prison Abu Ghraib destroyed any credibility the U.S. ever had. But legalized terror was not limited to foreigners, as "itchy-trigger-finger" syndrome was being diagnosed as early as this year.

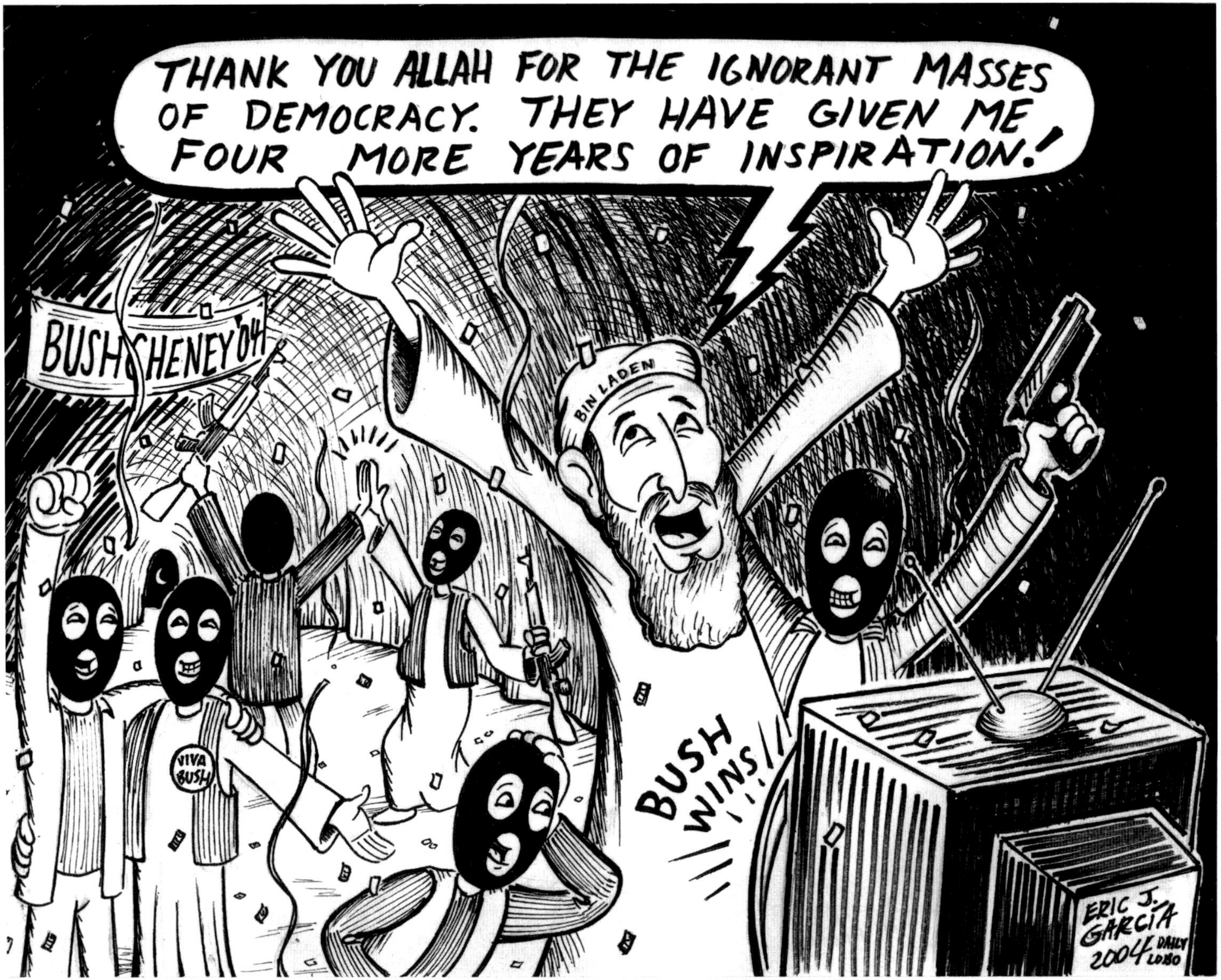
THANK YOU ALLAH FOR THE IGNORANT MASSES OF DEMOCRACY. THEY HAVE GIVEN ME FOUR MORE YEARS OF INSPIRATION!
BUSH CHENEY '04
BIN LADEN
VIVA BUSH
BUSH WINS!!!
ERIC J. GARCIA 2004 DAILY LOBO

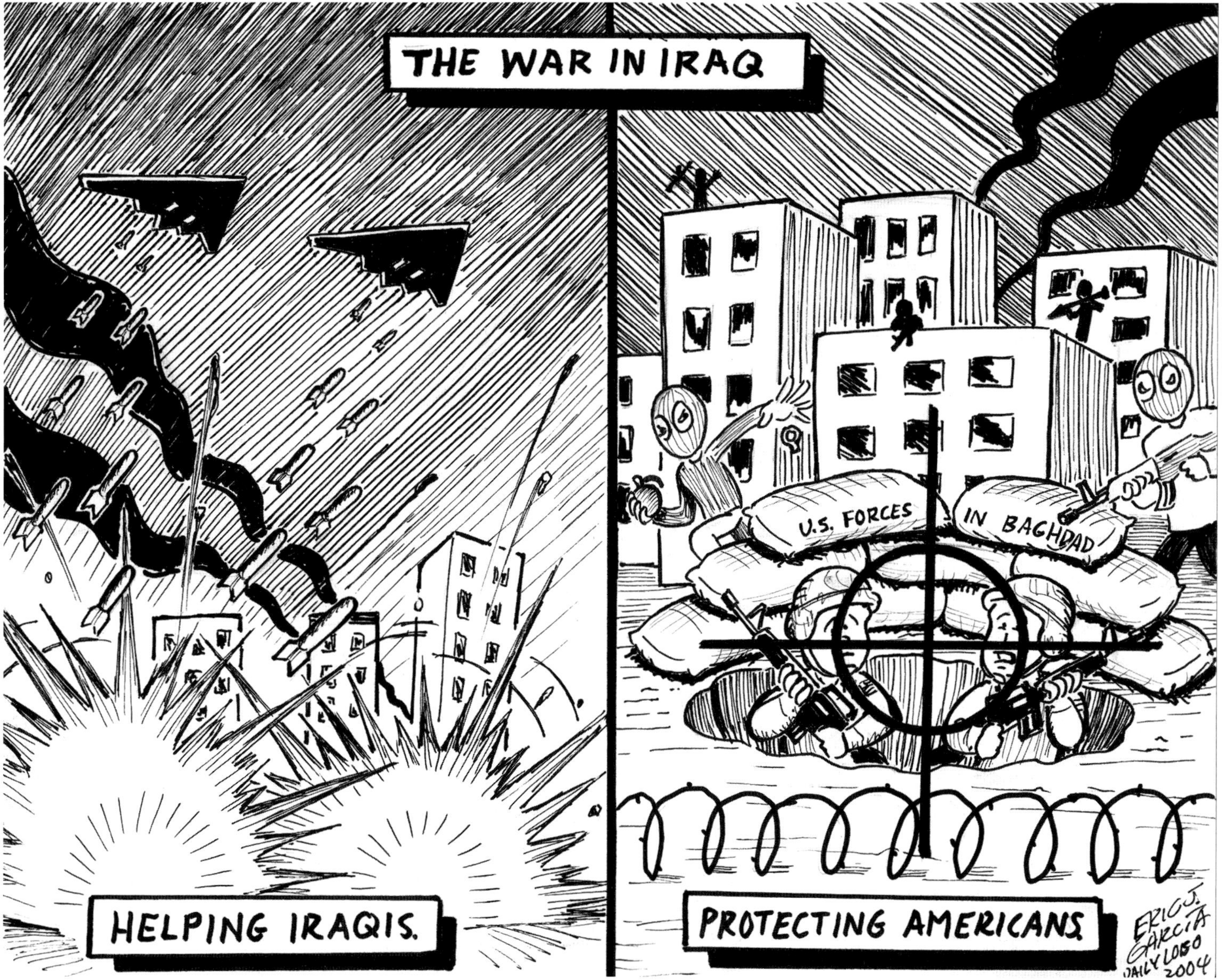
THE WAR IN IRAQ
HELPING IRAQIS.
U.S. FORCES
IN BAGHDAD
PROTECTING AMERICANS.
ERIC J. GARCIA
DAILY LOBO
2004

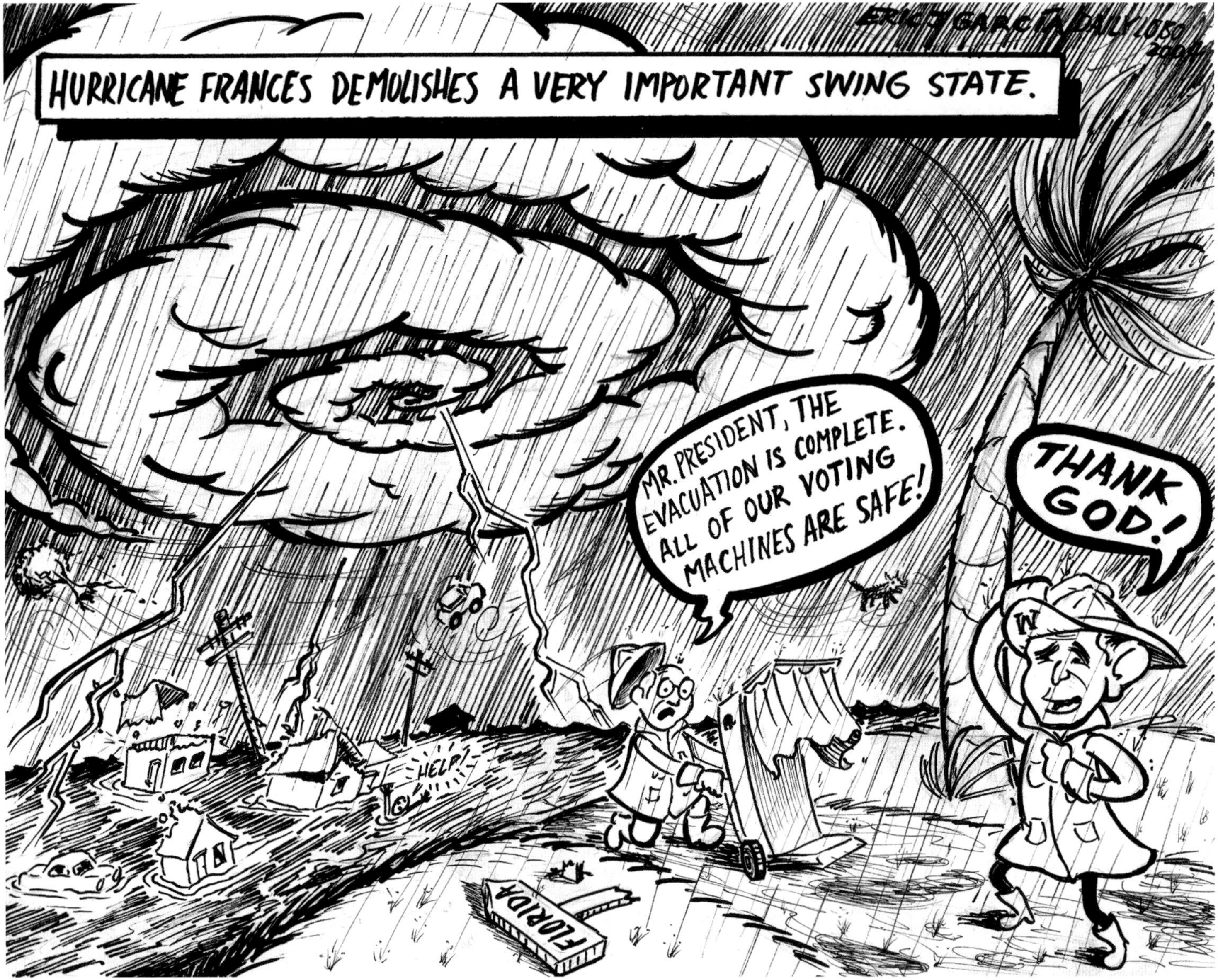
ERIC J GARCIA DAILY LOBO 2004
HURRICANE FRANCES DEMOLISHES A VERY IMPORTANT SWING STATE.
HELP!
MR. PRESIDENT, THE EVACUATION IS COMPLETE. ALL OF OUR VOTING MACHINES ARE SAFE!
THANK GOD!
W
FLORIDA

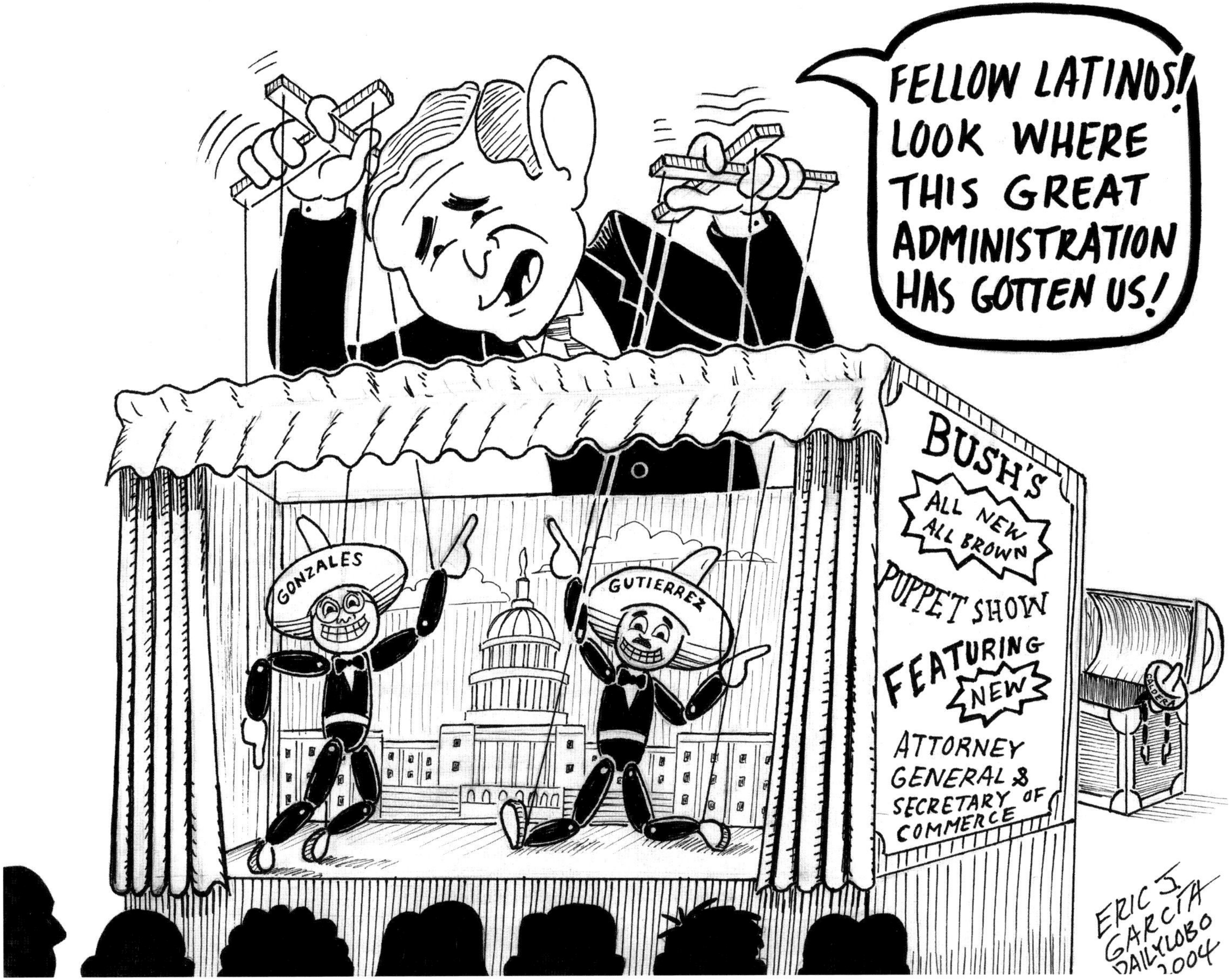
FELLOW LATINOS! LOOK WHERE THIS GREAT ADMINISTRATION HAS GOTTEN US!
BUSH'S
ALL NEW ALL BROWN
PUPPET SHOW
FEATURING
NEW
ATTORNEY GENERAL & SECRETARY OF COMMERCE
GONZALES
GUTIERREZ
CALDERA
ERIC J. GARCIA
DAILY LOBO
2004

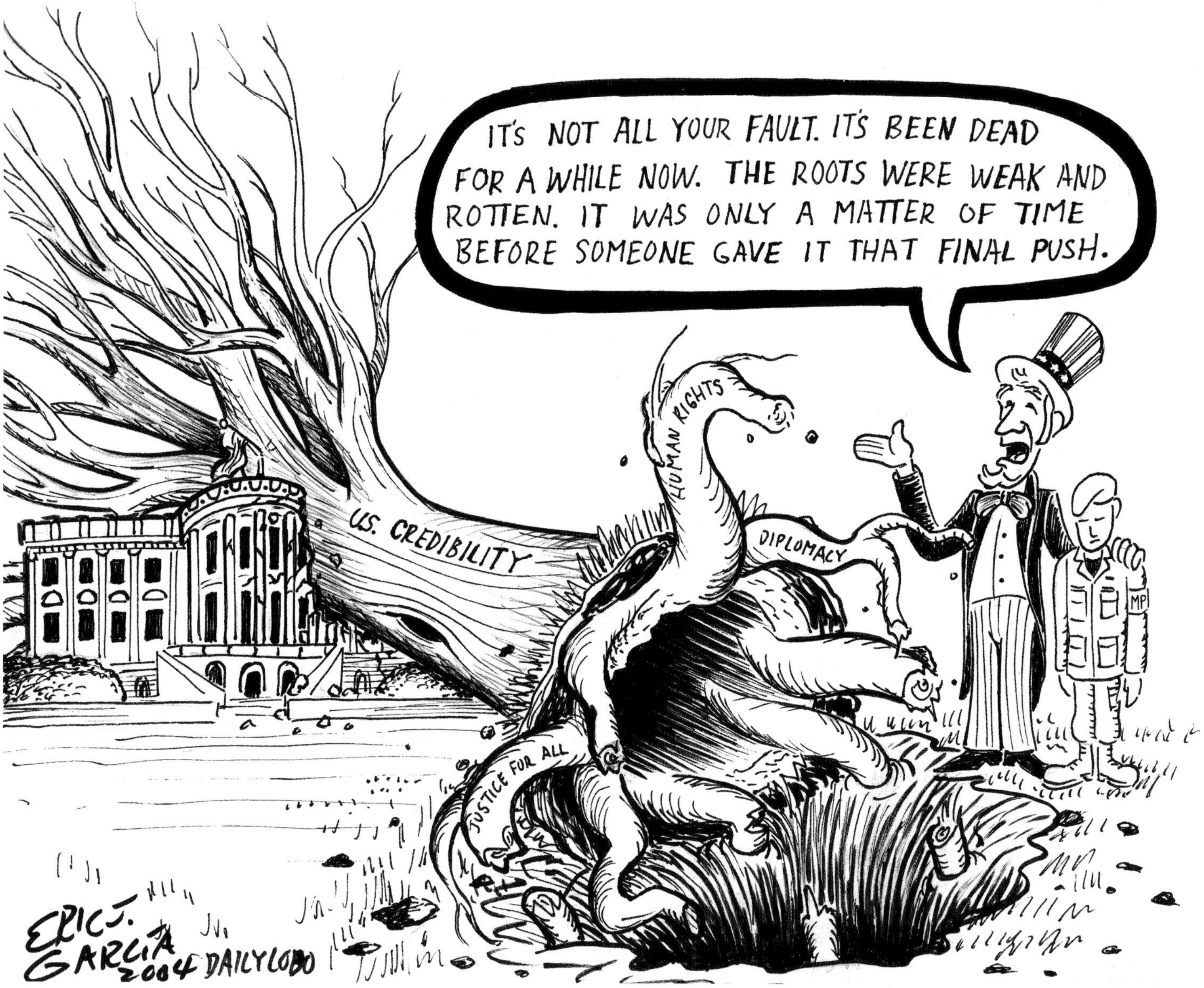
IT'S NOT ALL YOUR FAULT. IT'S BEEN DEAD FOR A WHILE NOW. THE ROOTS WERE WEAK AND ROTTEN. IT WAS ONLY A MATTER OF TIME BEFORE SOMEONE GAVE IT THAT FINAL PUSH.
U.S. CREDIBILITY
HUMAN RIGHTS
DIPLOMACY
JUSTICE FOR ALL
MP
ERIC J. GARCIA 2004 DAILY LOBO

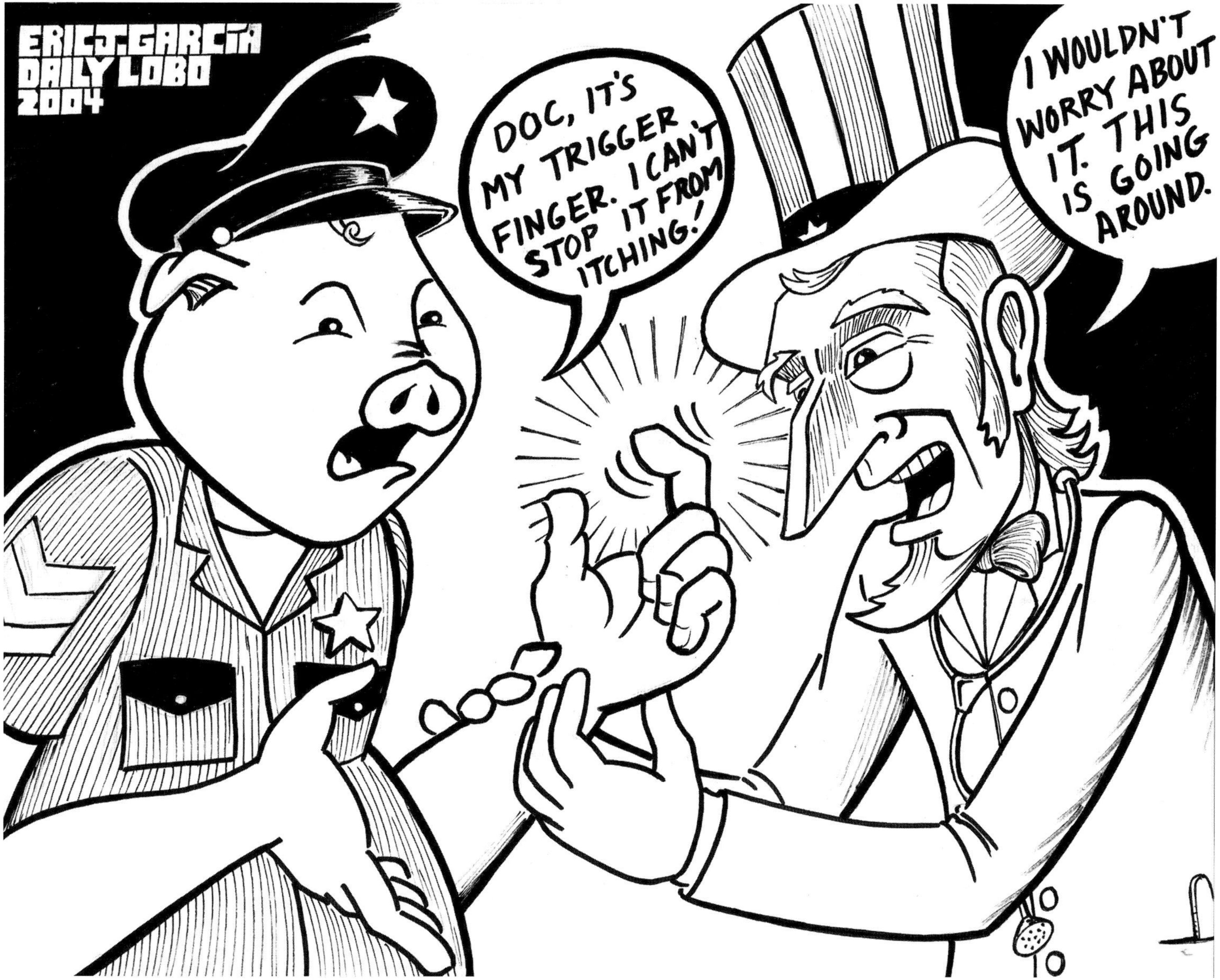
ERIC J. GARCIA
DAILY LOBO
2004
DOC, IT'S MY TRIGGER FINGER. I CAN'T STOP IT FROM ITCHING!
I WOULDN'T WORRY ABOUT IT. THIS IS GOING AROUND.

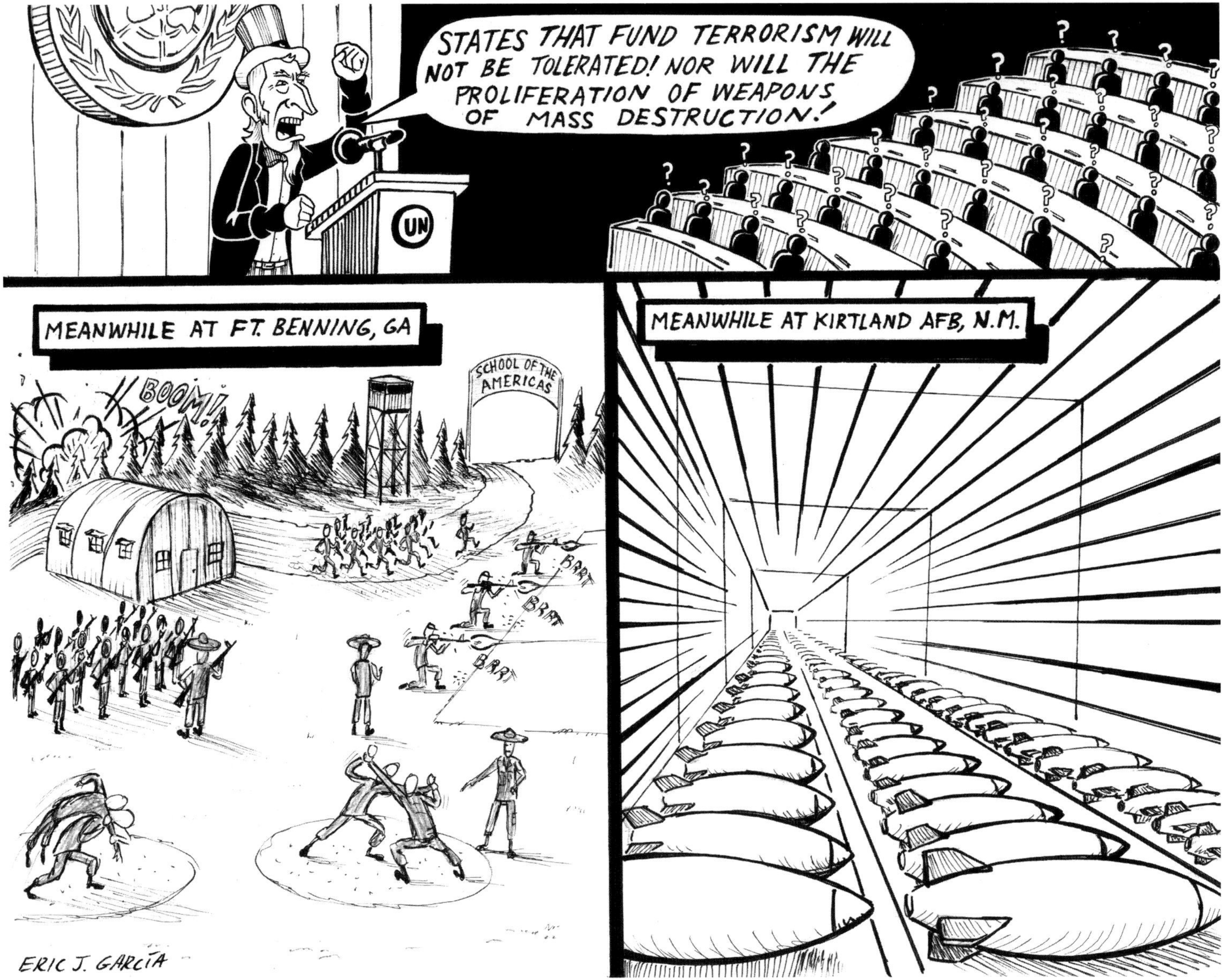

STATES THAT FUND TERRORISM WILL NOT BE TOLERATED! NOR WILL THE PROLIFERATION OF WEAPONS OF MASS DESTRUCTION!
UN
MEANWHILE AT FT. BENNING, GA
BOOM!
SCHOOL OF THE AMERICAS
BRRT
BRRT
BRRT
BRRT
MEANWHILE AT KIRTLAND AFB, N.M.
ERIC J. GARCÍA

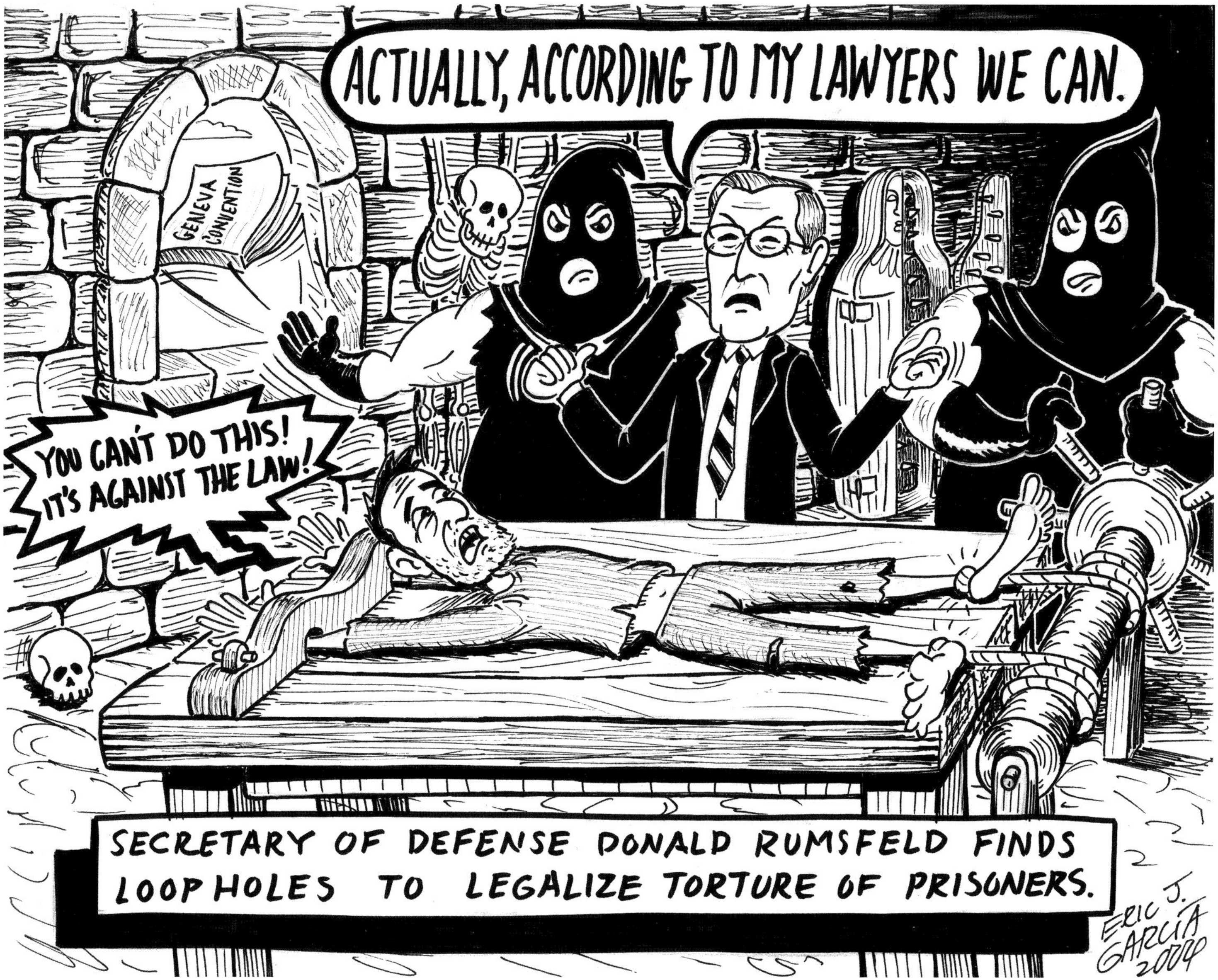
GENEVA CONVENTION
ACTUALLY, ACCORDING TO MY LAWYERS WE CAN.
YOU CAN'T DO THIS! IT'S AGAINST THE LAW!
SECRETARY OF DEFENSE DONALD RUMSFELD FINDS LOOPHOLES TO LEGALIZE TORTURE OF PRISONERS.
ERIC J. GARCIA 2004

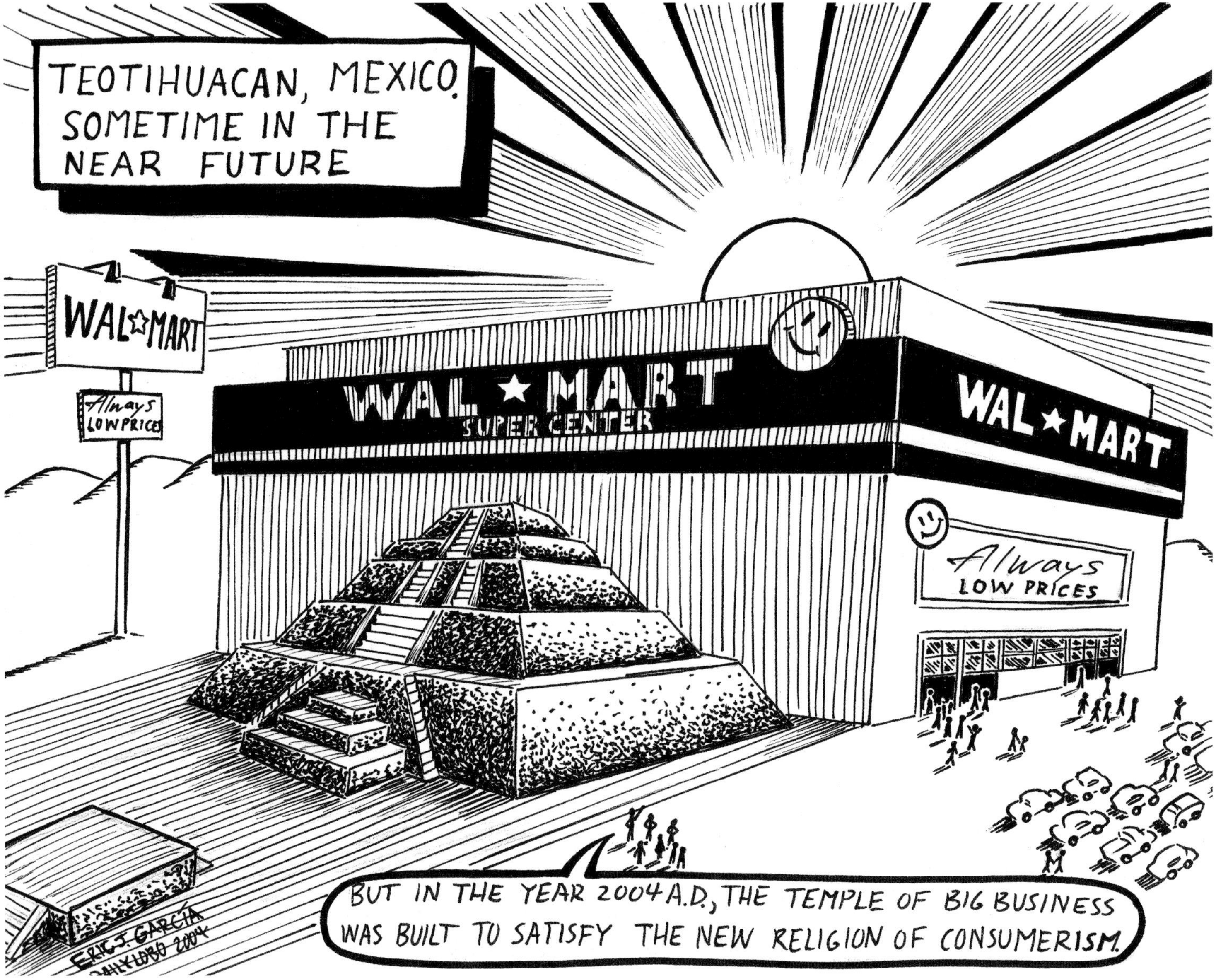
TEOTIHUACAN, MEXICO. SOMETIME IN THE NEAR FUTURE
WAL★MART
Always LOW PRICES
WAL★MART SUPER CENTER
WAL★MART
Always LOW PRICES
BUT IN THE YEAR 2004 A.D., THE TEMPLE OF BIG BUSINESS WAS BUILT TO SATISFY THE NEW RELIGION OF CONSUMERISM.
ERIC J. GARCIA DAILY LOBO 2004

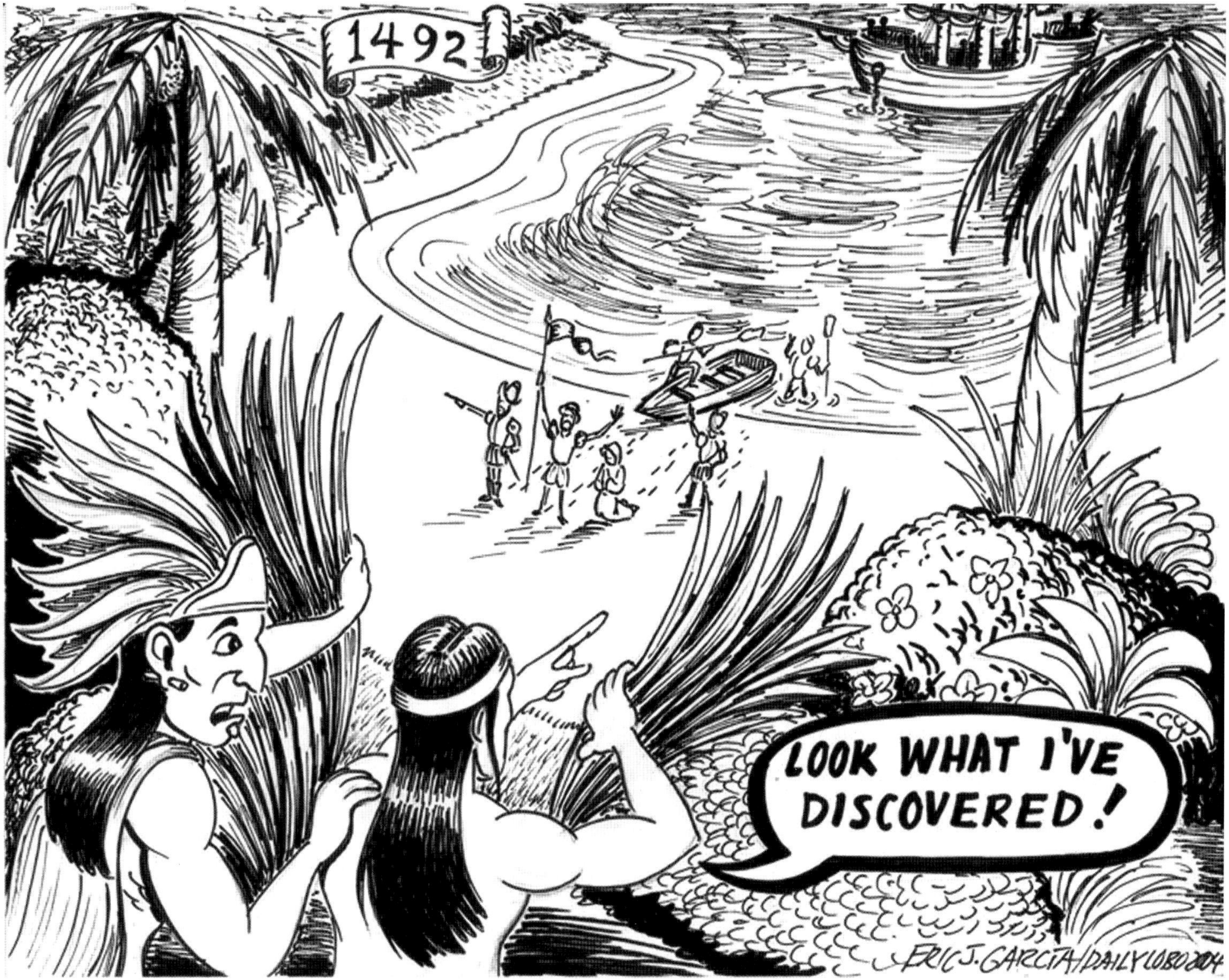
1492
LOOK WHAT I'VE DISCOVERED!
ERIC J. GARCIA/DAILY LOBO 2004

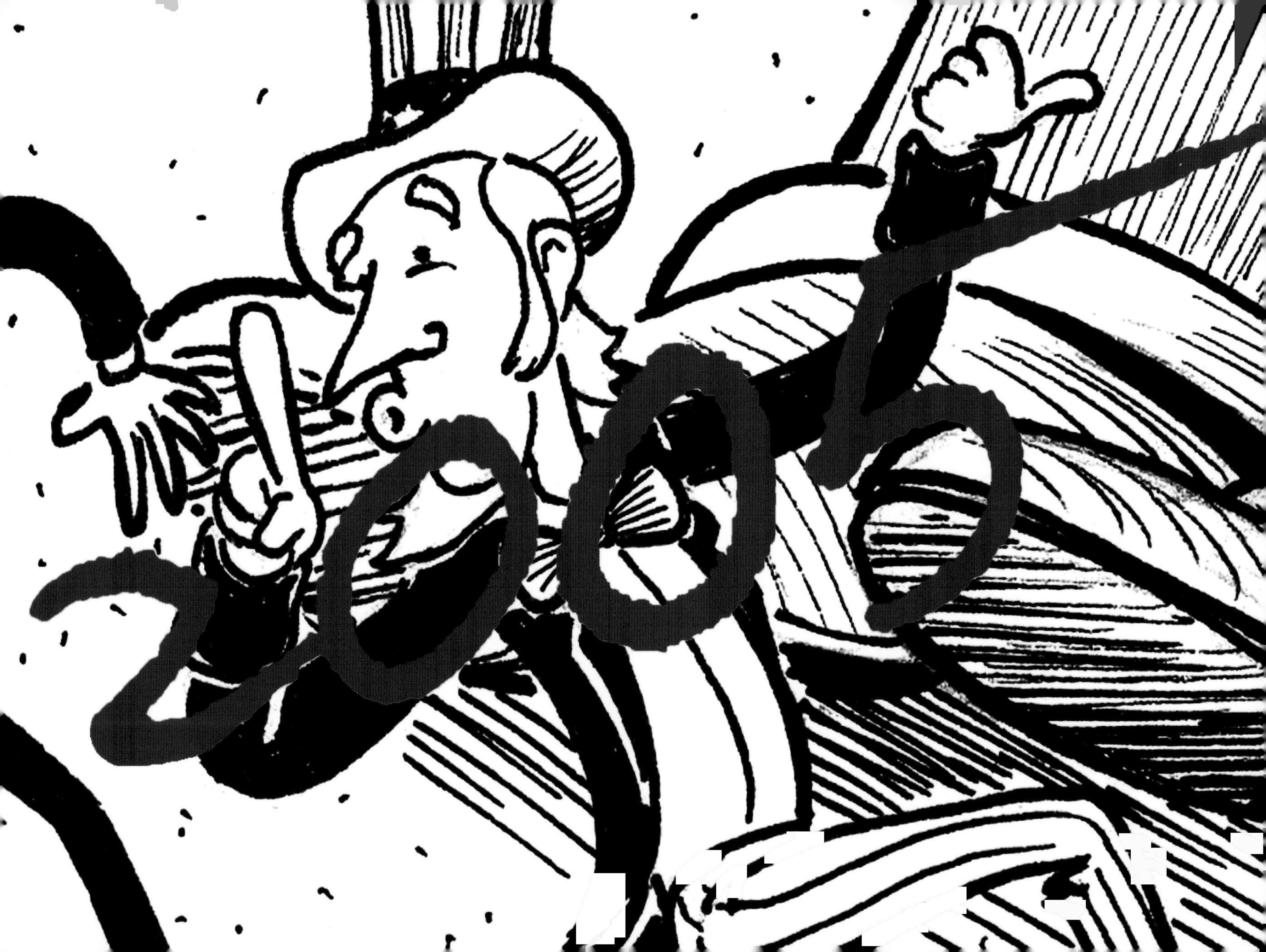

2005

Three years into the invasion of Iraq, and the U.S. was still on the hunt for those weapons of mass destruction. Luckily for George W. Bush, Hurricane Katrina distracted the public from one disaster to another. The 9/11 terrorist attacks had become an excuse to conjure up fear about the Mexican/U.S. border being a gateway for terrorists. White supremacists capitalized on that hysteria to justify their racist manhunts for undocumented immigrants. Meanwhile, south of the border the real terror continued with hundreds of women mysteriously found dead in the Chihuahuan desert.

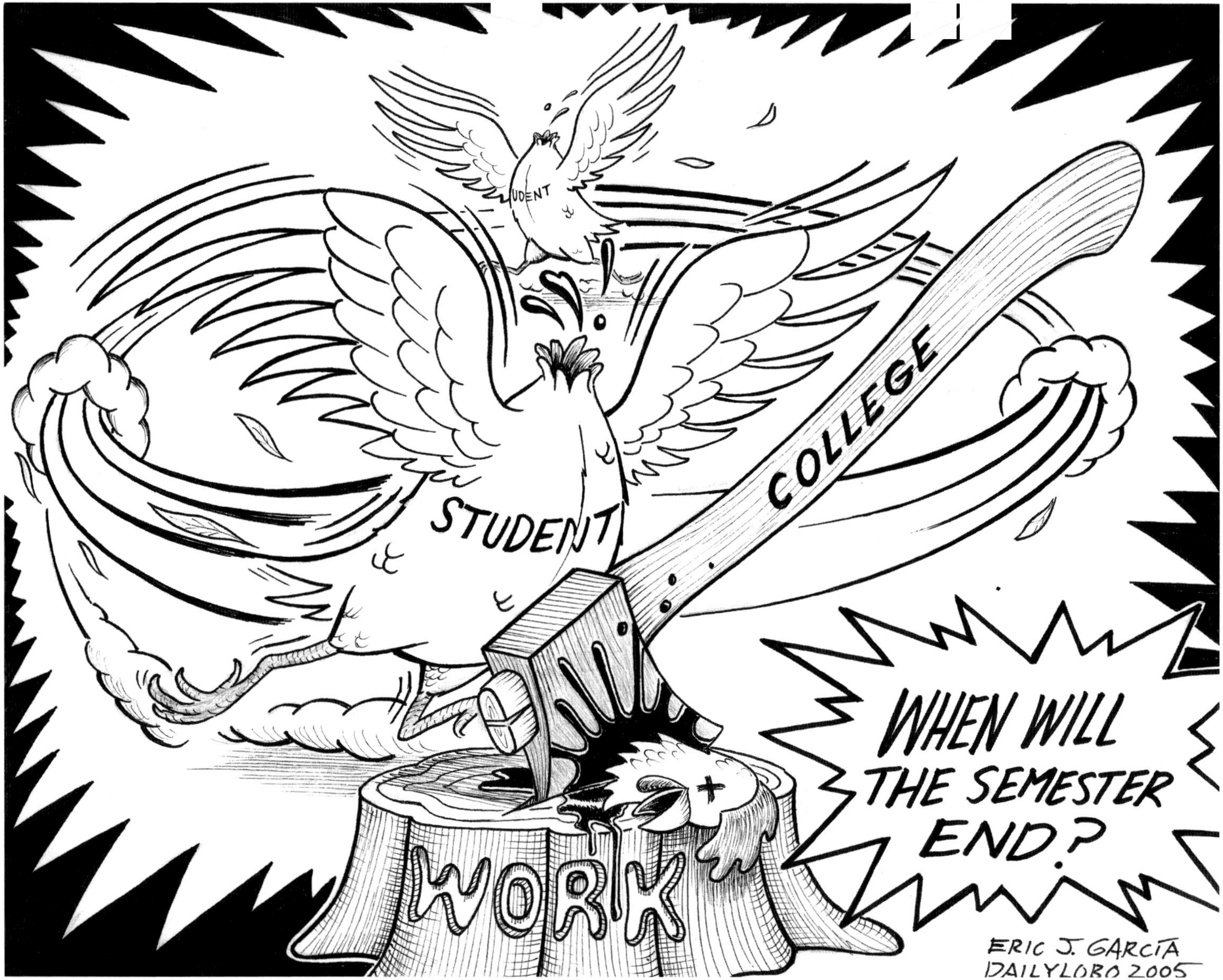

UDENT
STUDENT
COLLEGE
WORK
WHEN WILL THE SEMESTER END?
ERIC J. GARCIA
DAILYLOBO 2005

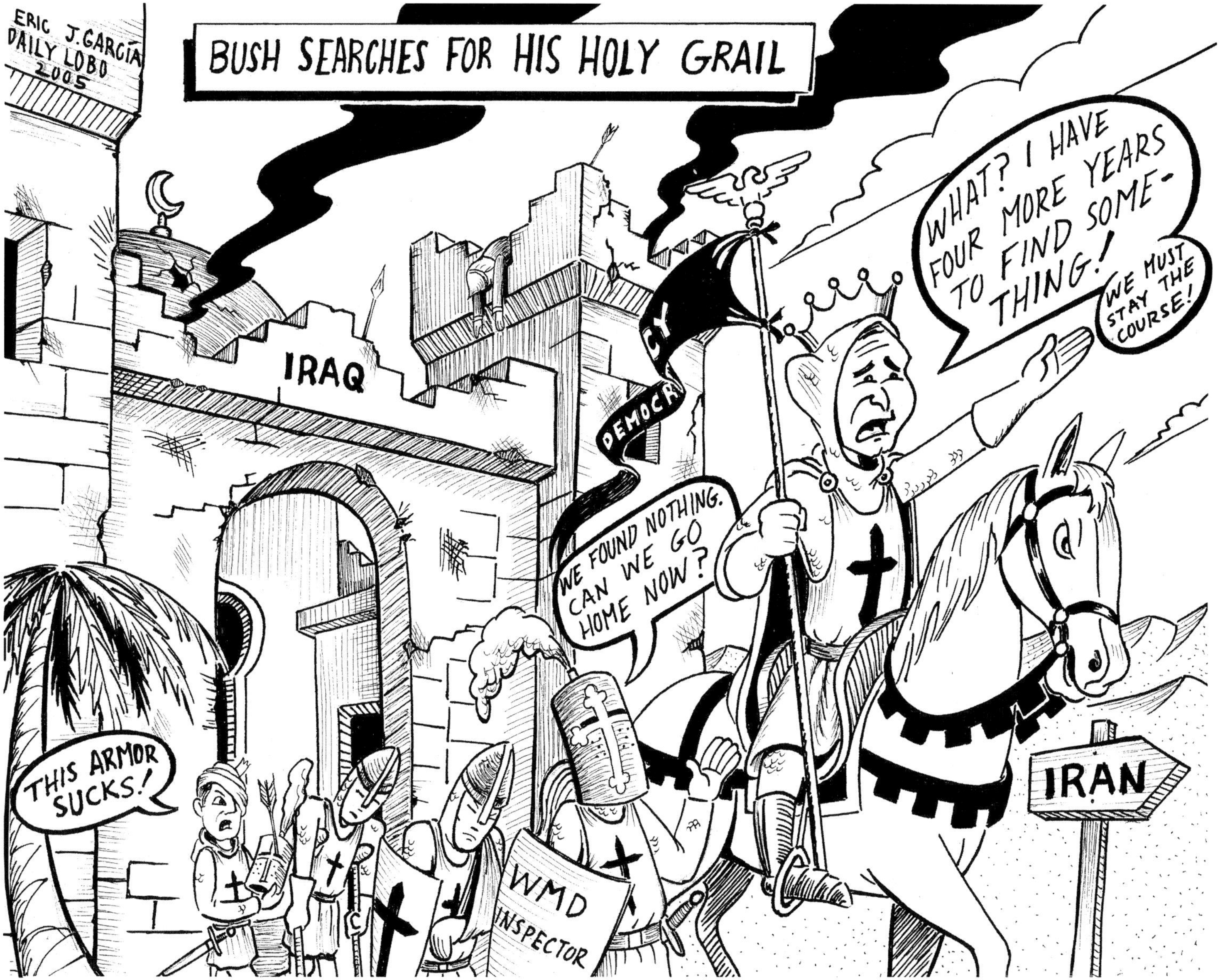
ERIC J. GARCÍA DAILY LOBO 2005
BUSH SEARCHES FOR HIS HOLY GRAIL
IRAQ
DEMOCRACY
WHAT? I HAVE FOUR MORE YEARS TO FIND SOME-THING!
WE MUST STAY THE COURSE!
WE FOUND NOTHING. CAN WE GO HOME NOW?
THIS ARMOR SUCKS!
WMD INSPECTOR
IRAN

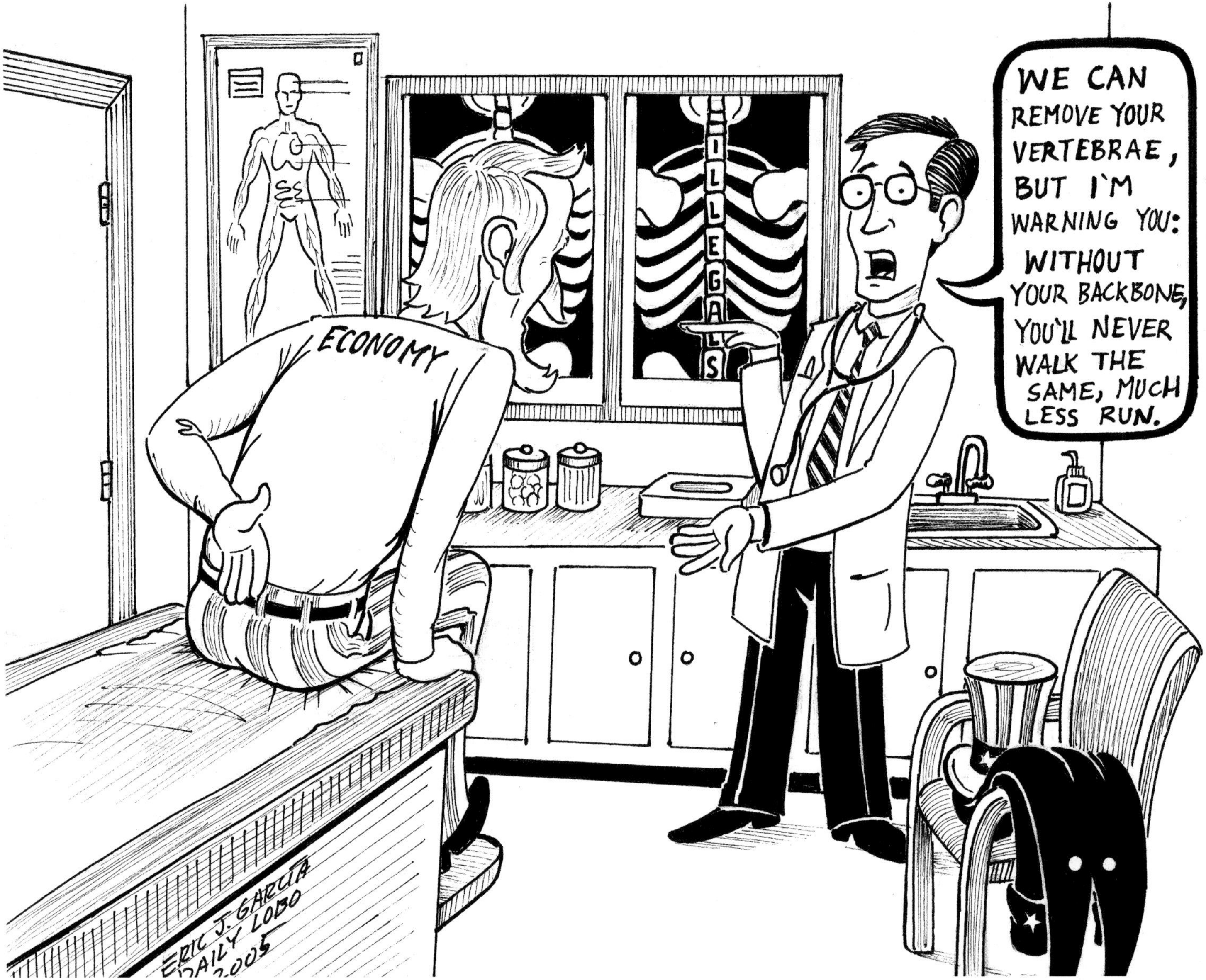
ECONOMY
ILLEGALS
WE CAN REMOVE YOUR VERTEBRAE, BUT I'M WARNING YOU: WITHOUT YOUR BACKBONE, YOU'LL NEVER WALK THE SAME, MUCH LESS RUN.
ERIC J. GARCIA DAILY LOBO 2005

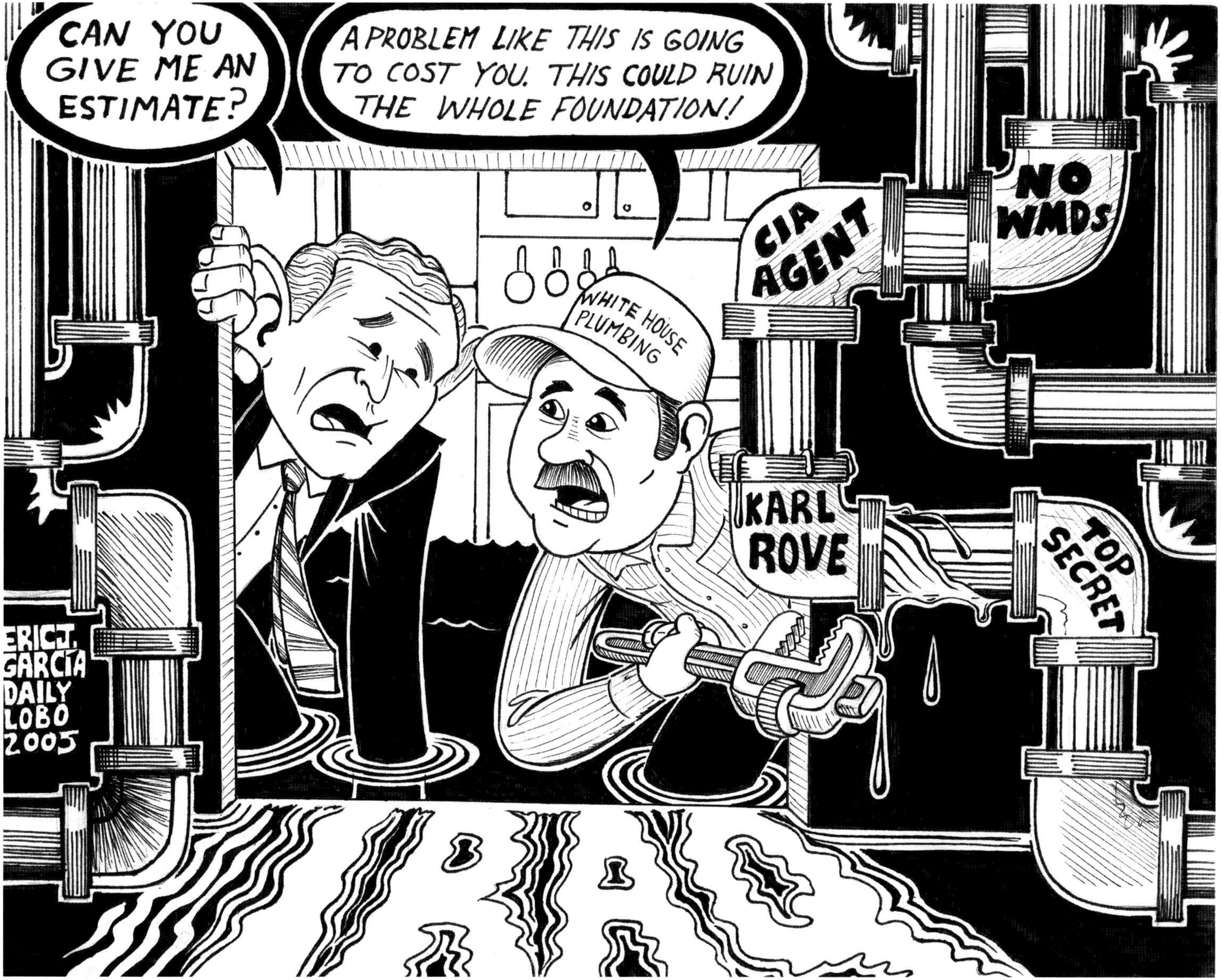
CAN YOU GIVE ME AN ESTIMATE?
A PROBLEM LIKE THIS IS GOING TO COST YOU. THIS COULD RUIN THE WHOLE FOUNDATION!
WHITE HOUSE PLUMBING
CIA AGENT
NO WMDS
KARL ROVE
TOP SECRET
ERIC J. GARCIA DAILY LOBO 2005

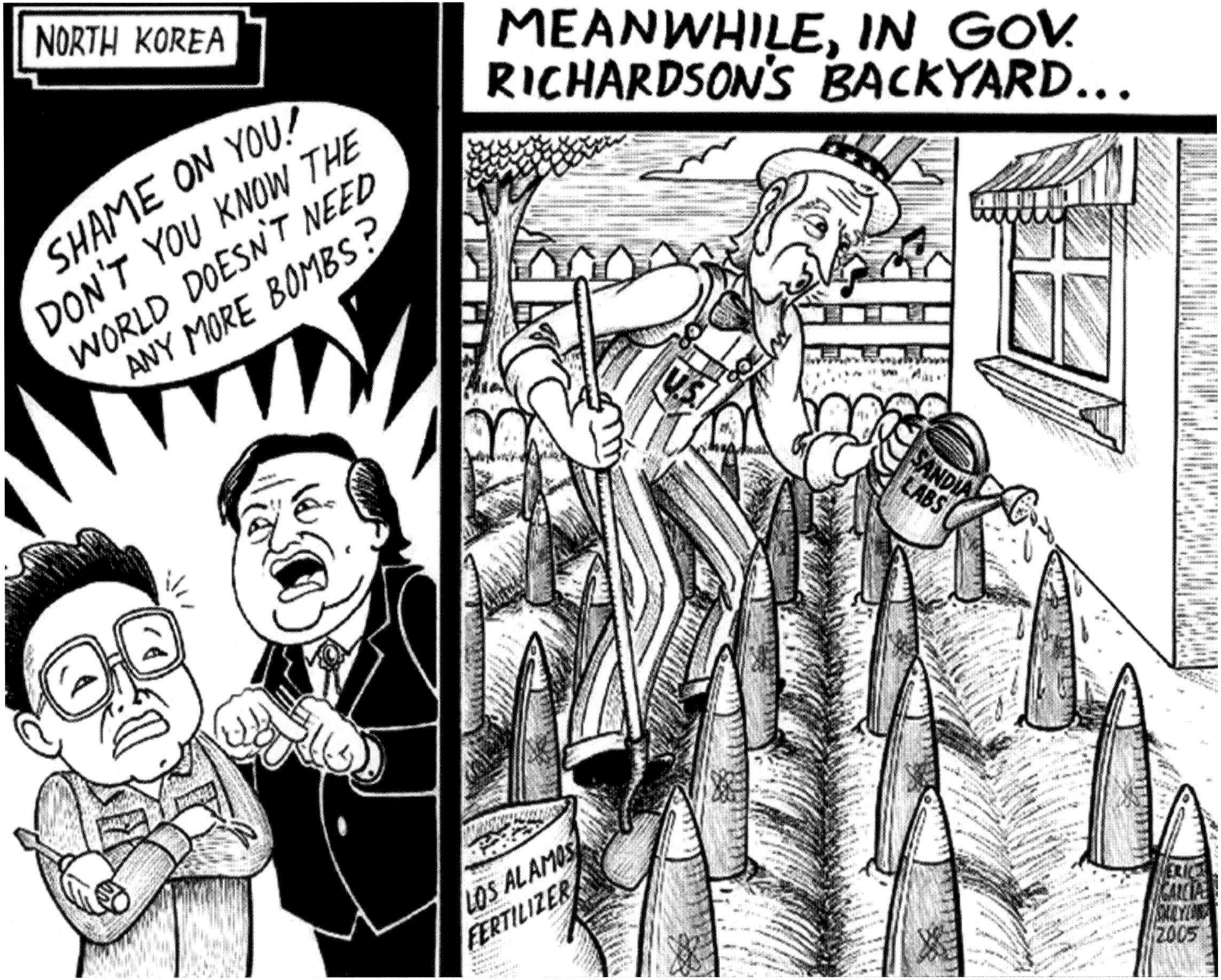
NORTH KOREA
SHAME ON YOU! DON'T YOU KNOW THE WORLD DOESN'T NEED ANY MORE BOMBS?
MEANWHILE, IN GOV. RICHARDSON'S BACKYARD...
U.S.
SANDIA LABS
LOS ALAMOS FERTILIZER

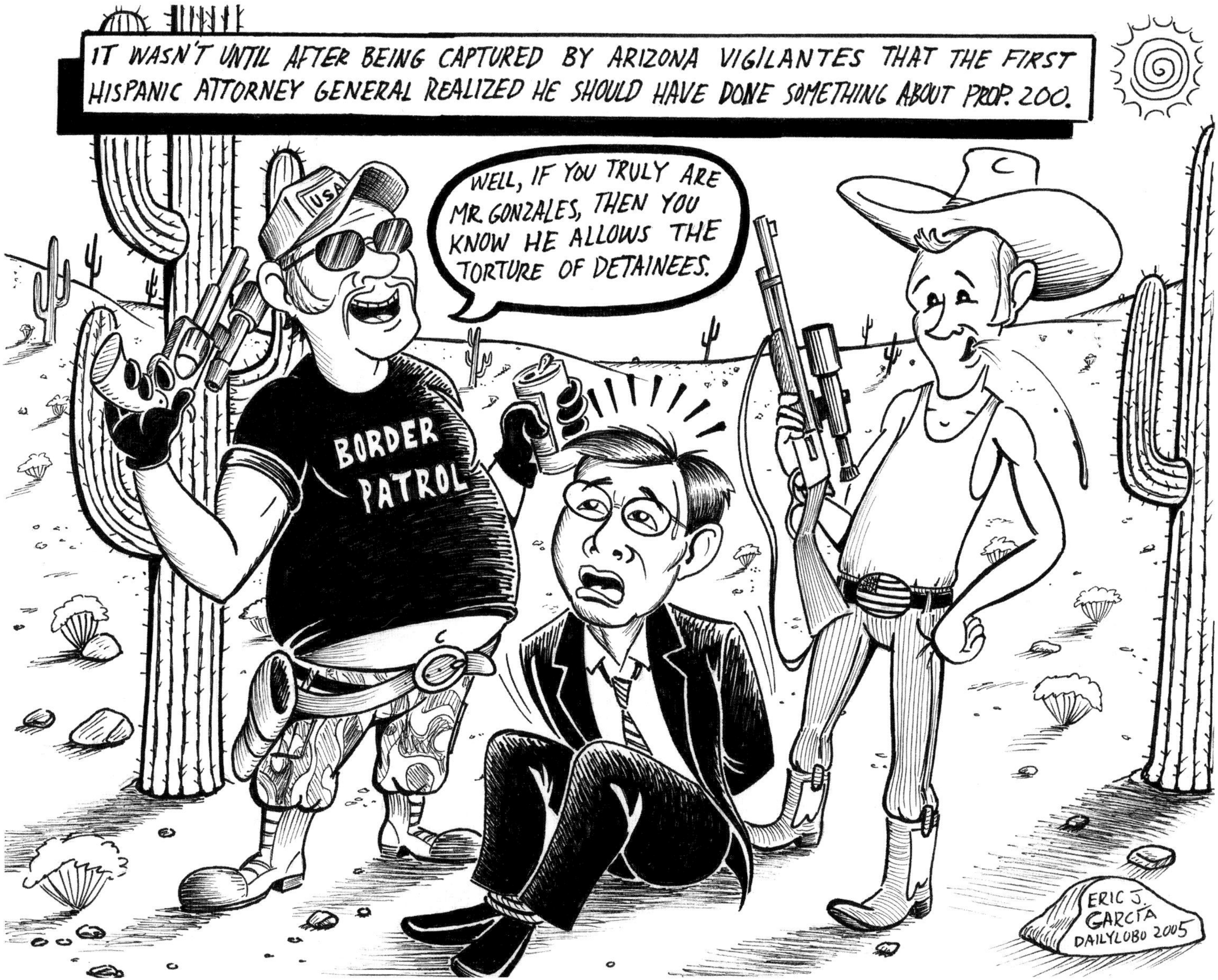
IT WASN'T UNTIL AFTER BEING CAPTURED BY ARIZONA VIGILANTES THAT THE FIRST HISPANIC ATTORNEY GENERAL REALIZED HE SHOULD HAVE DONE SOMETHING ABOUT PROP. 200.
WELL, IF YOU TRULY ARE MR. GONZALES, THEN YOU KNOW HE ALLOWS THE TORTURE OF DETAINEES.
USA
BORDER PATROL
ERIC J. GARCIA DAILYLOBO 2005

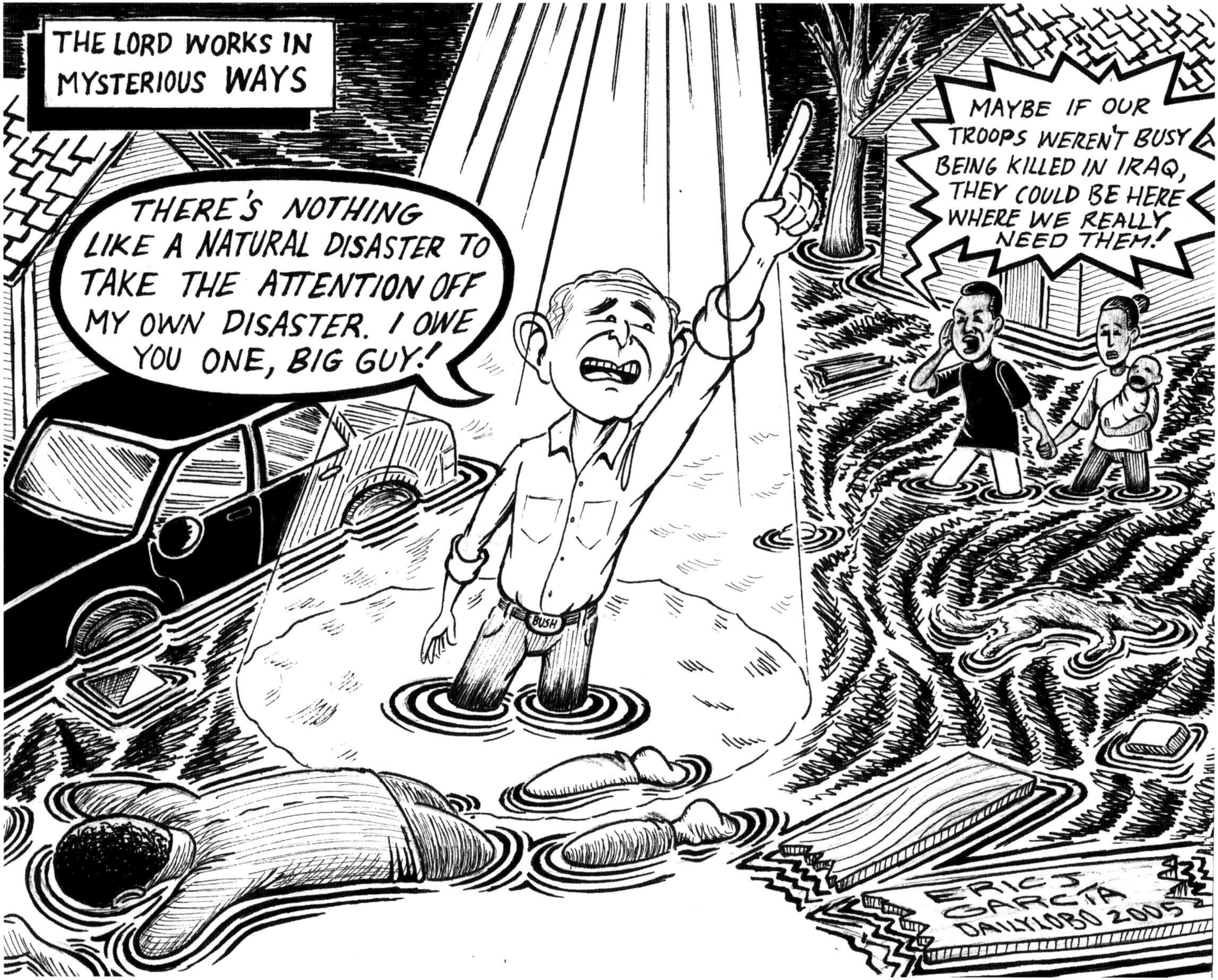
THE LORD WORKS IN MYSTERIOUS WAYS
THERE'S NOTHING LIKE A NATURAL DISASTER TO TAKE THE ATTENTION OFF MY OWN DISASTER. I OWE YOU ONE, BIG GUY!
MAYBE IF OUR TROOPS WEREN'T BUSY BEING KILLED IN IRAQ, THEY COULD BE HERE WHERE WE REALLY NEED THEM!
BUSH
ERIC J GARCIA DAILYLOBO 2005

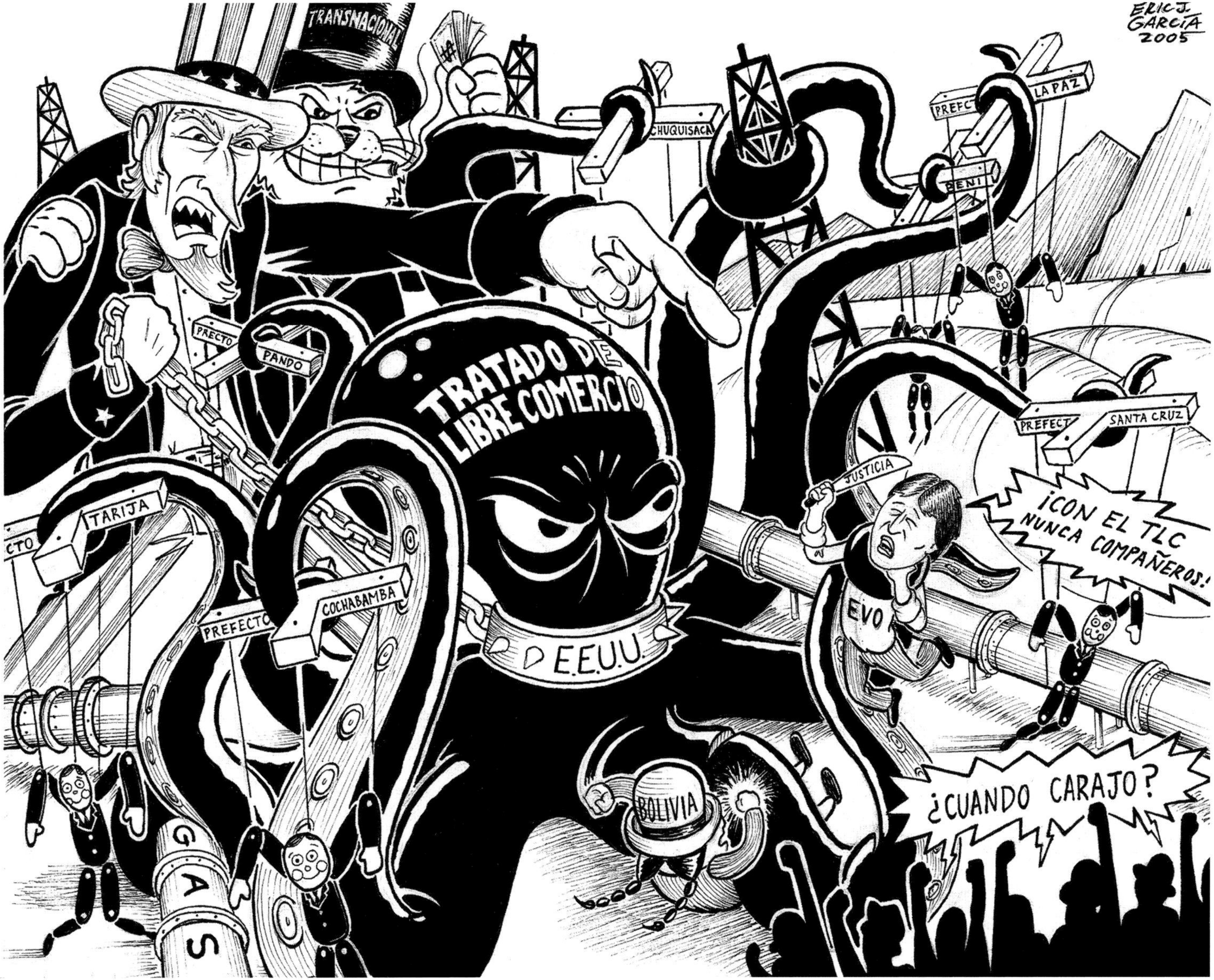
ERIC J. GARCÍA 2005
TRANSNACIONAL
CHUQUISACA
PREFECT
LA PAZ
BENI
PRECTO
PANDO
TRATADO DE LIBRE COMERCIO
PREFECT
SANTA CRUZ
JUSTICIA
TARIJA
CTO
¡CON EL TLC NUNCA COMPAÑEROS!
PREFECTO
COCHABAMBA
E.E.U.U.
EVO
BOLIVIA
¿CUANDO CARAJO?
GAS

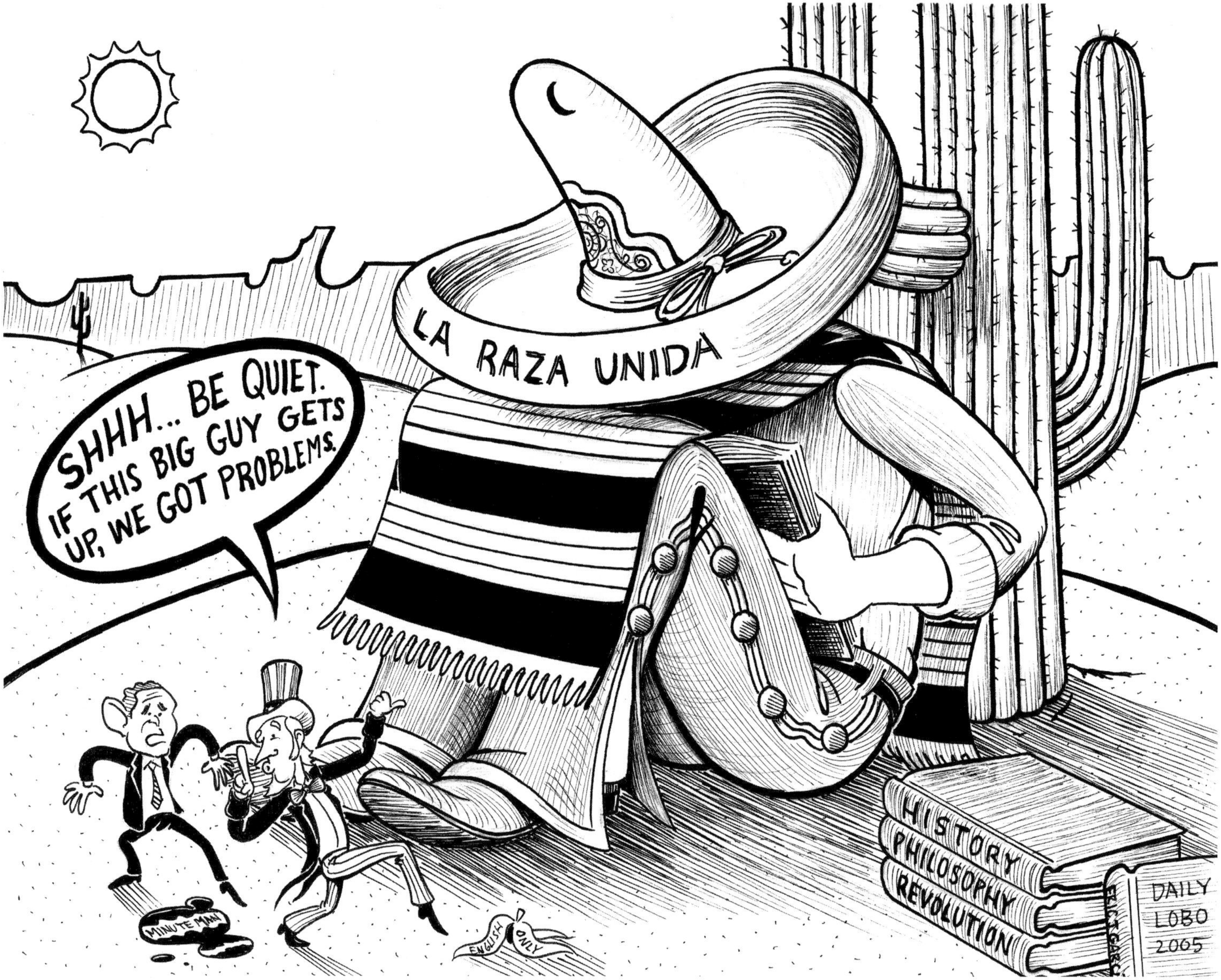
LA RAZA UNIDA
SHHH... BE QUIET. IF THIS BIG GUY GETS UP, WE GOT PROBLEMS.
MINUTE MAN
ENGLISH ONLY
HISTORY
PHILOSOPHY
REVOLUTION
DAILY LOBO 2005

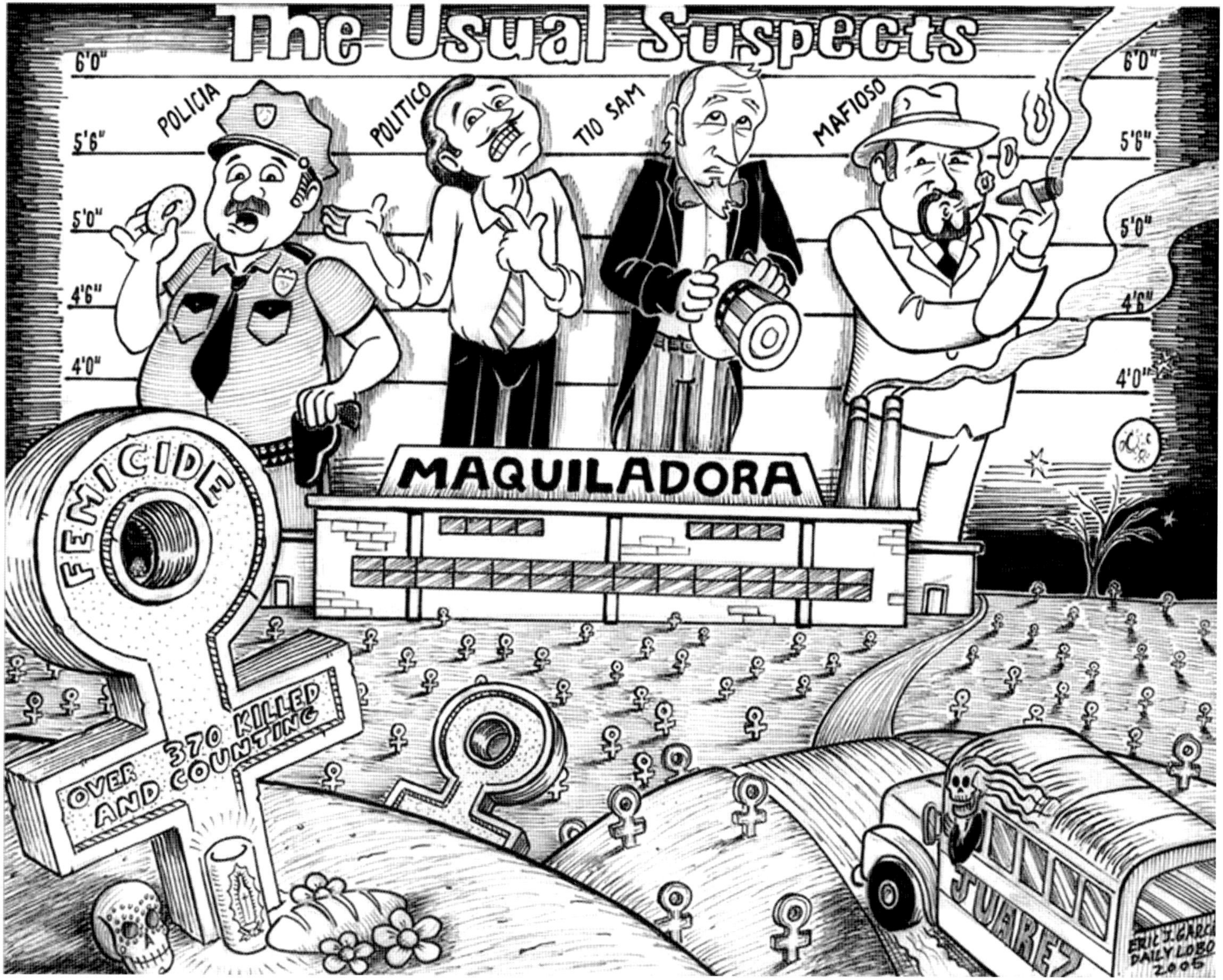
The Usual Suspects
6'0"
5'6"
5'0"
4'6"
4'0"
POLICIA
POLITICO
TIO SAM
MAFIOSO
MAQUILADORA
FEMICIDE
OVER 370 KILLED AND COUNTING
JUAREZ
ERIC J. GARCIA DAILY LOBO 2005

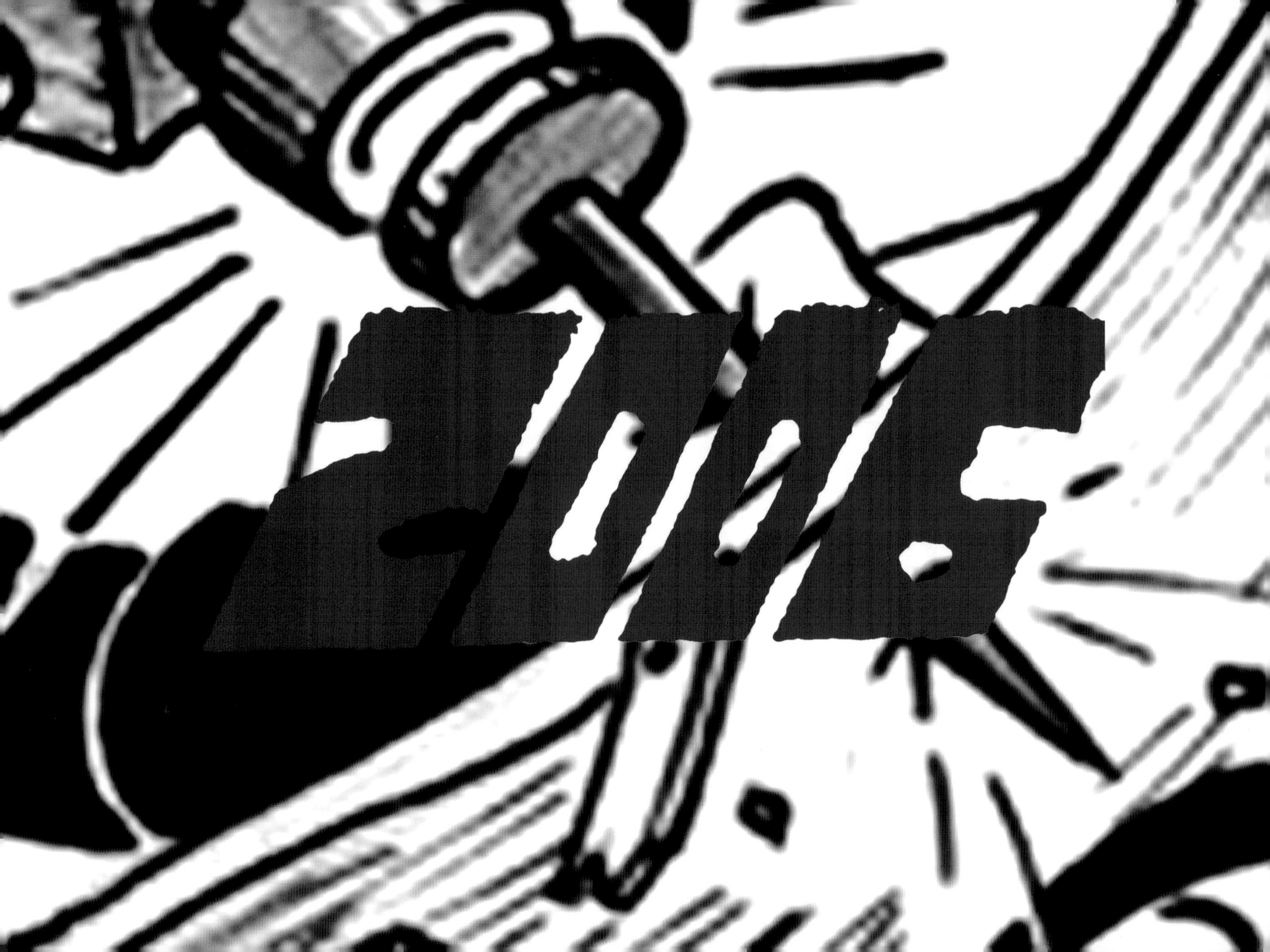
2006

2006

The debates on immigration continued to politically and physically divide Latino communities, often pitting Mexican-Americans against Mexicans. Assimilation tactics such as "English Only" legislation and the whitewashing of history manipulated people of color to not only oppress people of other nations but also oppress people of this nation. Why is it that Uncle Sam's destructive foreign policy is never taken into account during the discussions as to why people flee their countries for the stability of United States?

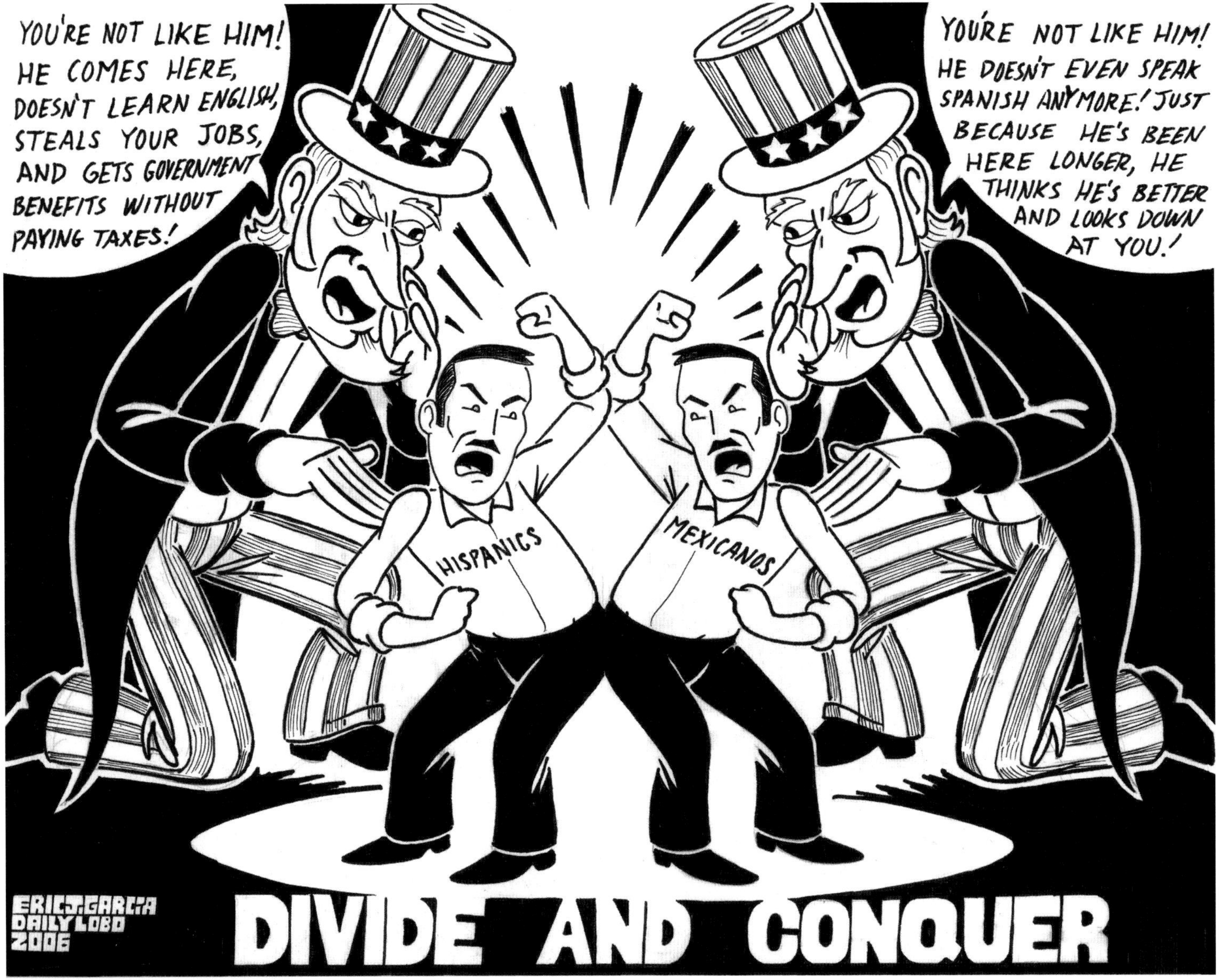
YOU'RE NOT LIKE HIM! HE COMES HERE, DOESN'T LEARN ENGLISH, STEALS YOUR JOBS, AND GETS GOVERNMENT BENEFITS WITHOUT PAYING TAXES!
YOU'RE NOT LIKE HIM! HE DOESN'T EVEN SPEAK SPANISH ANYMORE! JUST BECAUSE HE'S BEEN HERE LONGER, HE THINKS HE'S BETTER AND LOOKS DOWN AT YOU!
HISPANICS
MEXICANOS
ERIC J. GARCIA
DAILY LOBO
2006
DIVIDE AND CONQUER

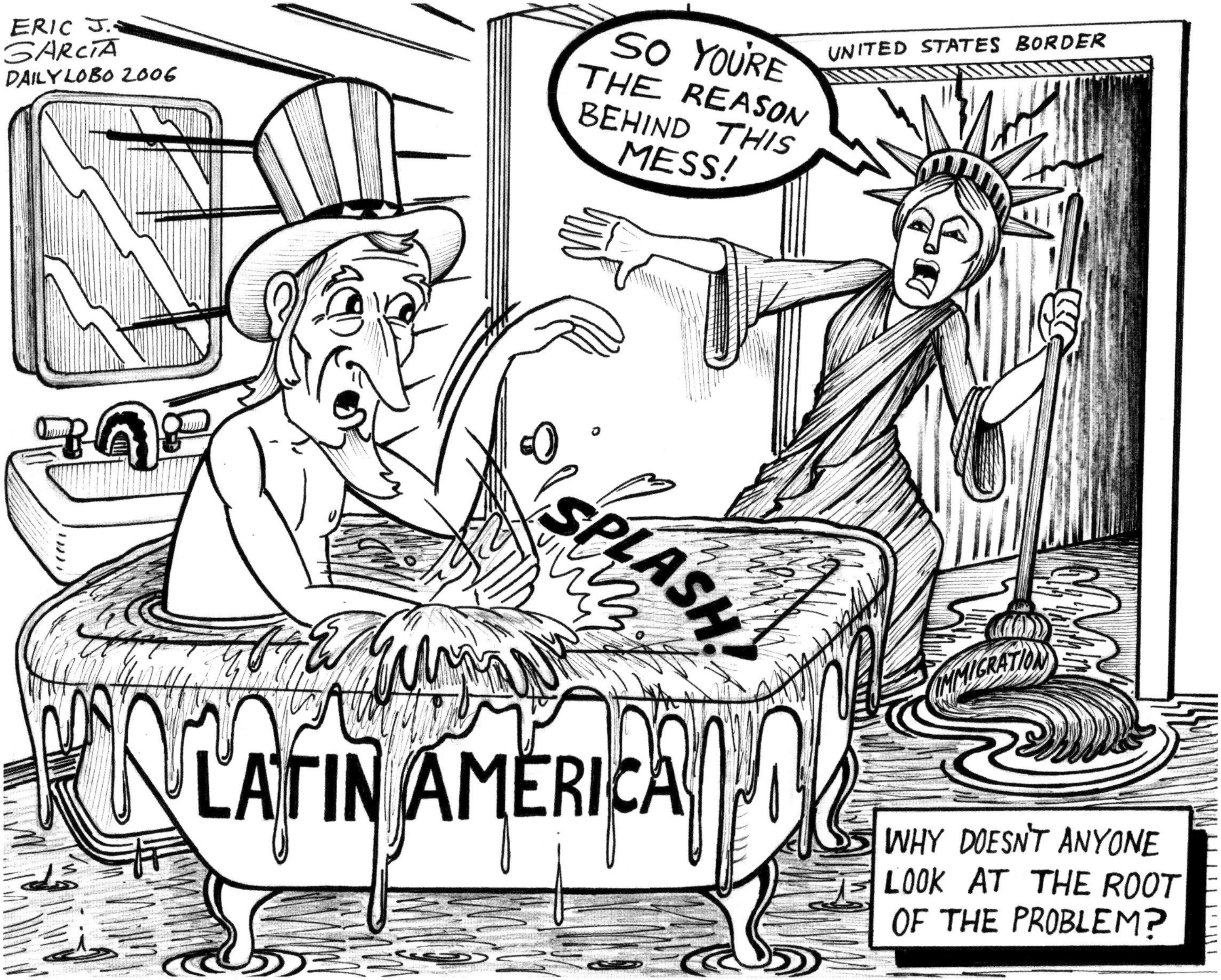
ERIC J. GARCIA
DAILYLOBO 2006
SO YOU'RE THE REASON BEHIND THIS MESS!
UNITED STATES BORDER
SPLASH!
IMMIGRATION
LATIN AMERICA
WHY DOESN'T ANYONE LOOK AT THE ROOT OF THE PROBLEM?

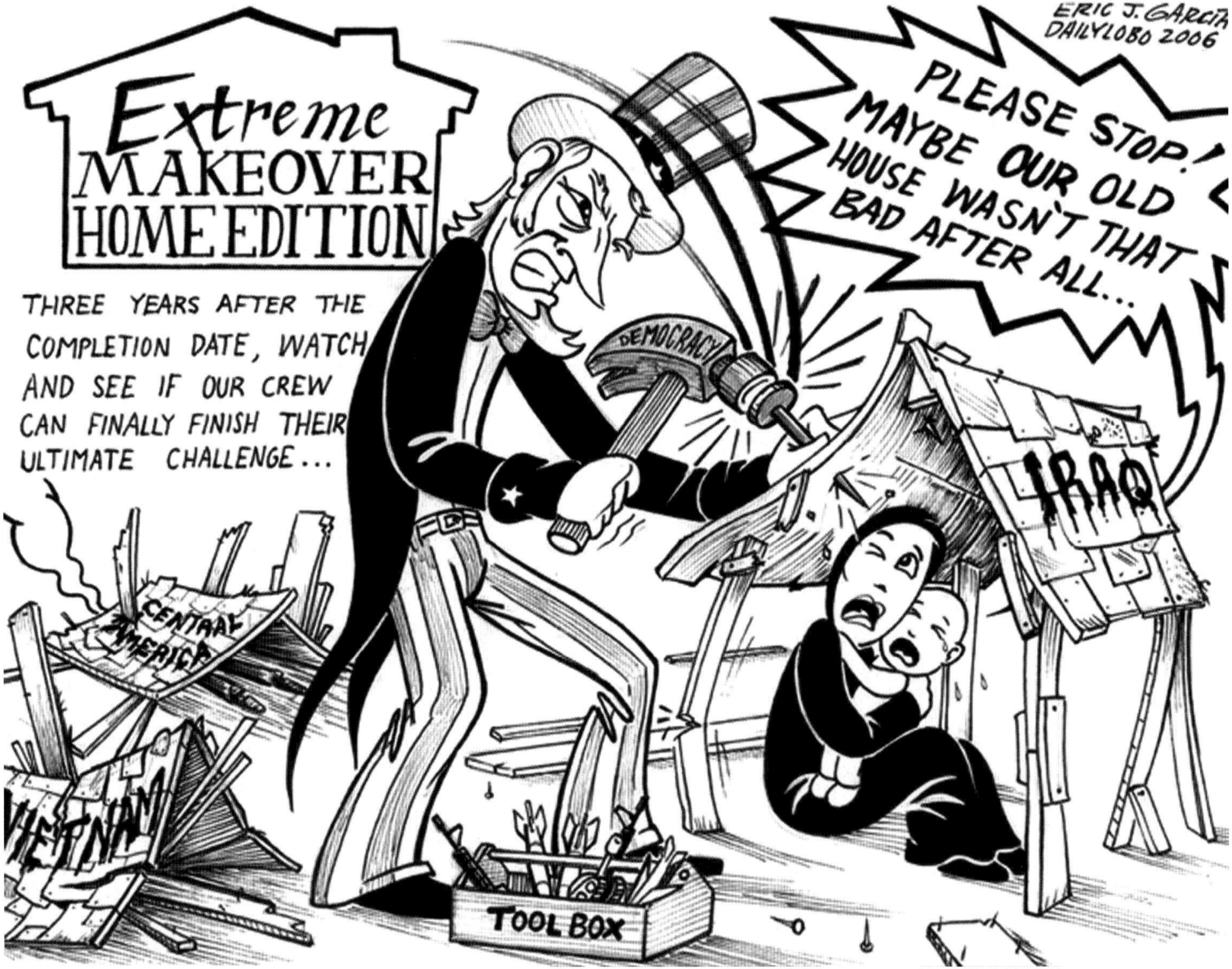
Extreme MAKEOVER HOME EDITION
THREE YEARS AFTER THE COMPLETION DATE, WATCH AND SEE IF OUR CREW CAN FINALLY FINISH THEIR ULTIMATE CHALLENGE...
PLEASE STOP! MAYBE OUR OLD HOUSE WASN'T THAT BAD AFTER ALL...
ERIC J. GARCIA DAILYLOBO 2006
DEMOCRACY
IRAQ
CENTRAL AMERICA
VIETNAM
TOOL BOX

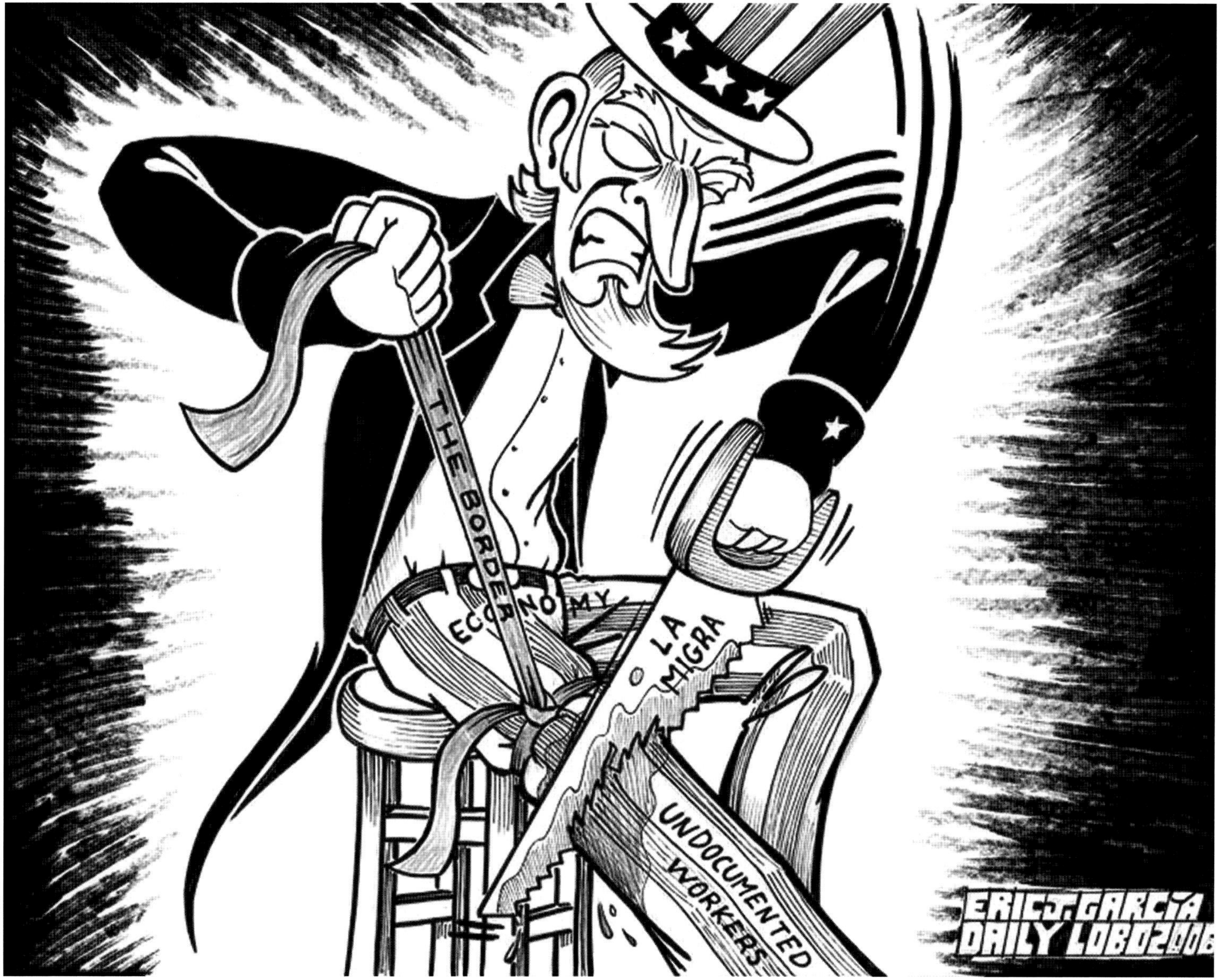
THE BORDER
ECONOMY
LA MIGRA
UNDOCUMENTED WORKERS
ERIC J. GARCIA
DAILY LOBO 2006

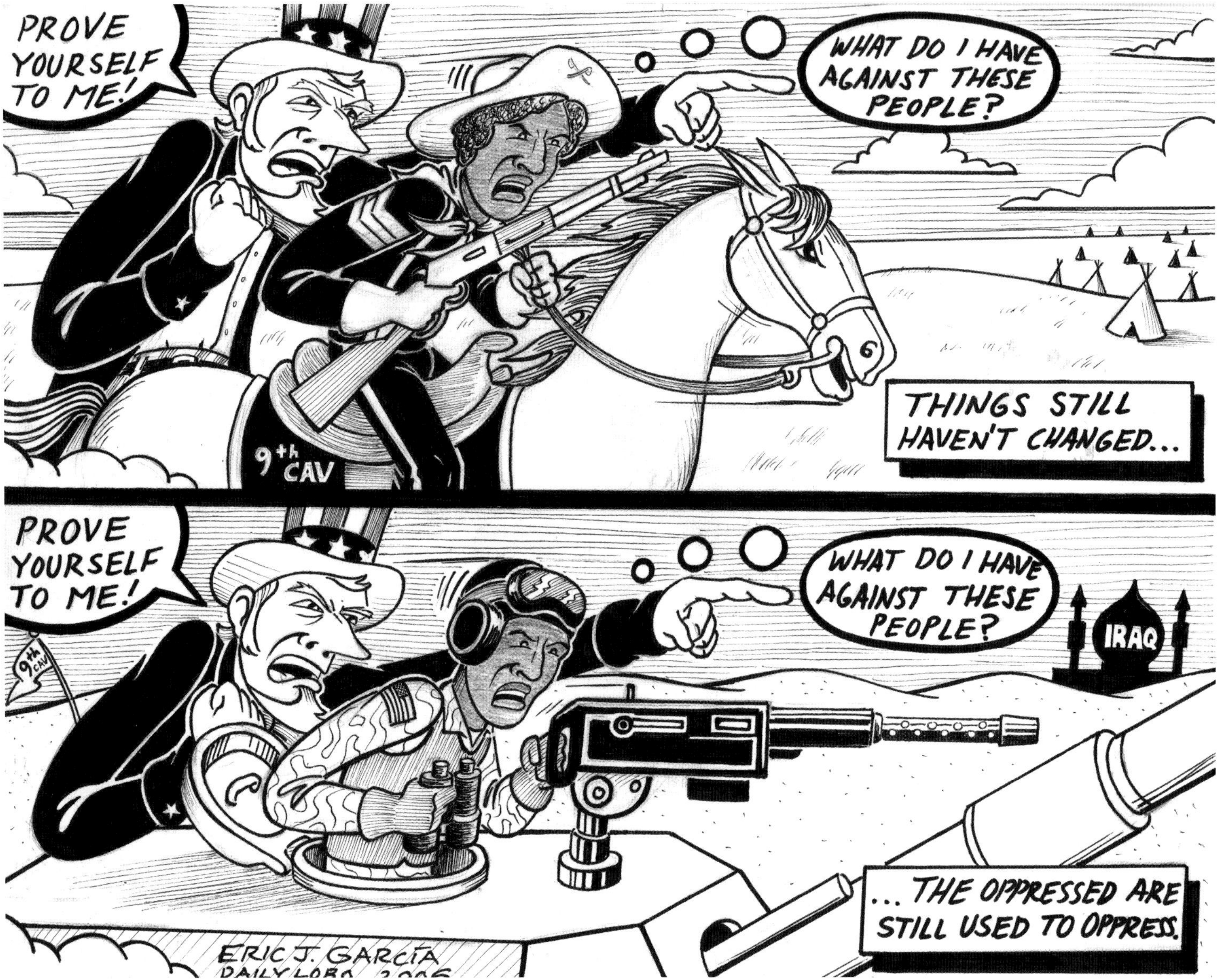
PROVE YOURSELF TO ME!
WHAT DO I HAVE AGAINST THESE PEOPLE?
9th CAV
THINGS STILL HAVEN'T CHANGED...
PROVE YOURSELF TO ME!
WHAT DO I HAVE AGAINST THESE PEOPLE?
9th CAV
IRAQ
...THE OPPRESSED ARE STILL USED TO OPPRESS.
ERIC J. GARCIA
DAILY LOBO 2006

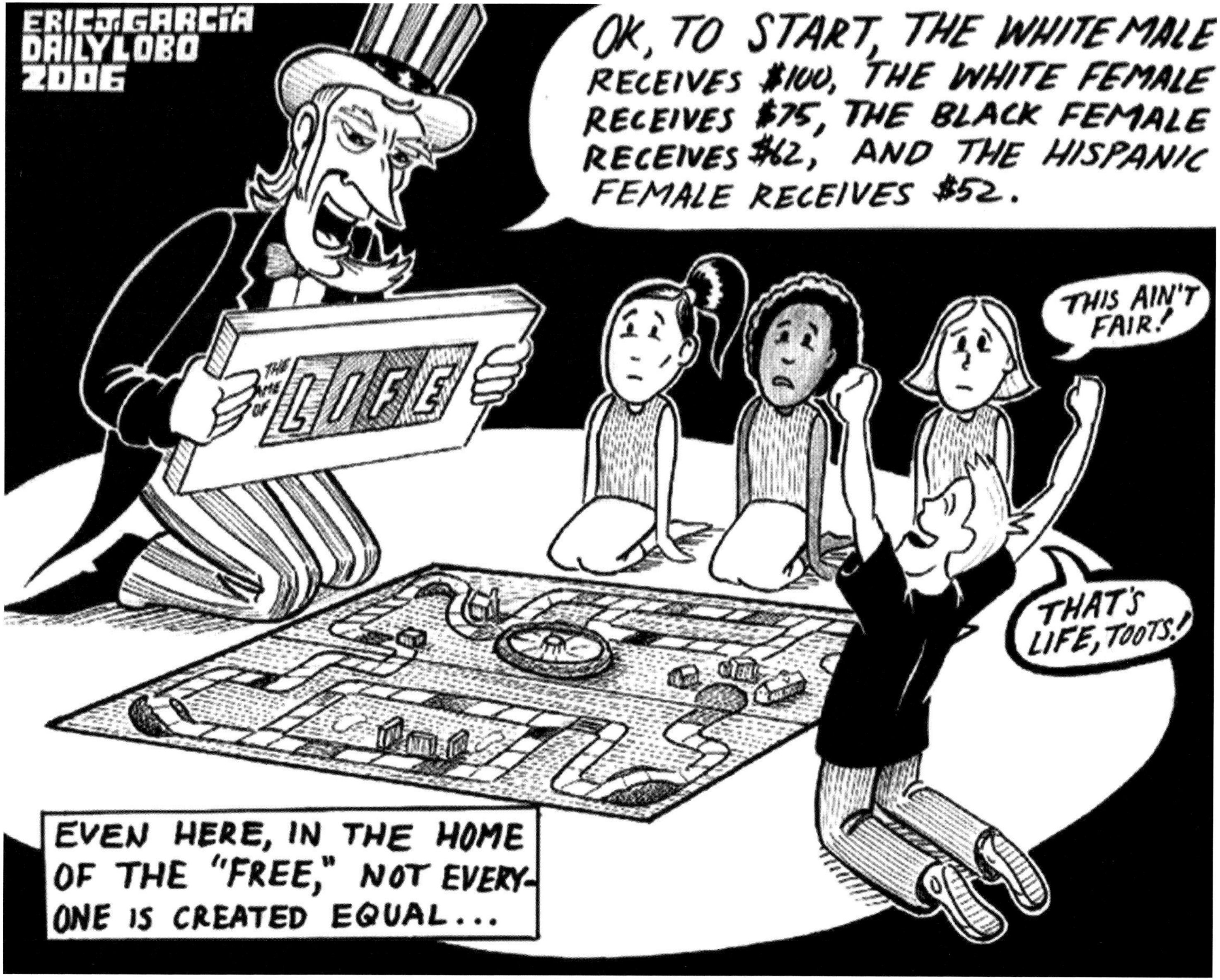
ERIC J. GARCIA
DAILY LOBO
2006
OK, TO START, THE WHITE MALE RECEIVES $100, THE WHITE FEMALE RECEIVES $75, THE BLACK FEMALE RECEIVES $62, AND THE HISPANIC FEMALE RECEIVES $52.
THE GAME OF LIFE
THIS AIN'T FAIR!
THAT'S LIFE, TOOTS!
EVEN HERE, IN THE HOME OF THE "FREE," NOT EVERY-ONE IS CREATED EQUAL...

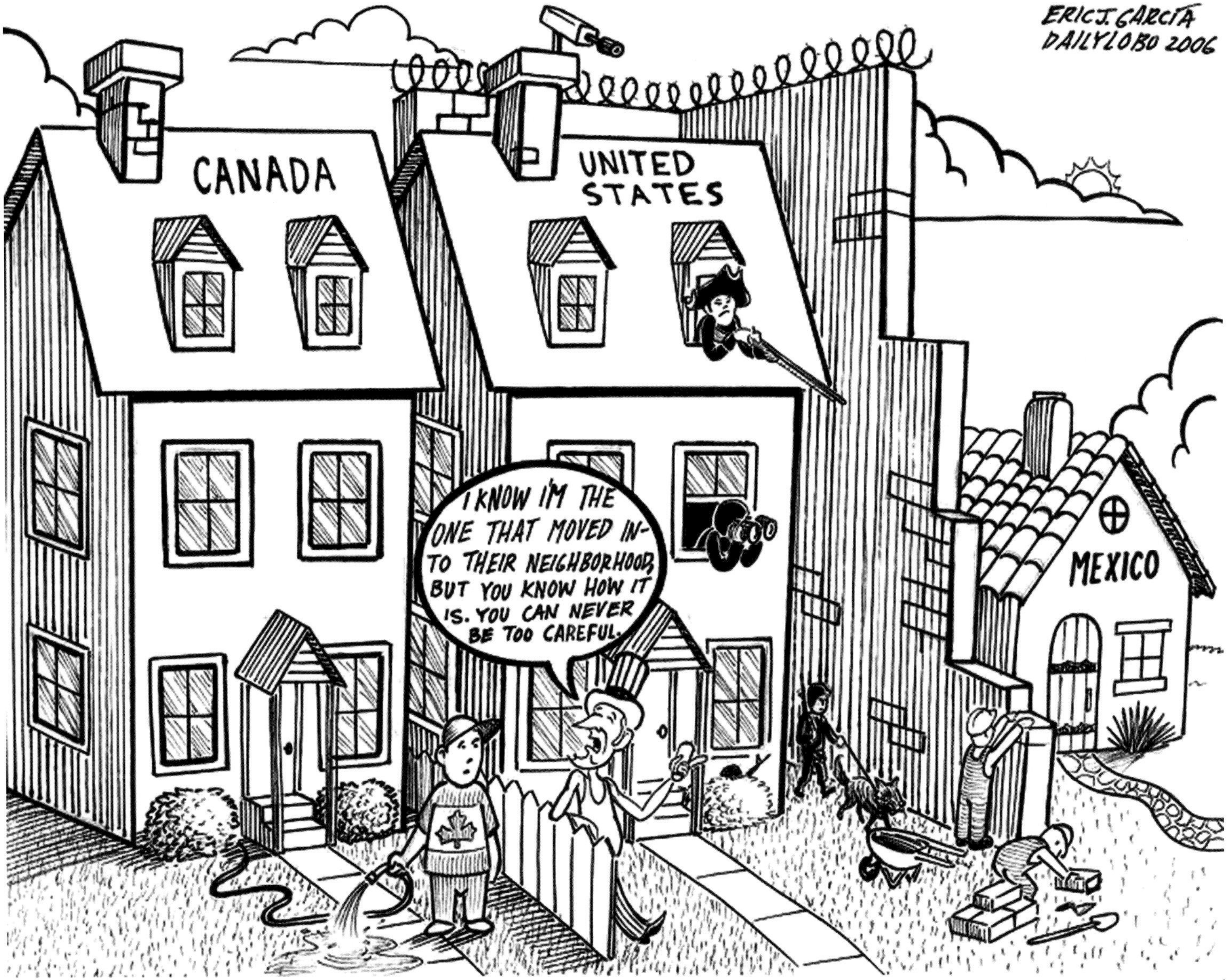
ERIC J. GARCÍA
DAILY LOBO 2006
CANADA
UNITED STATES
MEXICO
I KNOW I'M THE ONE THAT MOVED INTO THEIR NEIGHBORHOOD, BUT YOU KNOW HOW IT IS. YOU CAN NEVER BE TOO CAREFUL.

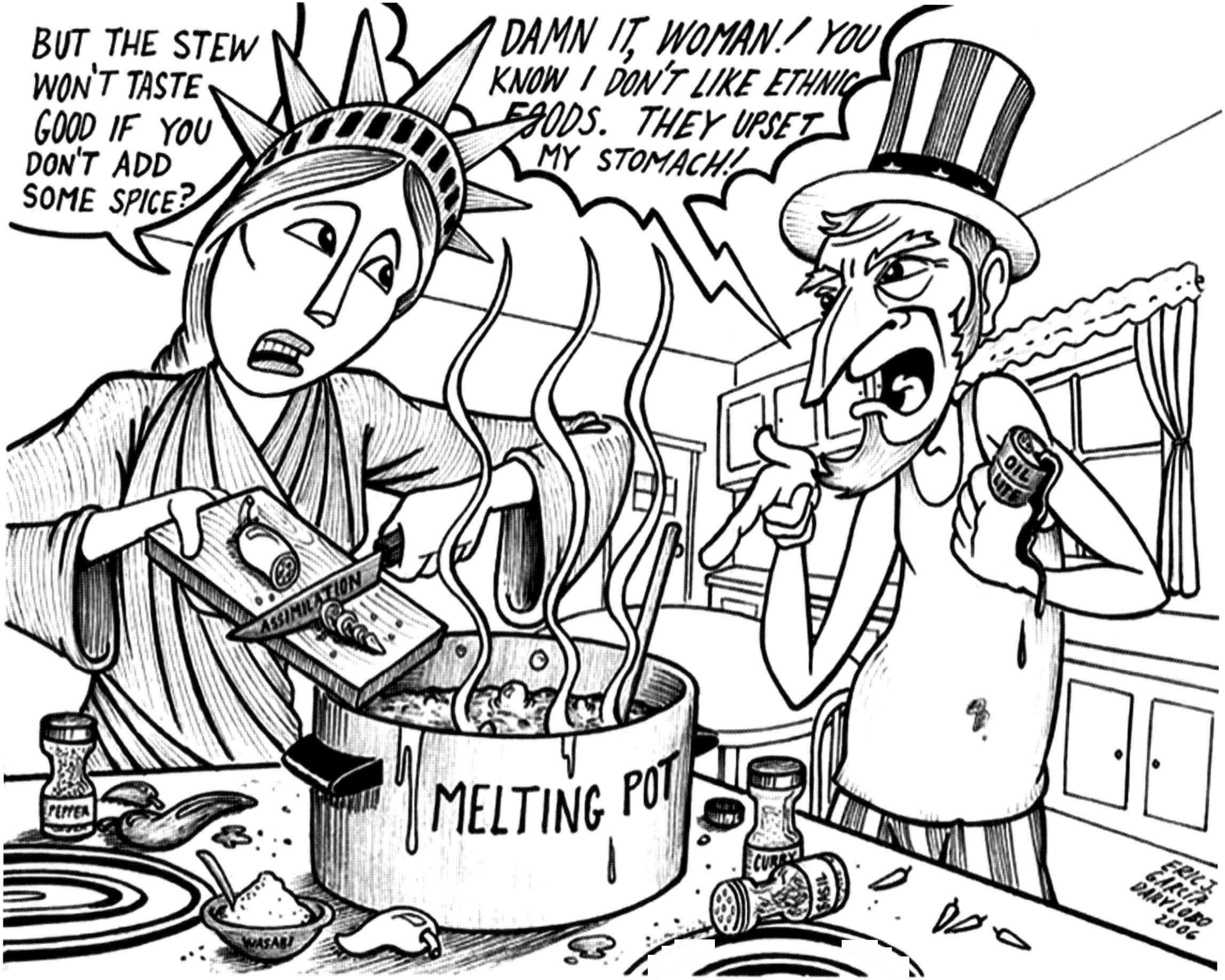
BUT THE STEW WON'T TASTE GOOD IF YOU DON'T ADD SOME SPICE?
DAMN IT, WOMAN! YOU KNOW I DON'T LIKE ETHNIC FOODS. THEY UPSET MY STOMACH!
ASSIMILATION
MELTING POT
OIL LITE
PEPPER
WASABI
CURRY
BASIL
ERIC J. GARCIA DARYLOBO 2006

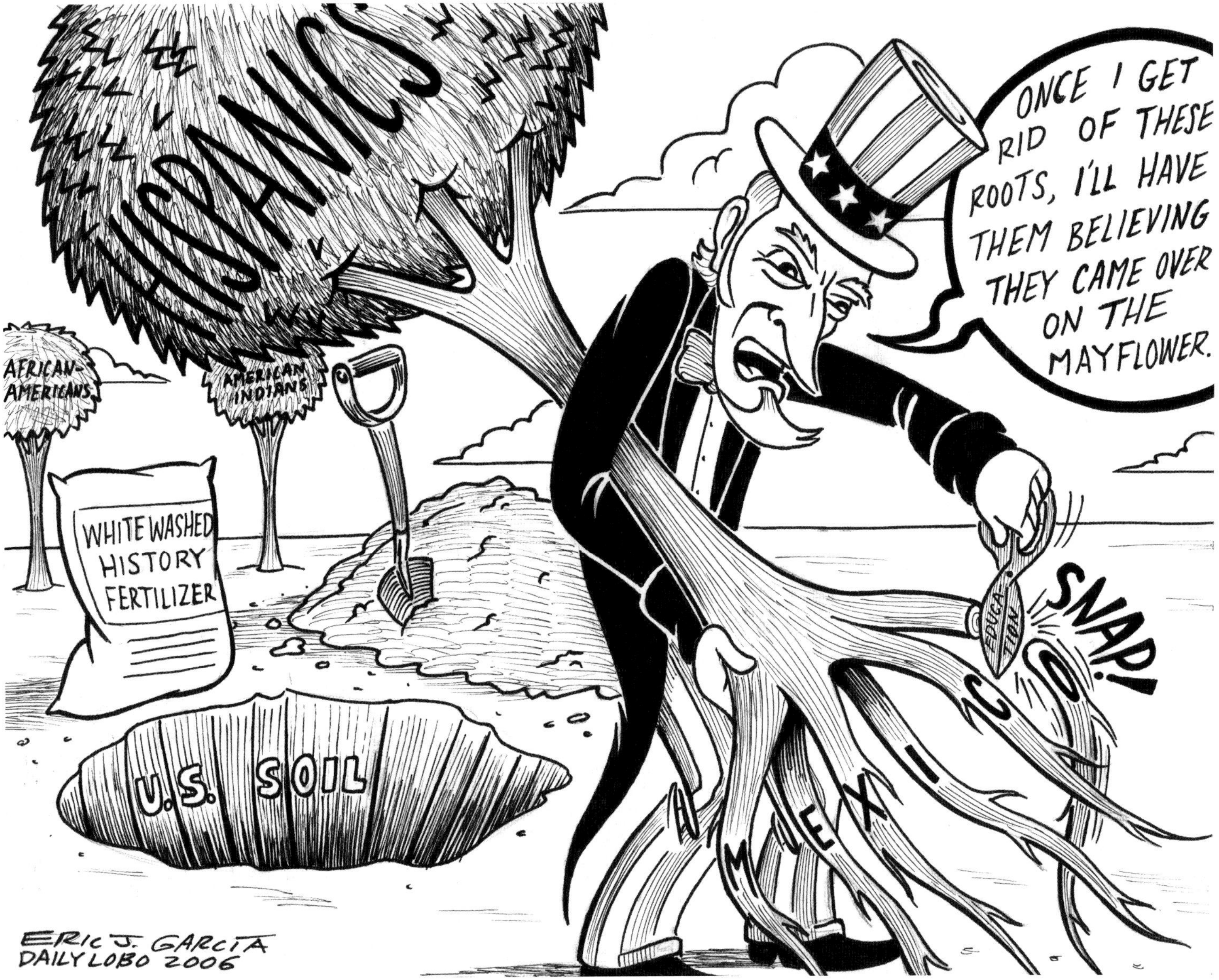
HISPANICS
AFRICAN-AMERICANS
AMERICAN INDIANS
ONCE I GET RID OF THESE ROOTS, I'LL HAVE THEM BELIEVING THEY CAME OVER ON THE MAYFLOWER.
WHITE WASHED HISTORY FERTILIZER
U.S. SOIL
EDUCATION
SNAP!
MEXICO
ERIC J. GARCIA
DAILY LOBO 2006

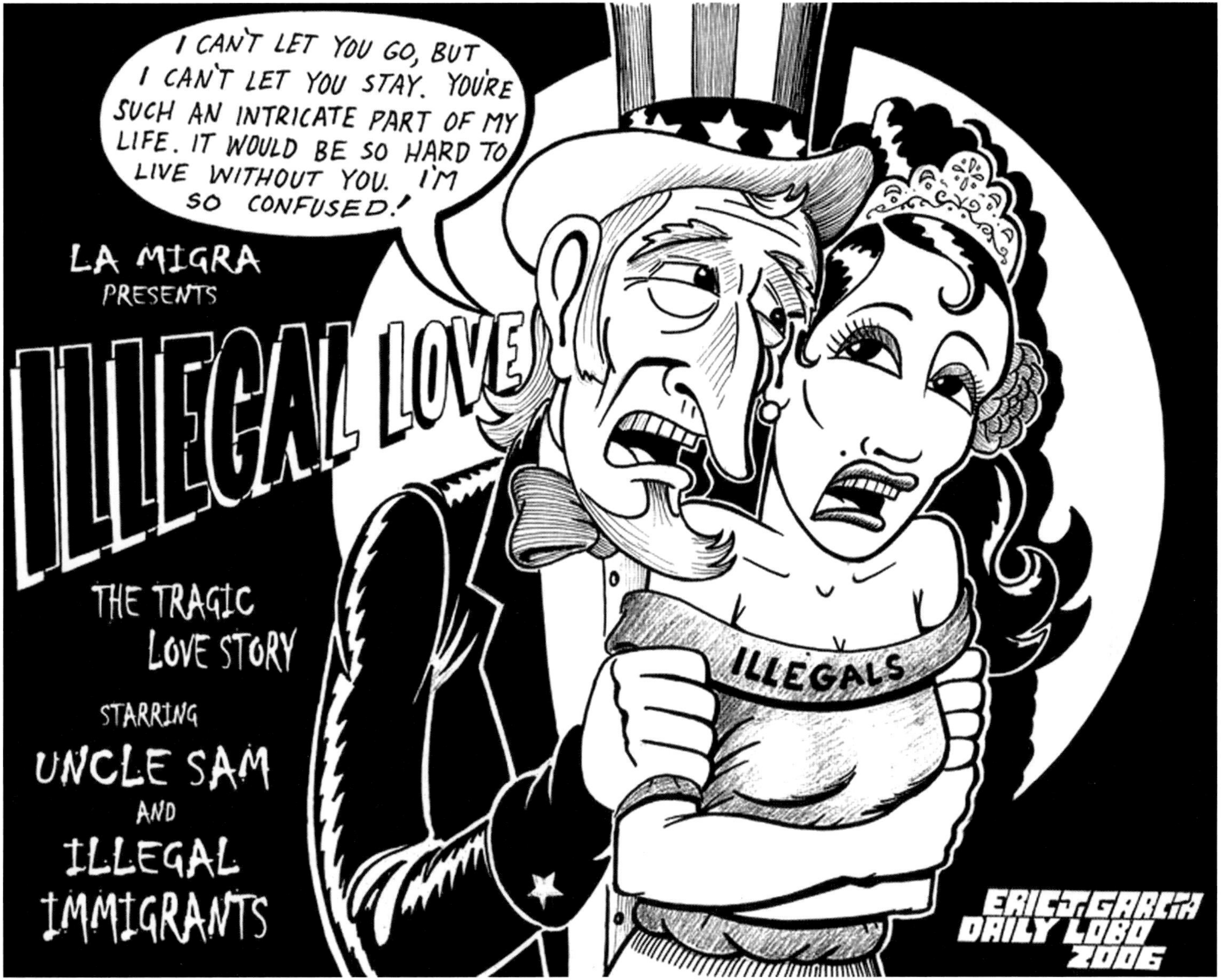
I CAN'T LET YOU GO, BUT I CAN'T LET YOU STAY. YOU'RE SUCH AN INTRICATE PART OF MY LIFE. IT WOULD BE SO HARD TO LIVE WITHOUT YOU. I'M SO CONFUSED!
LA MIGRA PRESENTS
ILLEGAL LOVE
THE TRAGIC LOVE STORY
STARRING
UNCLE SAM
AND
ILLEGAL IMMIGRANTS
ILLEGALS
ERIC J. GARCIA
DAILY LOBO
2006

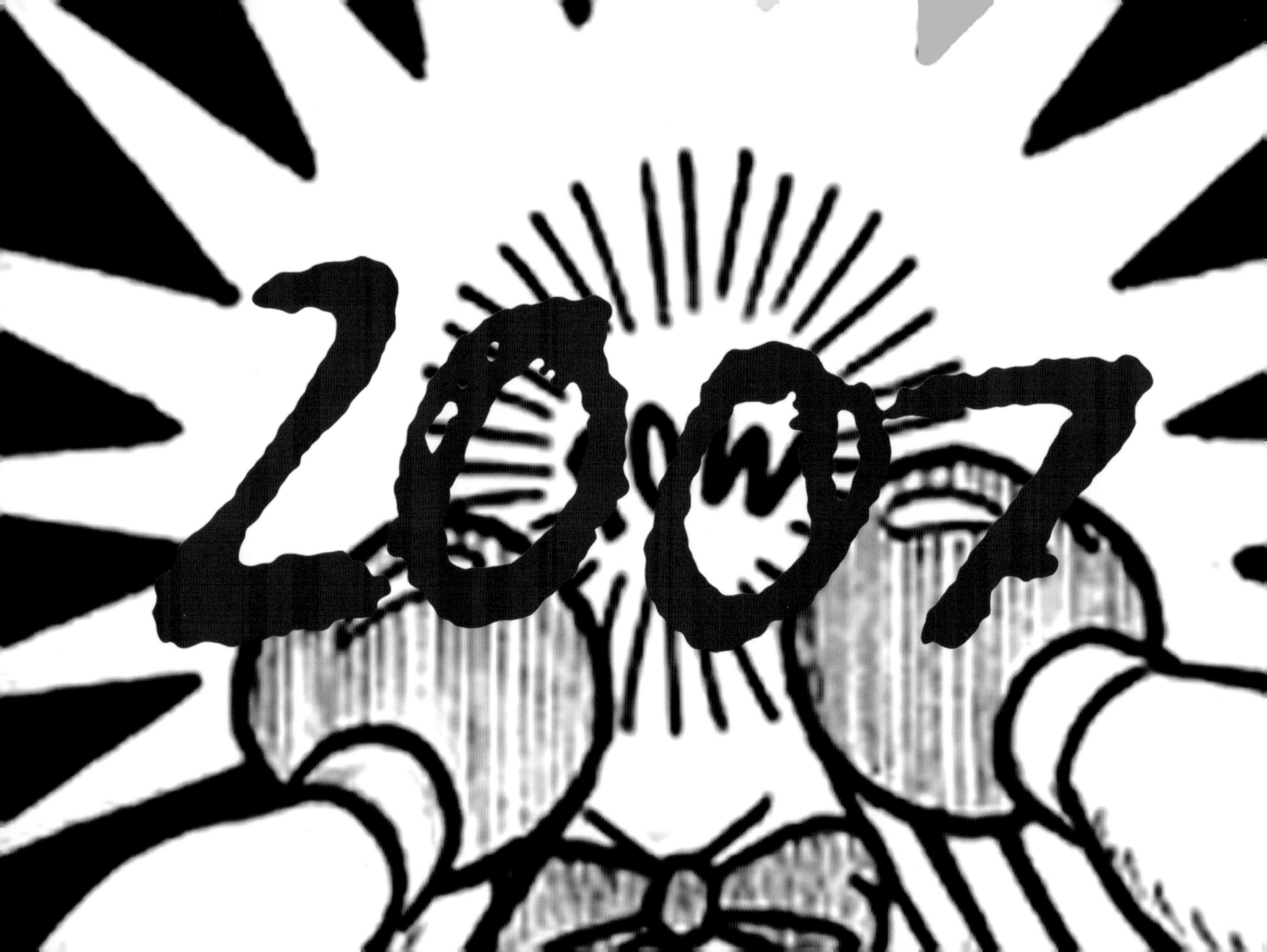
2007

2007

Big Business continued to flourish thanks to the destruction of the earth that provides its resources. In Iraq, the body count on both sides continued to grow exponentially. Luckily for the U.S. military, reinforcements came in the shape of highly paid and better-equipped private security forces hired by our government. U.S. officials and lawyers used these private armies, such as Blackwater, as a loophole to escape prosecution under the Uniform Code of Military Justice.

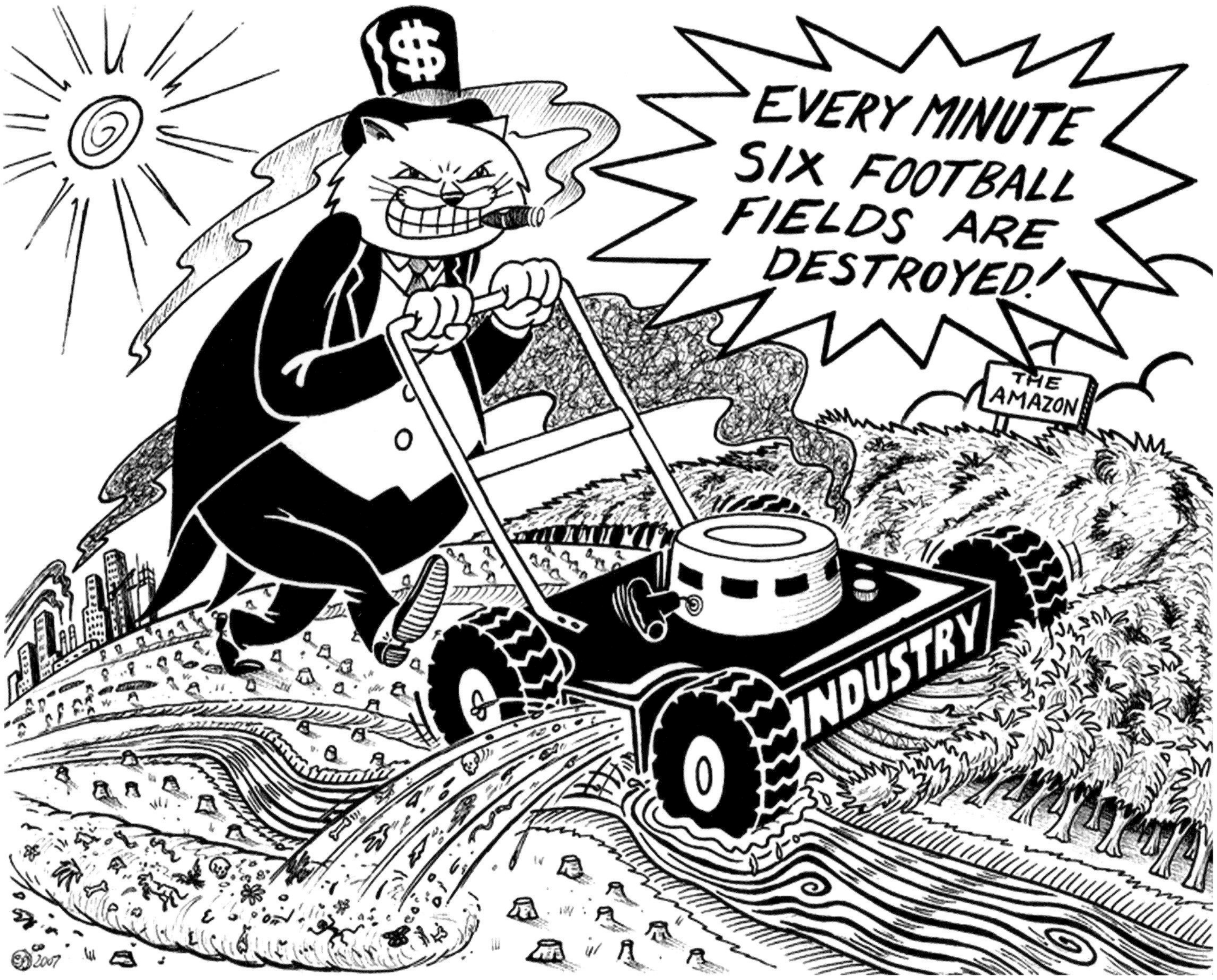
EVERY MINUTE SIX FOOTBALL FIELDS ARE DESTROYED!
THE AMAZON
INDUSTRY
$
©2007

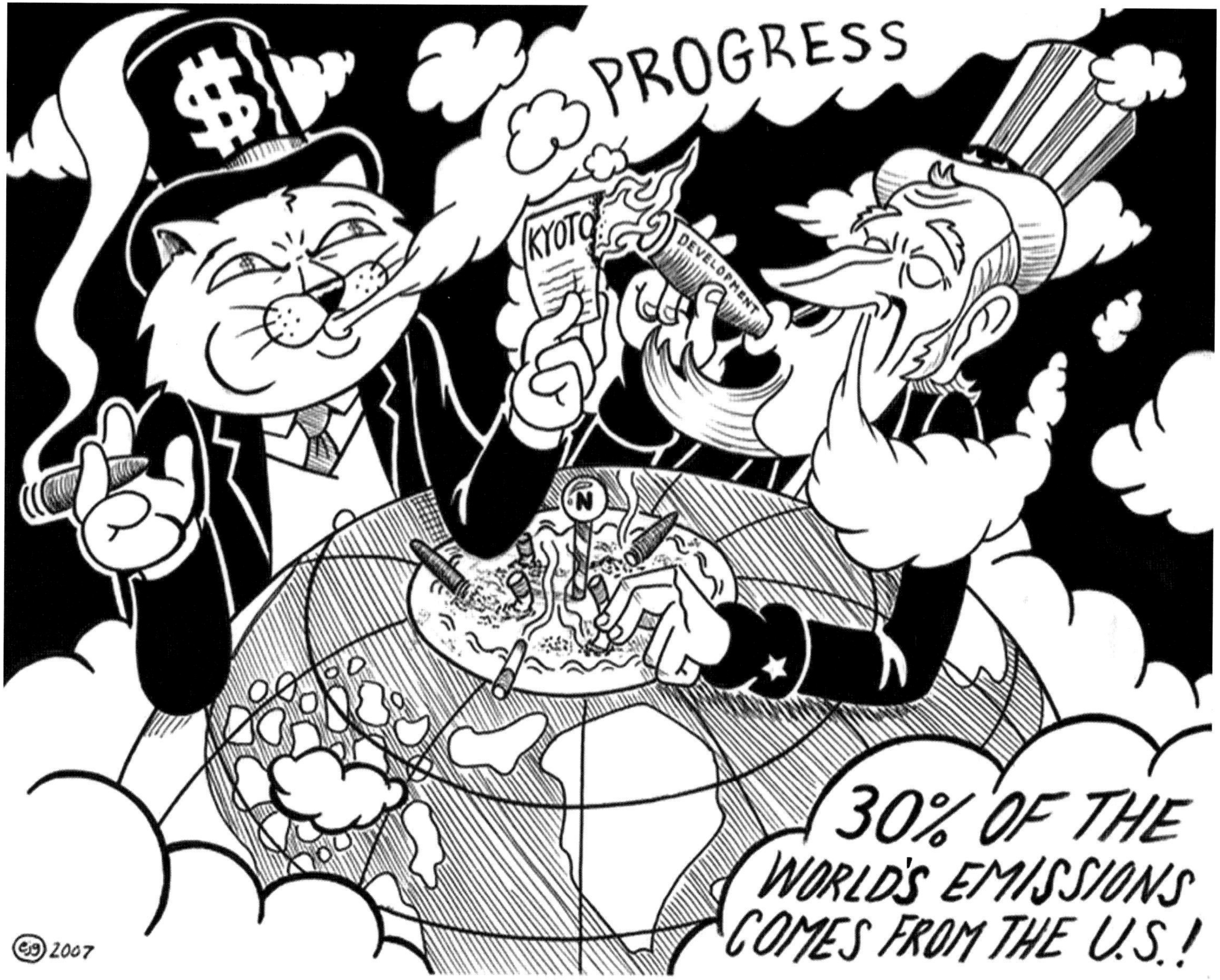
PROGRESS
$
KYOTO
DEVELOPMENT
N
30% OF THE WORLD'S EMISSIONS COMES FROM THE U.S.!
©eg 2007

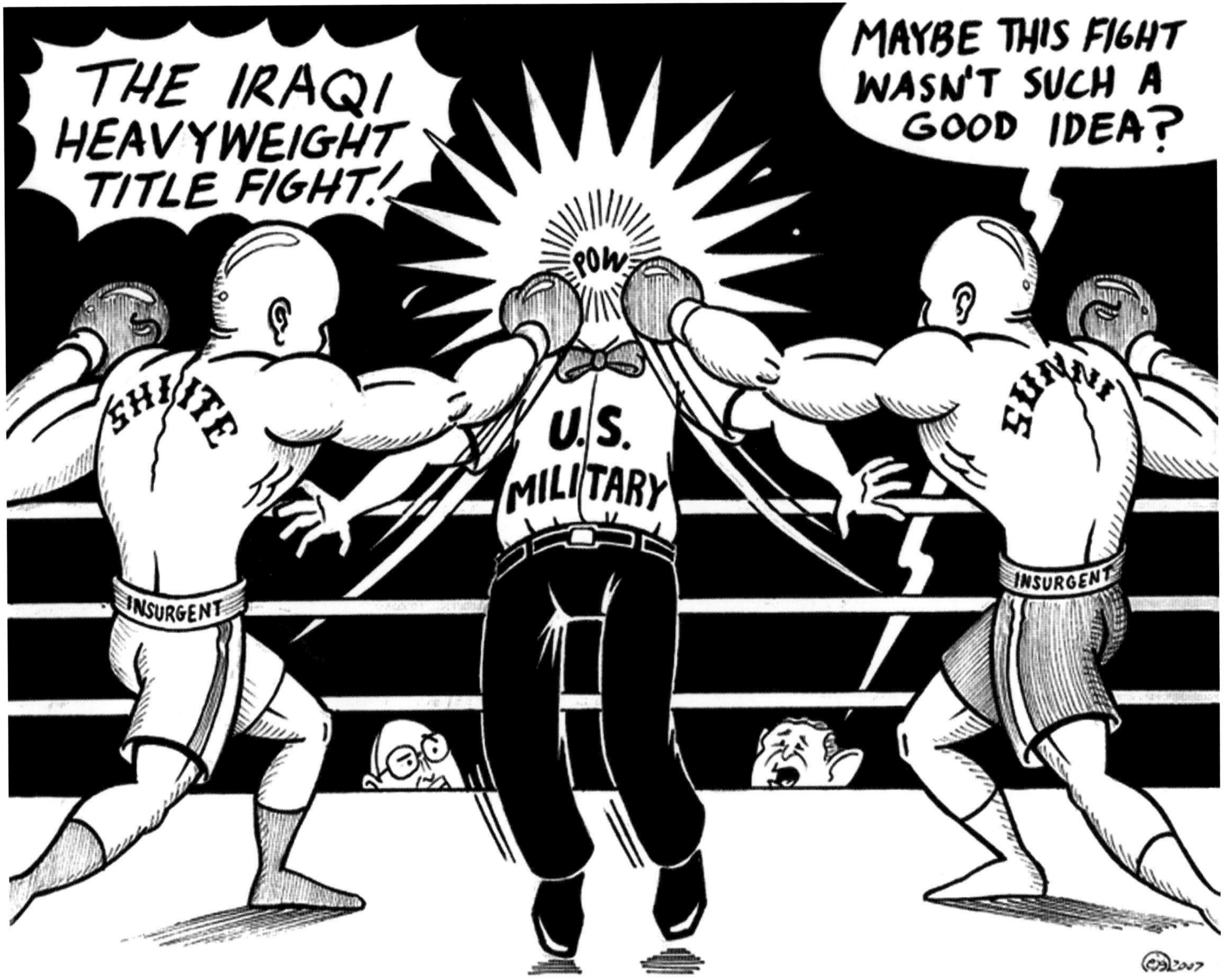
THE IRAQI HEAVYWEIGHT TITLE FIGHT!
MAYBE THIS FIGHT WASN'T SUCH A GOOD IDEA?
POW
SHIITE
U.S. MILITARY
SUNNI
INSURGENT
INSURGENT

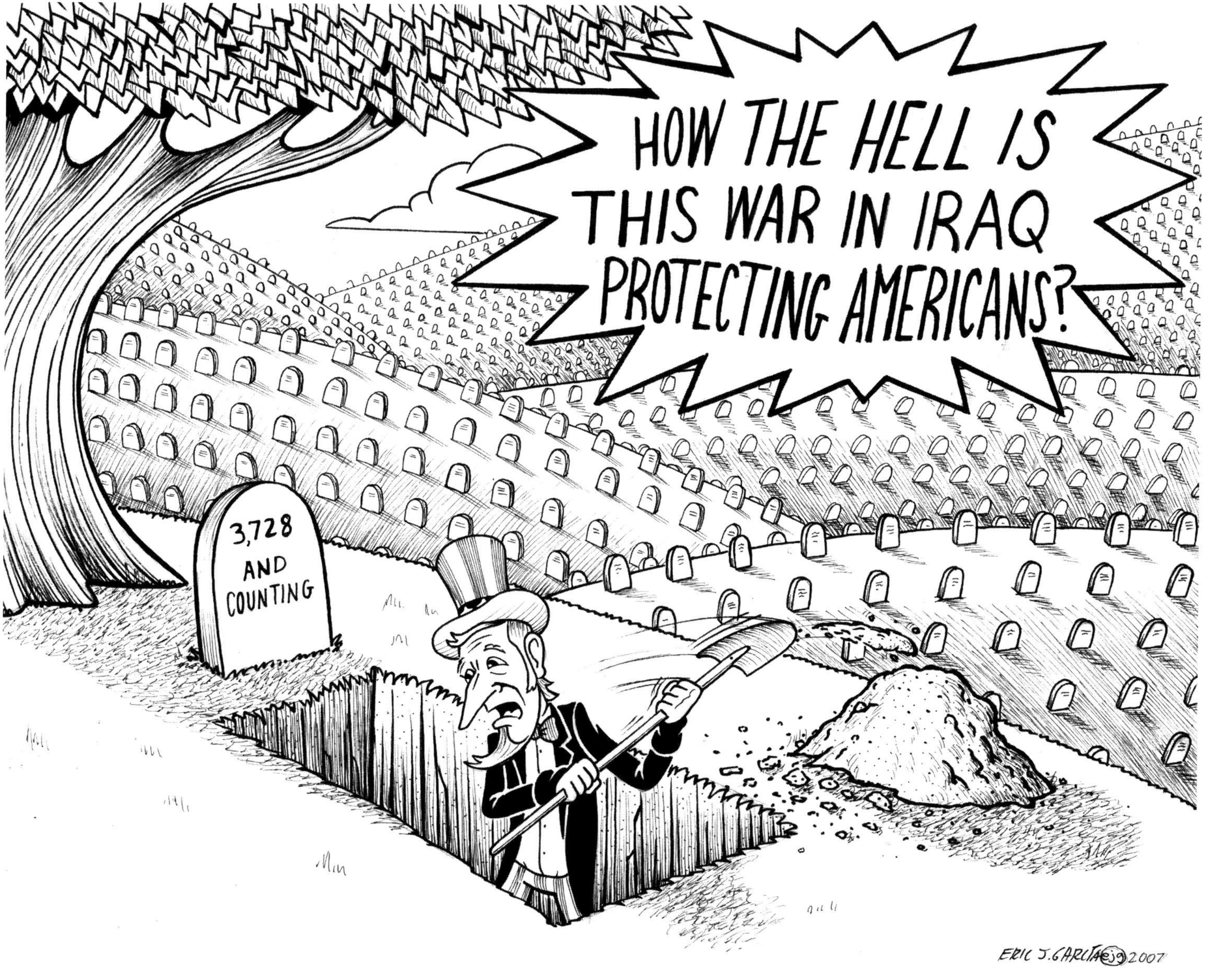
HOW THE HELL IS THIS WAR IN IRAQ PROTECTING AMERICANS?
3,728 AND COUNTING
ERIC J. GARCIA 2007

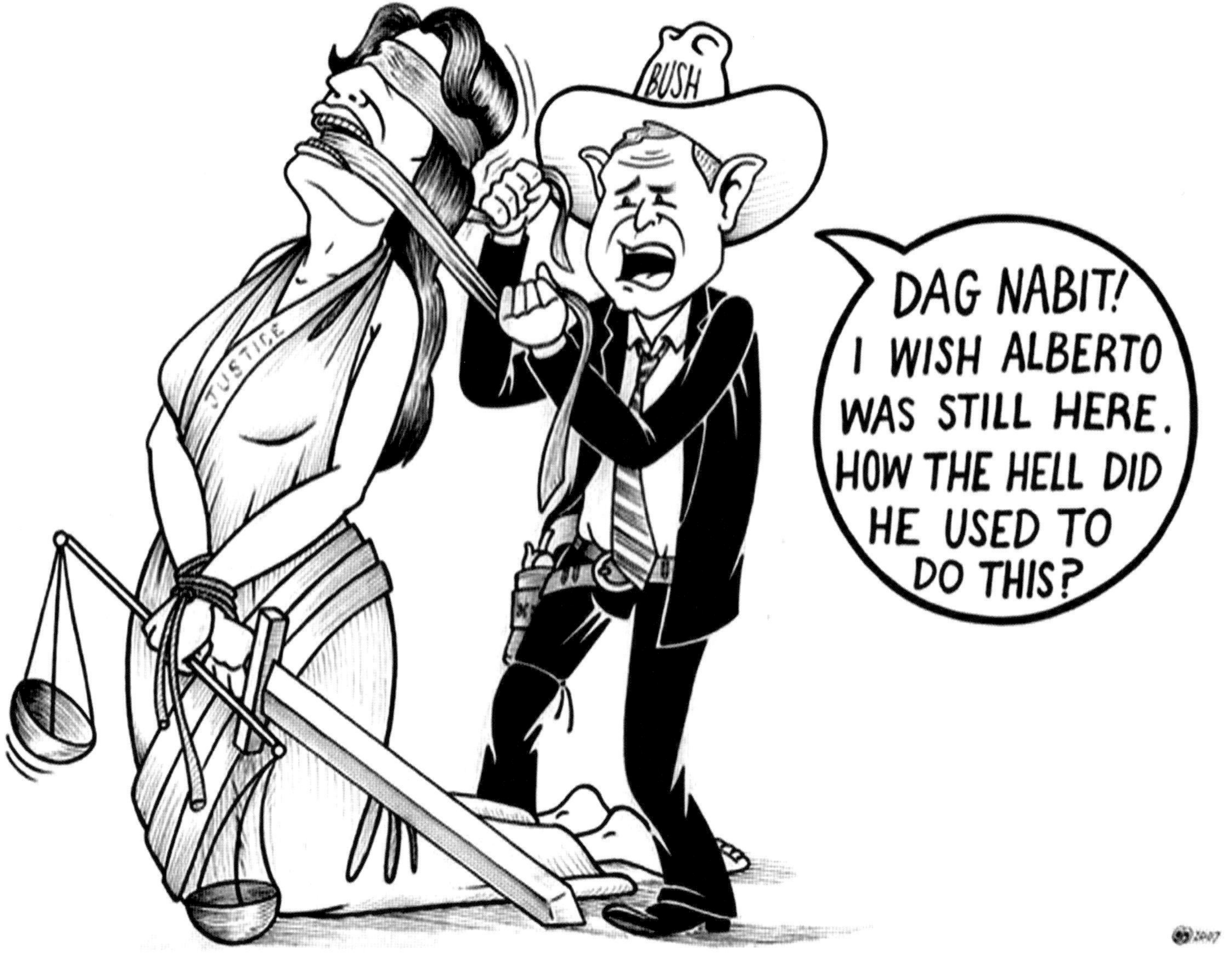
BUSH
JUSTICE
DAG NABIT! I WISH ALBERTO WAS STILL HERE. HOW THE HELL DID HE USED TO DO THIS?
2007

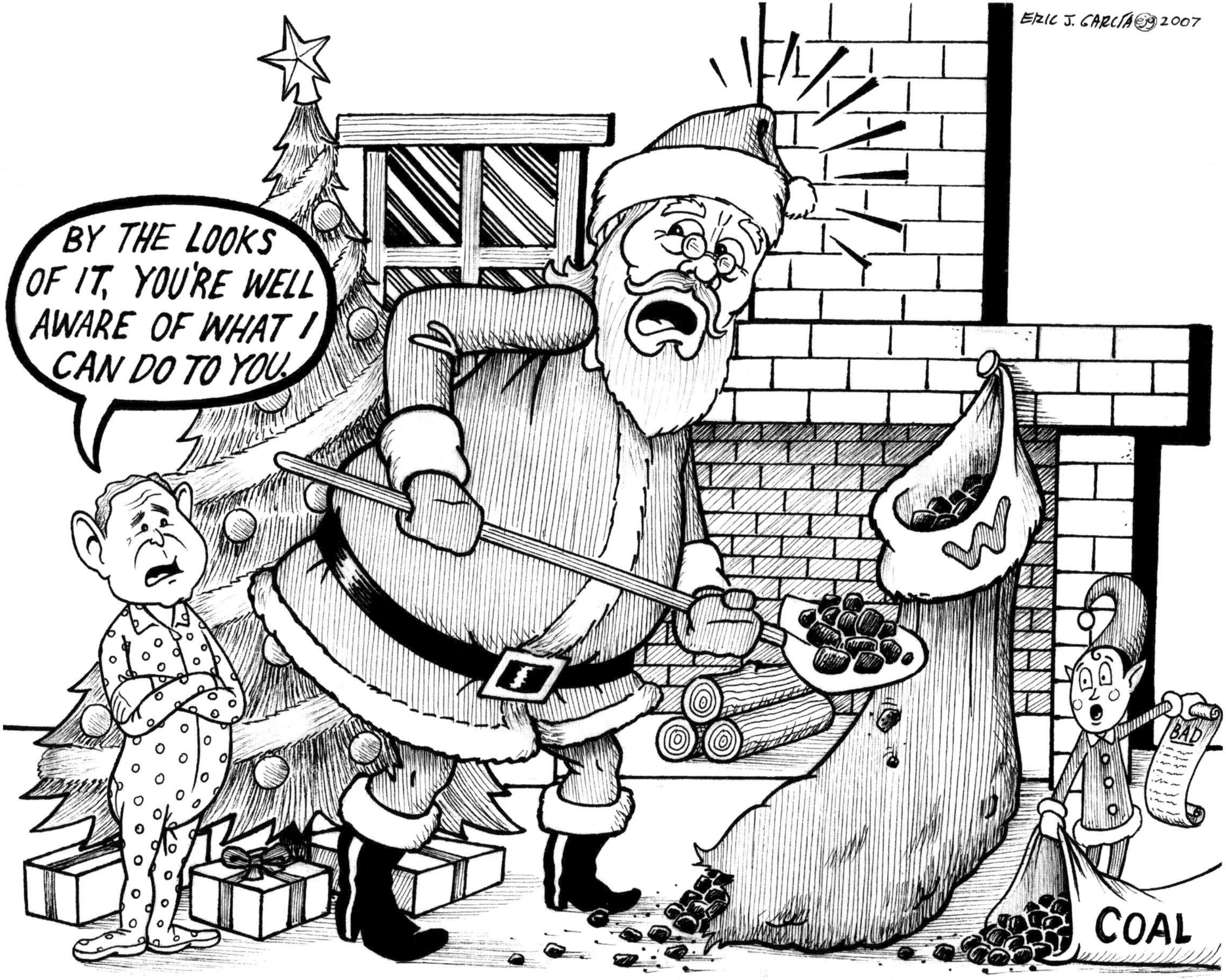
ERIC J. GARCIA ©2007
BY THE LOOKS OF IT, YOU'RE WELL AWARE OF WHAT I CAN DO TO YOU.
W
BAD
COAL

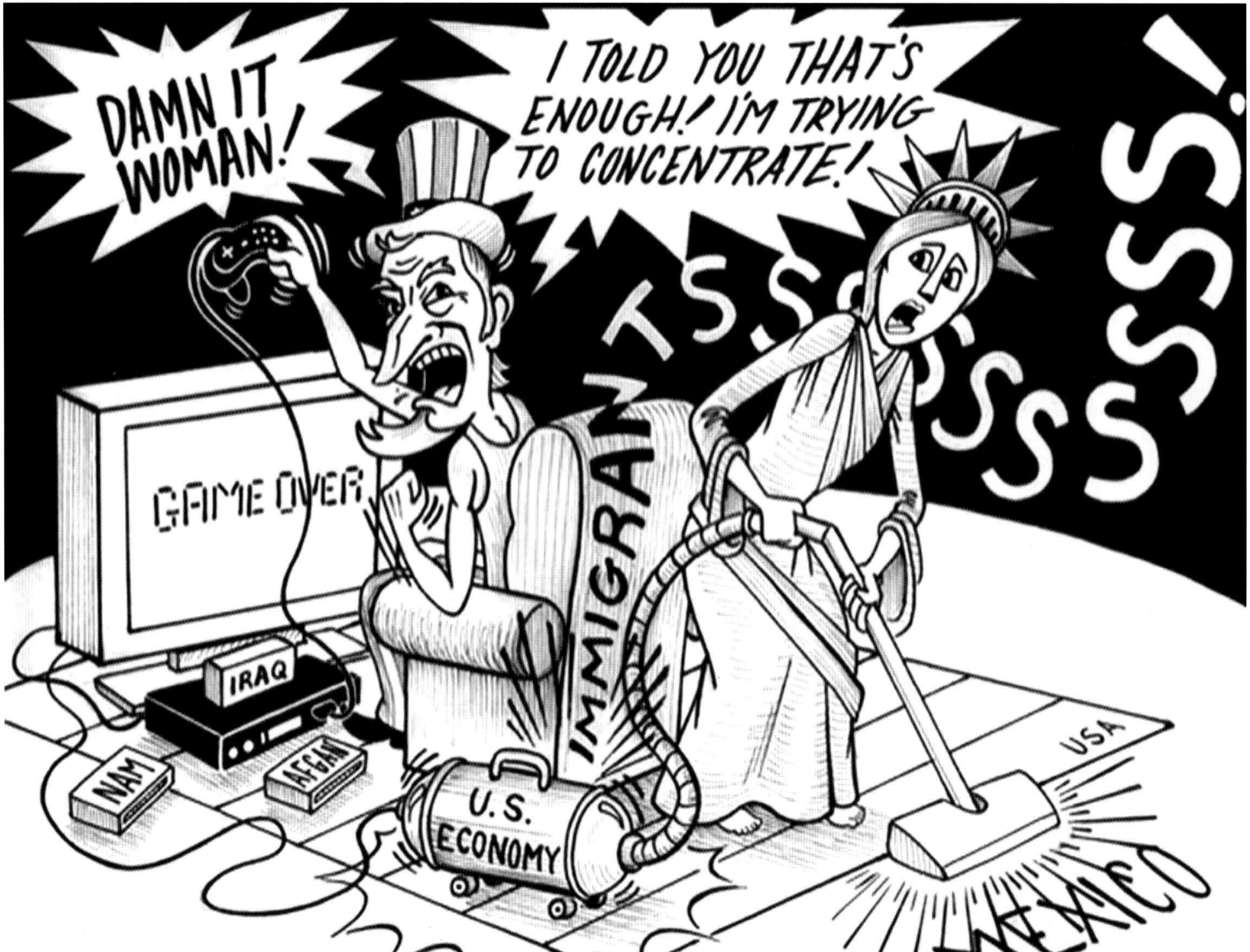
DAMN IT WOMAN!
I TOLD YOU THAT'S ENOUGH! I'M TRYING TO CONCENTRATE!
TSSSSSSSSSS!
GAME OVER
IRAQ
NAM
AFGAN
IMMIGRANT
U.S. ECONOMY
USA
MEXICO

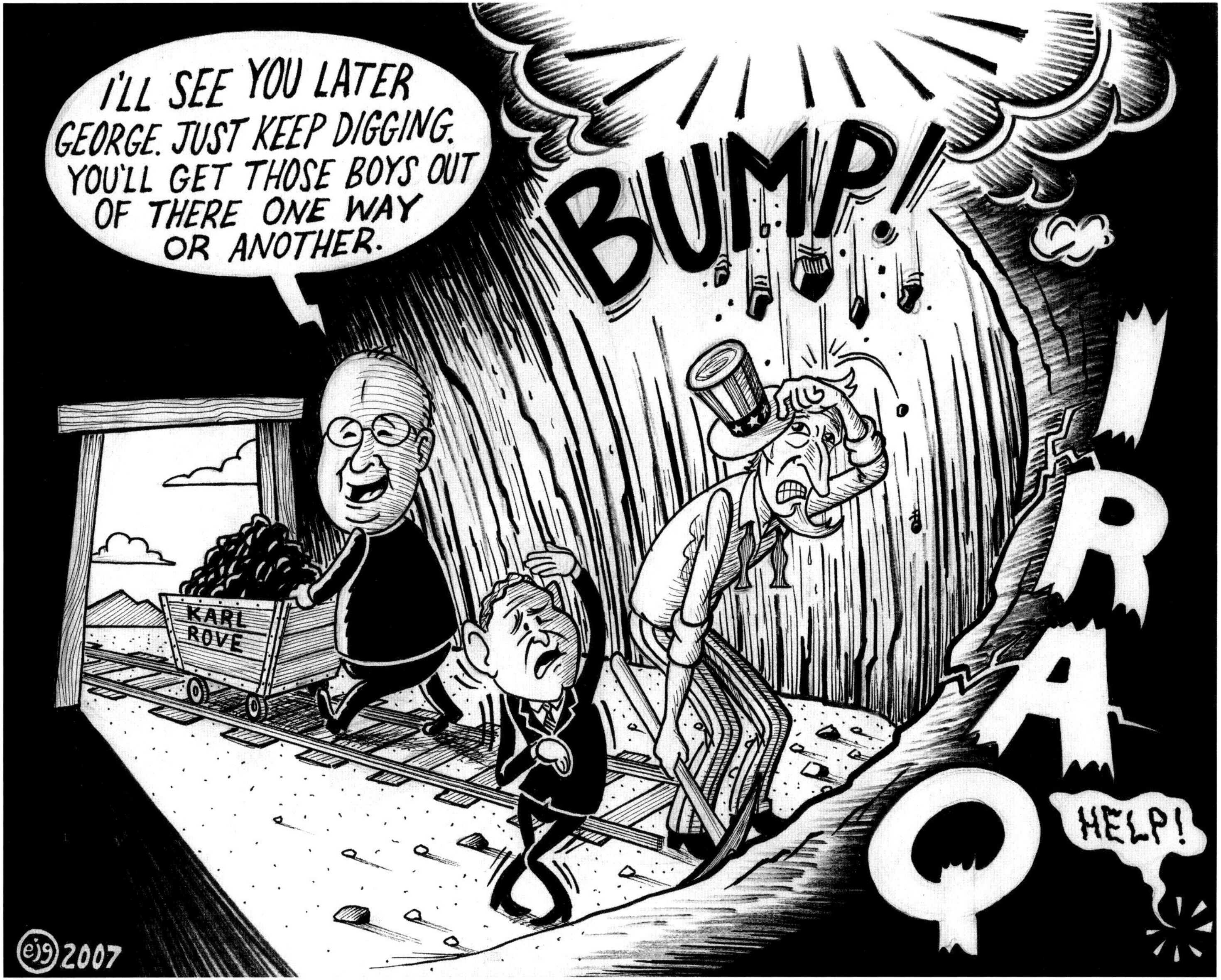
I'LL SEE YOU LATER GEORGE. JUST KEEP DIGGING. YOU'LL GET THOSE BOYS OUT OF THERE ONE WAY OR ANOTHER.
BUMP!
KARL ROVE
IRAQ
HELP!
ejg 2007

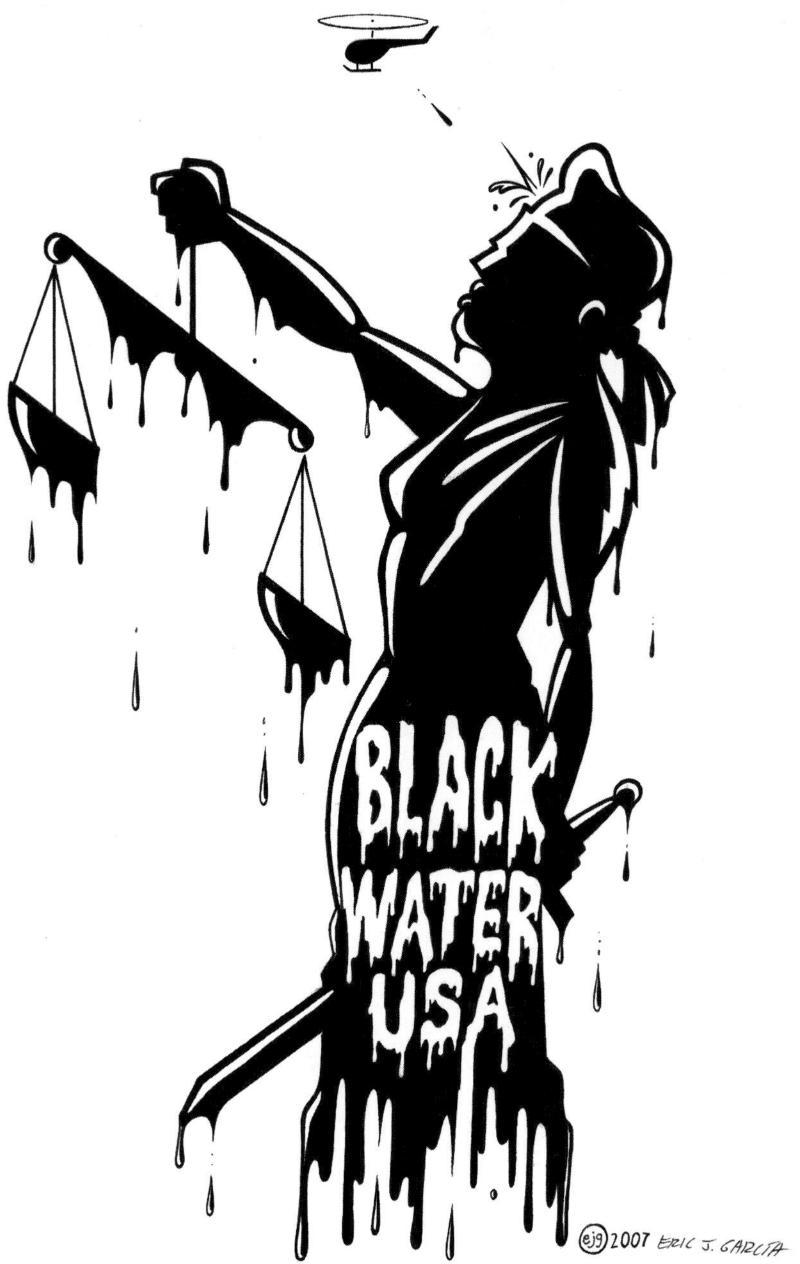
BLACK
WATER
USA
ejg 2007 ERIC J. GARCIA

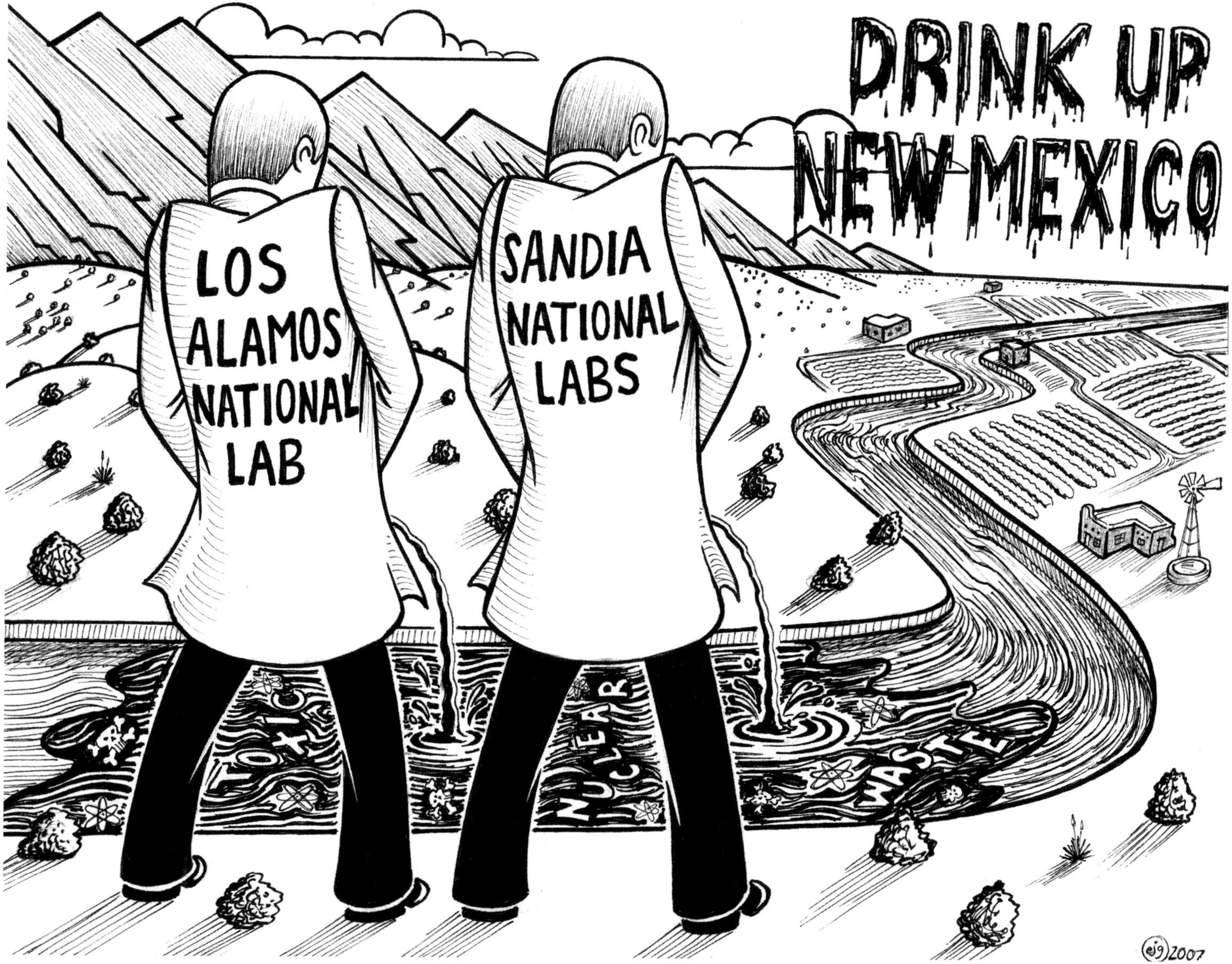
DRINK UP NEW MEXICO
LOS ALAMOS NATIONAL LAB
SANDIA NATIONAL LABS
TOXIC
NUCLEAR
WASTE
ejg 2007

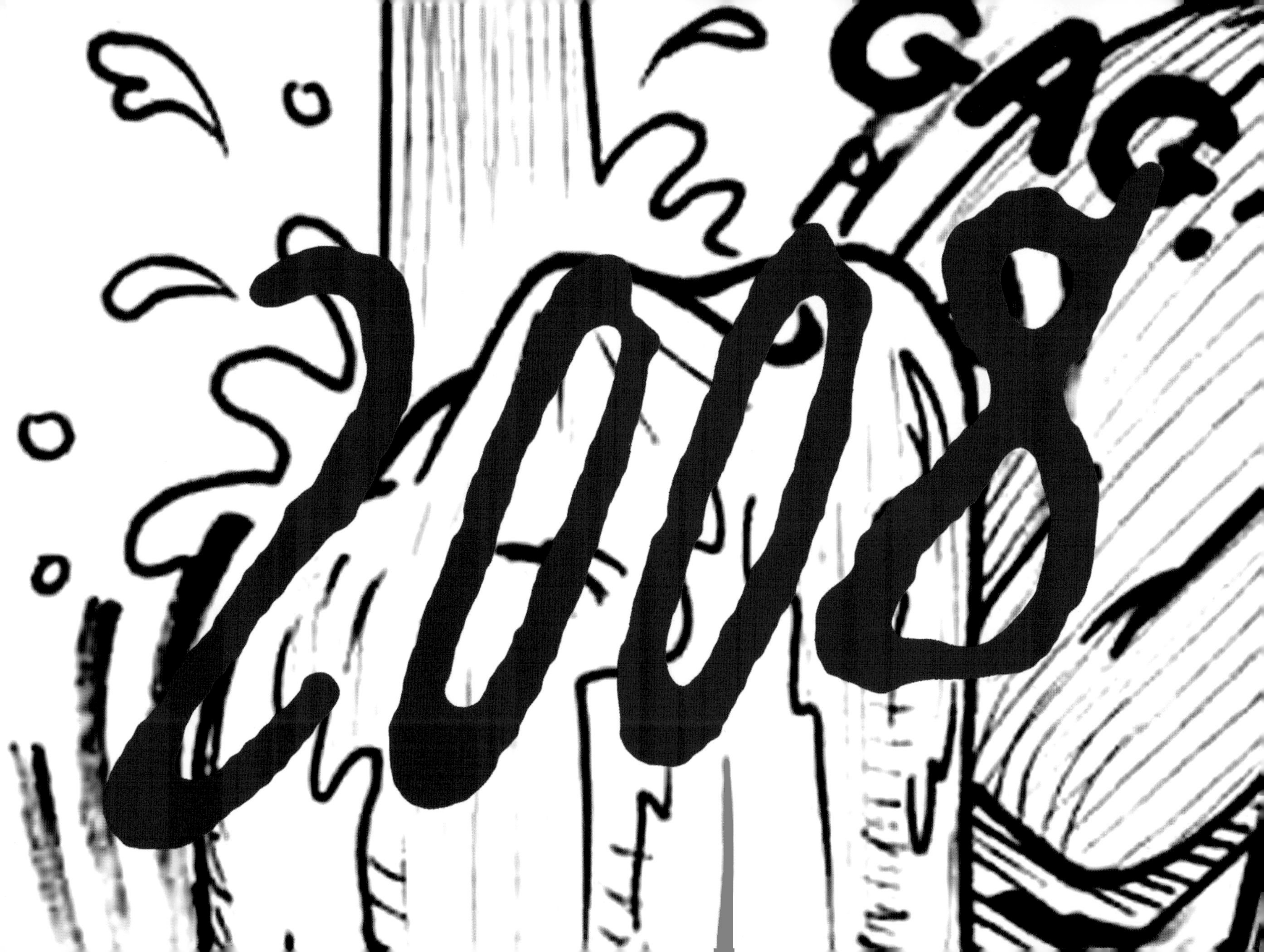
GAG...
2008

2008

The presidential elections distracted the nation from not only its financial crisis but also from the news of its torturous secret prisons. The elections also brought a closing to the era of the George W. Bush gang, but left behind a wake of tragedies that included ill-fated progress in Iraq and an economic disaster here at home. Communities in New Orleans attempted to rebuild after Hurricane Katrina, and once again greedy corporations pitted people of color against each other. Needing and wanting to rebuild their city, African-Americans were now forced to compete for jobs with even lower paid migrants who were specifically shipped by corporations like Halliburton to lower the price of labor.

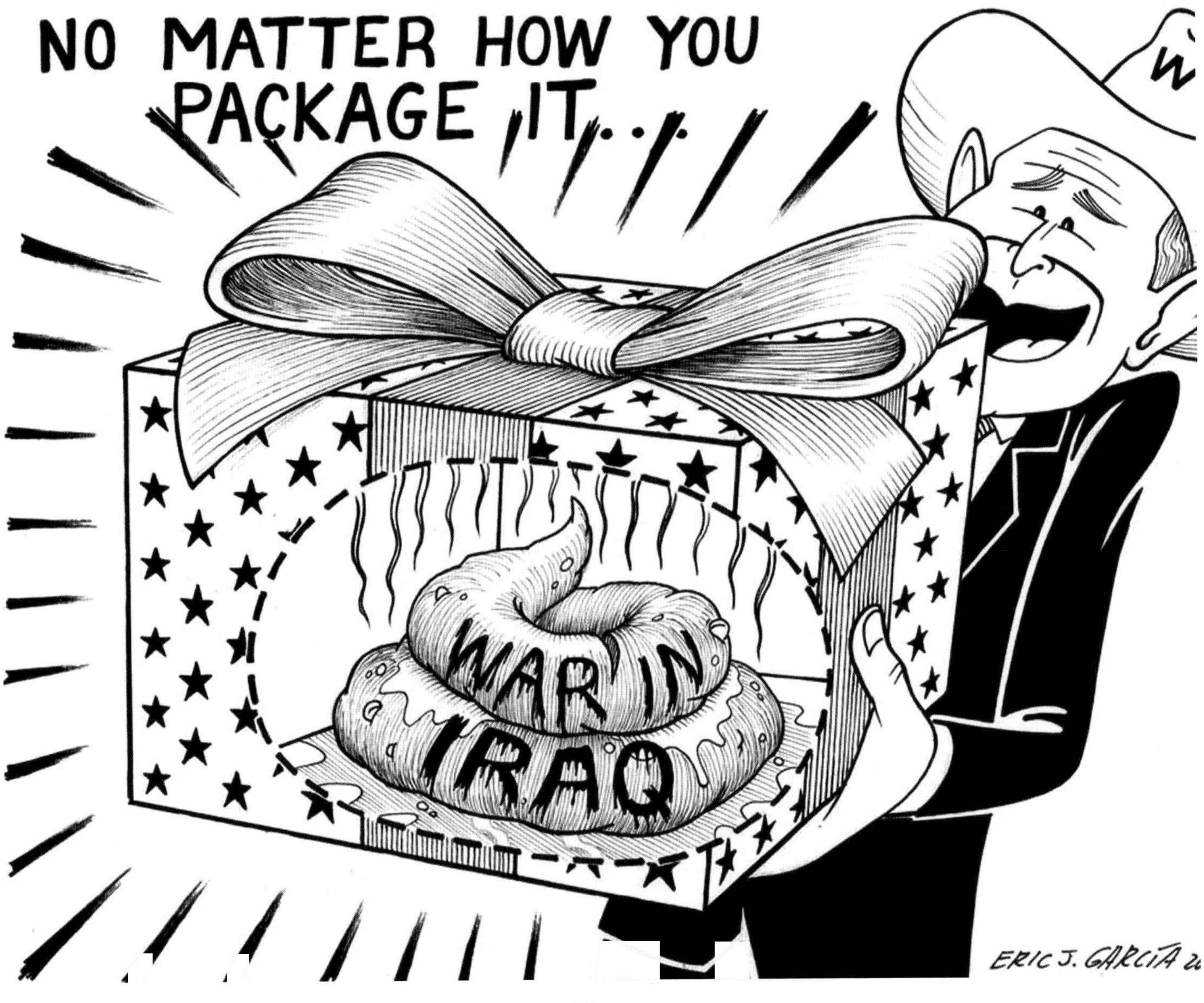
NO MATTER HOW YOU PACKAGE IT...
W
WAR IN IRAQ
ERIC J. GARCÍA

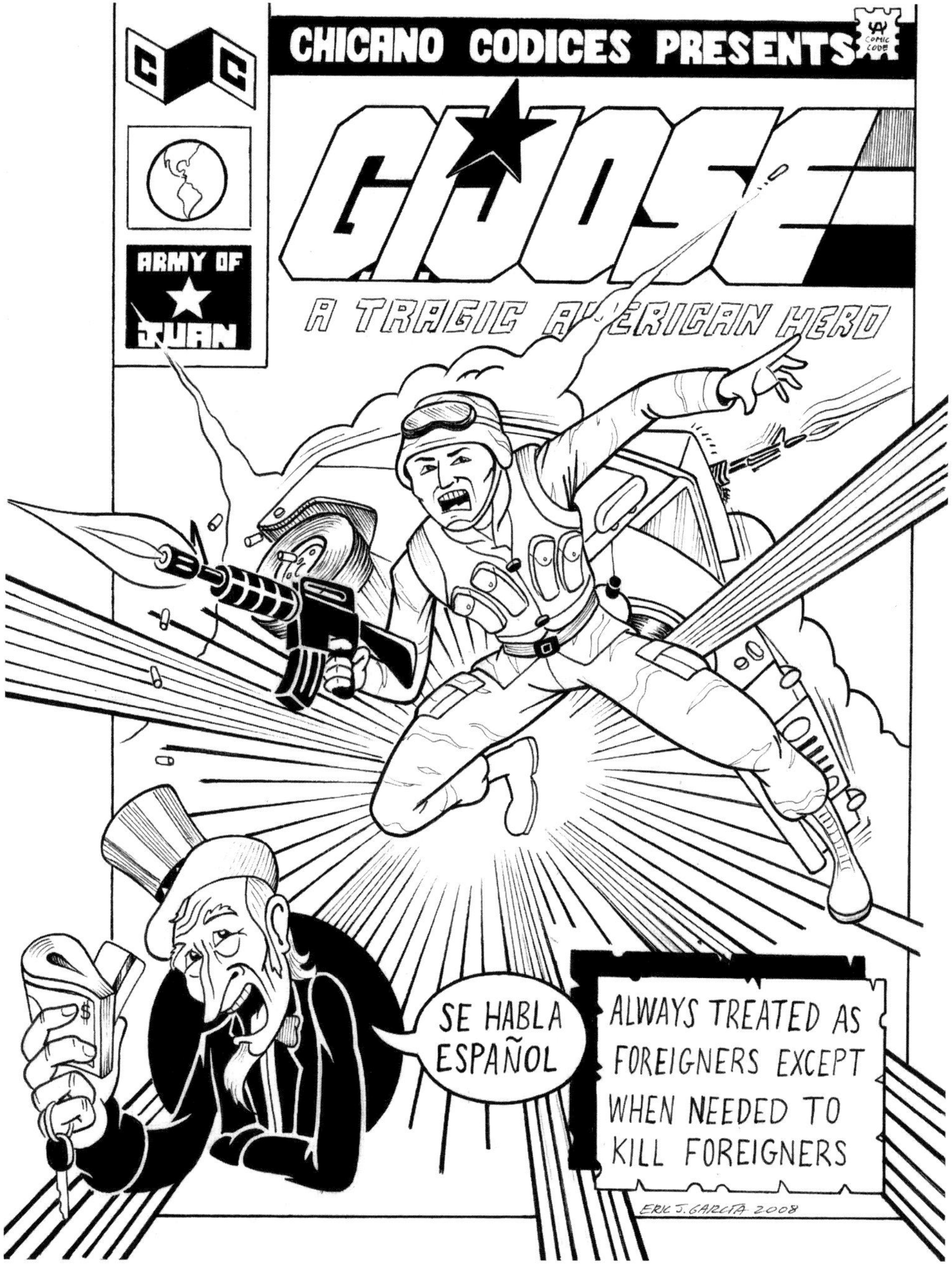
CHICANO CODICES PRESENTS
COMIC CODE
C C
ARMY OF JUAN
G.I. JOSE
A TRAGIC AMERICAN HERO
SE HABLA ESPAÑOL
ALWAYS TREATED AS FOREIGNERS EXCEPT WHEN NEEDED TO KILL FOREIGNERS
ERIC J. GARCIA 2008

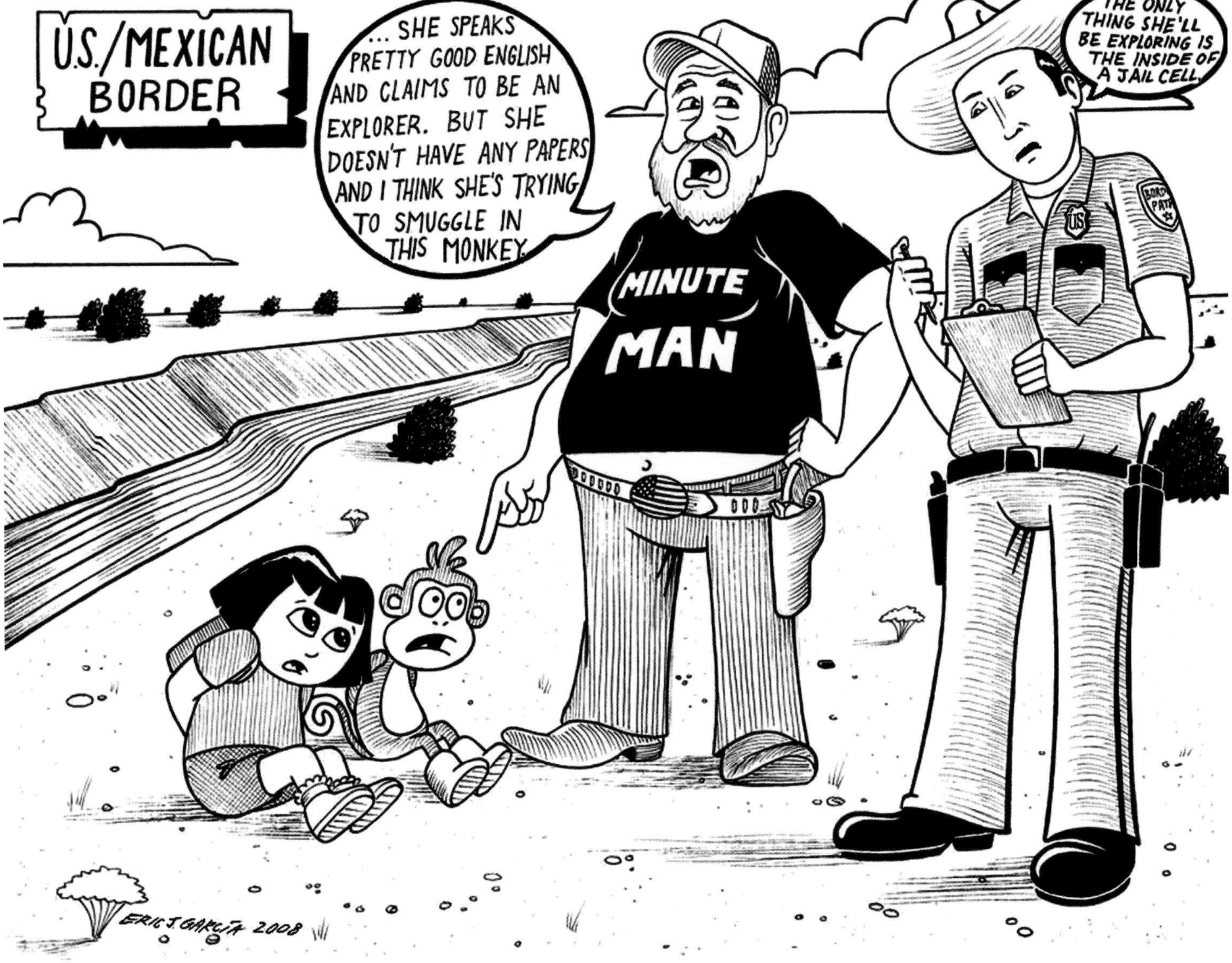
U.S./MEXICAN BORDER
... SHE SPEAKS PRETTY GOOD ENGLISH AND CLAIMS TO BE AN EXPLORER. BUT SHE DOESN'T HAVE ANY PAPERS AND I THINK SHE'S TRYING TO SMUGGLE IN THIS MONKEY.
THE ONLY THING SHE'LL BE EXPLORING IS THE INSIDE OF A JAIL CELL.
MINUTE MAN
US
ERIC J. GARCIA 2008

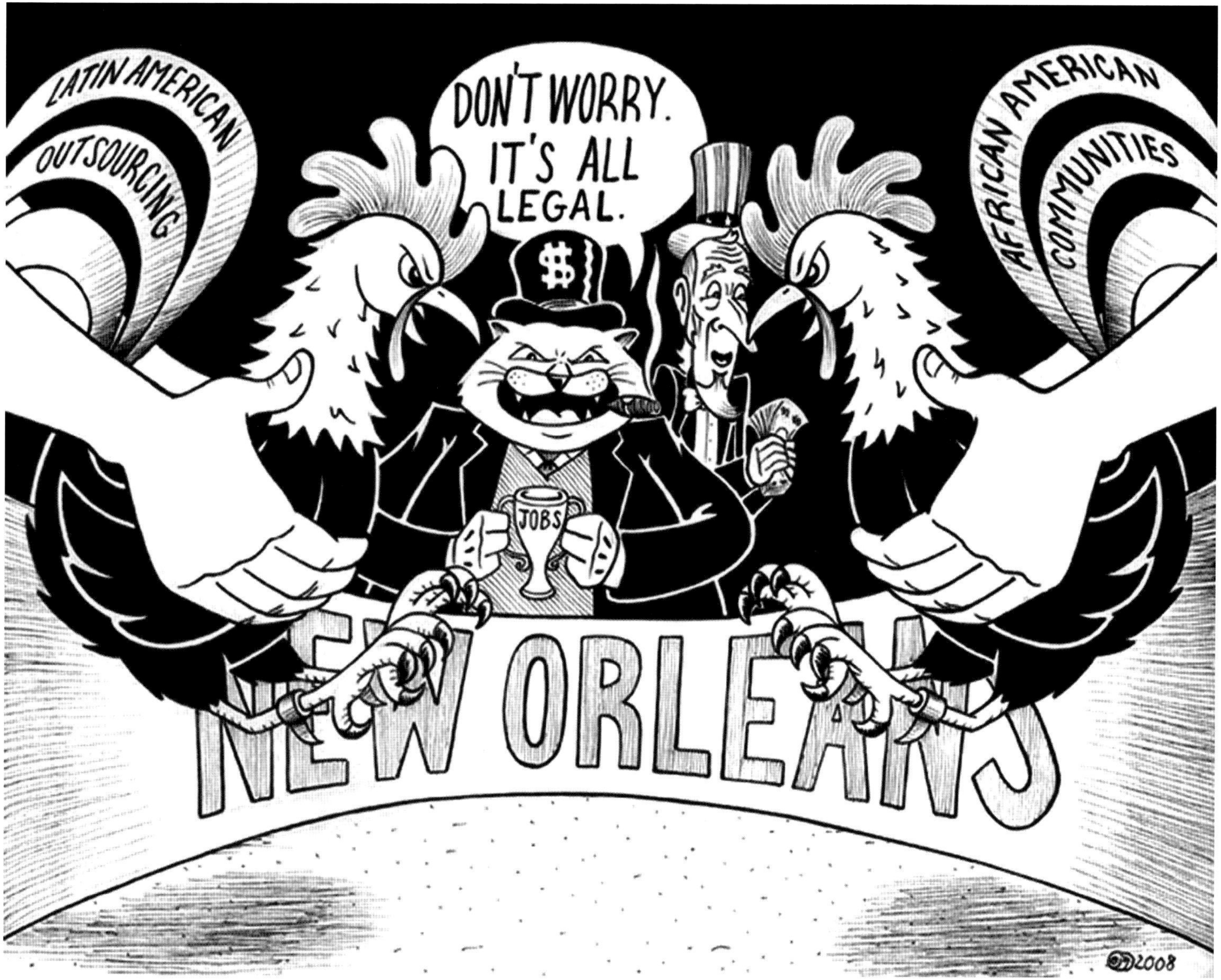
LATIN AMERICAN
OUTSOURCING
DON'T WORRY. IT'S ALL LEGAL.
AFRICAN AMERICAN
COMMUNITIES
$
JOBS
NEW ORLEANS
2008

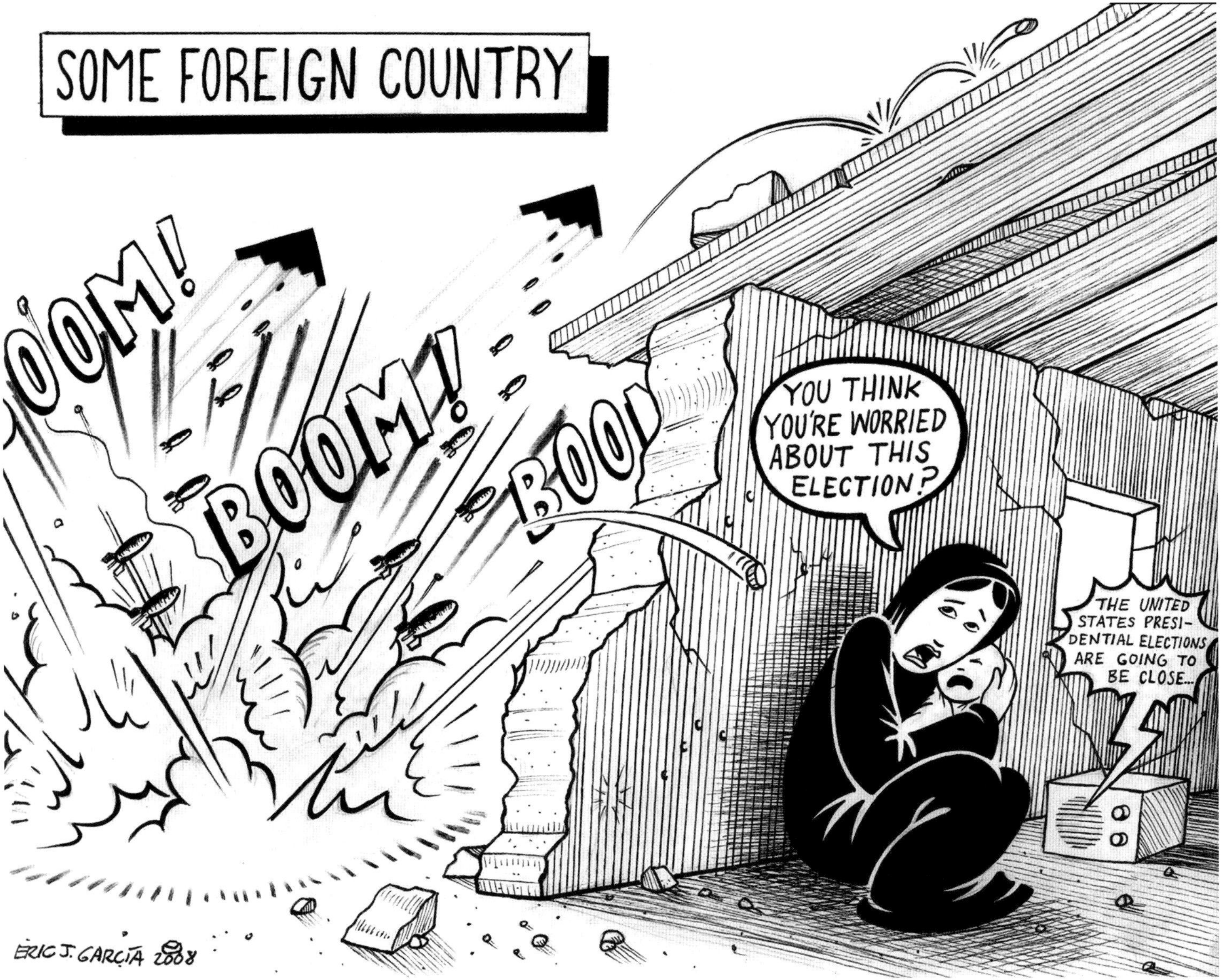
SOME FOREIGN COUNTRY
OOM!
BOOM!
BOO
YOU THINK YOU'RE WORRIED ABOUT THIS ELECTION?
THE UNITED STATES PRESI-DENTIAL ELECTIONS ARE GOING TO BE CLOSE...
ERIC J. GARCIA 2008

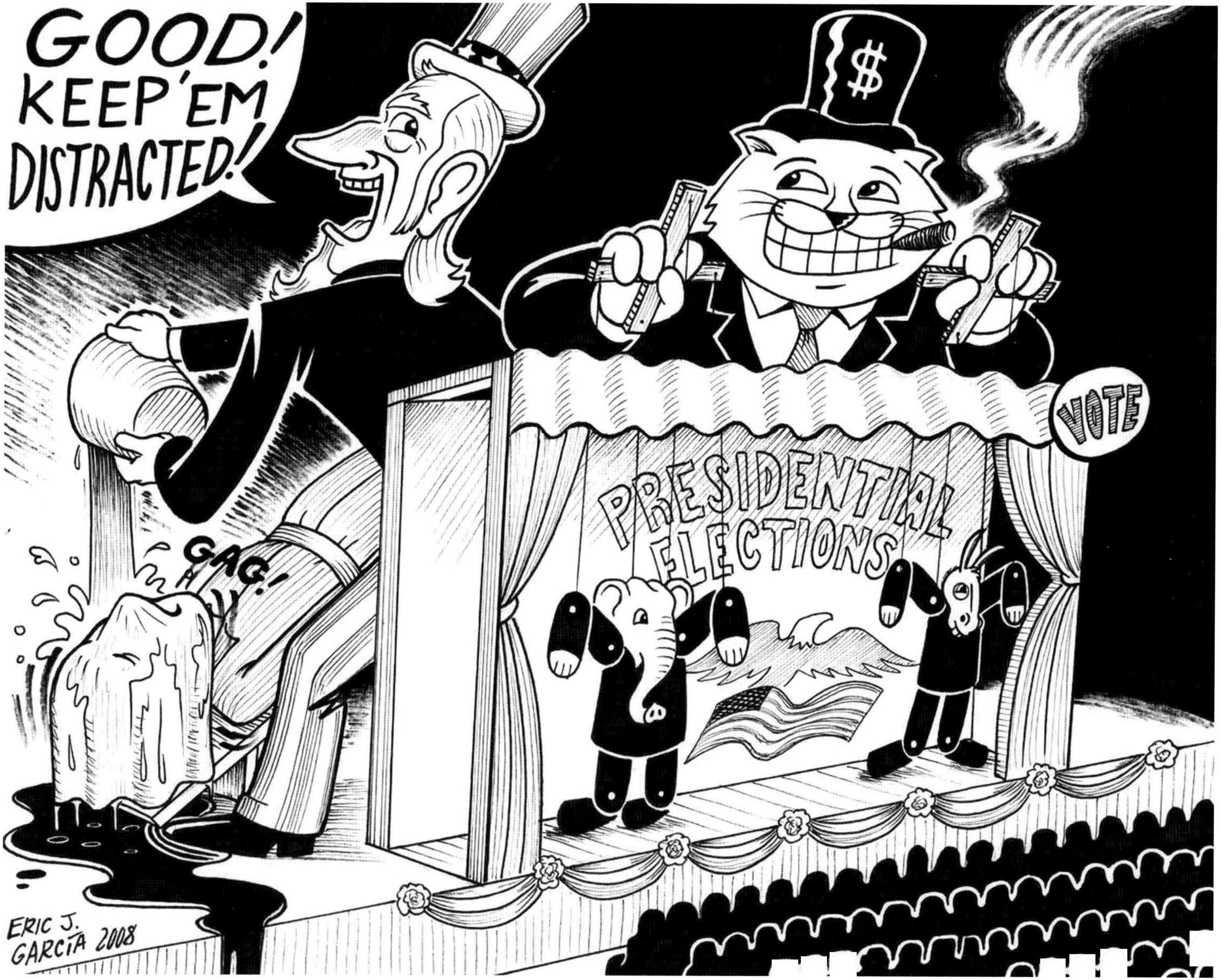
GOOD! KEEP 'EM DISTRACTED!
$
GAG!
VOTE
PRESIDENTIAL ELECTIONS
ERIC J. GARCIA 2008

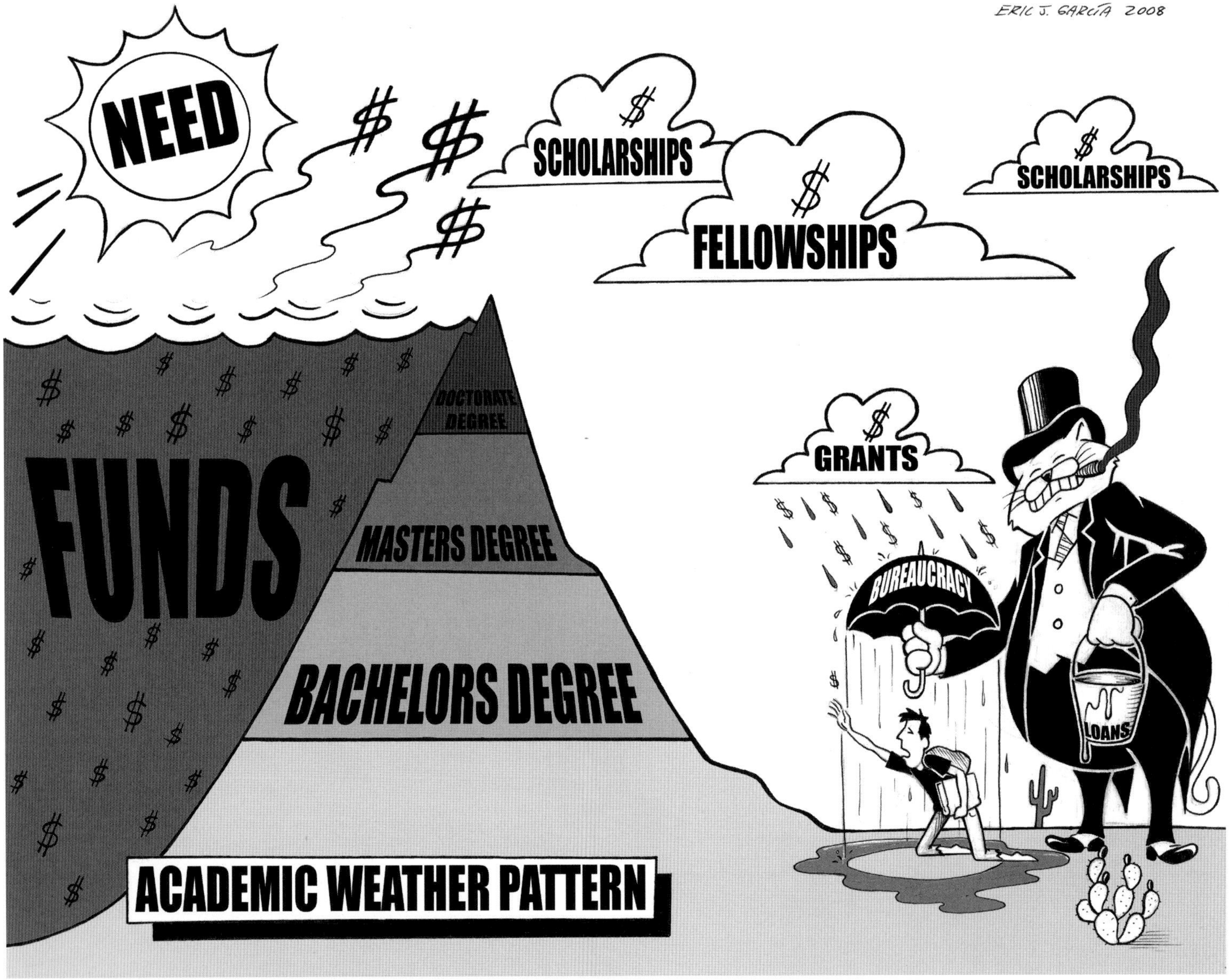
ERIC J. GARCIA 2008
NEED
SCHOLARSHIPS
FELLOWSHIPS
SCHOLARSHIPS
FUNDS
DOCTORATE DEGREE
MASTERS DEGREE
BACHELORS DEGREE
GRANTS
BUREAUCRACY
LOANS
ACADEMIC WEATHER PATTERN

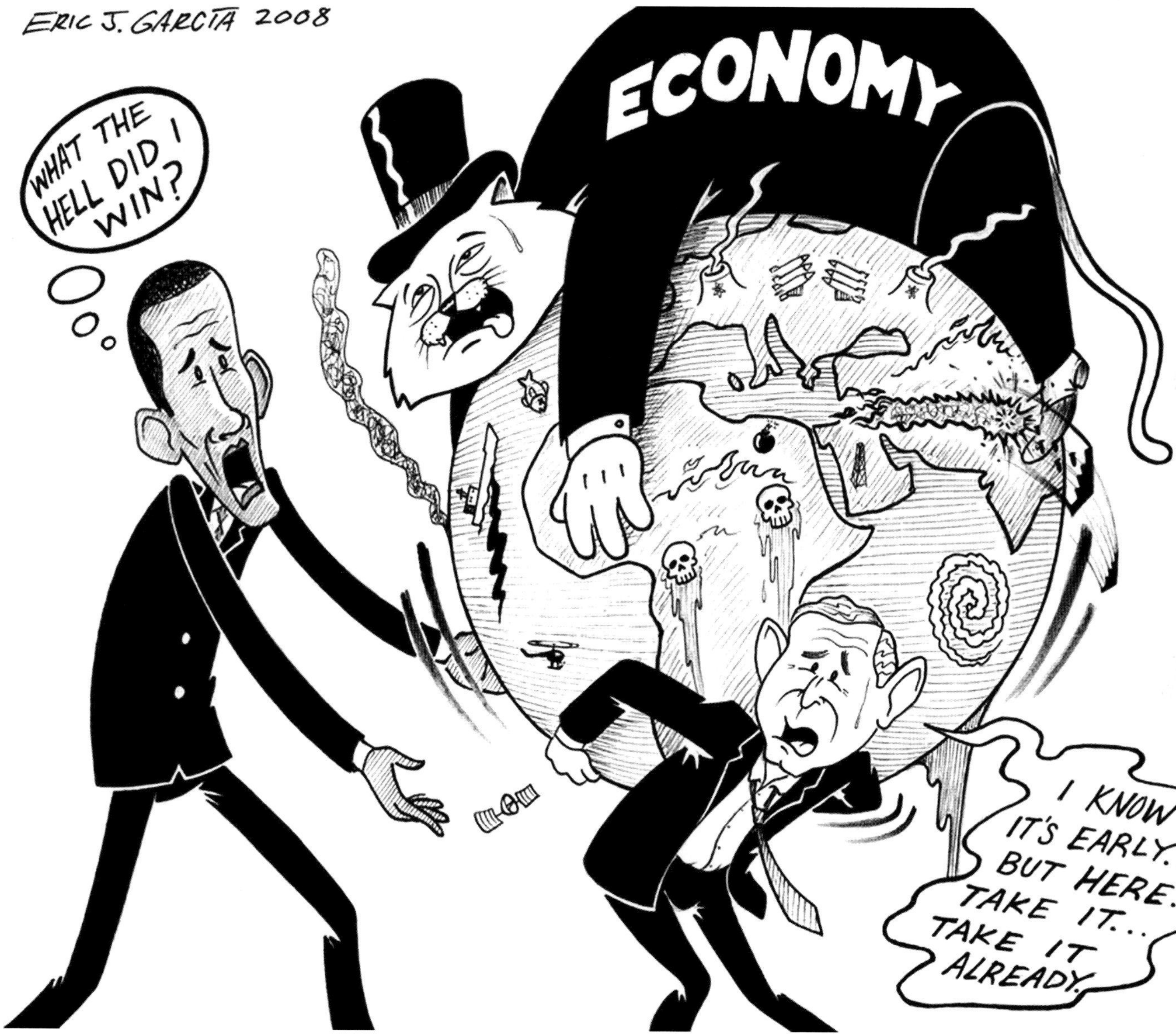
ERIC J. GARCIA 2008
ECONOMY
WHAT THE HELL DID I WIN?
I KNOW IT'S EARLY... BUT HERE... TAKE IT... TAKE IT ALREADY.

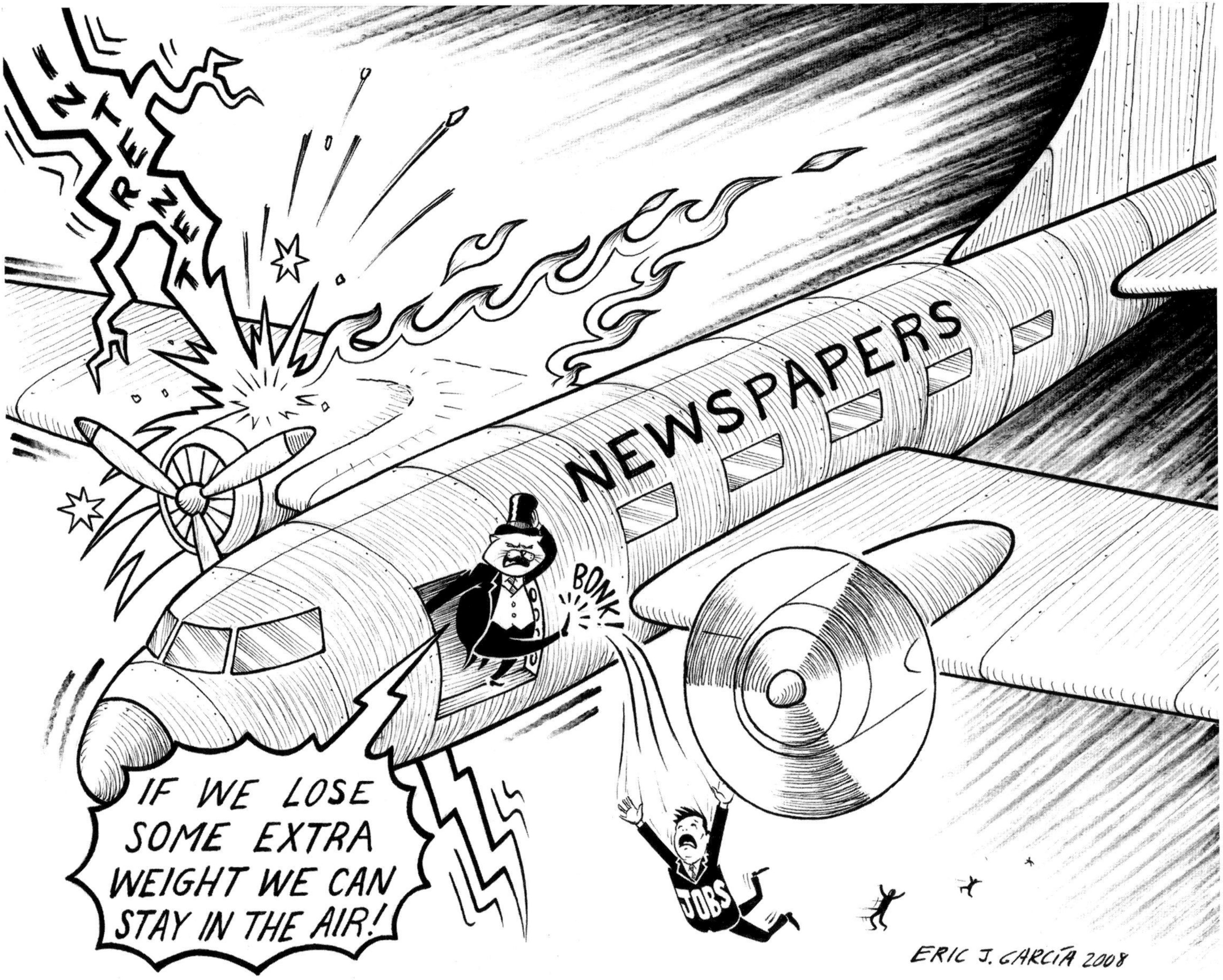
INTERNET
NEWSPAPERS
BONK!
JOBS
IF WE LOSE SOME EXTRA WEIGHT WE CAN STAY IN THE AIR!
ERIC J. GARCIA 2008

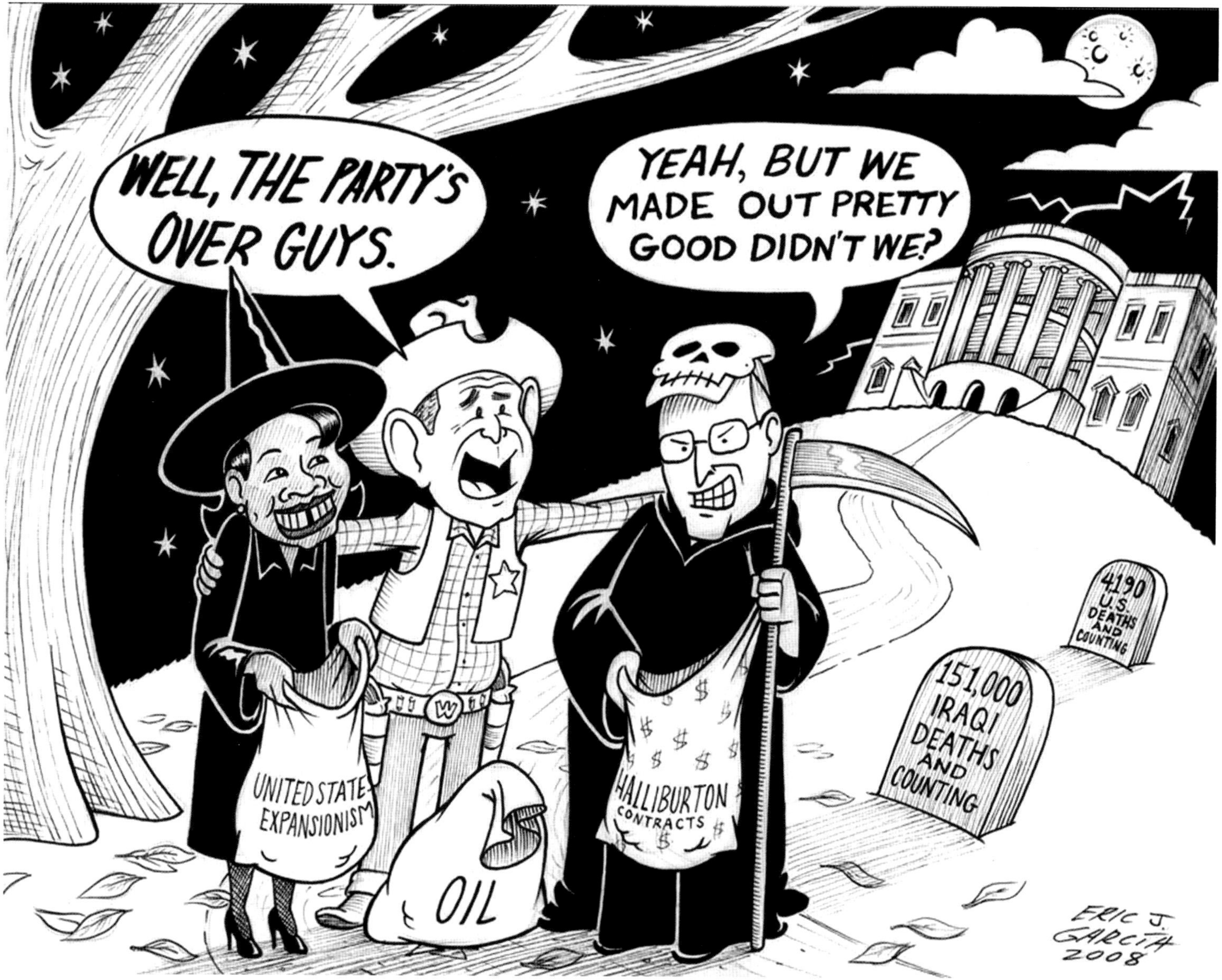
WELL, THE PARTY'S OVER GUYS.
YEAH, BUT WE MADE OUT PRETTY GOOD DIDN'T WE?
4190 U.S. DEATHS AND COUNTING
151,000 IRAQI DEATHS AND COUNTING
UNITED STATES EXPANSIONISM
OIL
HALLIBURTON CONTRACTS
ERIC J. GARCIA 2008

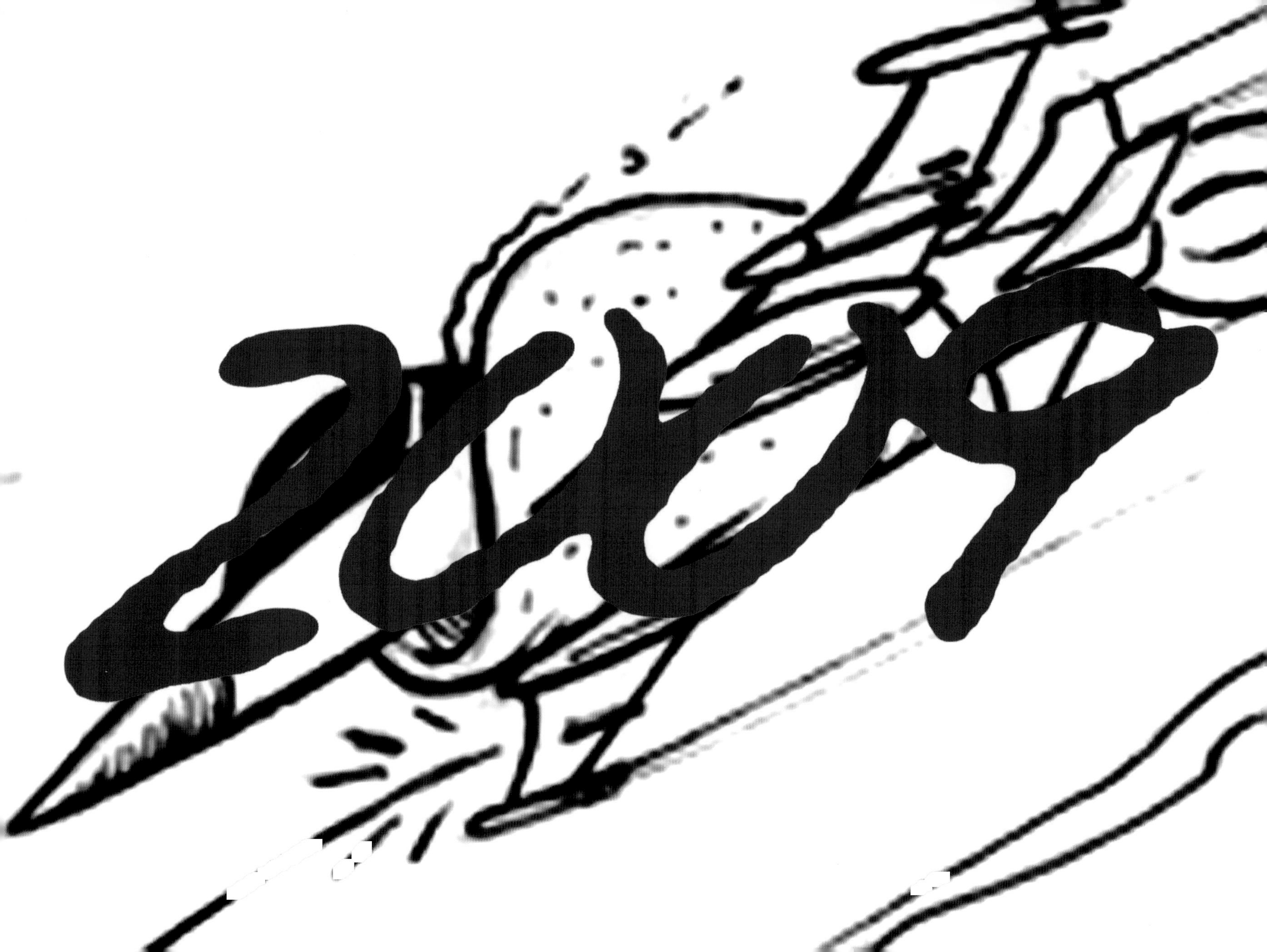
2009

2009

Unfortunately the presidential elections only brought about minor change, such as averting the public's awareness of the disaster in Iraq to focusing on the war in Afghanistan. Both wars were still supported by the blind faith of the Christian Right and corporations like Dick Cheney's Halliburton, which profited from the war. At the same time, south of the border, the Drug War raging in Mexico was nothing more than drug lords competing for the unquenchable markets of the U.S. Back stateside, college students dare not step out of line, as they'd become indentured servants trying to win back their financial freedom.

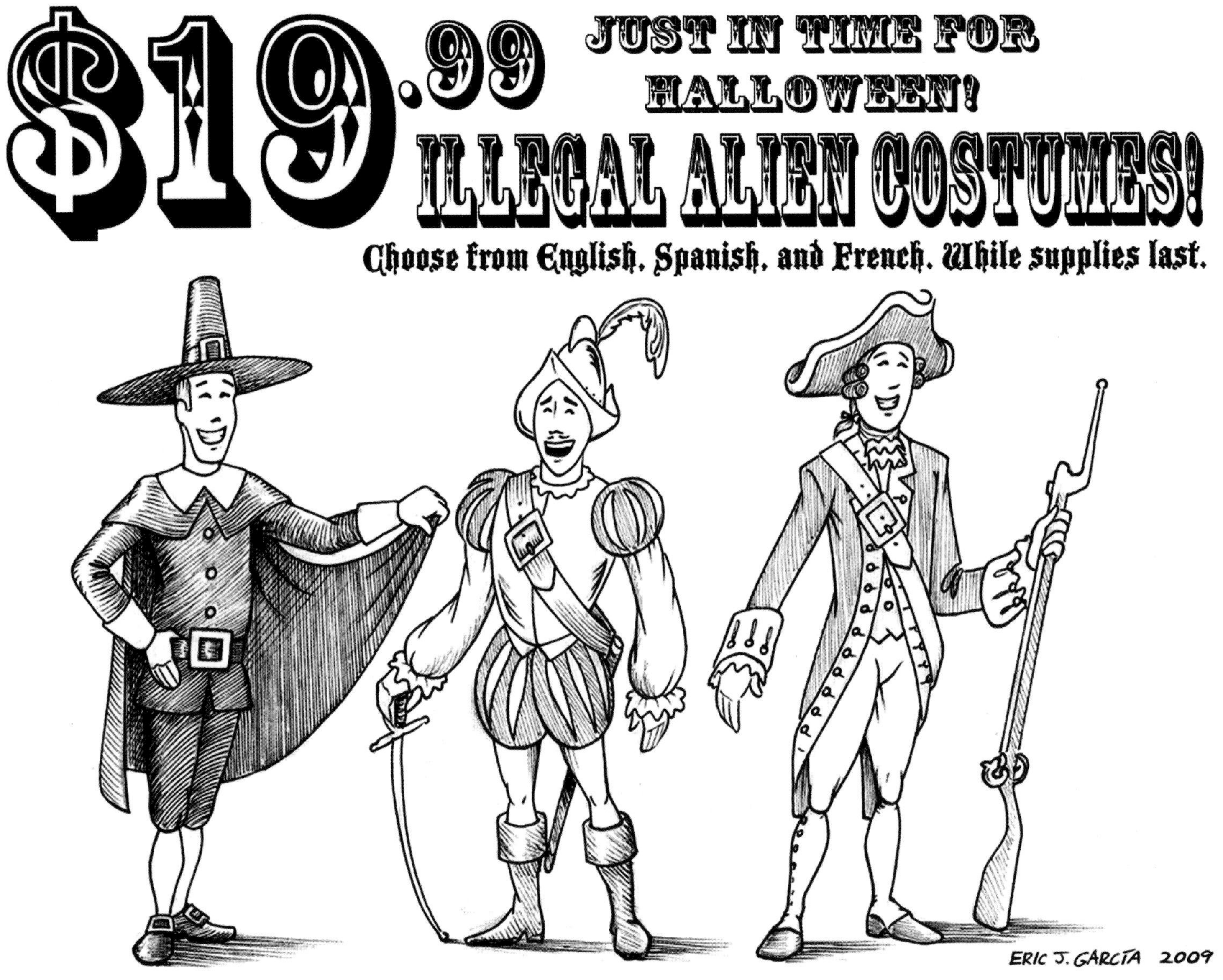
$19.99
JUST IN TIME FOR HALLOWEEN!
ILLEGAL ALIEN COSTUMES!
Choose from English, Spanish, and French. While supplies last.
ERIC J. GARCIA 2009

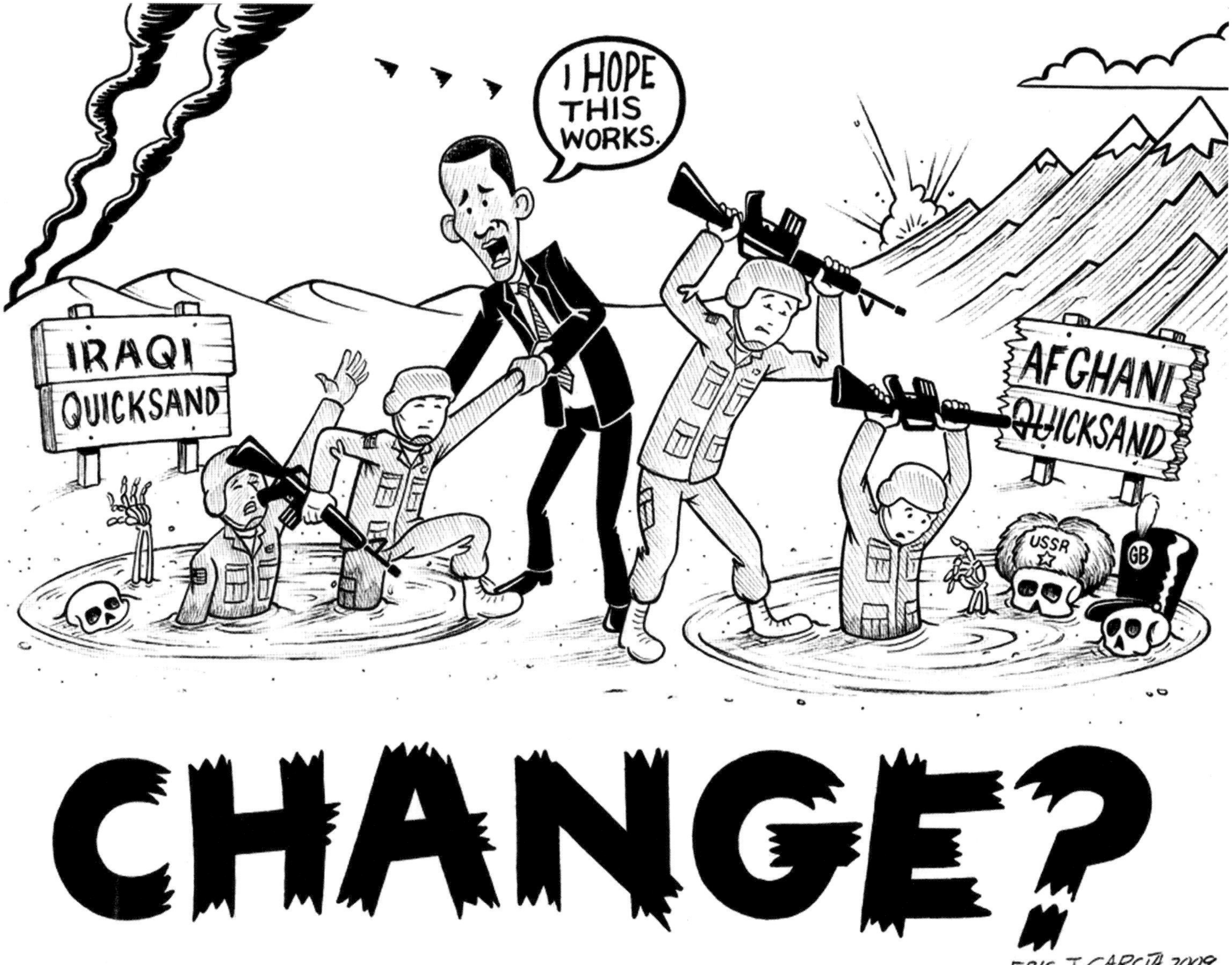

I HOPE THIS WORKS.
IRAQI QUICKSAND
AFGHANI QUICKSAND
USSR
GB
CHANGE?
ERIC J. GARCIA 2009

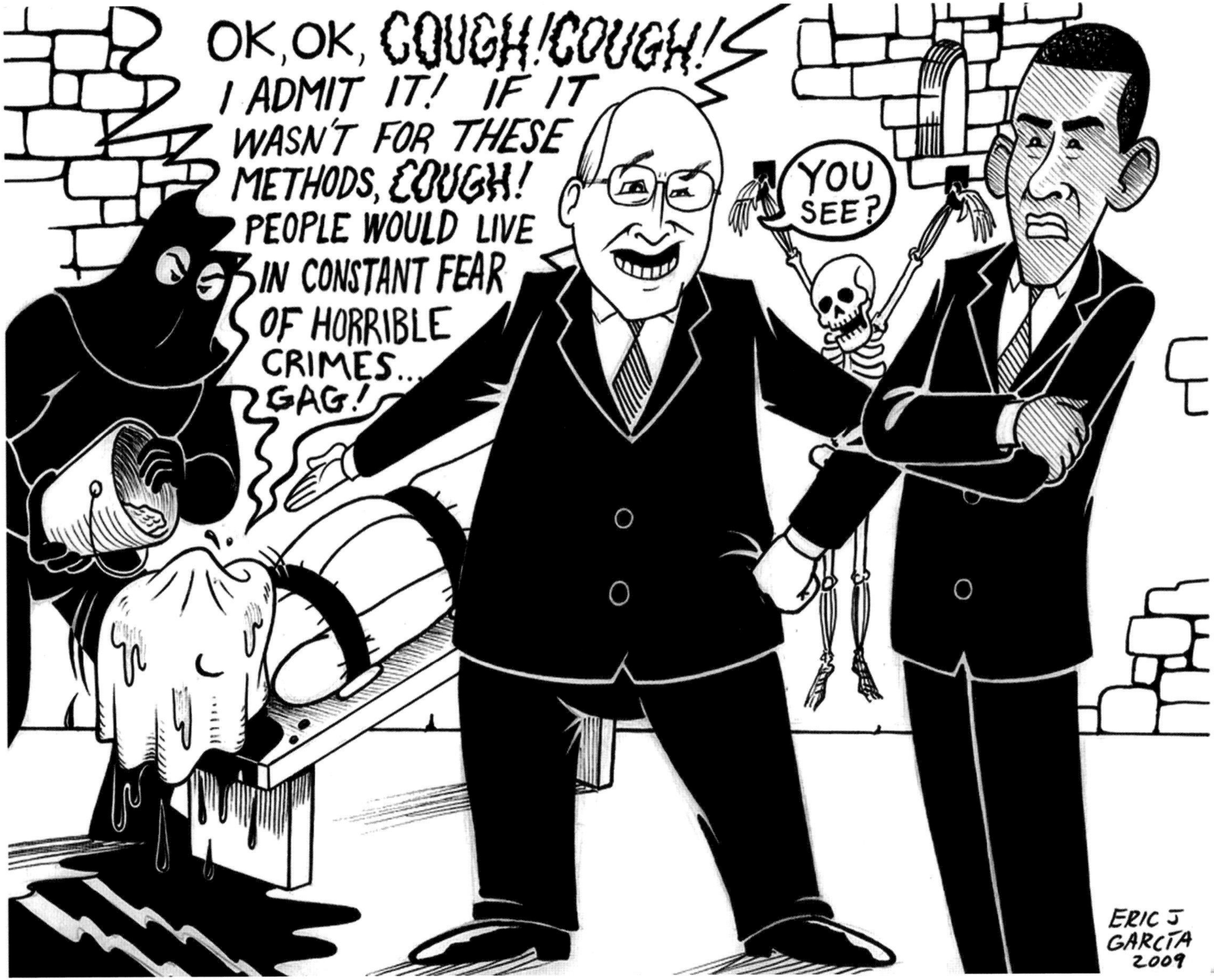
OK, OK, COUGH! COUGH! I ADMIT IT! IF IT WASN'T FOR THESE METHODS, COUGH! PEOPLE WOULD LIVE IN CONSTANT FEAR OF HORRIBLE CRIMES... GAG!
YOU SEE?
ERIC J GARCIA 2009

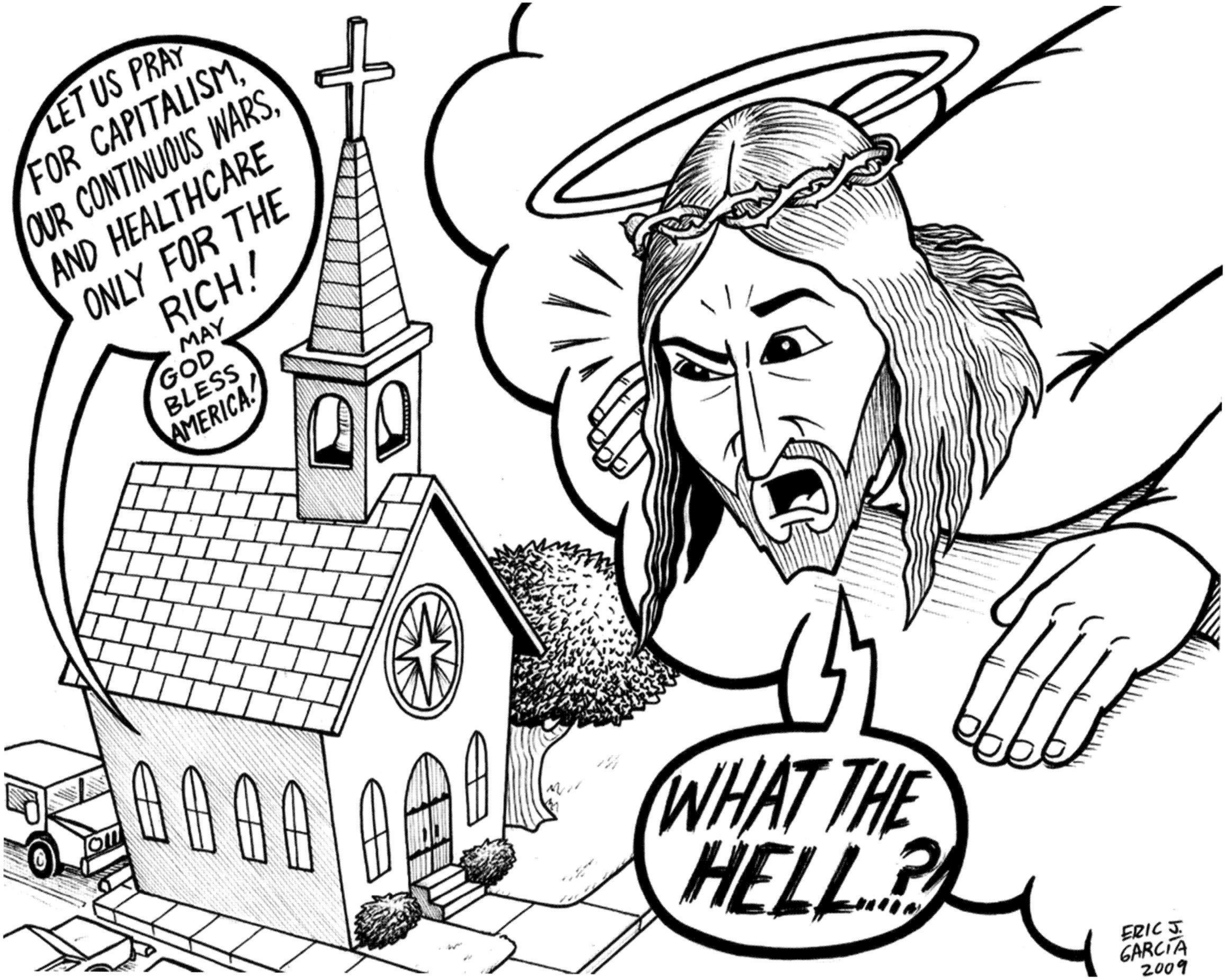
LET US PRAY FOR CAPITALISM, OUR CONTINUOUS WARS, AND HEALTHCARE ONLY FOR THE RICH!
MAY GOD BLESS AMERICA!
WHAT THE HELL...?!
ERIC J. GARCIA 2009

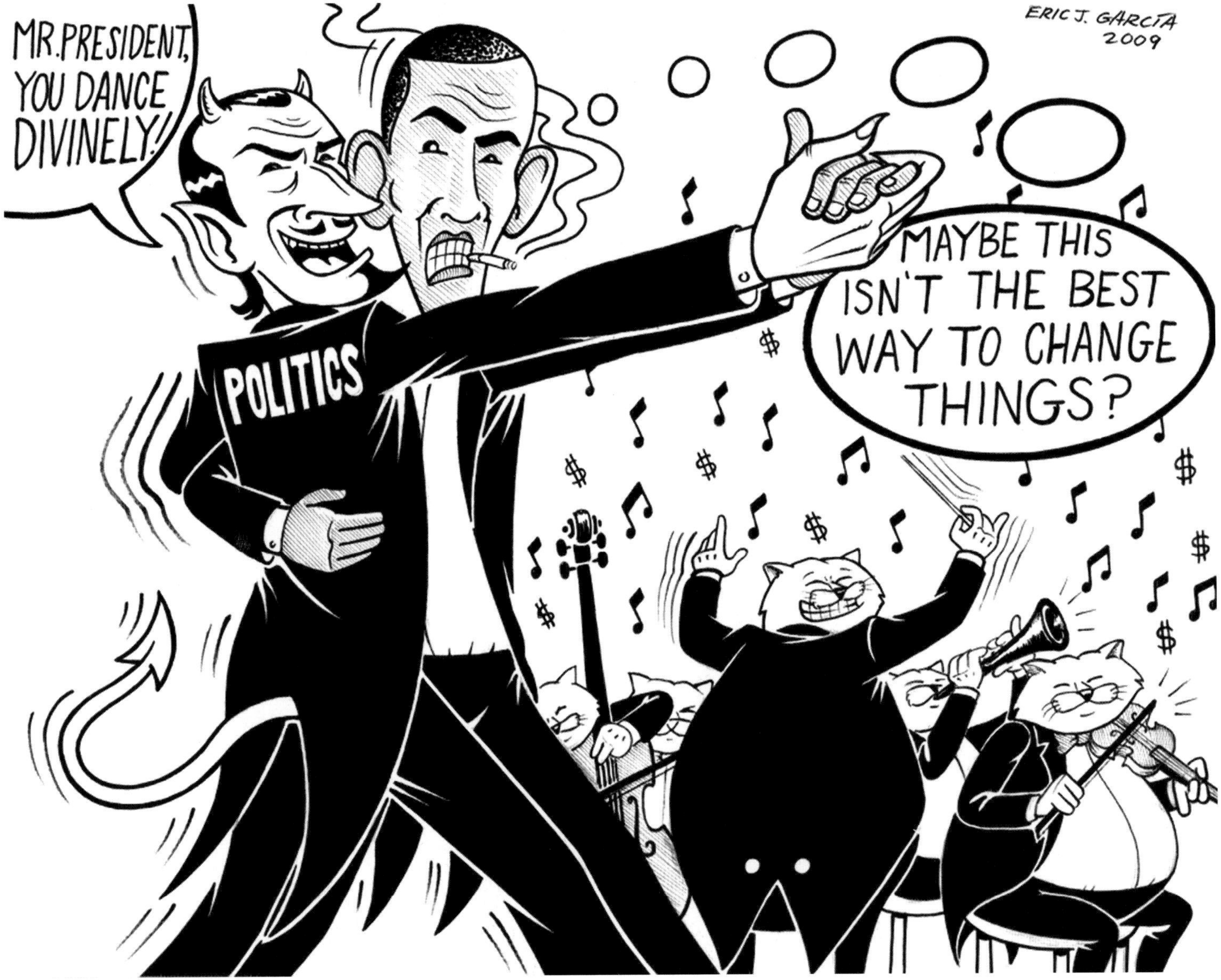
ERIC J. GARCIA
2009
MR. PRESIDENT, YOU DANCE DIVINELY!
POLITICS
MAYBE THIS ISN'T THE BEST WAY TO CHANGE THINGS?

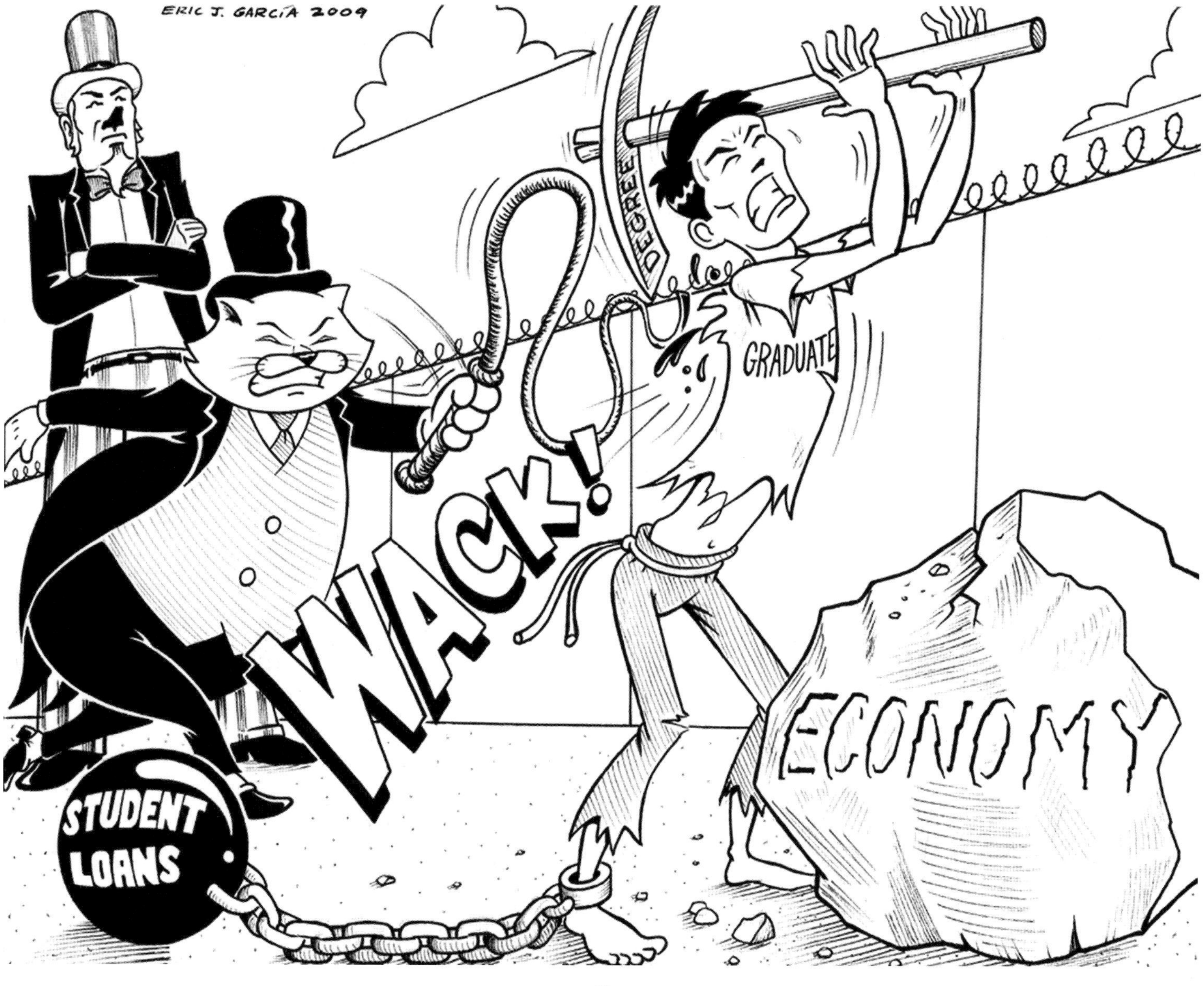
ERIC J. GARCÍA 2009
DEGREE
GRADUATE
WACK!
ECONOMY
STUDENT LOANS

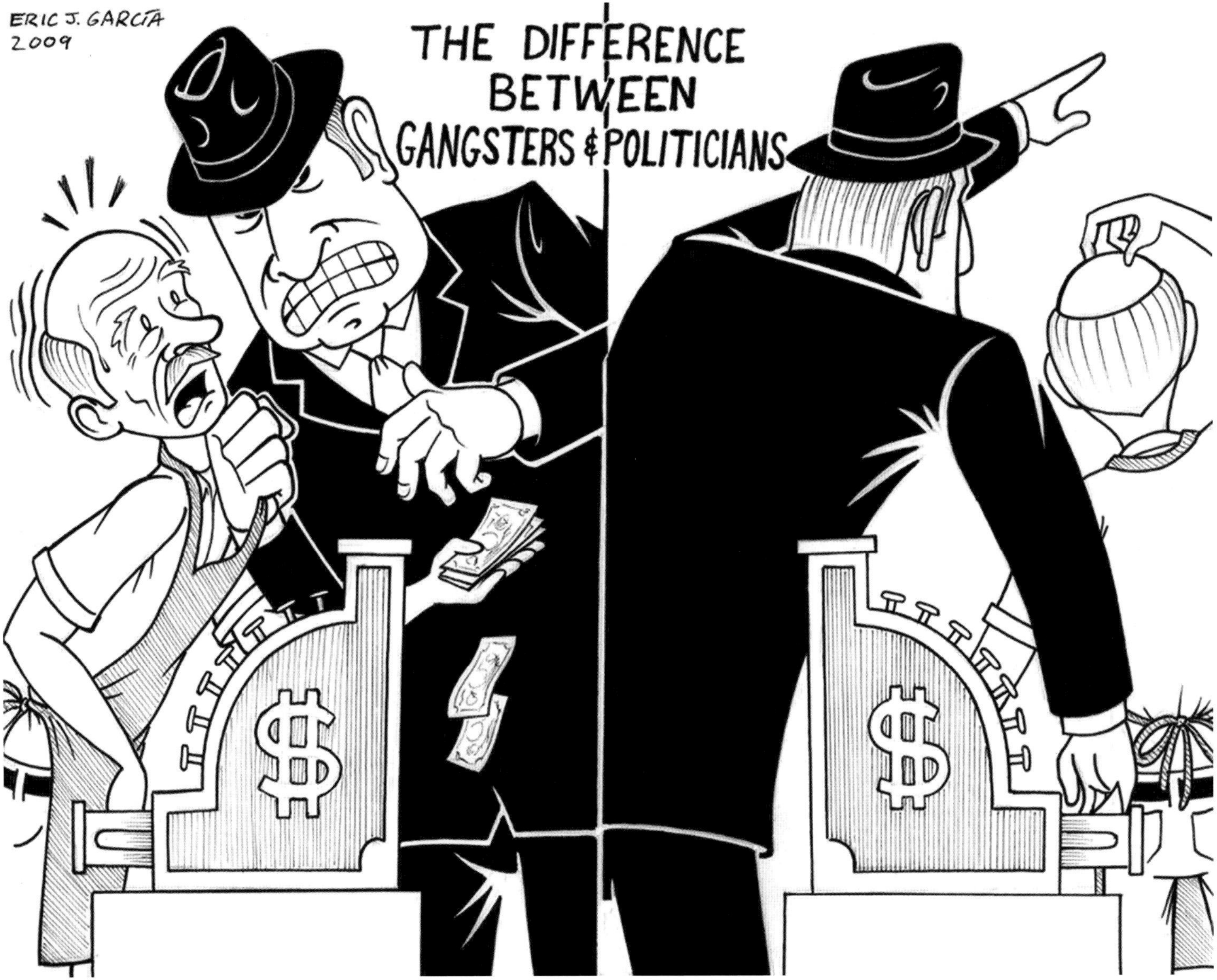
ERIC J. GARCÍA
2009
THE DIFFERENCE BETWEEN GANGSTERS & POLITICIANS

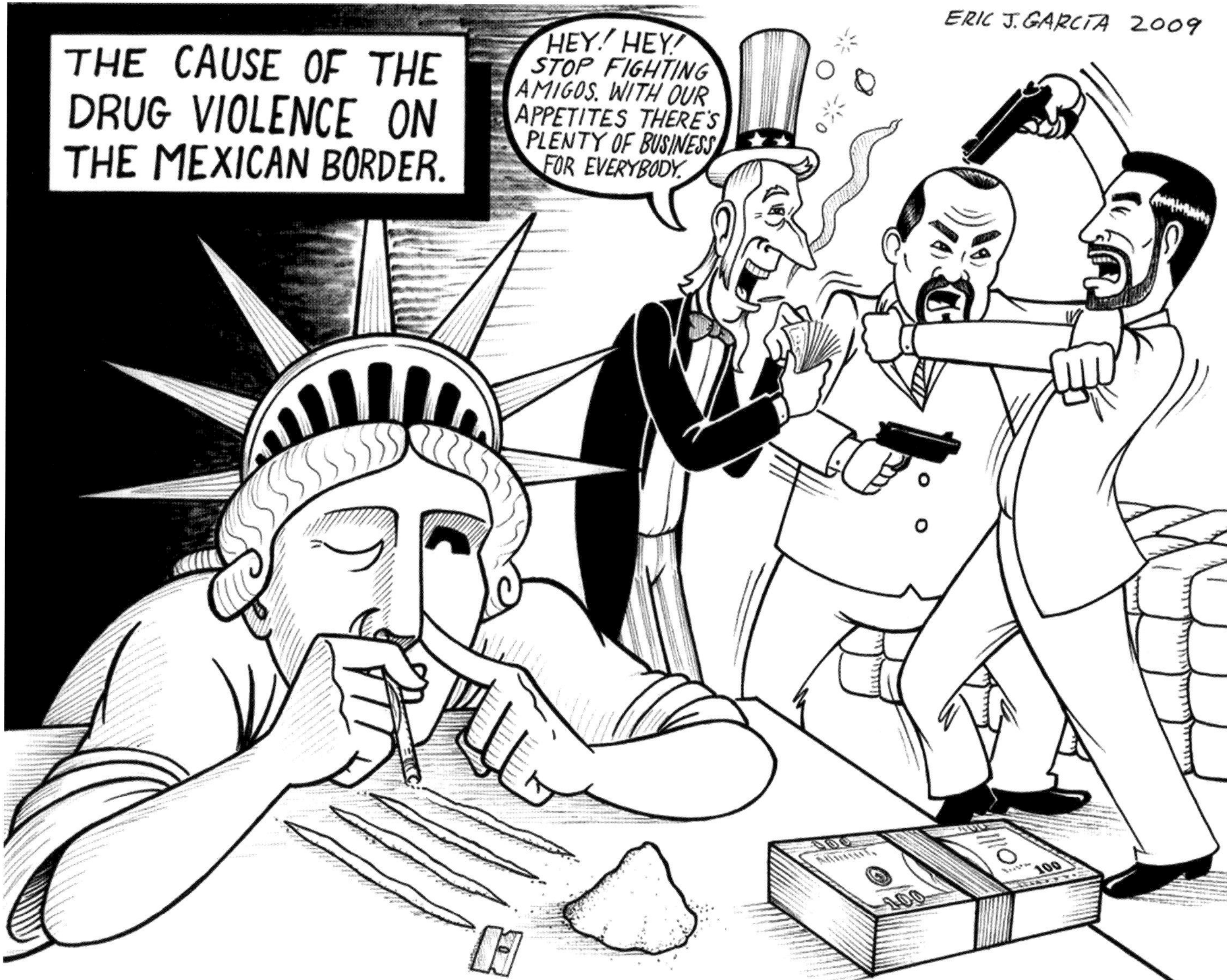
ERIC J. GARCIA 2009
THE CAUSE OF THE DRUG VIOLENCE ON THE MEXICAN BORDER.
HEY! HEY! STOP FIGHTING AMIGOS. WITH OUR APPETITES THERE'S PLENTY OF BUSINESS FOR EVERYBODY.

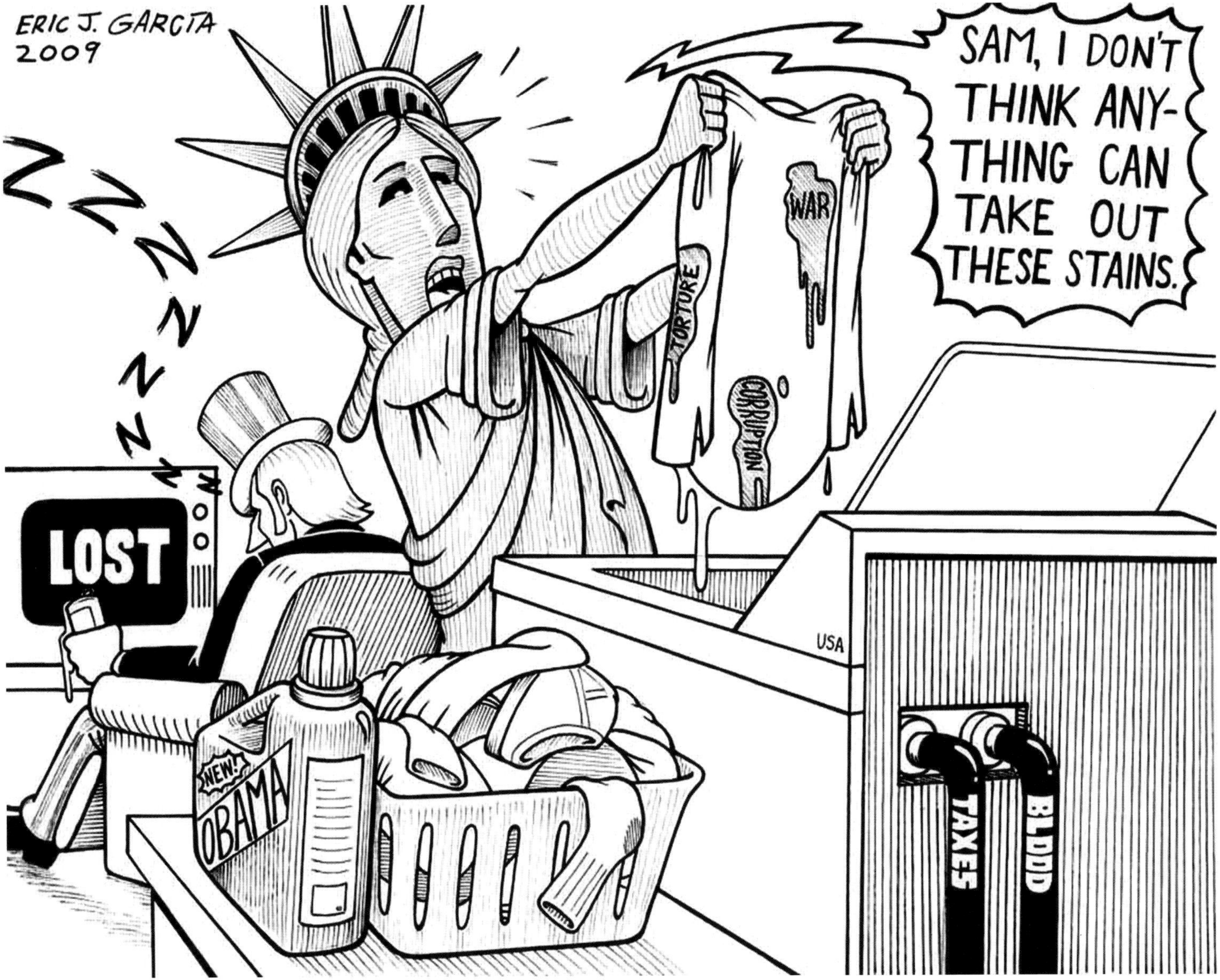
ERIC J. GARCIA
2009
SAM, I DON'T THINK ANY-THING CAN TAKE OUT THESE STAINS.
WAR
TORTURE
CORRUPTION
LOST
USA
NEW!
OBAMA
TAXES
BLOOD

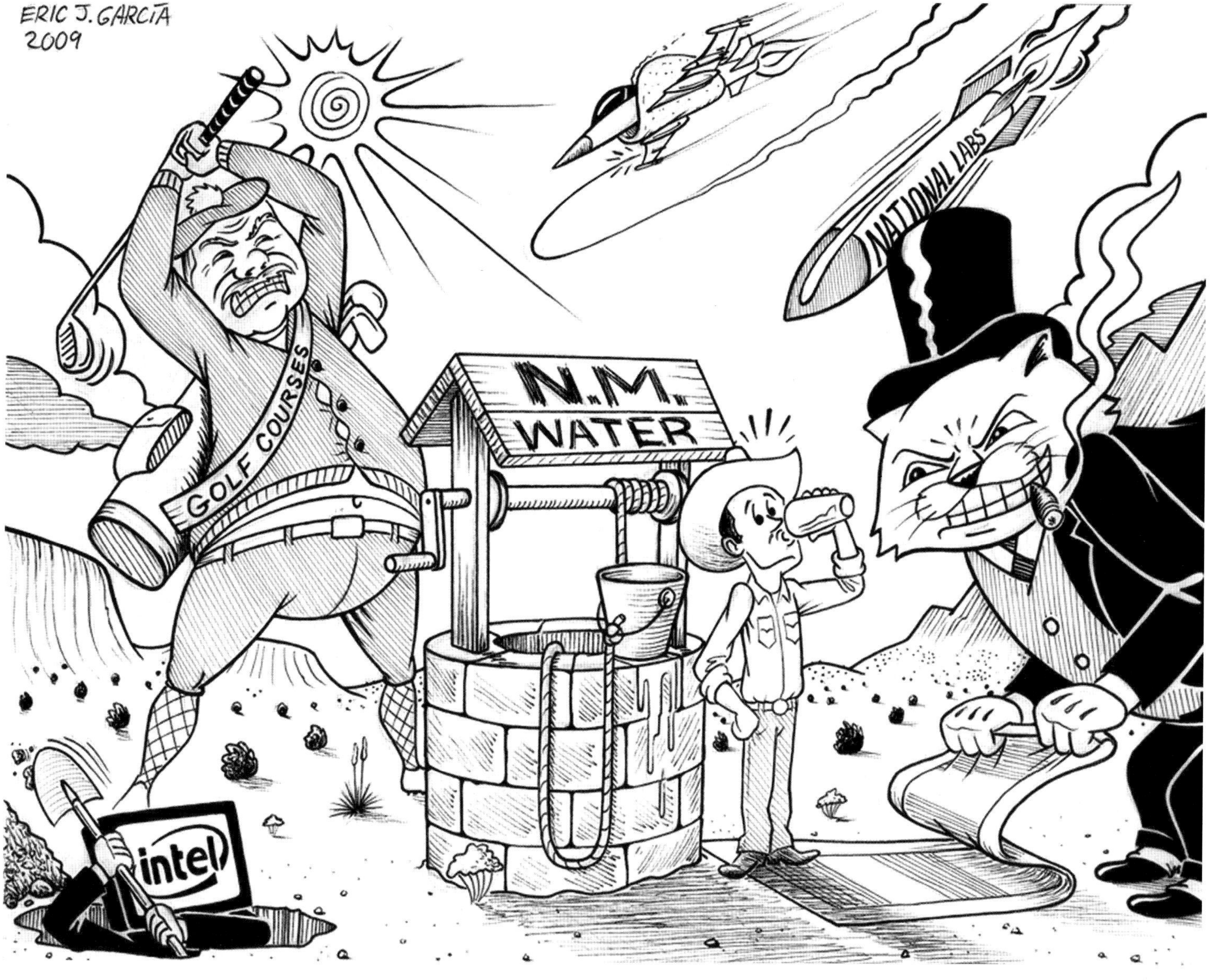
ERIC J. GARCIA
2009
NATIONAL LABS
N.M.
WATER
GOLF COURSES
intel

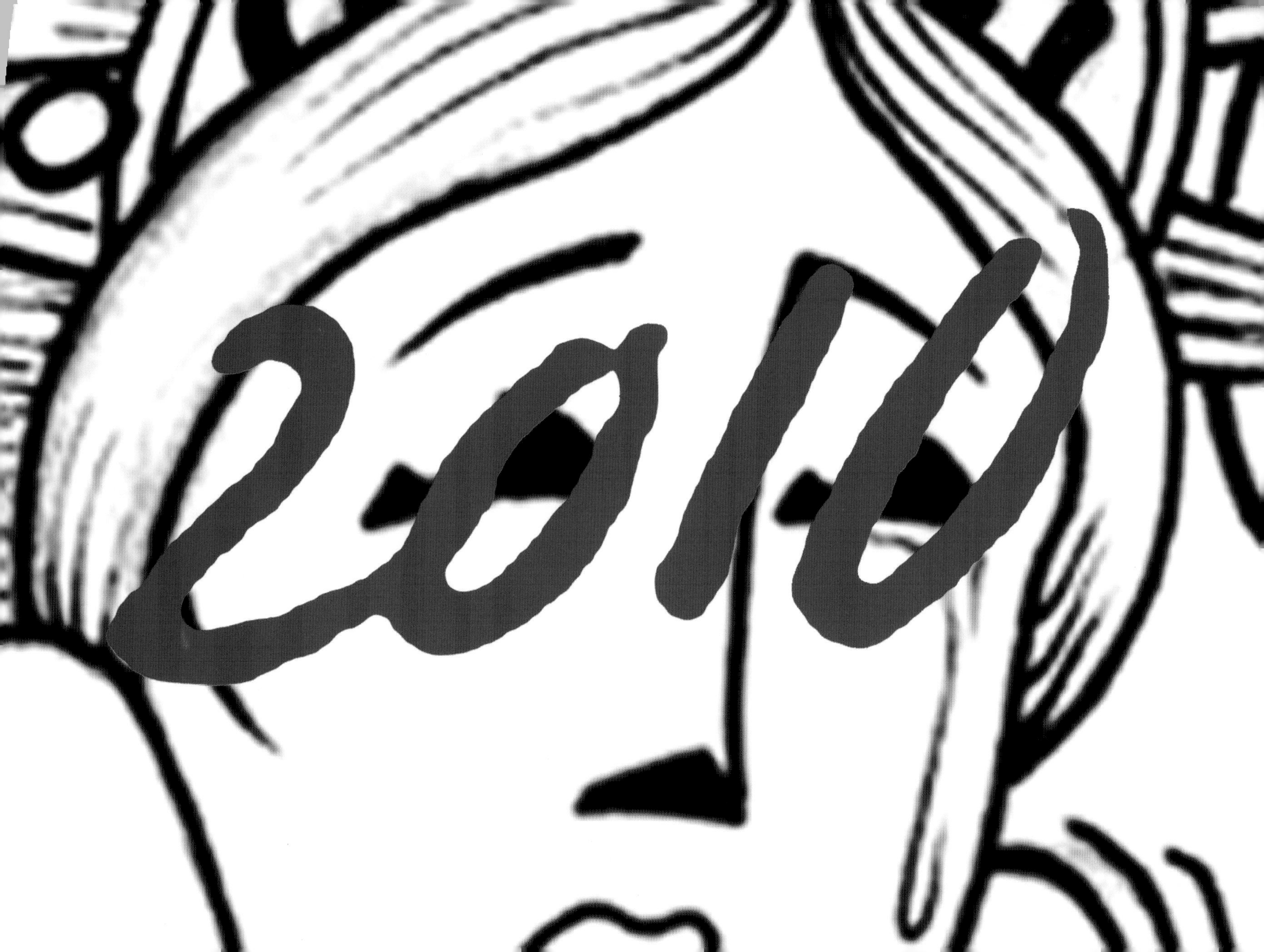
2010

2010

The national debt caused the United States to become dependent on Chinese handouts. Besides debt, the white-collar
crooks who caused the financial crisis got off with a mere
slap on the wrist thanks to their crooked government coun-
terparts. Out west, the Arizona anti-immigrant laws actually
created new migration routes as white supremacists flocked
to the border. In world news, the European-abused island of
Haiti was hit yet again, this time by a force of nature as a
catastrophic 7.0 earthquake rocked the country. And the war
in Iraq began to wind down but was far from over, as a priva-
tized army replaced the U.S. military forces. Soldiers started
to come home one way or another.

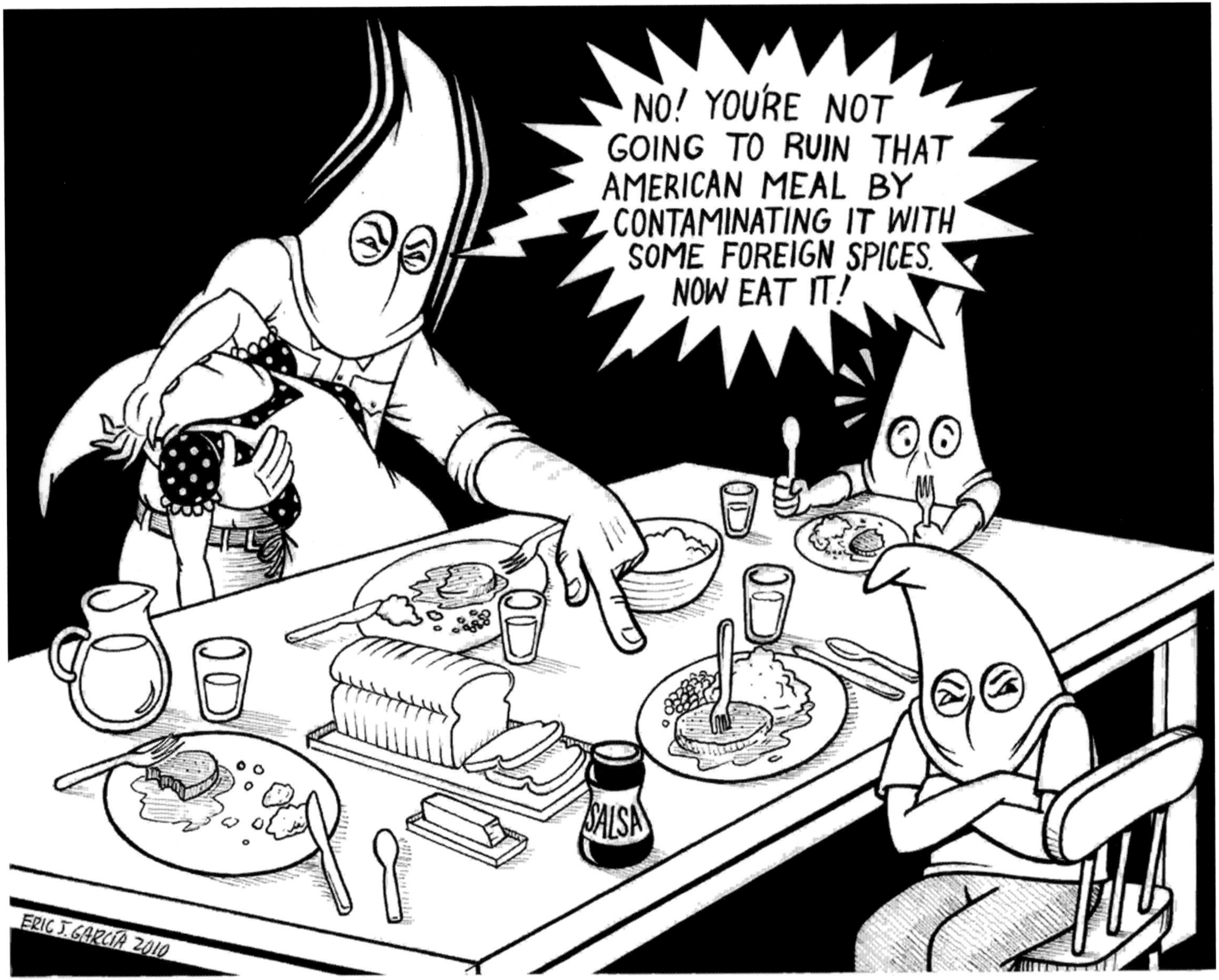
NO! YOU'RE NOT GOING TO RUIN THAT AMERICAN MEAL BY CONTAMINATING IT WITH SOME FOREIGN SPICES. NOW EAT IT!
SALSA
ERIC J. GARCÍA 2010

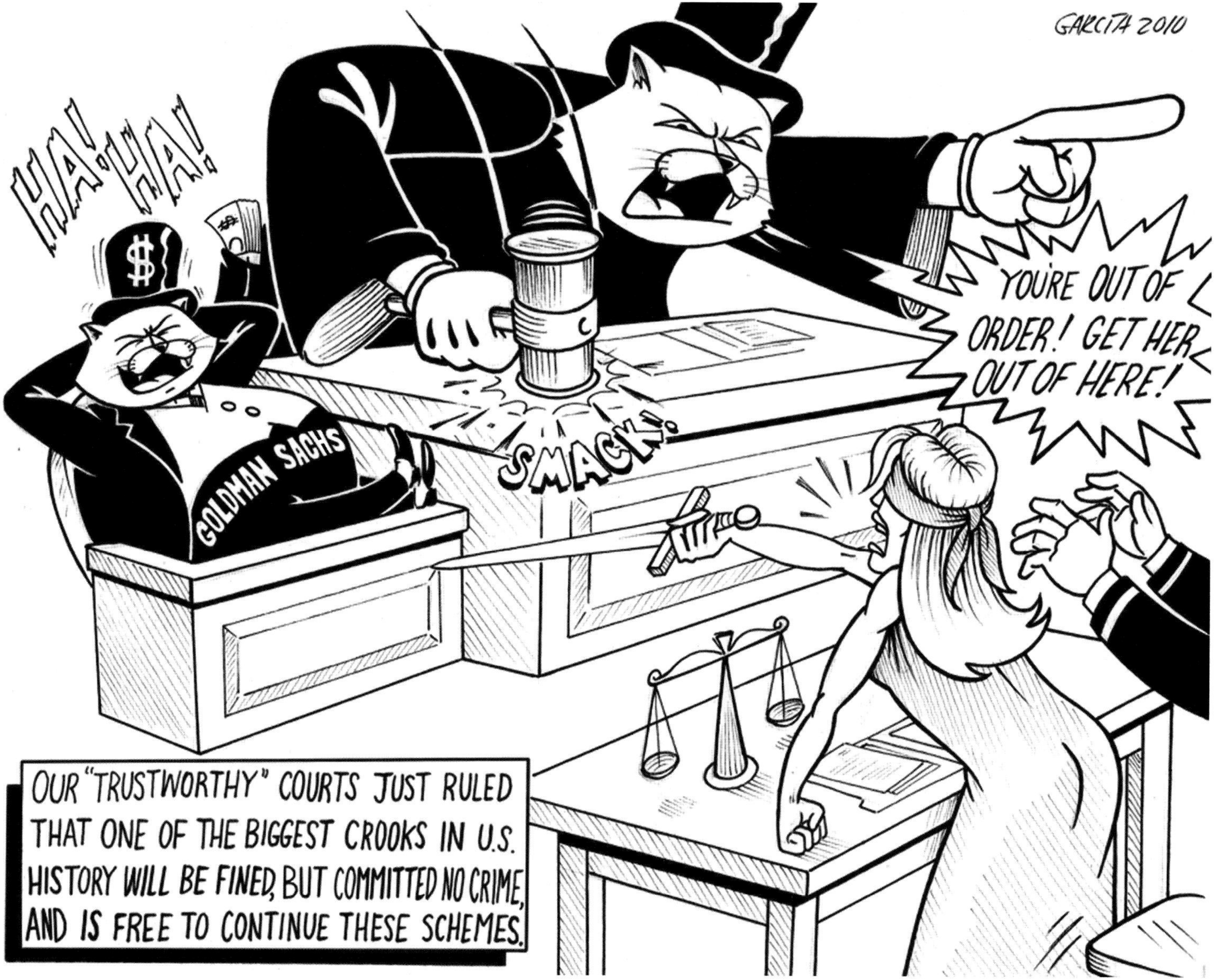
GARCIA 2010
HA! HA!
$
GOLDMAN SACHS
SMACK!
YOU'RE OUT OF ORDER! GET HER OUT OF HERE!
OUR "TRUSTWORTHY" COURTS JUST RULED THAT ONE OF THE BIGGEST CROOKS IN U.S. HISTORY WILL BE FINED, BUT COMMITTED NO CRIME, AND IS FREE TO CONTINUE THESE SCHEMES.

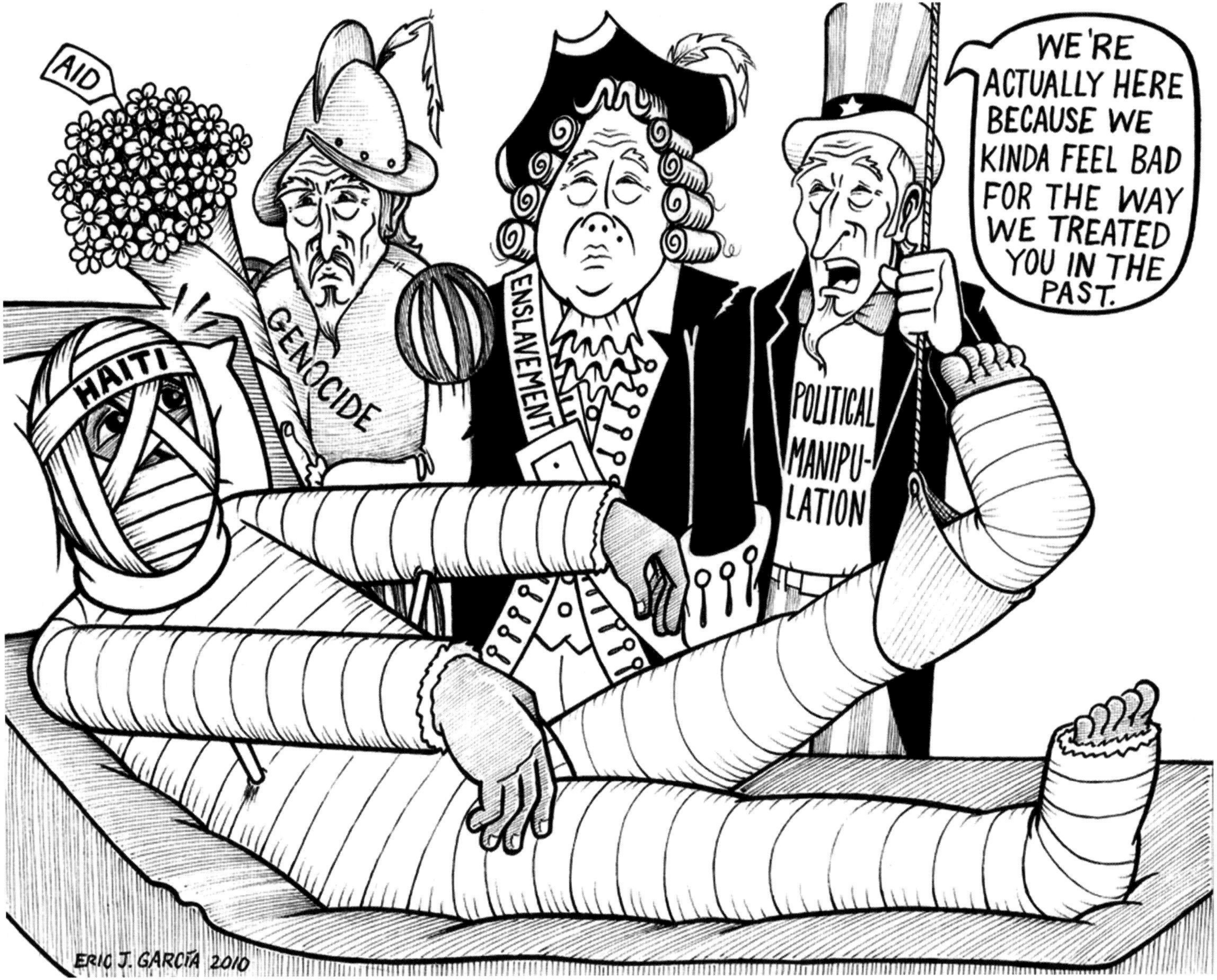
AID
HAITI
GENOCIDE
ENSLAVEMENT
POLITICAL MANIPU-LATION
WE'RE ACTUALLY HERE BECAUSE WE KINDA FEEL BAD FOR THE WAY WE TREATED YOU IN THE PAST.
ERIC J. GARCÍA 2010

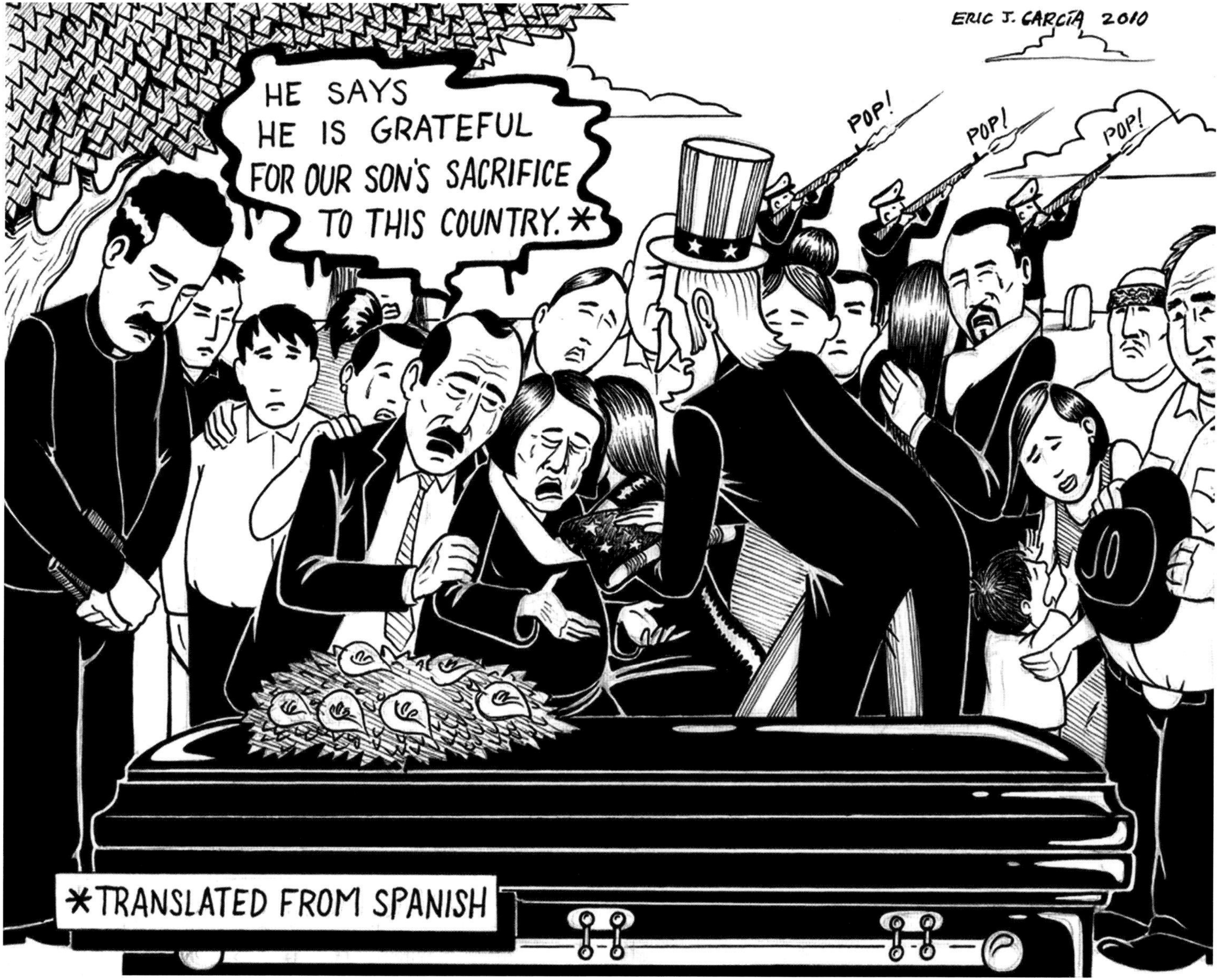
ERIC J. GARCIA 2010
HE SAYS HE IS GRATEFUL FOR OUR SON'S SACRIFICE TO THIS COUNTRY.*
POP!
POP!
POP!
*TRANSLATED FROM SPANISH

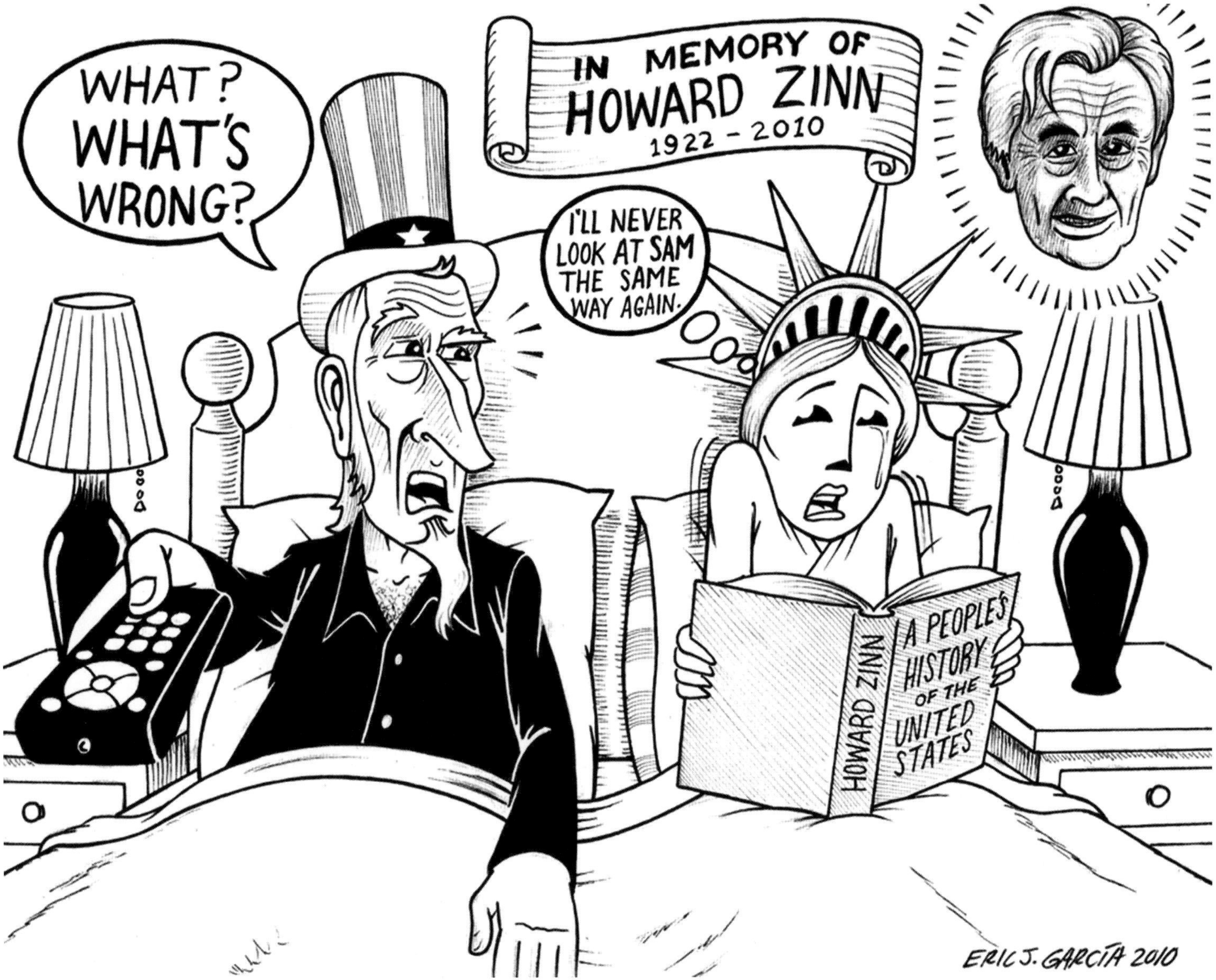
WHAT? WHAT'S WRONG?
IN MEMORY OF HOWARD ZINN 1922 - 2010
I'LL NEVER LOOK AT SAM THE SAME WAY AGAIN.
HOWARD ZINN
A PEOPLE'S HISTORY OF THE UNITED STATES
ERIC J. GARCIA 2010

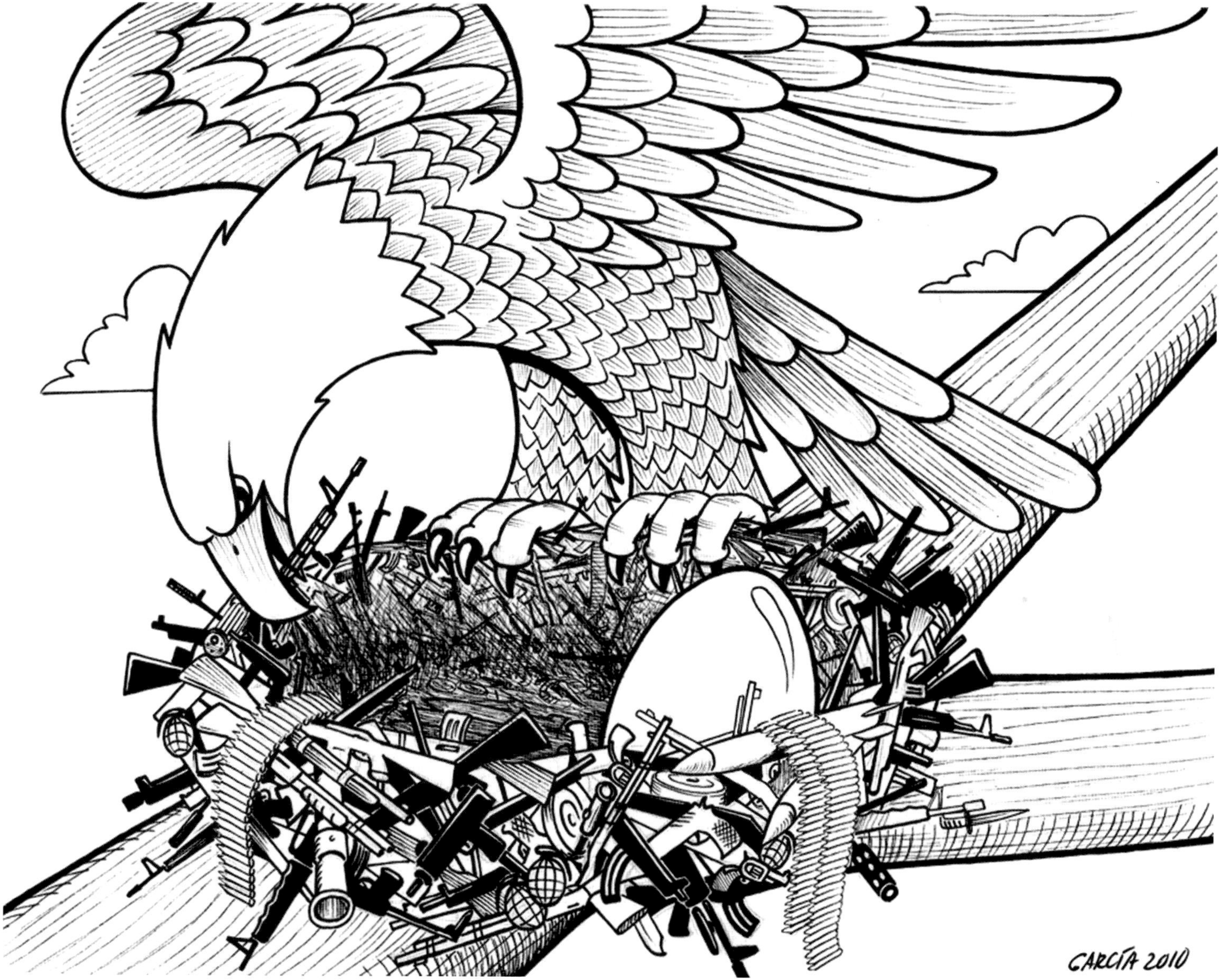
GARCÍA 2010

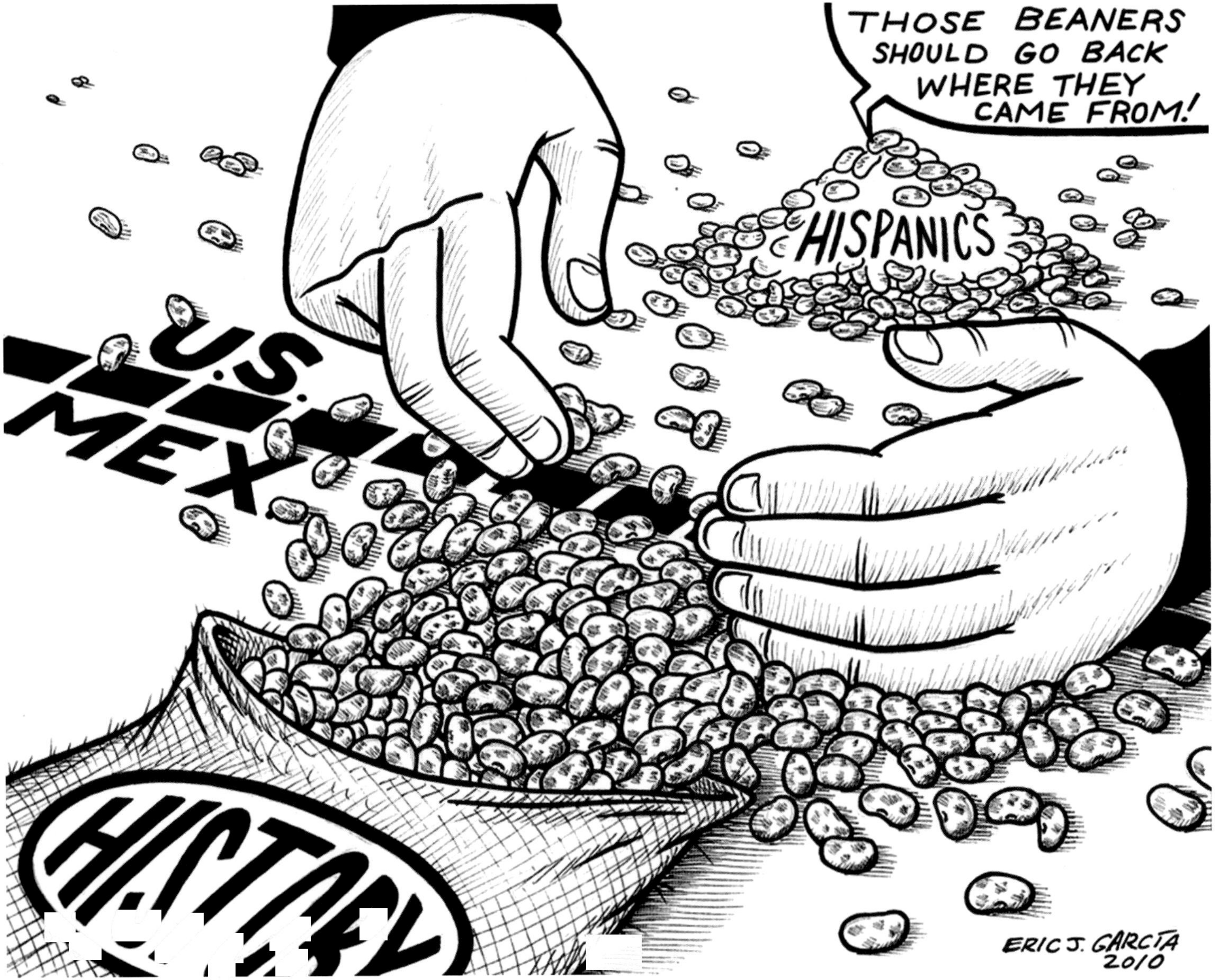
THOSE BEANERS SHOULD GO BACK WHERE THEY CAME FROM!
HISPANICS
U.S.
MEX
HISTORY
ERIC J. GARCIA 2010

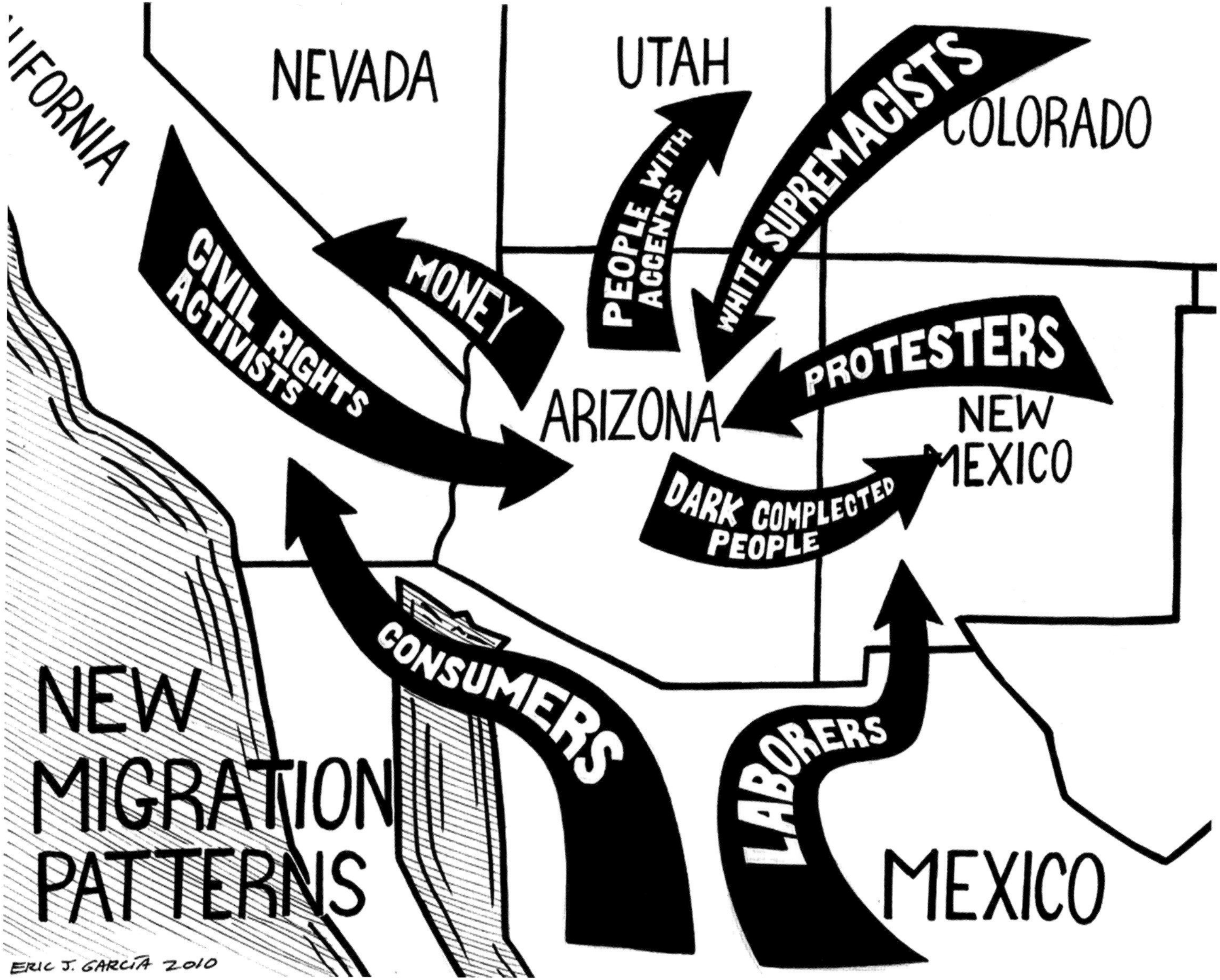
IFORNIA
NEVADA
UTAH
COLORADO
WHITE SUPREMACISTS
PEOPLE WITH ACCENTS
MONEY
CIVIL RIGHTS ACTIVISTS
ARIZONA
PROTESTERS
NEW MEXICO
DARK COMPLECTED PEOPLE
CONSUMERS
LABORERS
MEXICO
NEW MIGRATION PATTERNS
ERIC J. GARCIA 2010

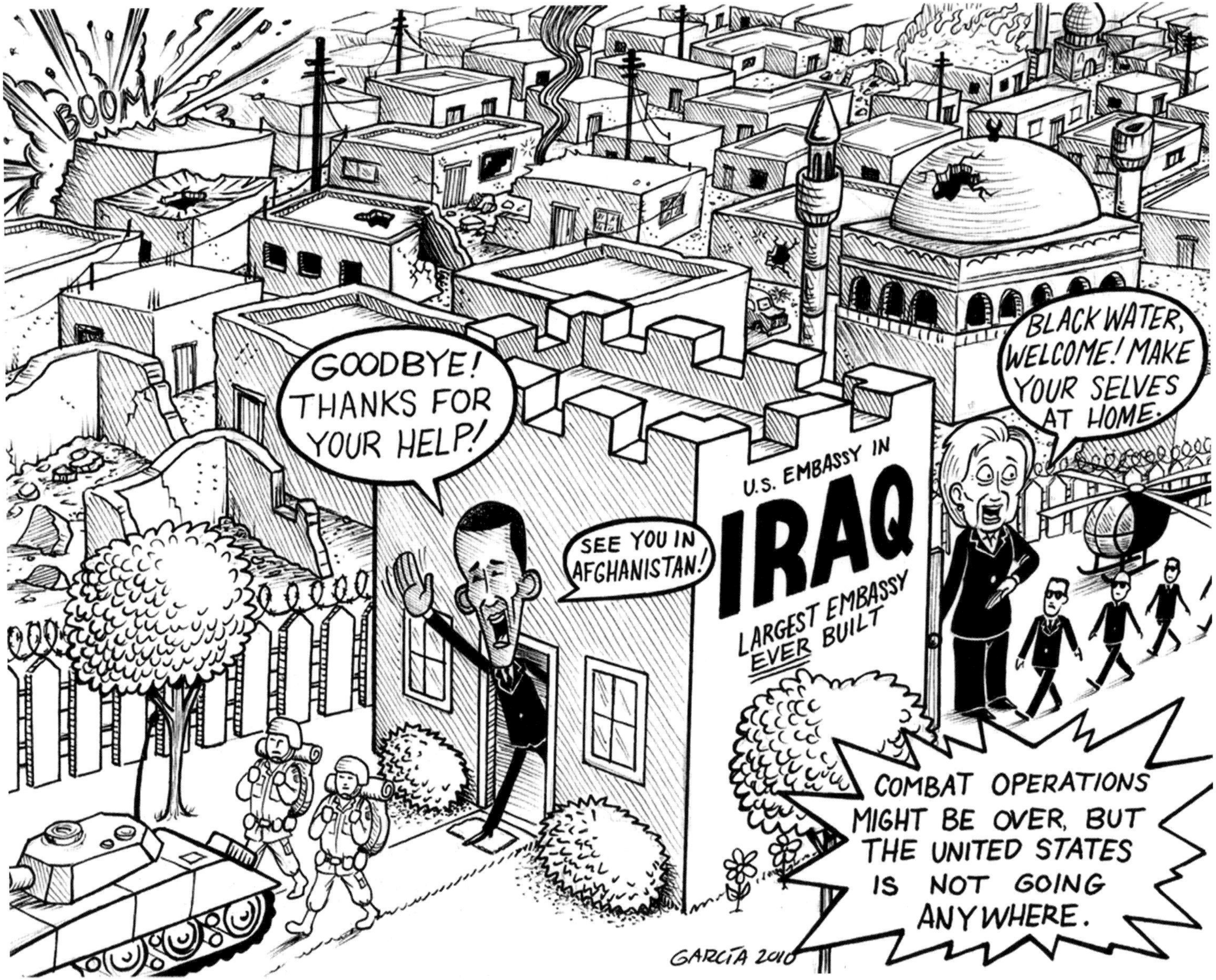
BOOM
GOODBYE! THANKS FOR YOUR HELP!
SEE YOU IN AFGHANISTAN!
U.S. EMBASSY IN IRAQ LARGEST EMBASSY EVER BUILT
BLACKWATER, WELCOME! MAKE YOUR SELVES AT HOME.
COMBAT OPERATIONS MIGHT BE OVER, BUT THE UNITED STATES IS NOT GOING ANYWHERE.
GARCIA 2010

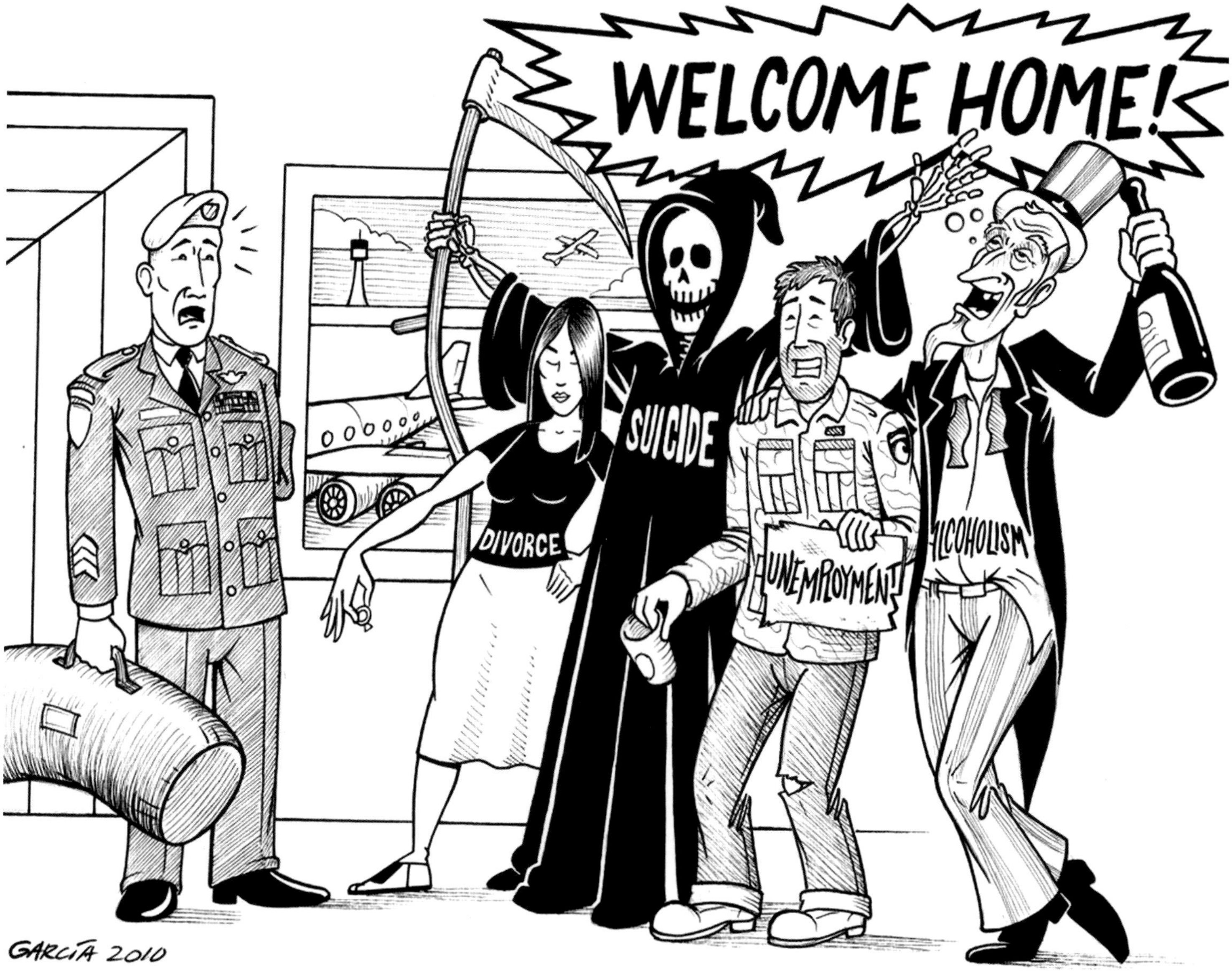
WELCOME HOME!
SUICIDE
DIVORCE
UNEMPLOYMENT
ALCOHOLISM
GARCÍA 2010

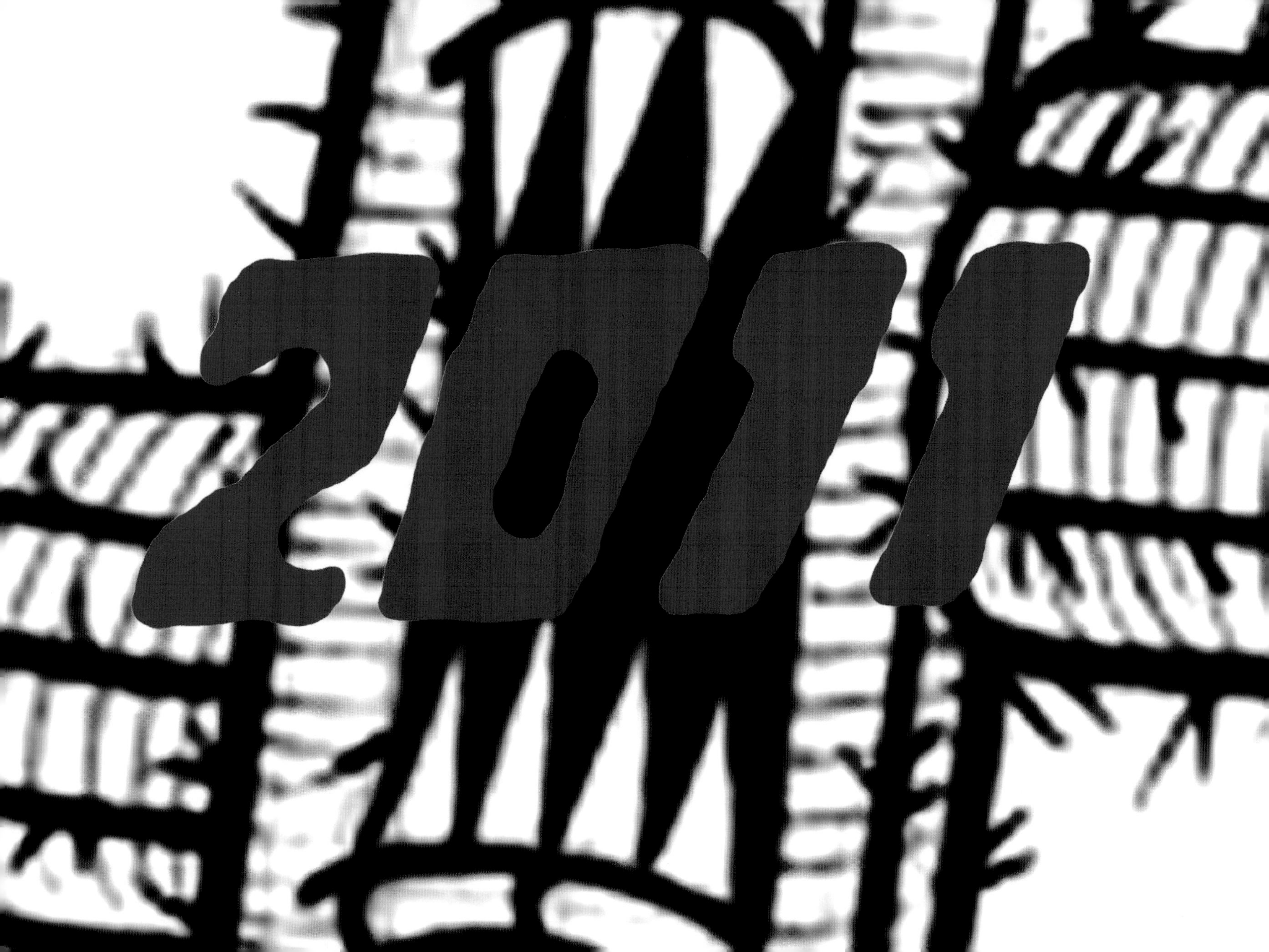
2011

2011

The 1% of the population seemed to be thriving during the recession as the government and police forces continued to protect them from the Occupy Movement. Undocumented workers tried to keep the economy running but were chased out by racist state laws that only hurt moneymaking industries that depend on their labor. On the flip side, the drug economy was thriving, as the leading consumer of the Latin American narcotics (the U.S.) was ironically "thanked" in a letter by none other than the drug dealers themselves. As the Drug War continued, so did the war in Afghanistan. But with the main objective of killing Osama bin Laden accomplished, why were we still there? Meanwhile at Guantanamo Bay Naval Base, suspects detained from the War on Terror were slowly being forgotten.

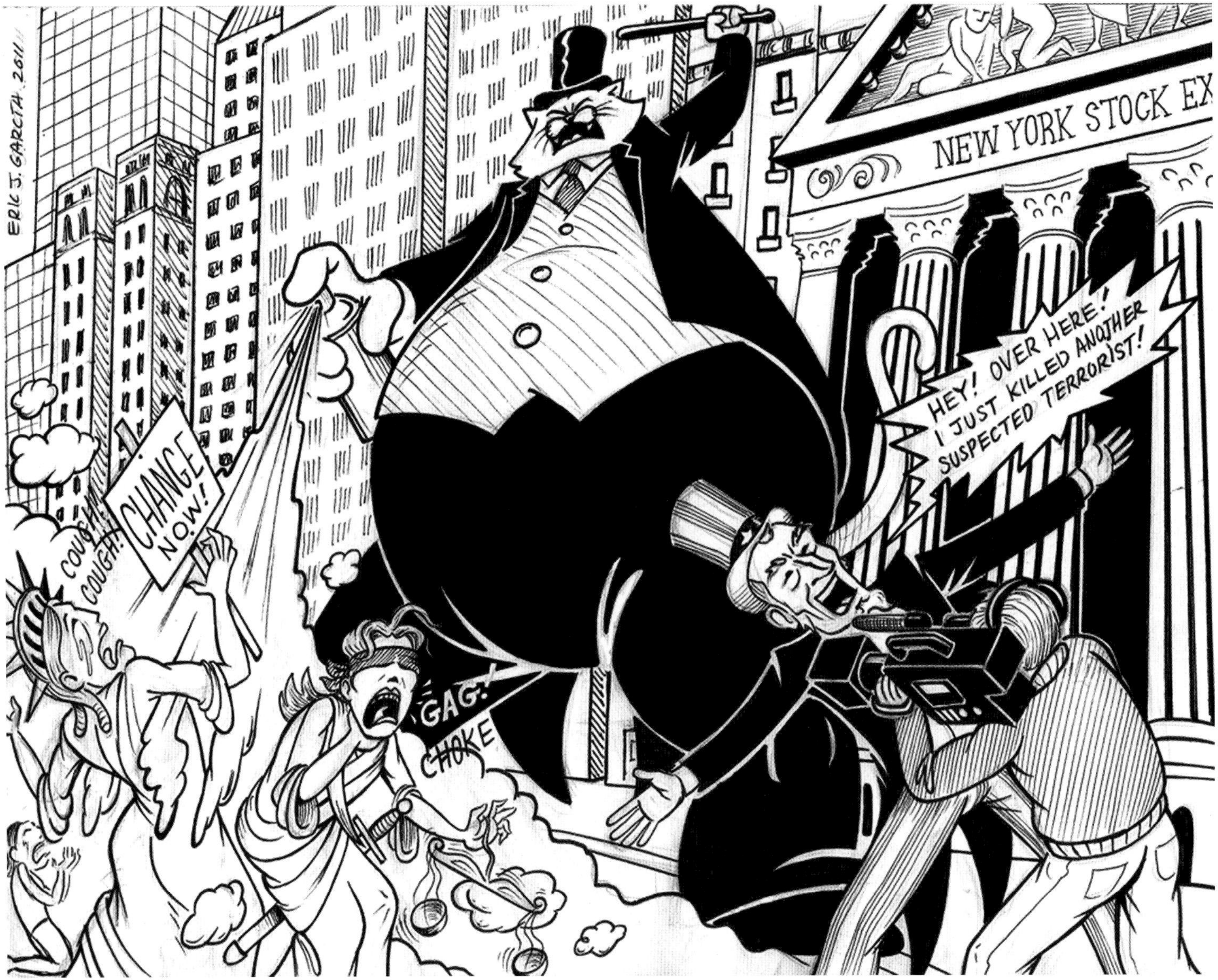
ERIC J. GARCIA 2011
NEW YORK STOCK EX
CHANGE NOW!
COUGH! COUGH!
GAG!
CHOKE
HEY! OVER HERE! I JUST KILLED ANOTHER SUSPECTED TERRORIST!

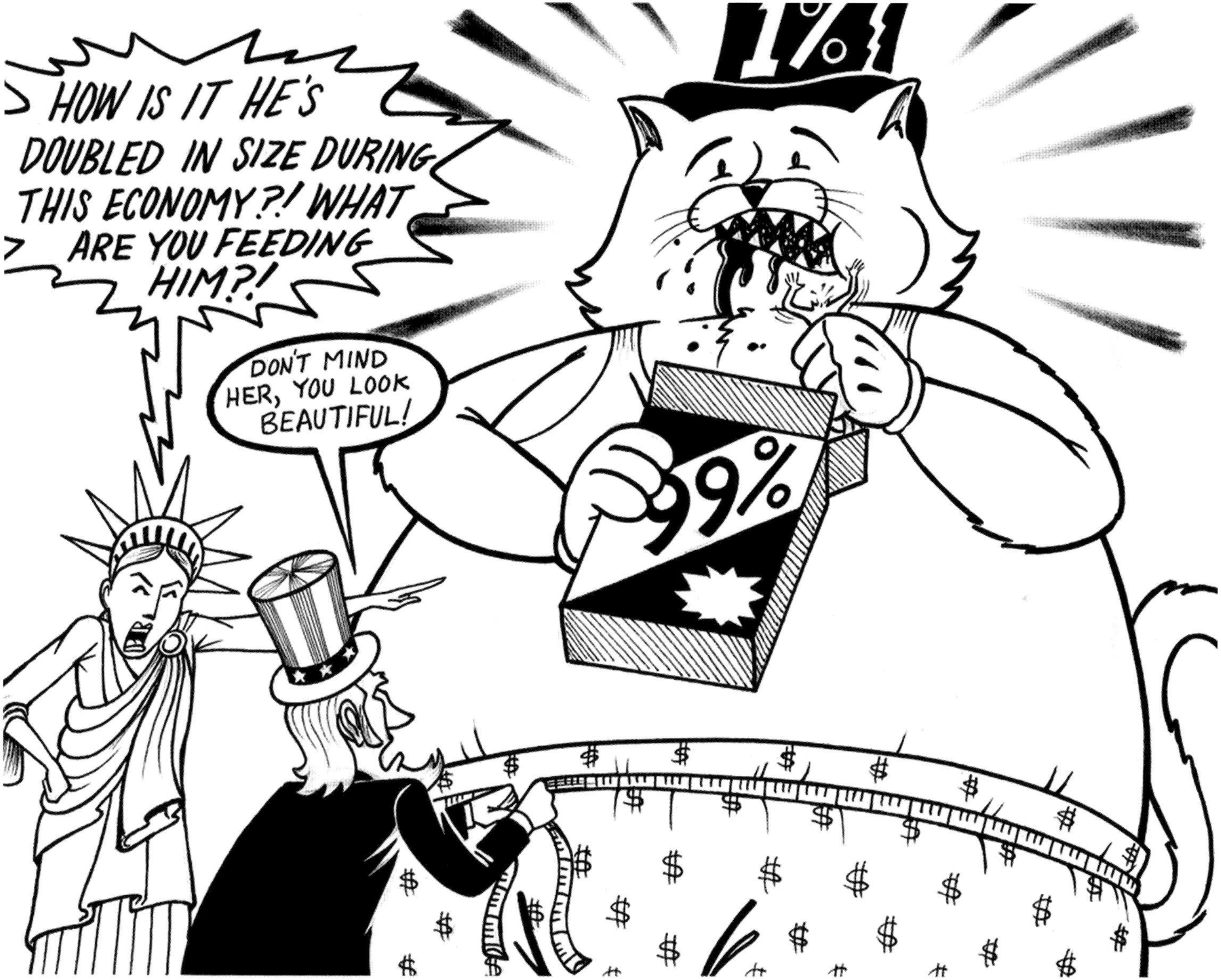
1%
HOW IS IT HE'S DOUBLED IN SIZE DURING THIS ECONOMY?! WHAT ARE YOU FEEDING HIM?!
DON'T MIND HER, YOU LOOK BEAUTIFUL!
99%

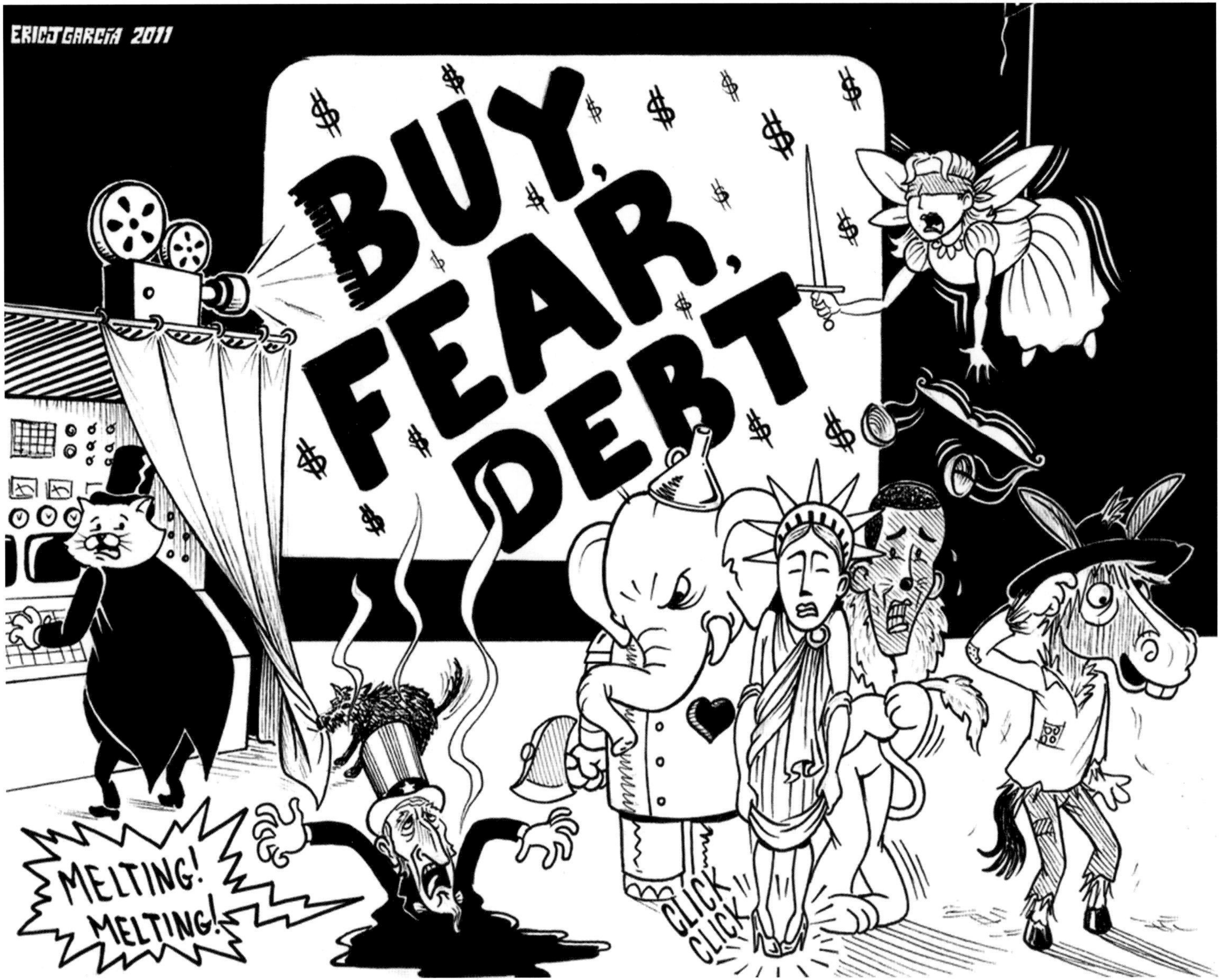
ERICJGARCIA 2011
BUY, FEAR, DEBT
MELTING! MELTING!
CLICK CLICK

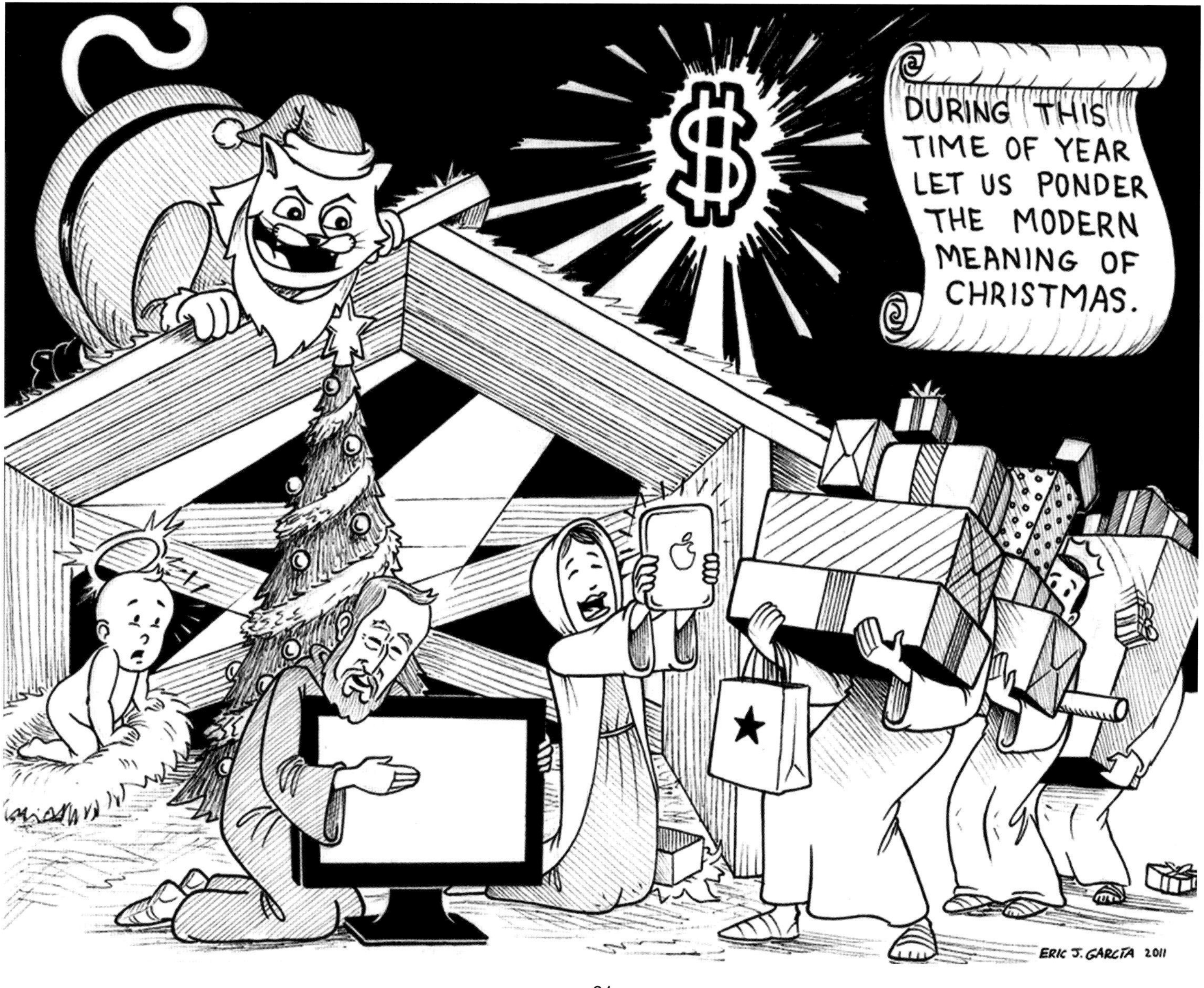
DURING THIS TIME OF YEAR LET US PONDER THE MODERN MEANING OF CHRISTMAS.
$
ERIC J. GARCIA 2011

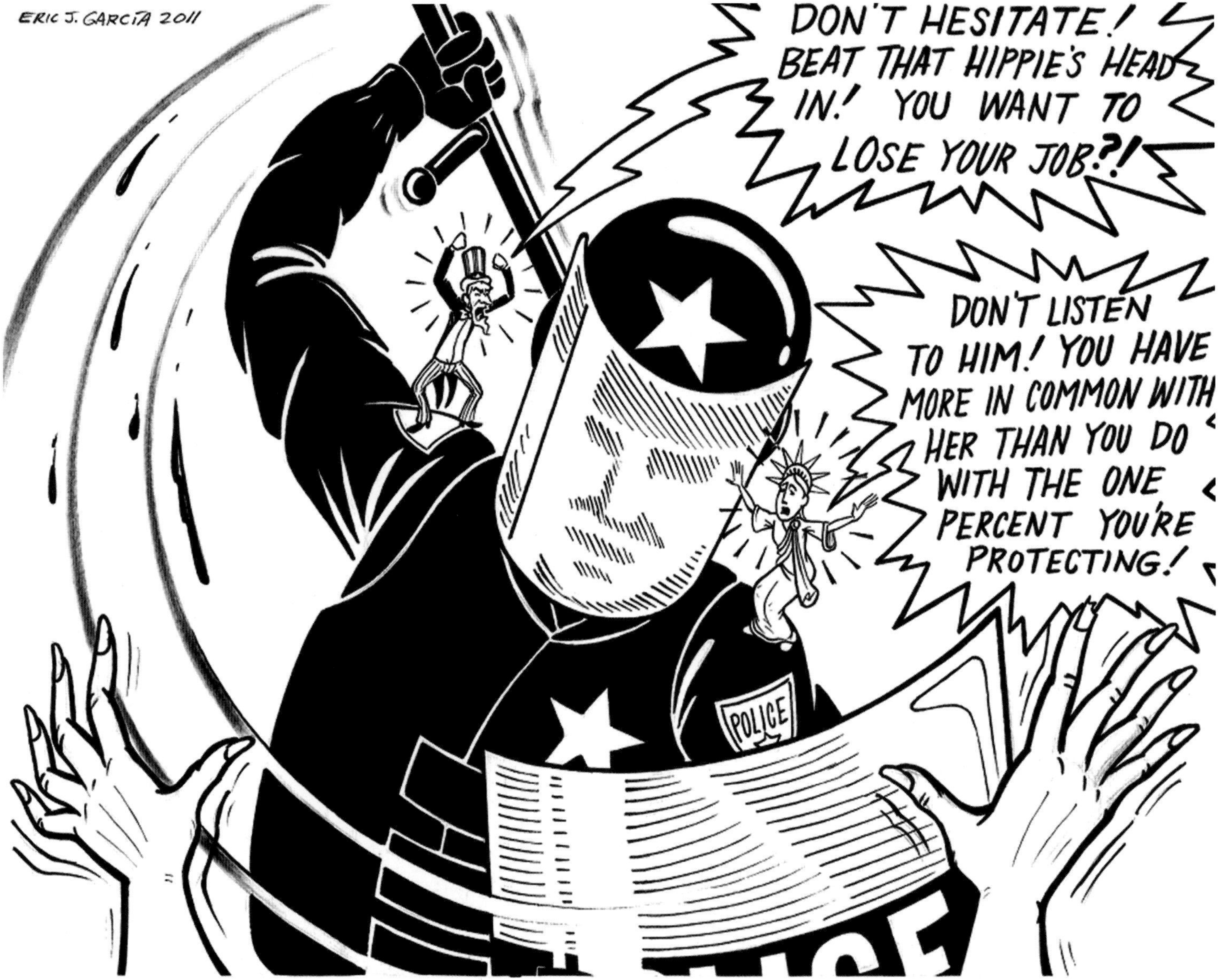
ERIC J. GARCIA 2011
DON'T HESITATE! BEAT THAT HIPPIE'S HEAD IN! YOU WANT TO LOSE YOUR JOB?!
DON'T LISTEN TO HIM! YOU HAVE MORE IN COMMON WITH HER THAN YOU DO WITH THE ONE PERCENT YOU'RE PROTECTING!
POLICE

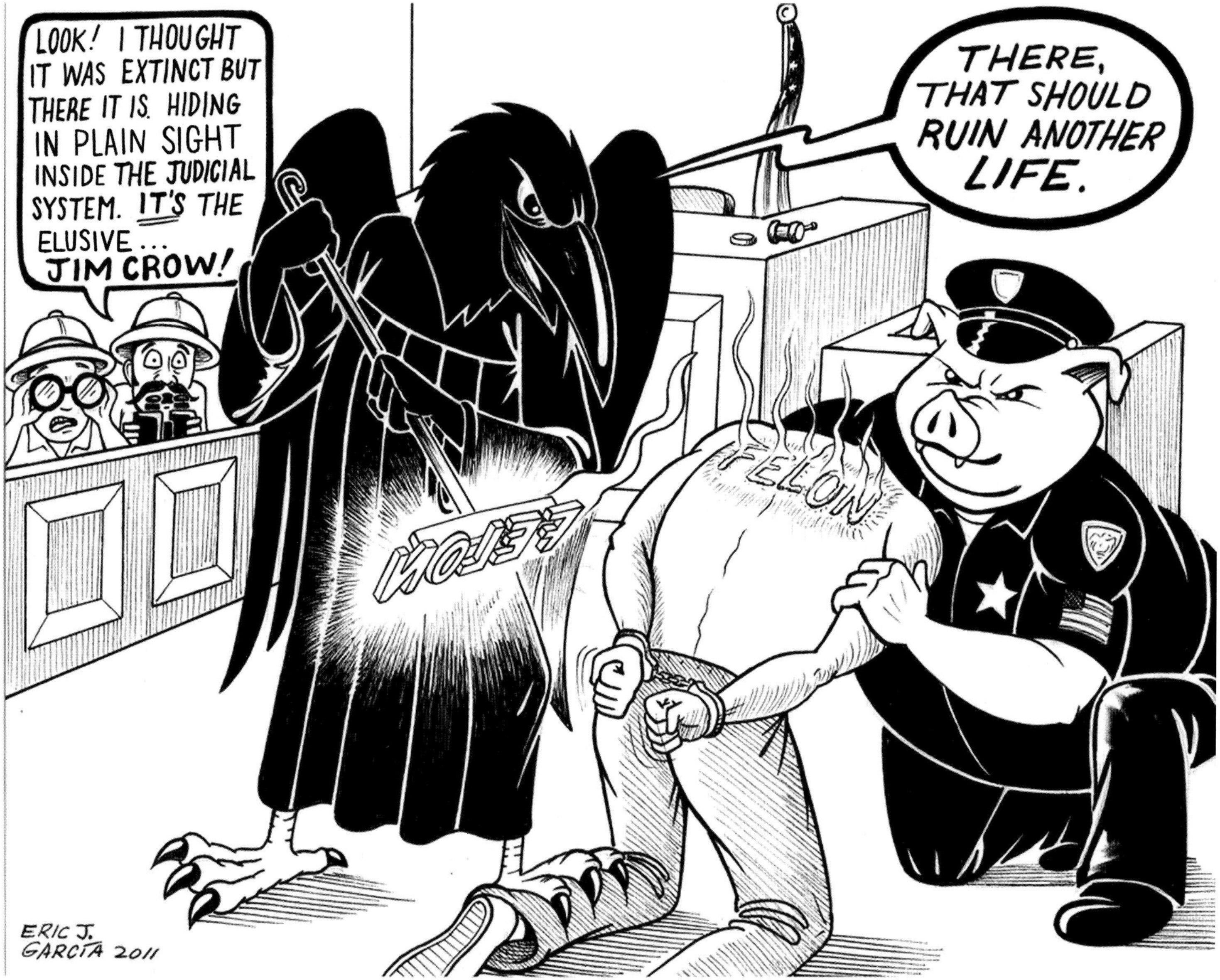
LOOK! I THOUGHT IT WAS EXTINCT BUT THERE IT IS. HIDING IN PLAIN SIGHT INSIDE THE JUDICIAL SYSTEM. IT'S THE ELUSIVE... JIM CROW!
THERE, THAT SHOULD RUIN ANOTHER LIFE.
FELON
FELON
ERIC J. GARCIA 2011

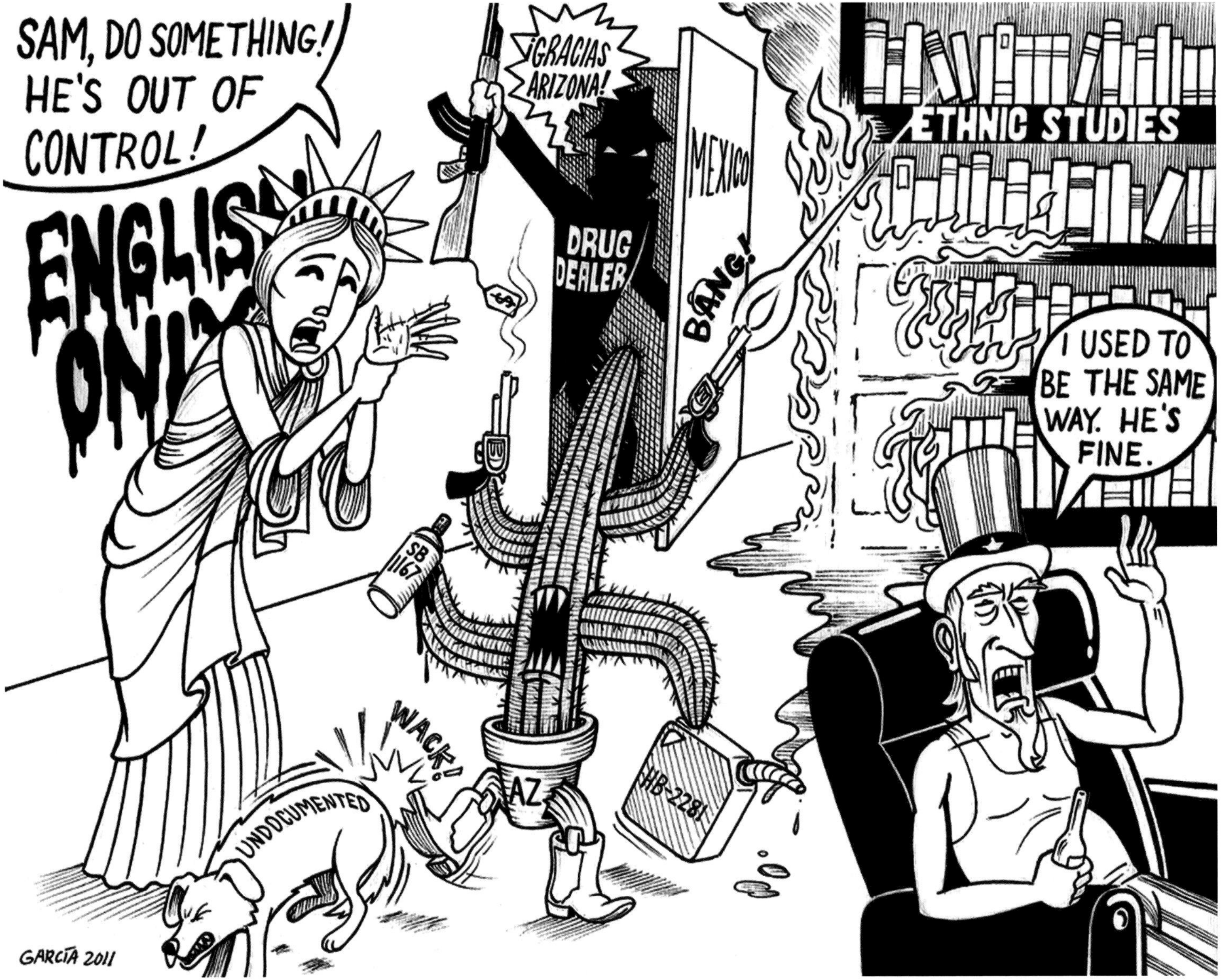
SAM, DO SOMETHING! HE'S OUT OF CONTROL!
¡GRACIAS ARIZONA!
MEXICO
DRUG DEALER
BANG!
ETHNIC STUDIES
I USED TO BE THE SAME WAY. HE'S FINE.
SB 1167
WACK!
UNDOCUMENTED
AZ
HB-2281
GARCÍA 2011

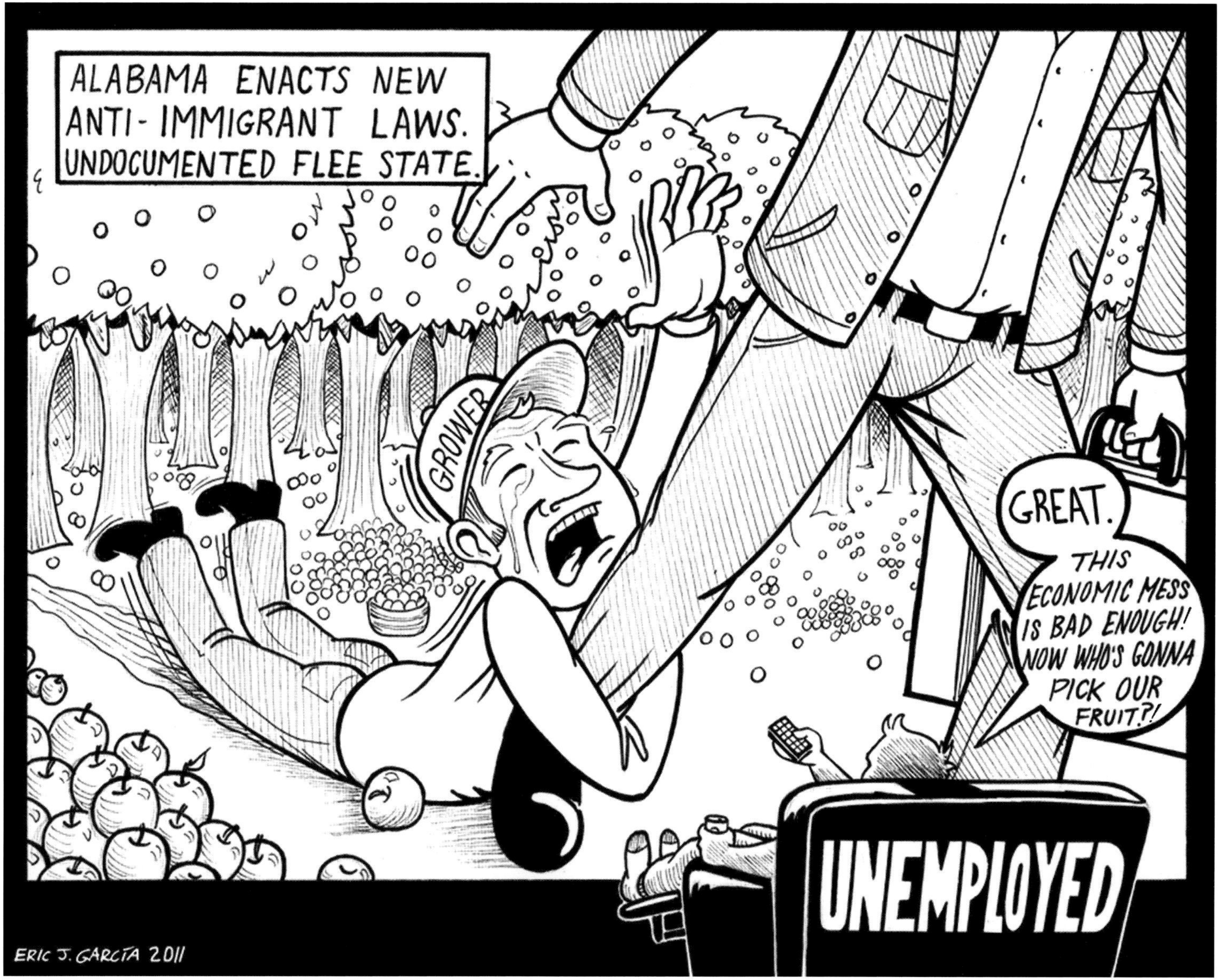
ALABAMA ENACTS NEW ANTI-IMMIGRANT LAWS. UNDOCUMENTED FLEE STATE.
GROWER
GREAT.
THIS ECONOMIC MESS IS BAD ENOUGH! NOW WHO'S GONNA PICK OUR FRUIT?!
UNEMPLOYED
ERIC J. GARCIA 2011

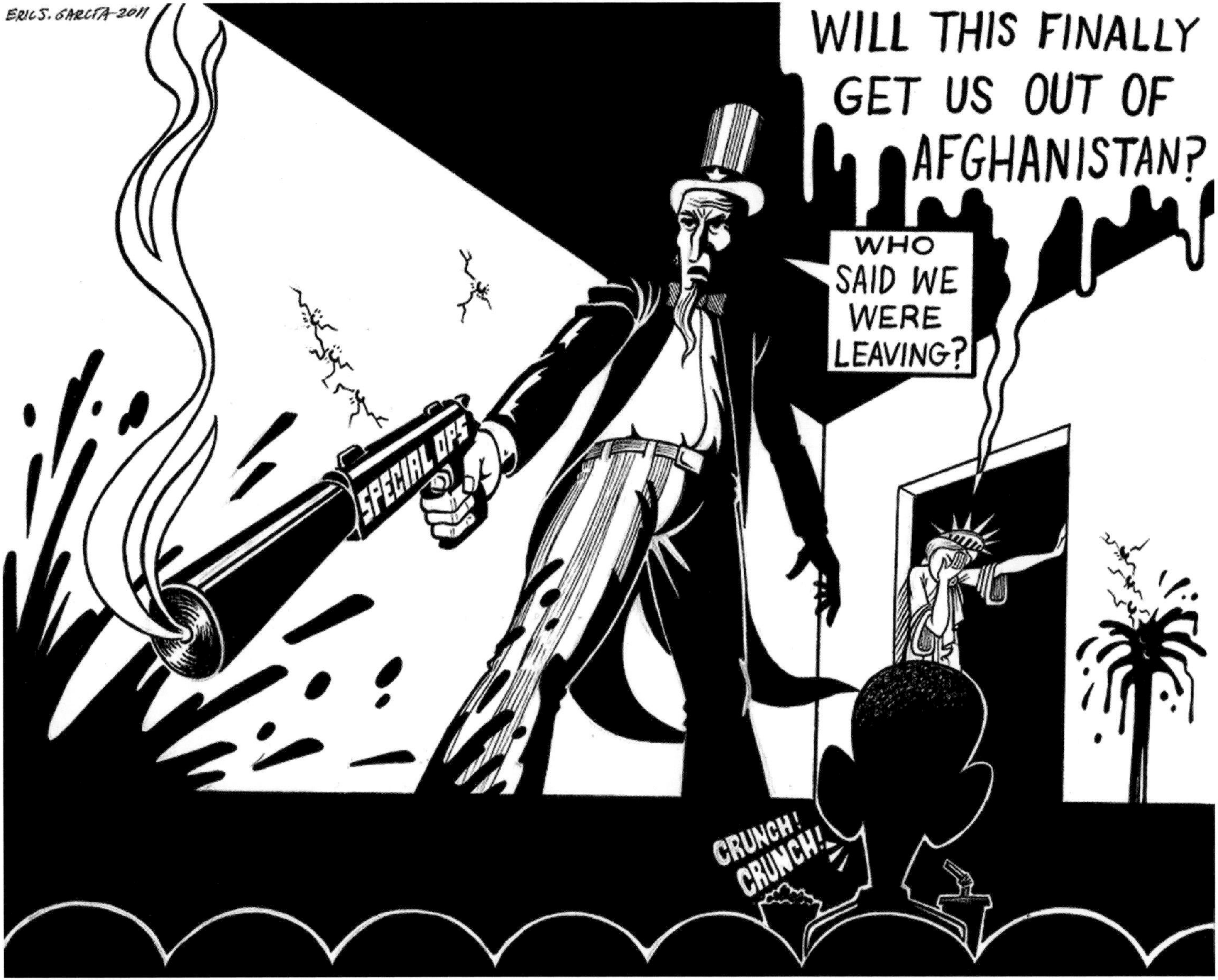
ERIC S. GARCIA 2011
WILL THIS FINALLY GET US OUT OF AFGHANISTAN?
WHO SAID WE WERE LEAVING?
SPECIAL OPS
CRUNCH! CRUNCH!

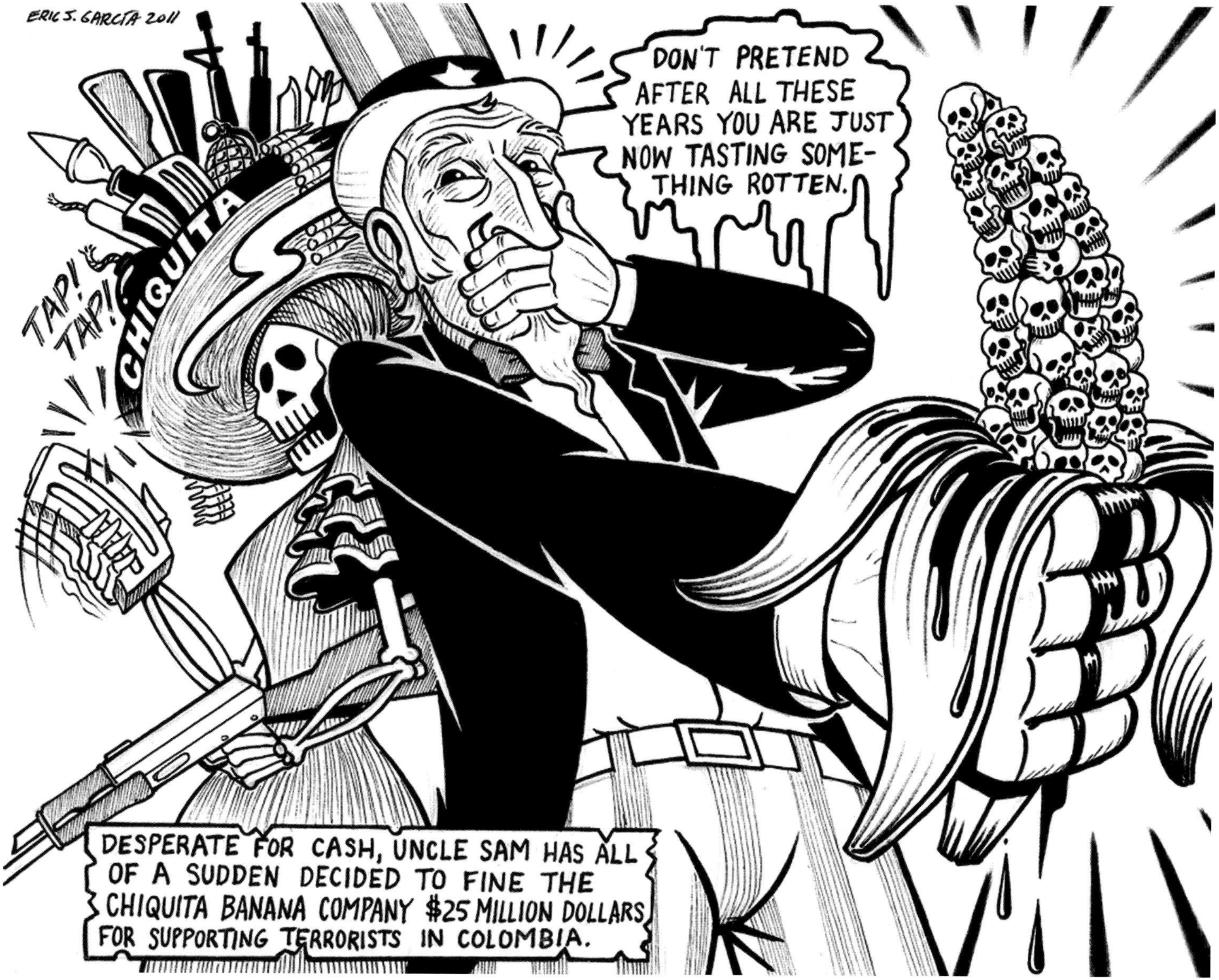
ERIC J. GARCIA 2011
DON'T PRETEND AFTER ALL THESE YEARS YOU ARE JUST NOW TASTING SOME-THING ROTTEN.
CHIQUITA
TAP! TAP!
DESPERATE FOR CASH, UNCLE SAM HAS ALL OF A SUDDEN DECIDED TO FINE THE CHIQUITA BANANA COMPANY $25 MILLION DOLLARS FOR SUPPORTING TERRORISTS IN COLOMBIA.

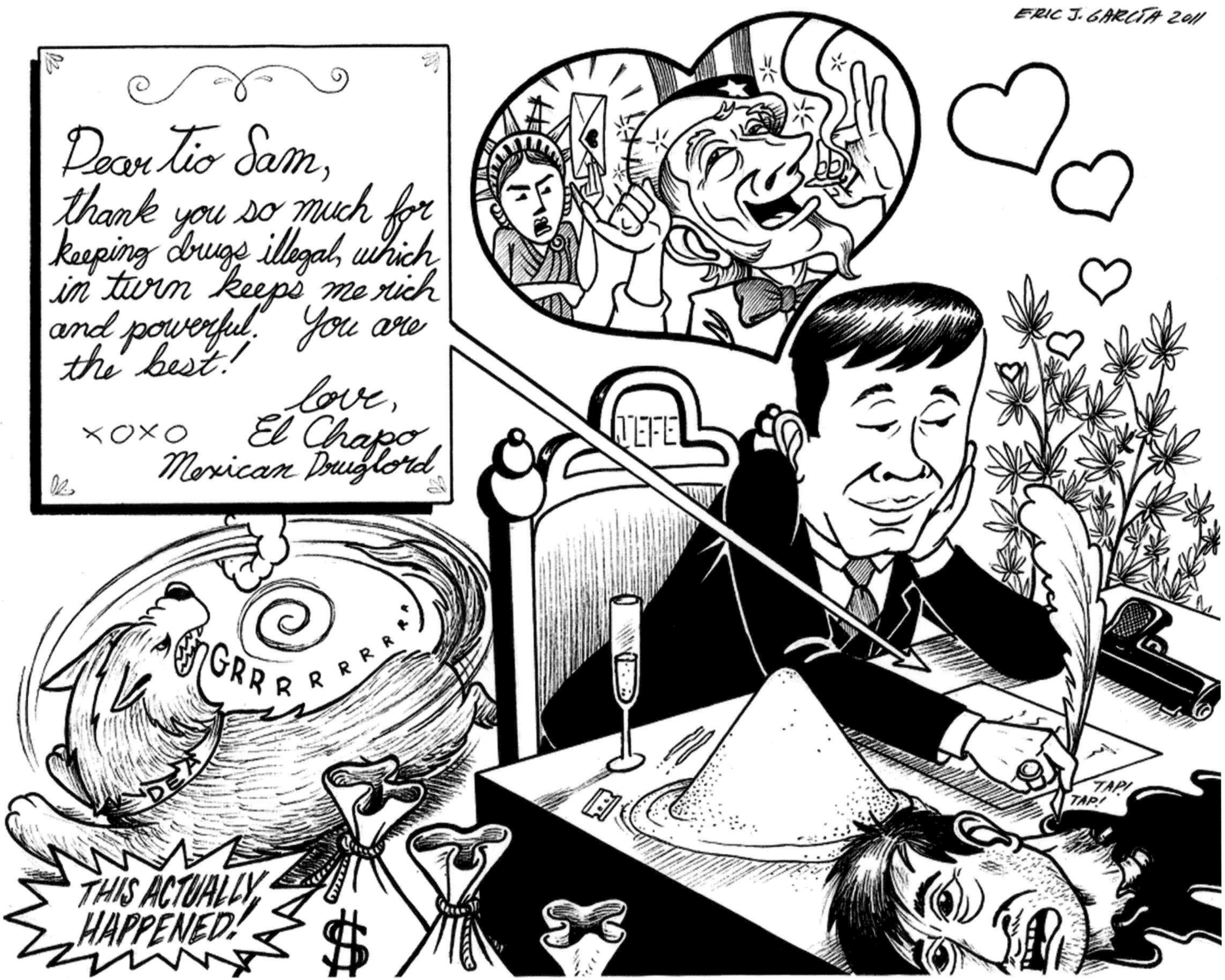
ERIC J. GARCÍA 2011
Dear tio Sam,
thank you so much for keeping drugs illegal, which in turn keeps me rich and powerful. You are the best!
love,
El Chapo
Mexican Druglord
XOXO
JEFE
DEA
GRRRRRRRRRR
TAP! TAP!
THIS ACTUALLY HAPPENED!
$

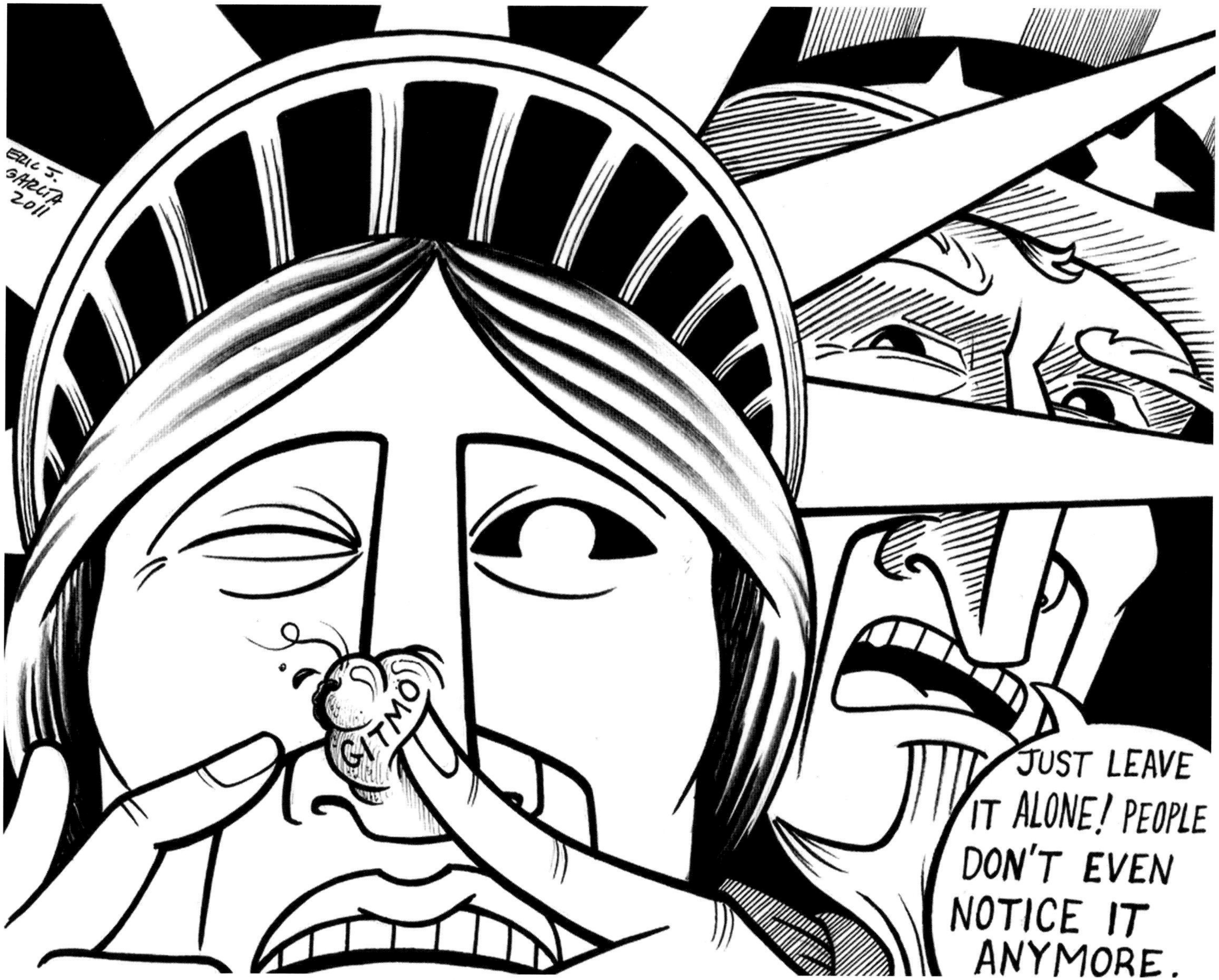
ERIC J. GARCIA 2011
GITMO
JUST LEAVE IT ALONE! PEOPLE DON'T EVEN NOTICE IT ANYMORE.

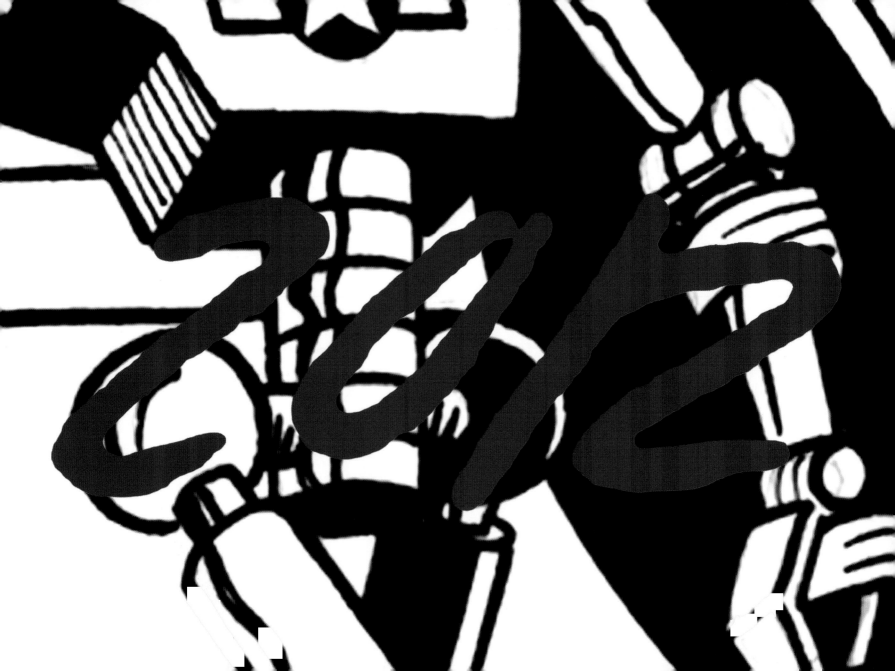

2012

The presidential elections had brought up important questions for male lawmakers who dictate female rights. "Democracy" also put Barack Obama back behind the joystick, as his drones continued to kill mercilessly without discrimination. Because of these expensive deadly toys and the billions of other tax dollars sent to support the wars in the Middle East, barely any funds were left to support the arts in our schools. The new Affordable Healthcare Act also came up short in many respects, as mental health was again left on the burner. This combination of nurturing a generation of violence and untreated mental health caused another gruesome school shooting, at Sandy Hook Elementary. Meanwhile ignorance and callousness were being demonstrated at the university level as sorority sisters mocked Mexicanos and flaunted the drugs coming from south of the border without realizing the true cost of their high.

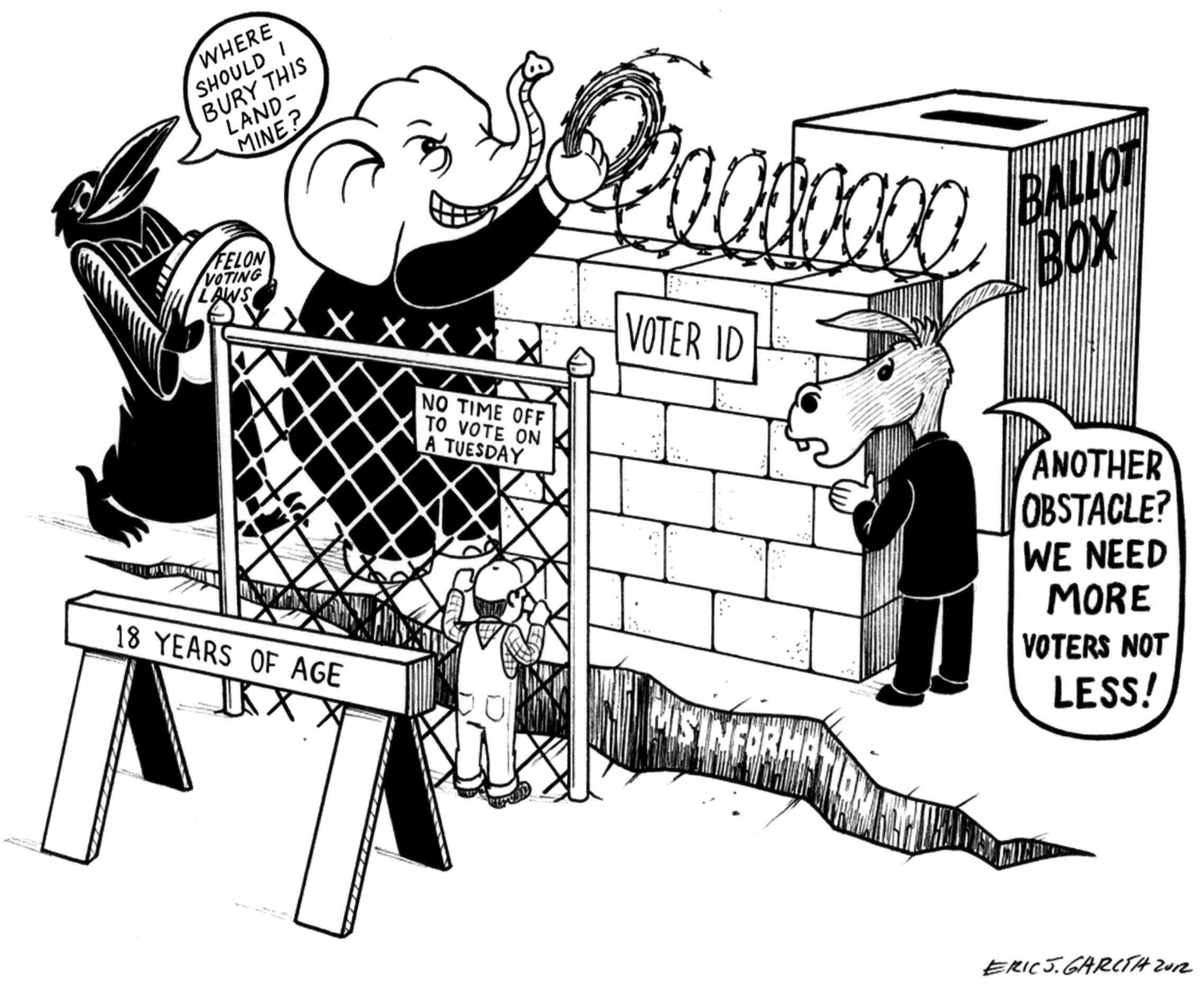
WHERE SHOULD I BURY THIS LAND-MINE?
FELON VOTING LAWS
BALLOT BOX
VOTER ID
NO TIME OFF TO VOTE ON A TUESDAY
ANOTHER OBSTACLE? WE NEED MORE VOTERS NOT LESS!
18 YEARS OF AGE
MISINFORMATION
ERIC J. GARCIA 2012

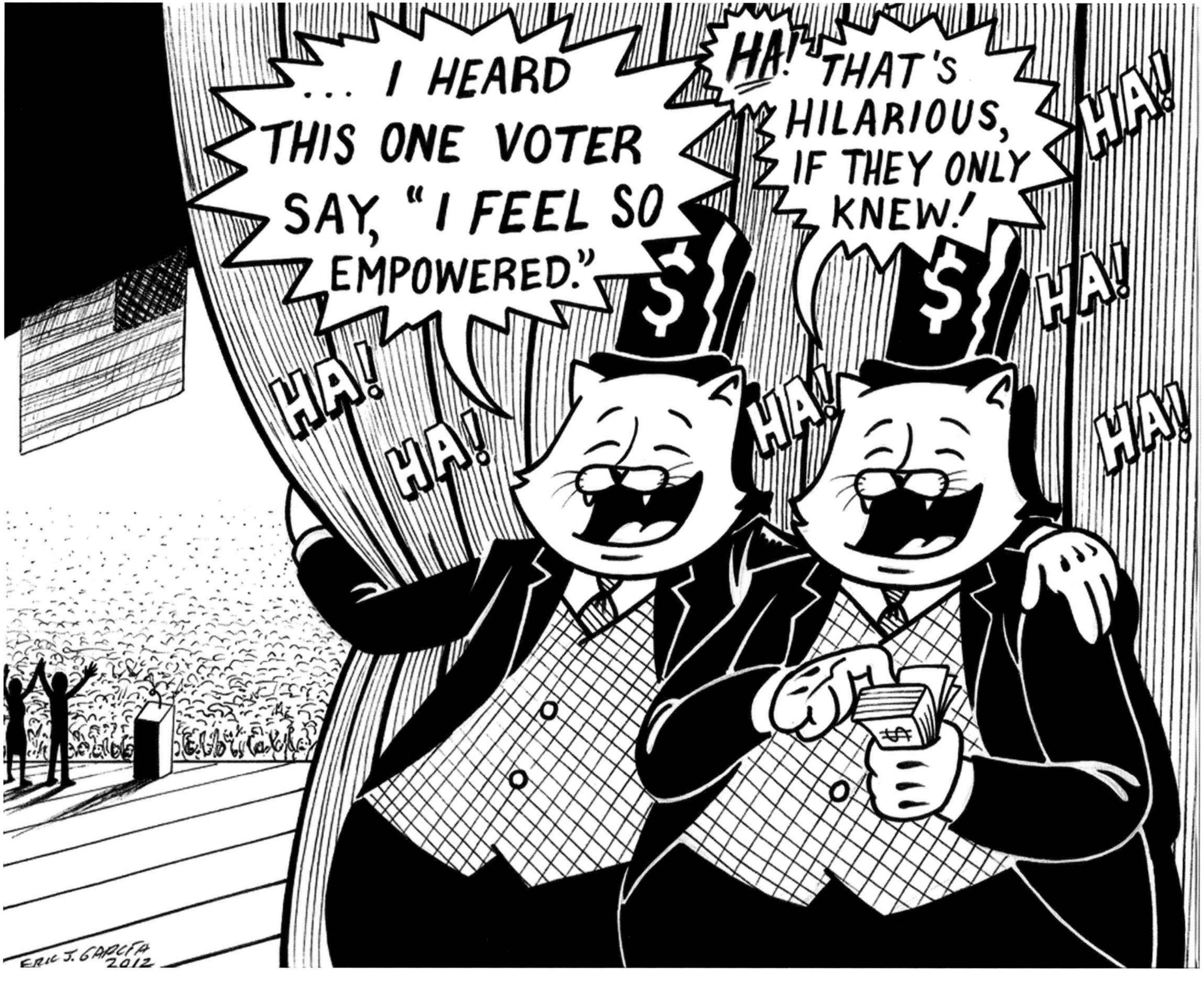
... I HEARD THIS ONE VOTER SAY, "I FEEL SO EMPOWERED."
HA! THAT'S HILARIOUS, IF THEY ONLY KNEW!
HA!
HA!
HA!
HA!
HA!
HA!
HA!
ERIC J. GARCIA 2012

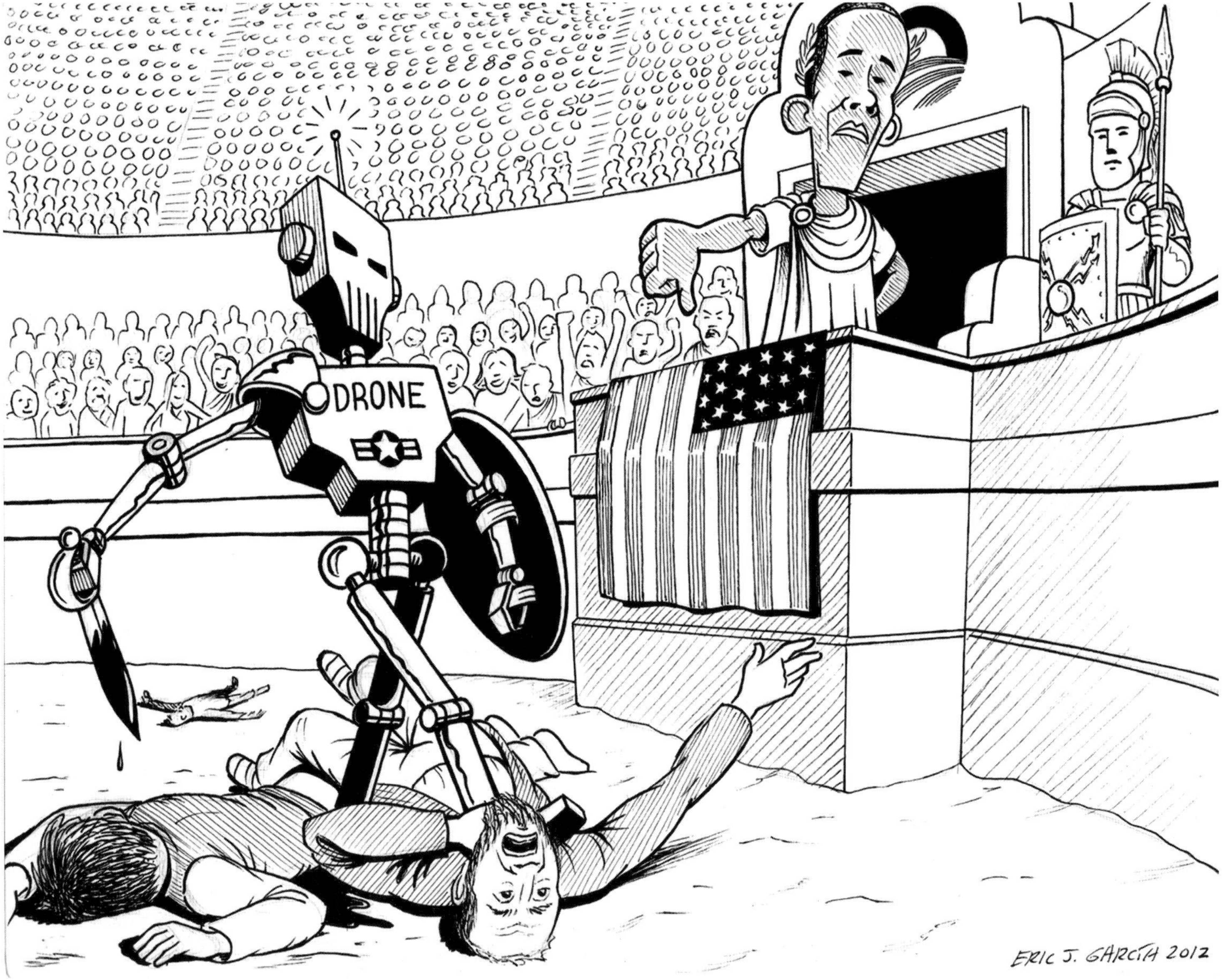
DRONE
ERIC J. GARCIA 2012

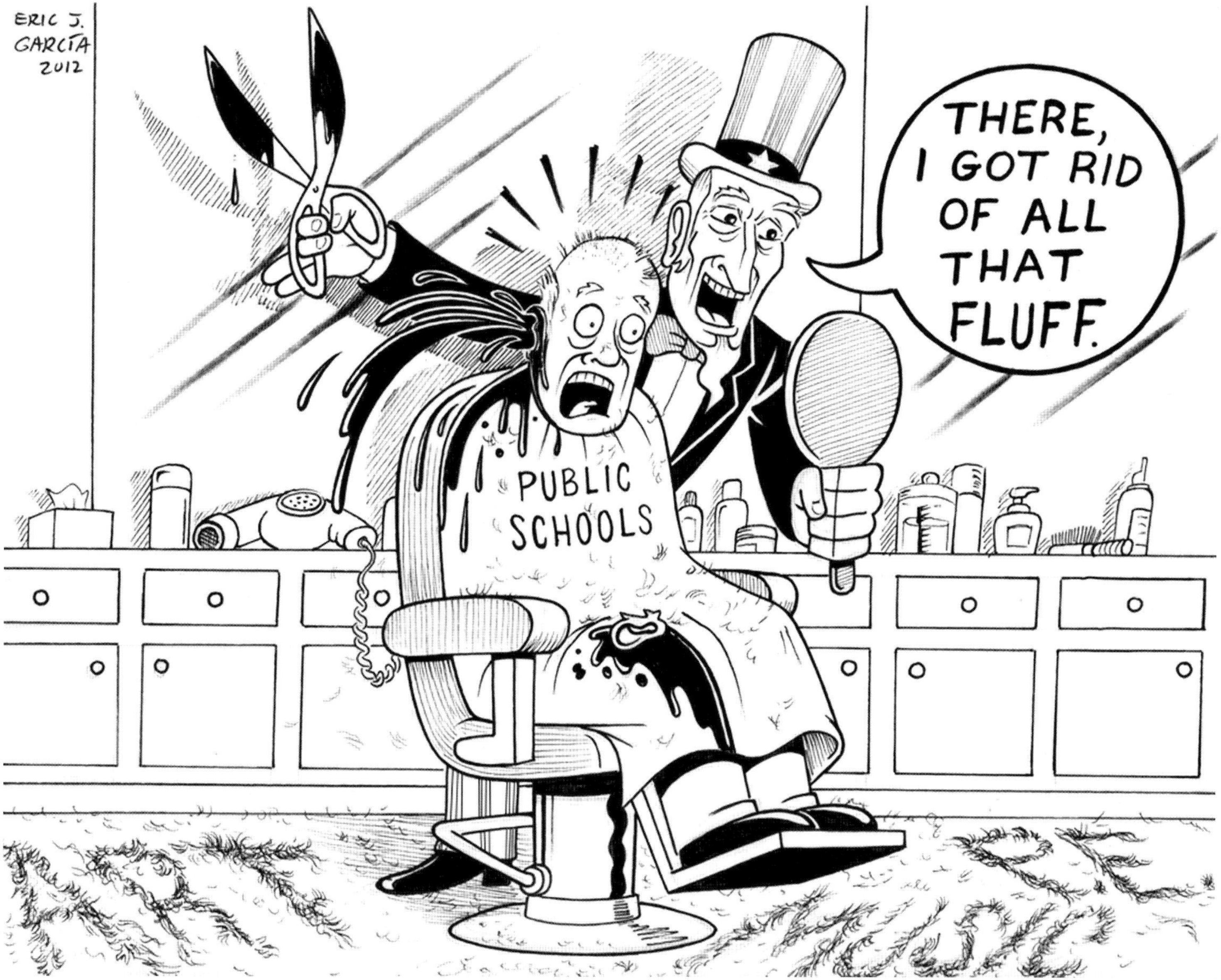
ERIC J. GARCIA 2012
THERE, I GOT RID OF ALL THAT FLUFF.
PUBLIC SCHOOLS

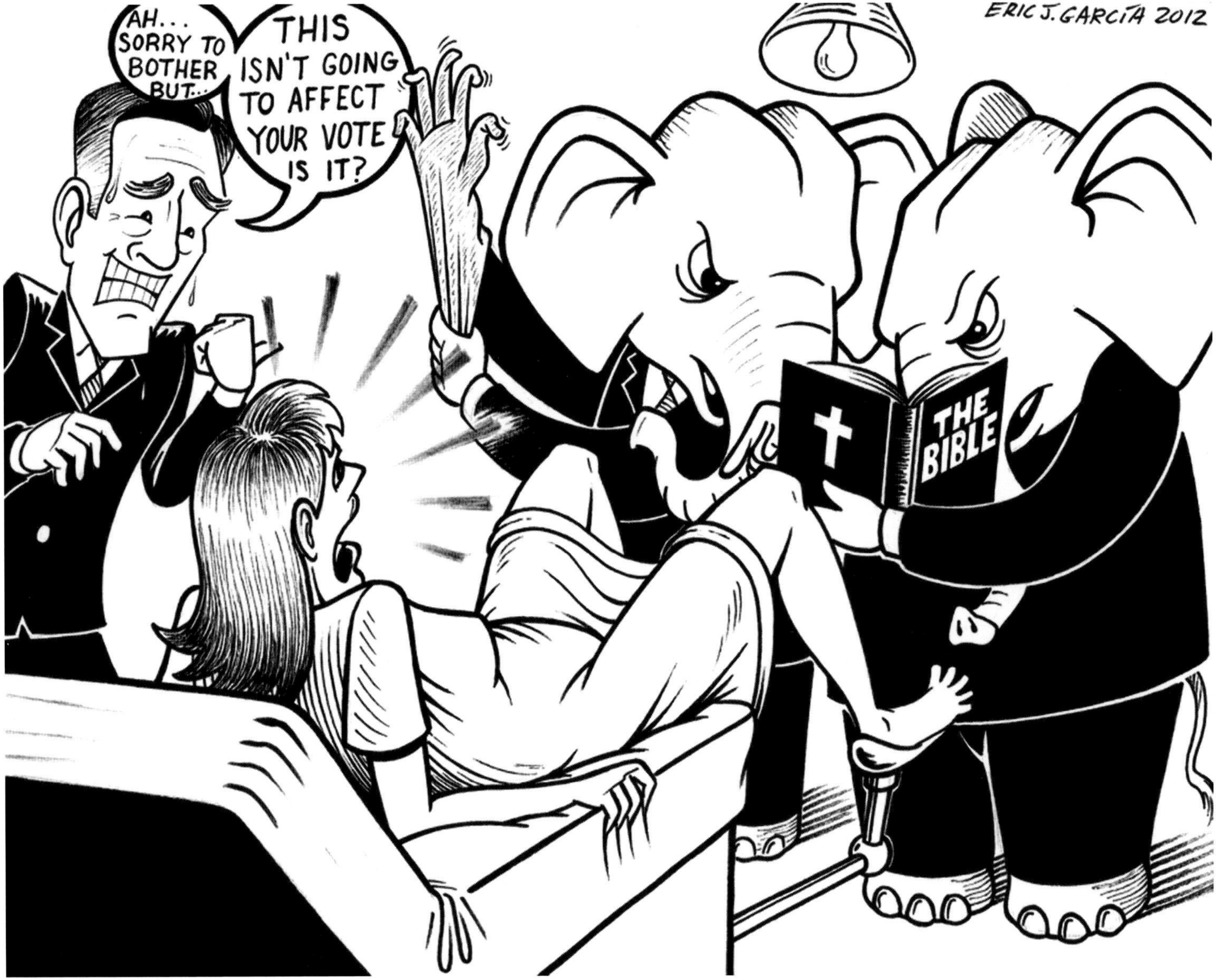
ERIC J. GARCIA 2012
AH... SORRY TO BOTHER BUT...
THIS ISN'T GOING TO AFFECT YOUR VOTE IS IT?
THE BIBLE

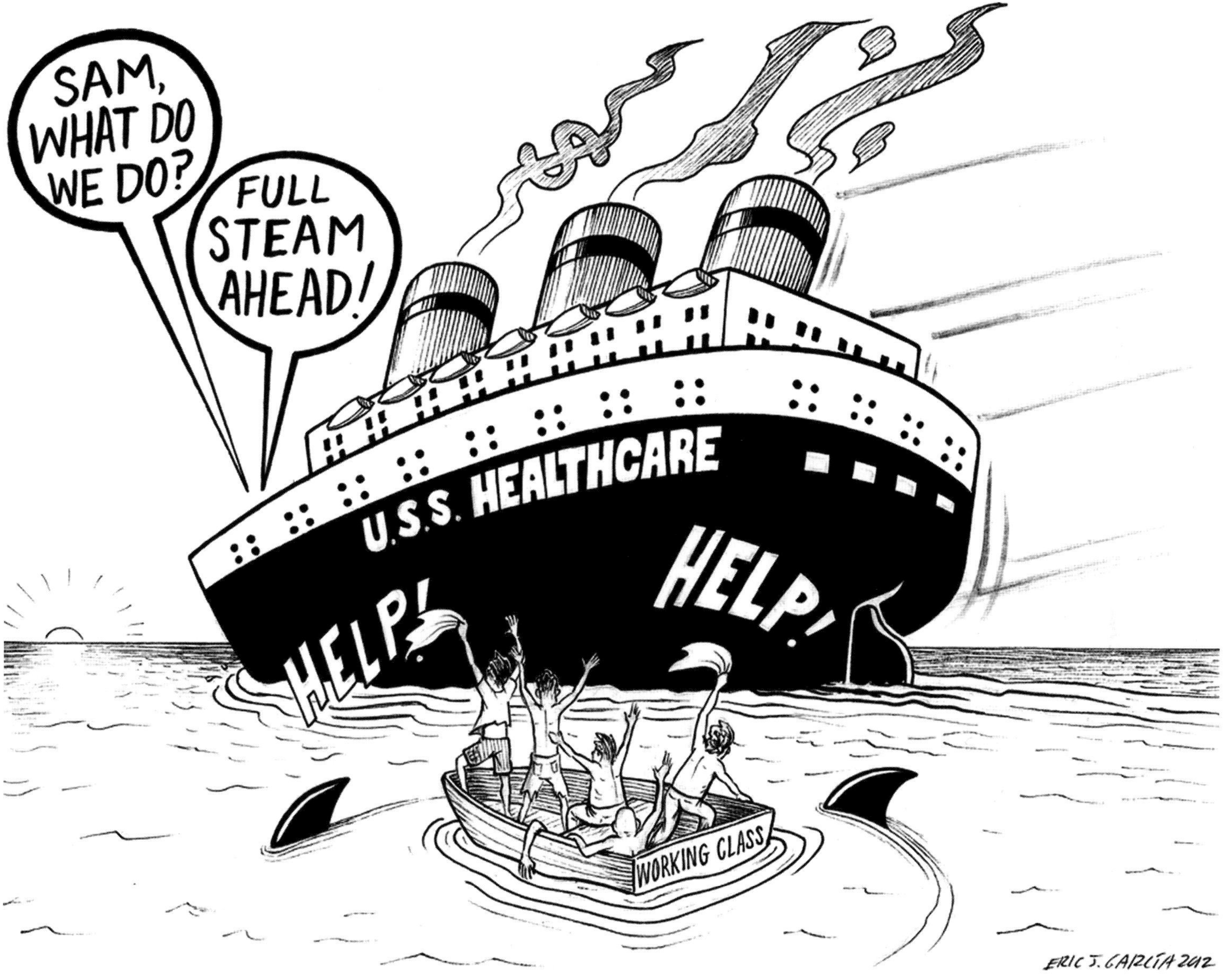
SAM, WHAT DO WE DO?
FULL STEAM AHEAD!
U.S.S. HEALTHCARE
HELP!
HELP!
WORKING CLASS
ERIC J. GARCÍA 2012

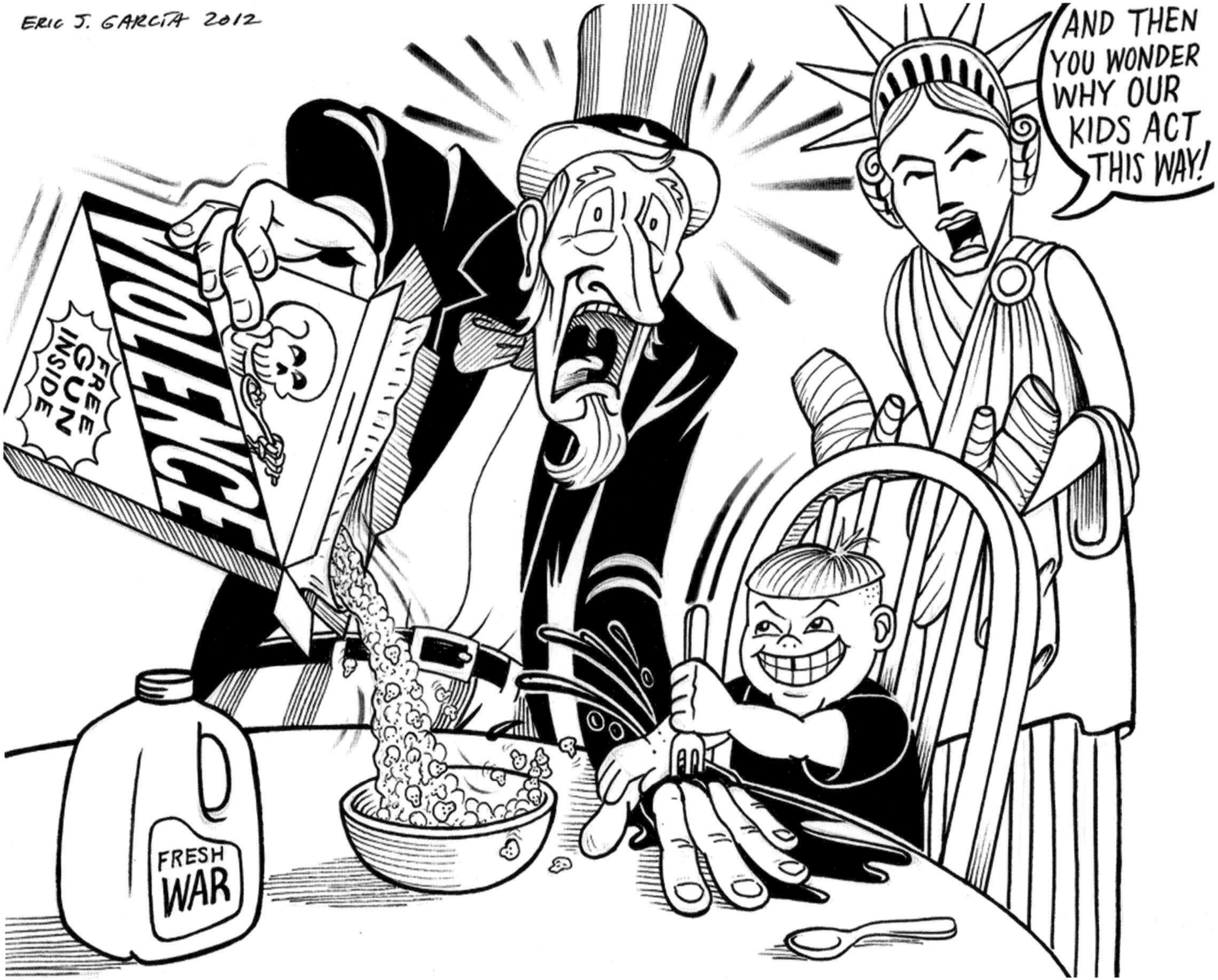
ERIC J. GARCIA 2012
AND THEN YOU WONDER WHY OUR KIDS ACT THIS WAY!
VIOLENCE
FREE GUN INSIDE
FRESH WAR

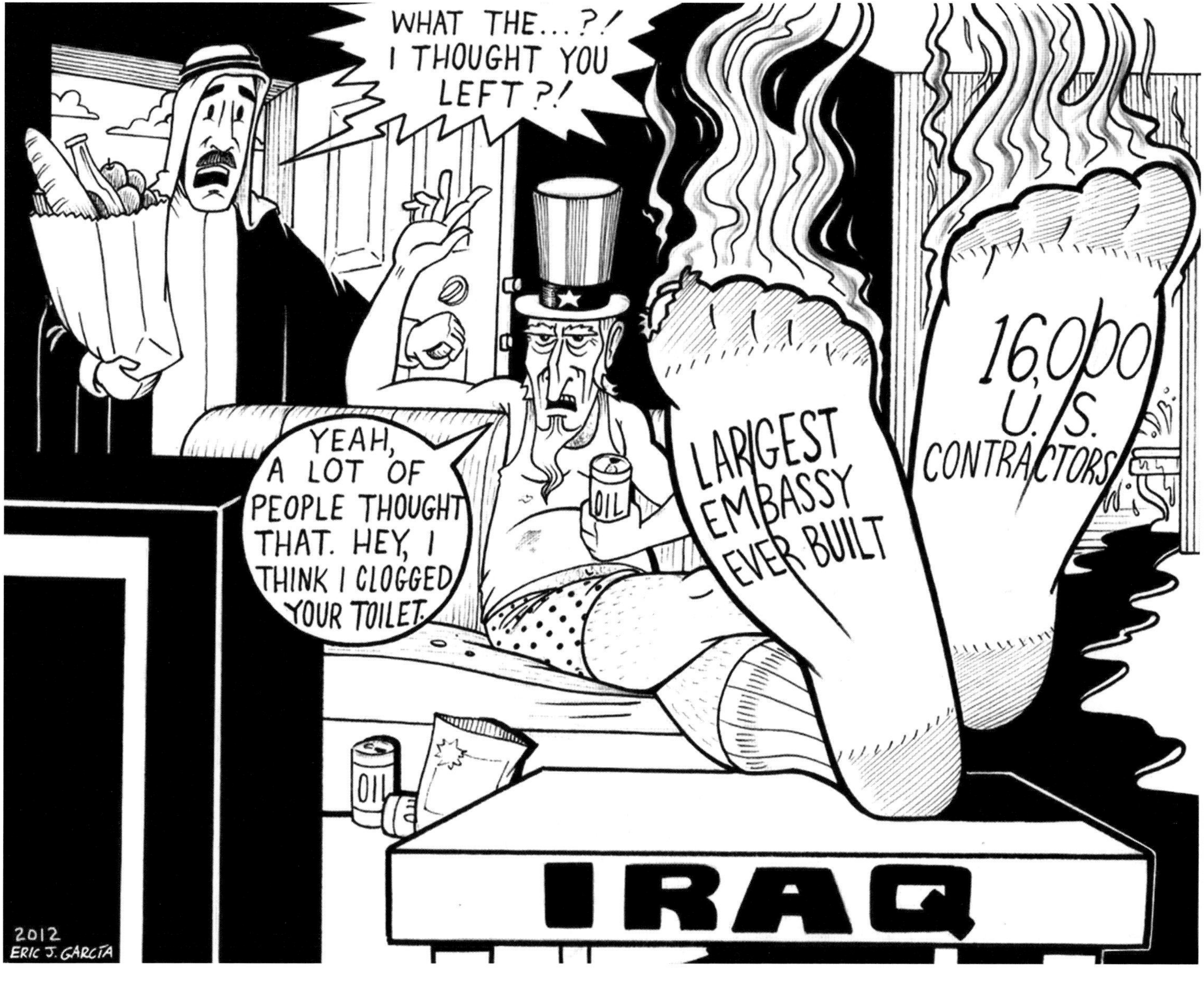
WHAT THE...?! I THOUGHT YOU LEFT?!
YEAH, A LOT OF PEOPLE THOUGHT THAT. HEY, I THINK I CLOGGED YOUR TOILET.
OIL
LARGEST EMBASSY EVER BUILT
16,000 U.S. CONTRACTORS
OIL
IRAQ
2012 ERIC J. GARCIA

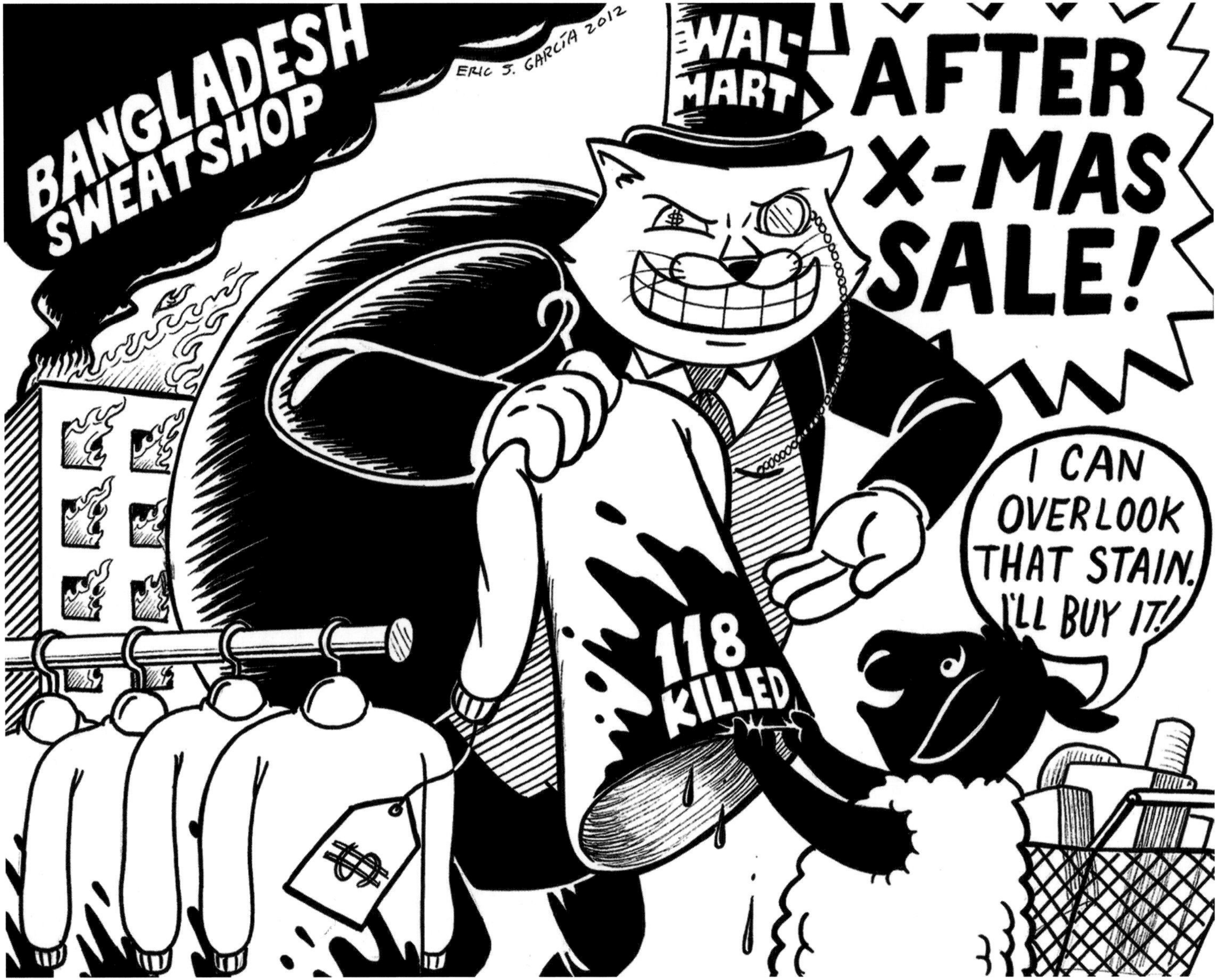
BANGLADESH SWEATSHOP
ERIC J. GARCÍA 2012
WAL-MART
AFTER X-MAS SALE!
118 KILLED
I CAN OVERLOOK THAT STAIN. I'LL BUY IT!

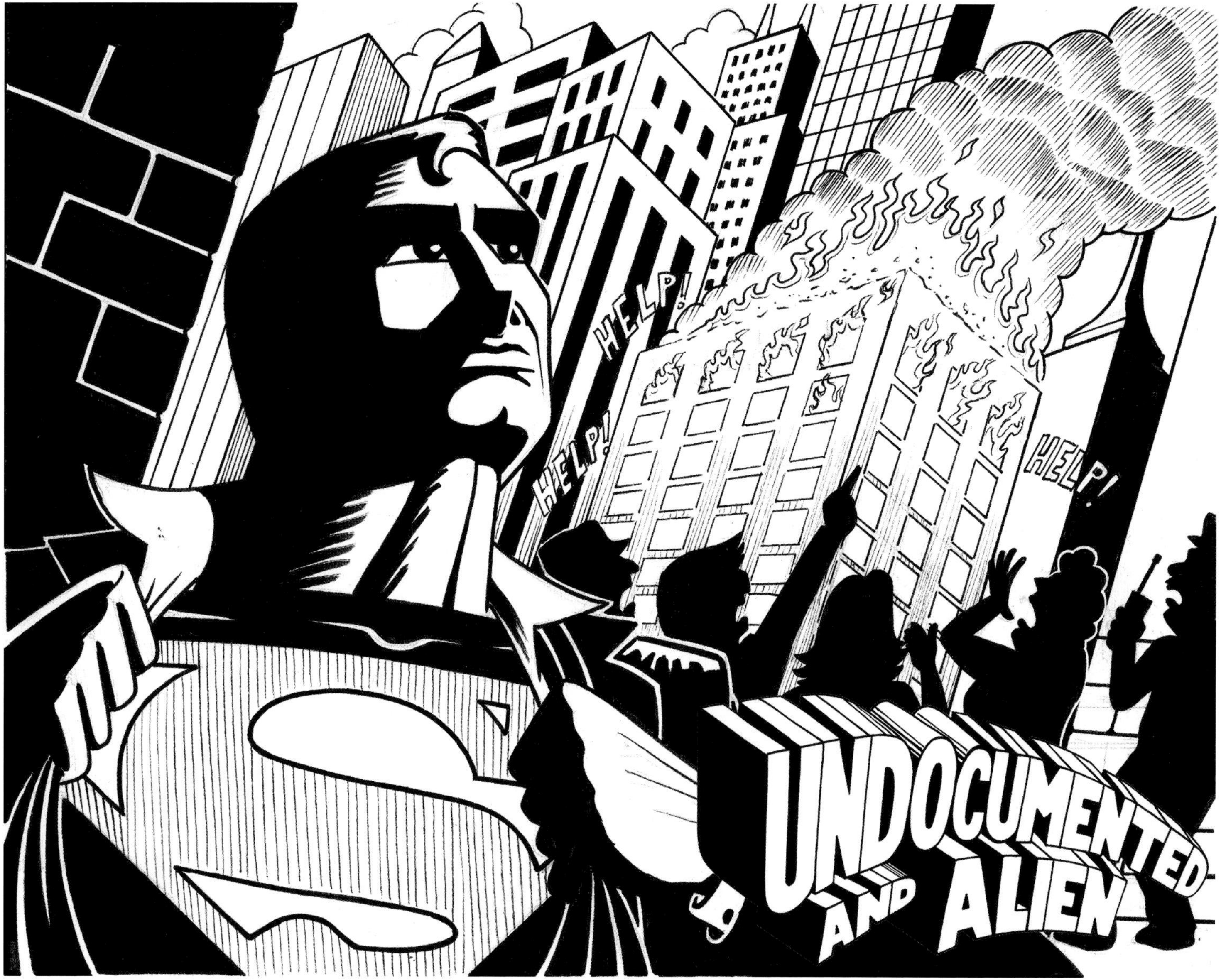
HELP!
HELP!
HELP!
UNDOCUMENTED AND ALIEN

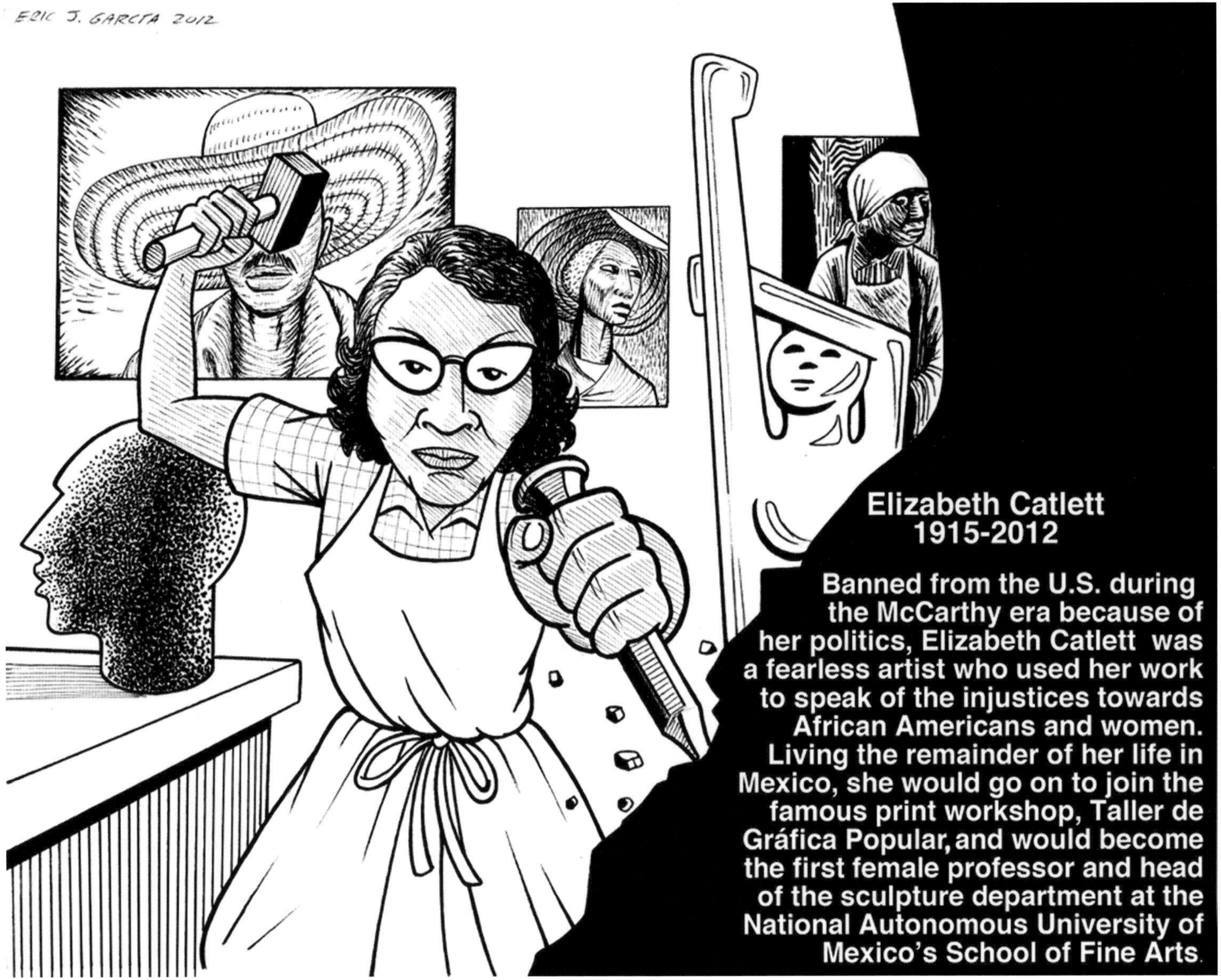
ERIC J. GARCIA 2012
Elizabeth Catlett
1915-2012
Banned from the U.S. during the McCarthy era because of her politics, Elizabeth Catlett was a fearless artist who used her work to speak of the injustices towards African Americans and women. Living the remainder of her life in Mexico, she would go on to join the famous print workshop, Taller de Gráfica Popular, and would become the first female professor and head of the sculpture department at the National Autonomous University of Mexico's School of Fine Arts.

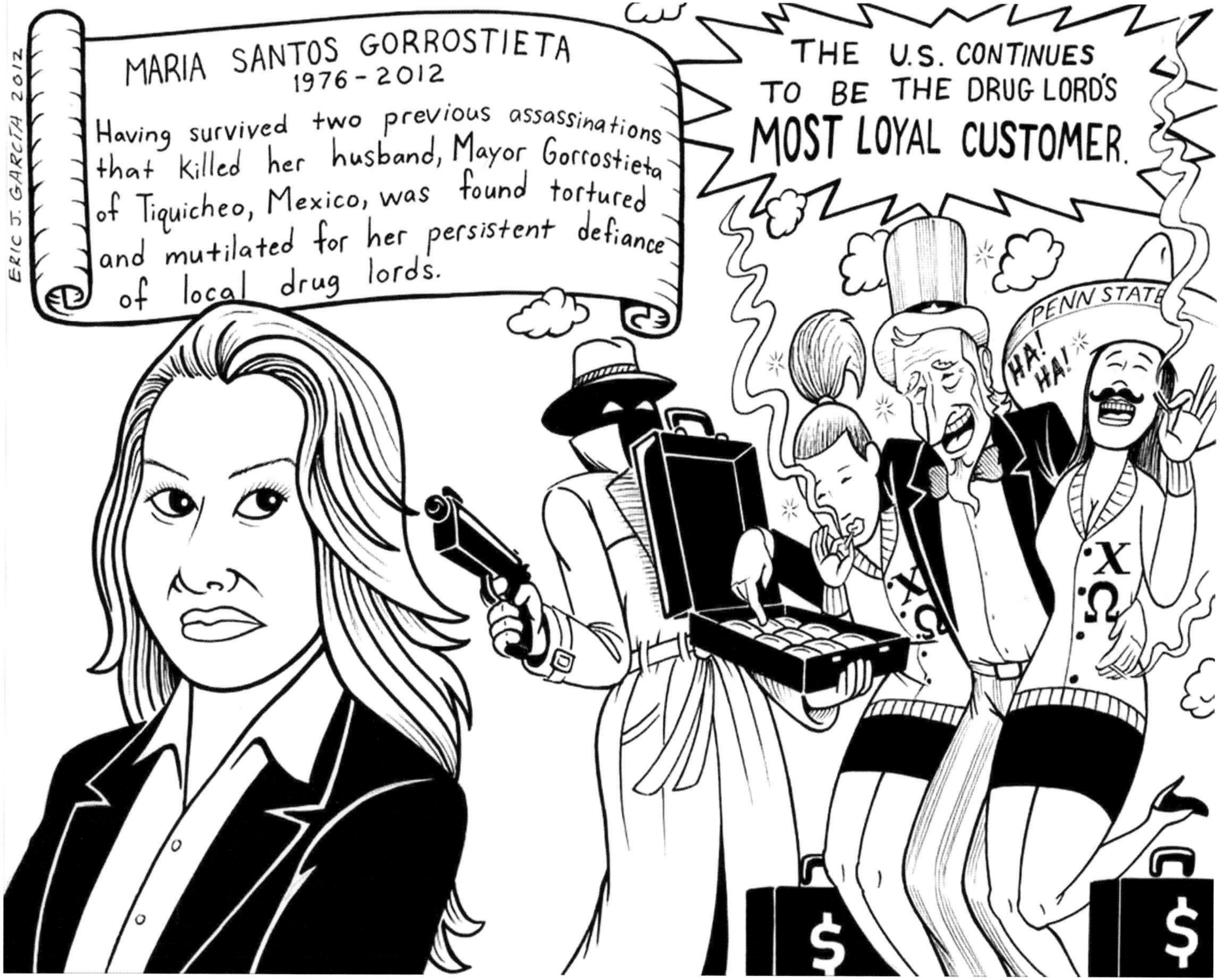
ERIC J. GARCIA 2012
MARIA SANTOS GORROSTIETA
1976 - 2012
Having survived two previous assassinations that killed her husband, Mayor Gorrostieta of Tiquicheo, Mexico, was found tortured and mutilated for her persistent defiance of local drug lords.
THE U.S. CONTINUES TO BE THE DRUG LORD'S MOST LOYAL CUSTOMER.
PENN STATE
HA! HA!
X Ω
X Ω
$
$

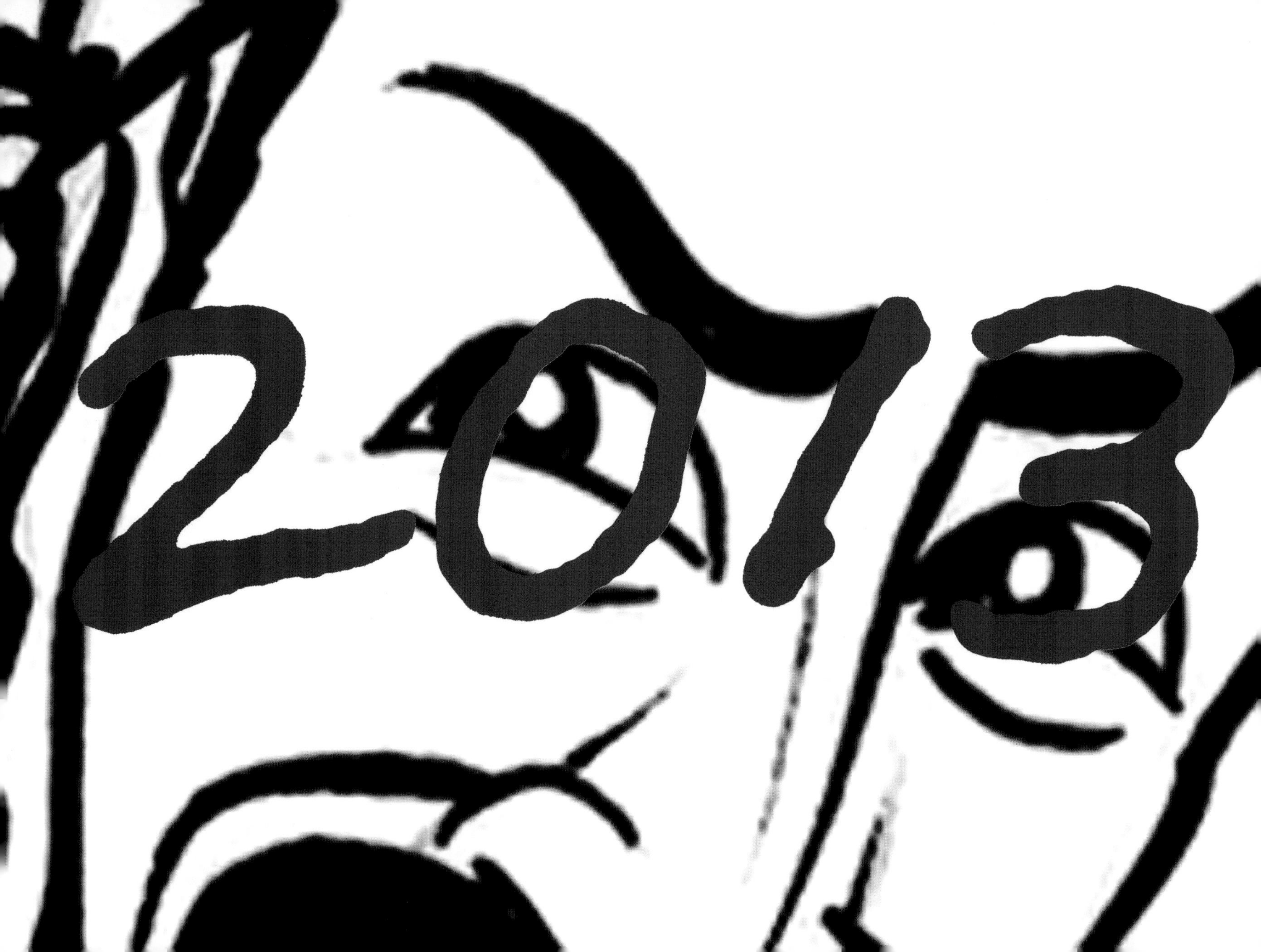
2013

2013

Biblical prophecies have come to pass as blasphemers are rained down upon by fire from the heavens. Or that's what the U.S. would like us to think as killer drones helped the United States become the new global god/government to be worshiped. But with the use of Osama bin Laden's ghost, the U.S. had created a state of fear. This fear was then used to destroy civil liberties, which actually played right into bin Laden's plan. This fear not only justified our military's violent actions globally but also the violent actions in our local neighborhoods, as in the case of Trayvon Martin. Greedy corporations like the prison industry fed off of this fear, and undocumented immigrants were swallowed up whole. Good thing activists like Dr. King weren't alive to see this, as we honored 50 years since his "I Have a Dream" speech.

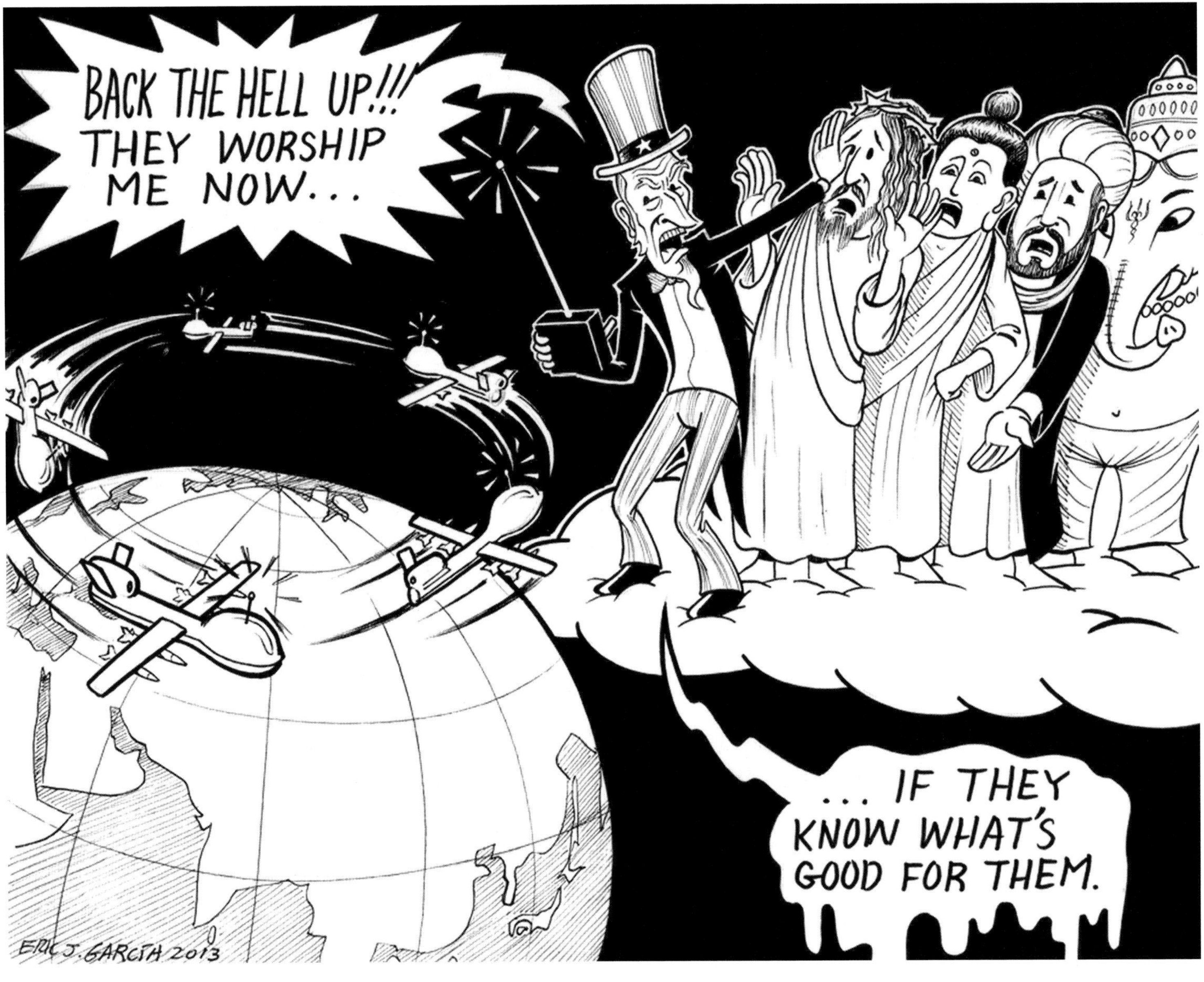
BACK THE HELL UP!!! THEY WORSHIP ME NOW...
... IF THEY KNOW WHAT'S GOOD FOR THEM.
ERIC J. GARCIA 2013

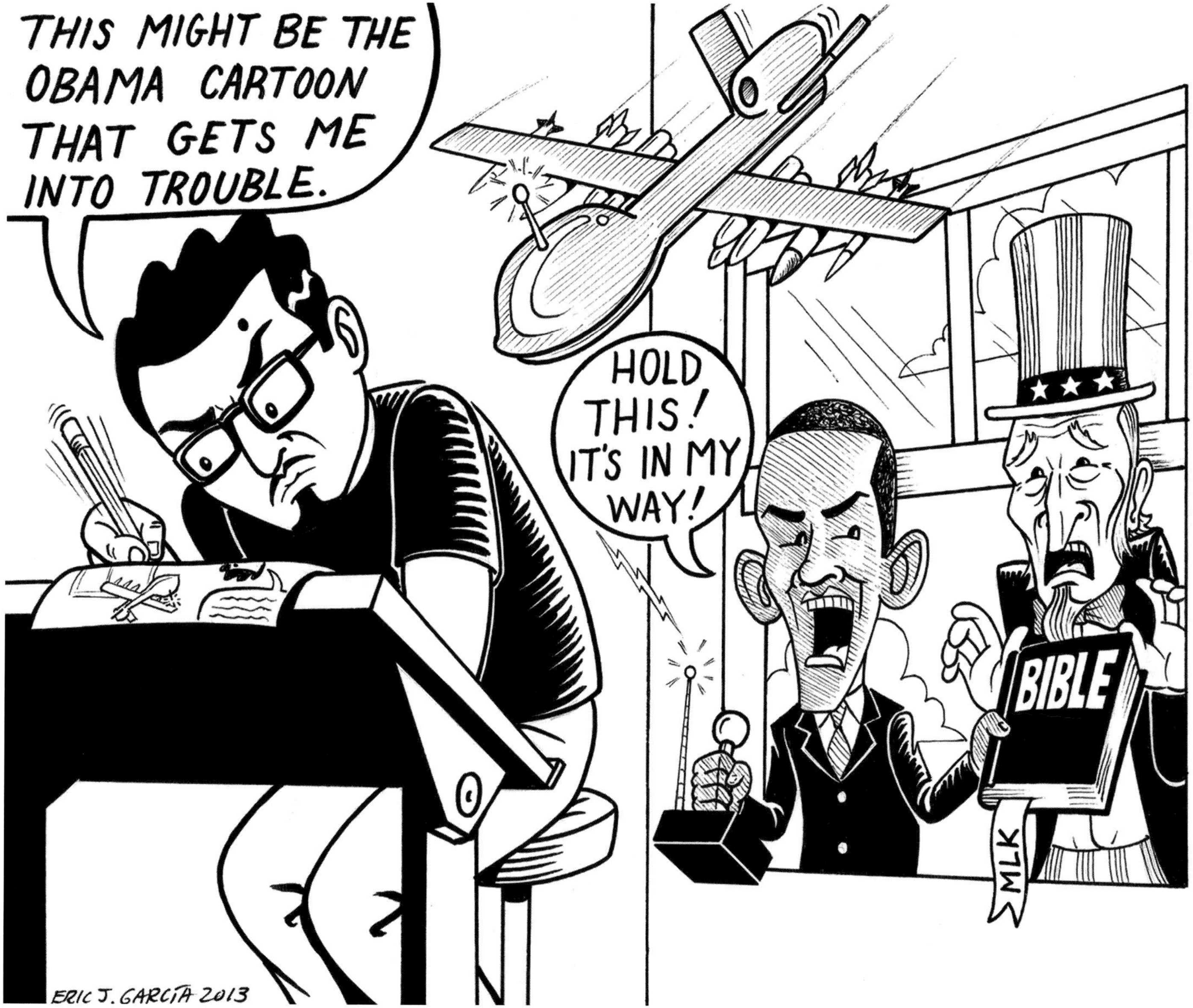
THIS MIGHT BE THE OBAMA CARTOON THAT GETS ME INTO TROUBLE.
HOLD THIS! IT'S IN MY WAY!
BIBLE
MLK
ERIC J. GARCIA 2013

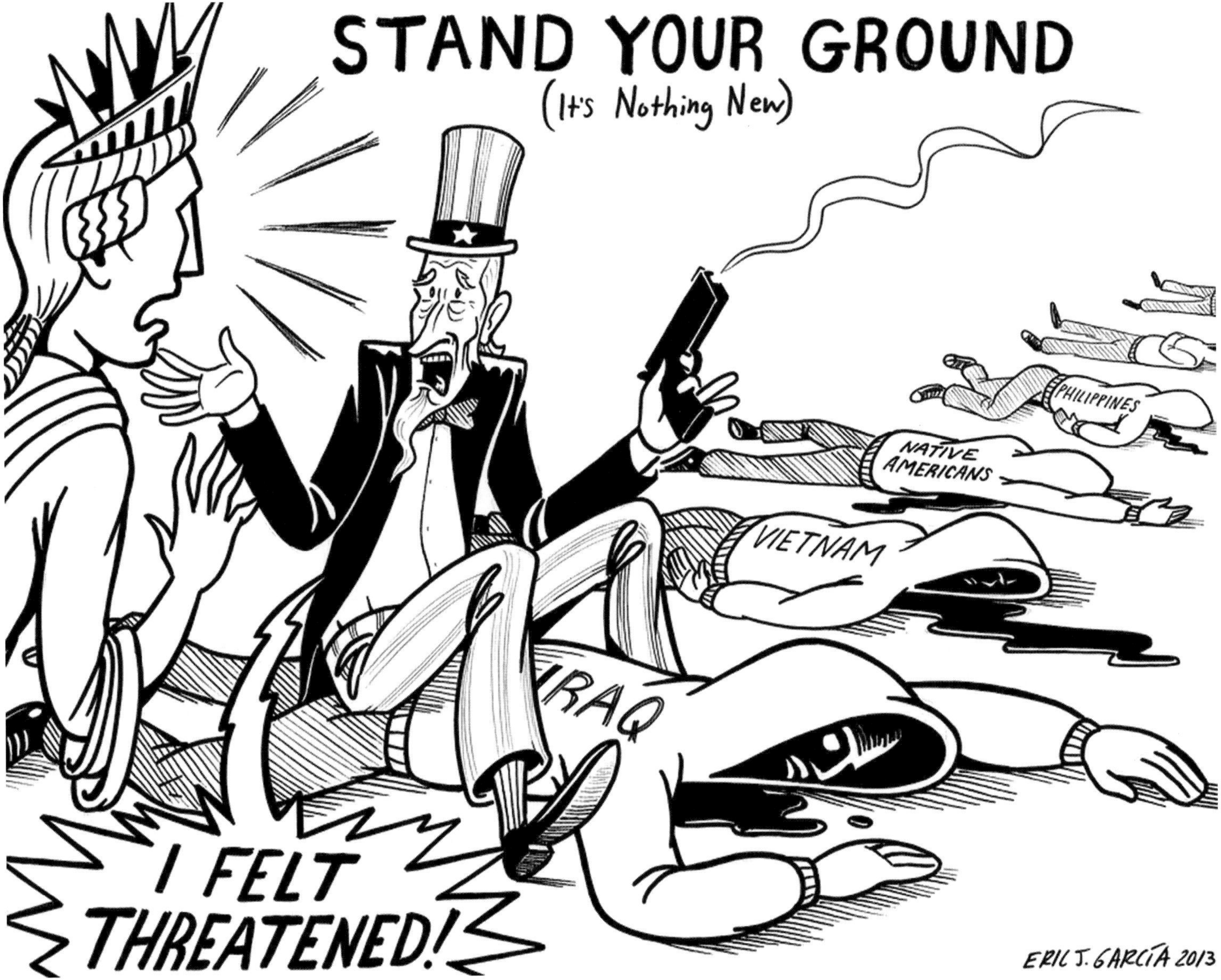
STAND YOUR GROUND
(It's Nothing New)
PHILIPPINES
NATIVE AMERICANS
VIETNAM
IRAQ
I FELT THREATENED!
ERIC J. GARCÍA 2013

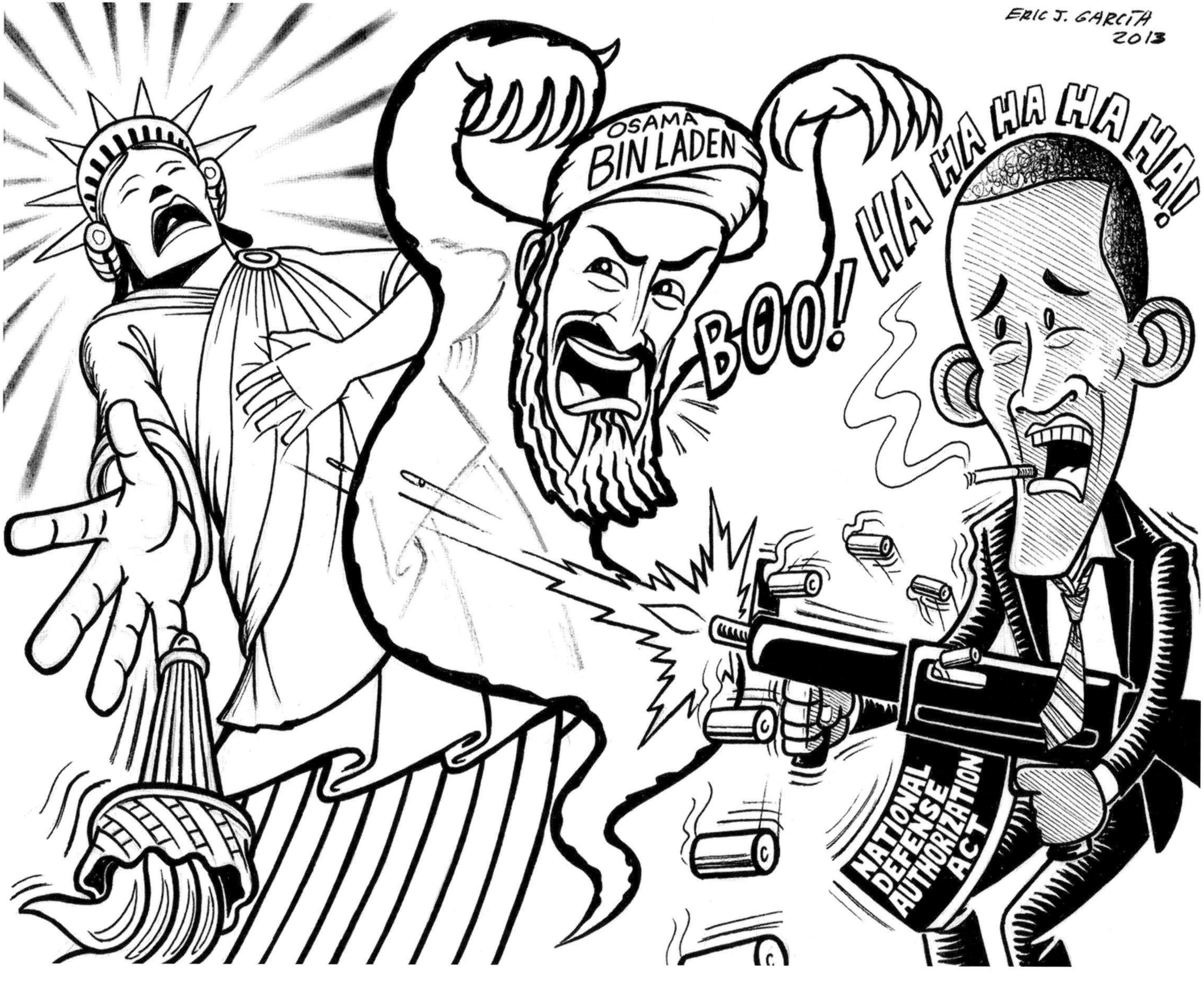
ERIC J. GARCIA
2013
OSAMA
BIN LADEN
BOO! HA HA HA HA HA HA!
NATIONAL
DEFENSE
AUTHORIZATION
ACT

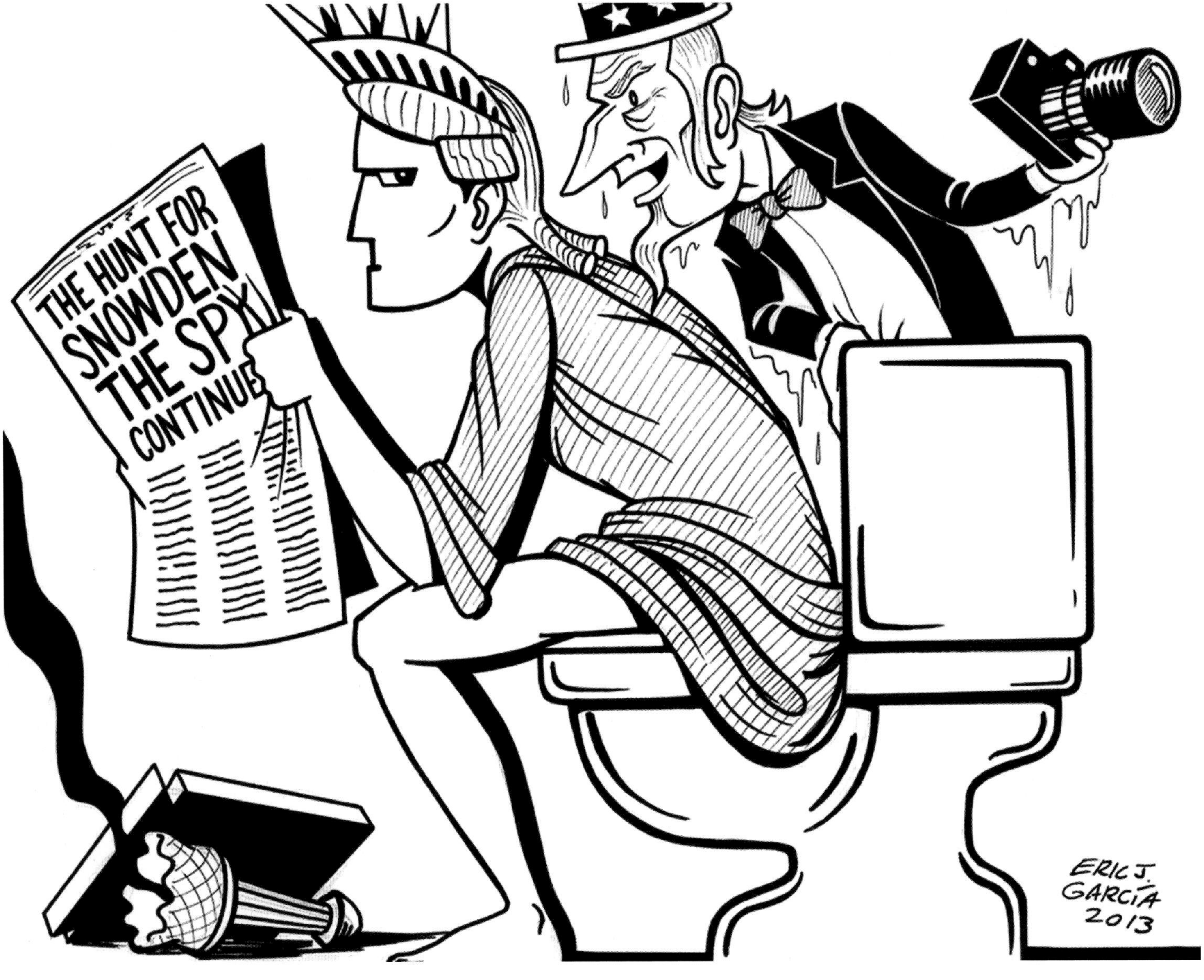
THE HUNT FOR SNOWDEN THE SPY CONTINUE
ERIC J. GARCÍA 2013

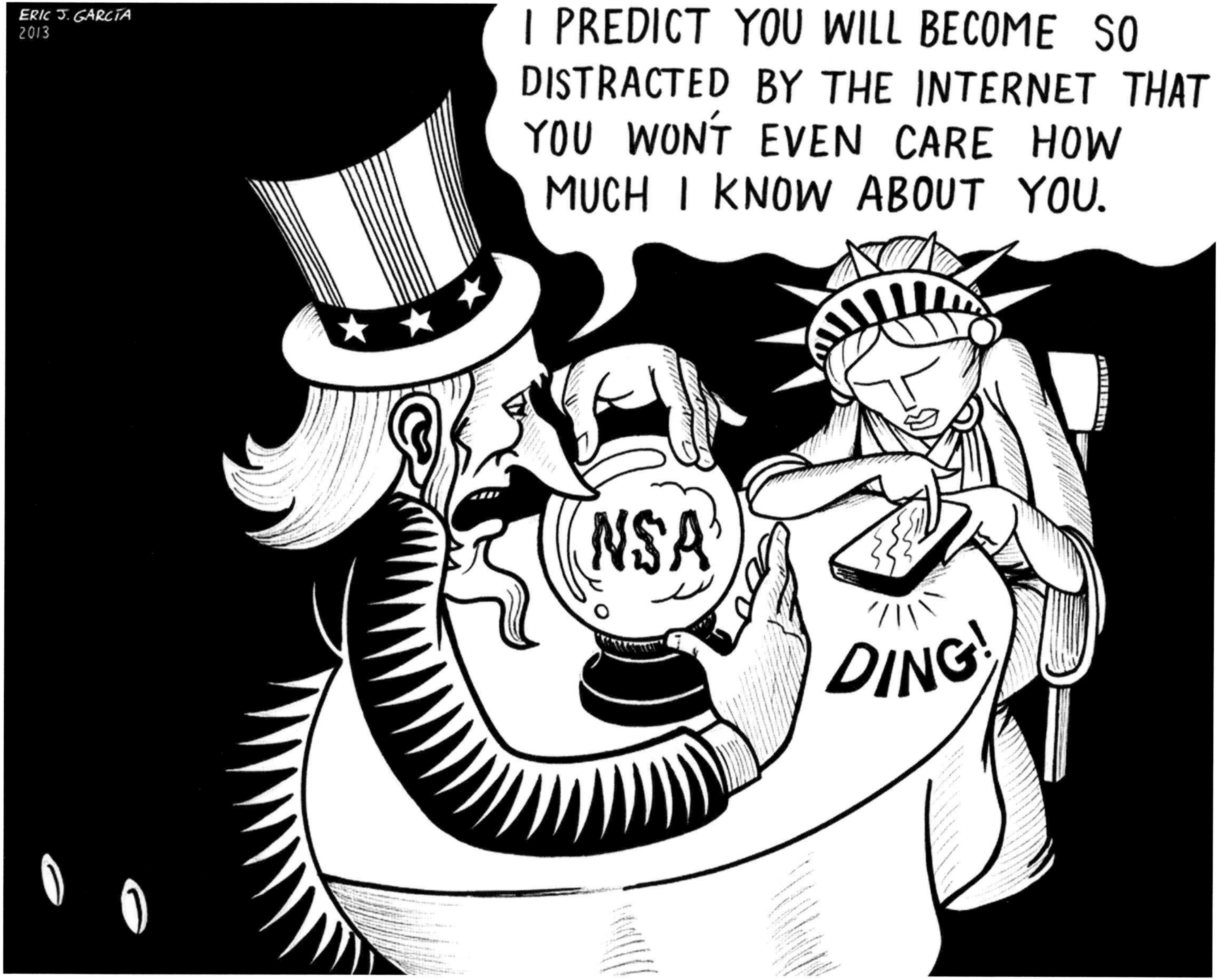
ERIC J. GARCÍA
2013
I PREDICT YOU WILL BECOME SO DISTRACTED BY THE INTERNET THAT YOU WON'T EVEN CARE HOW MUCH I KNOW ABOUT YOU.
NSA
DING!

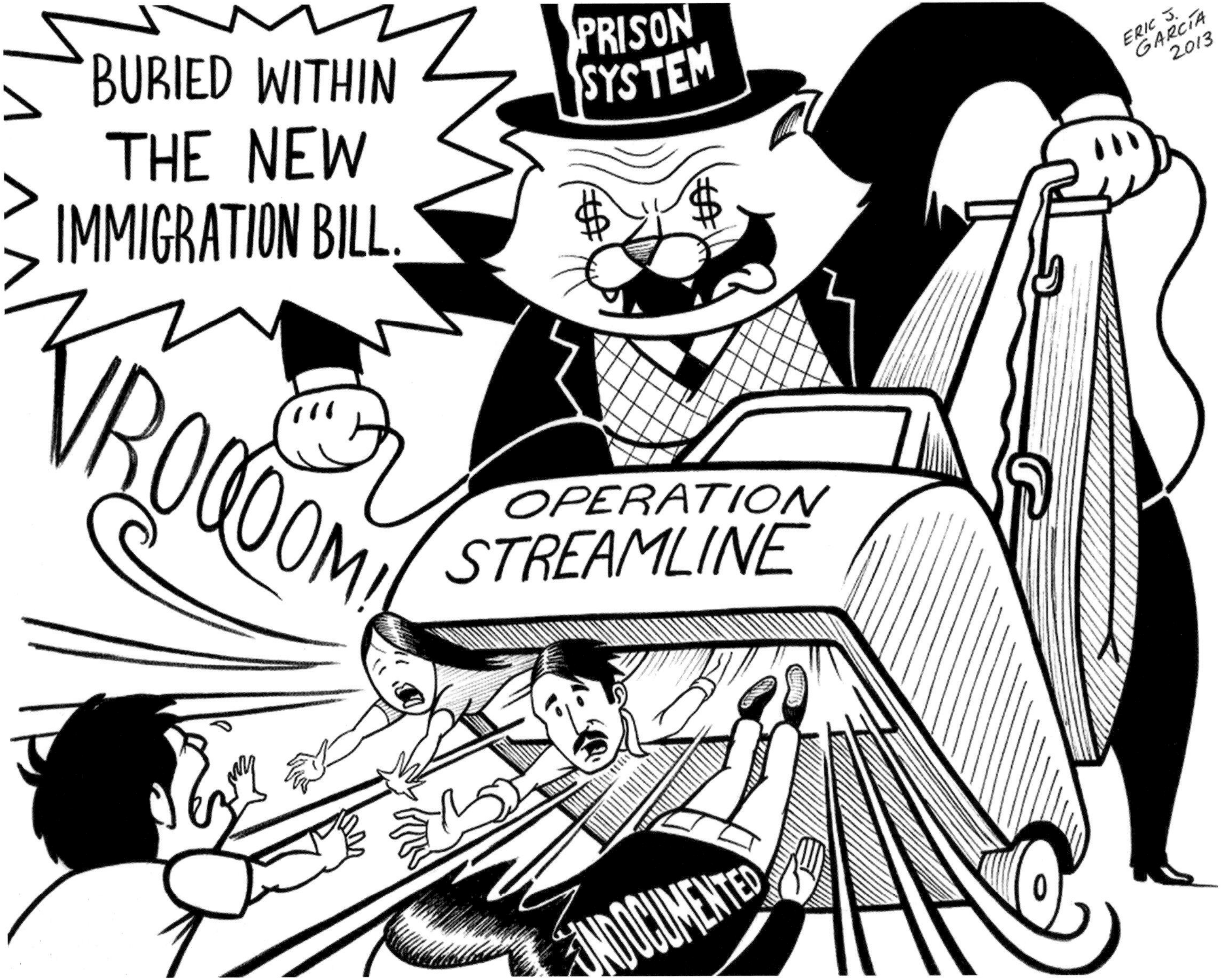
BURIED WITHIN THE NEW IMMIGRATION BILL.
PRISON SYSTEM
ERIC J. GARCIA 2013
VROOOOOM!
OPERATION STREAMLINE
UNDOCUMENTED

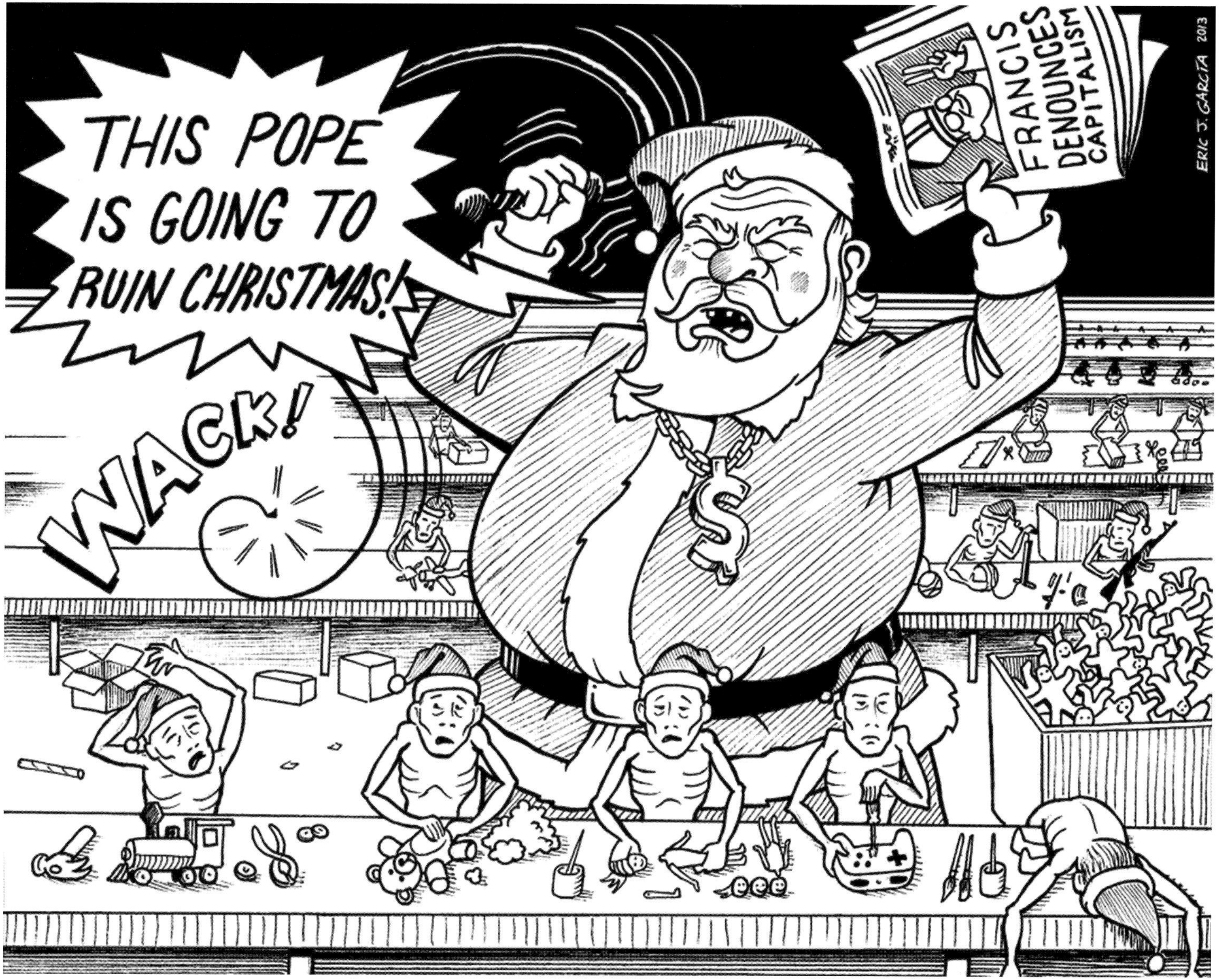
THIS POPE IS GOING TO RUIN CHRISTMAS!
WACK!
FRANCIS DENOUNCES CAPITALISM
ERIC J. GARCIA 2013

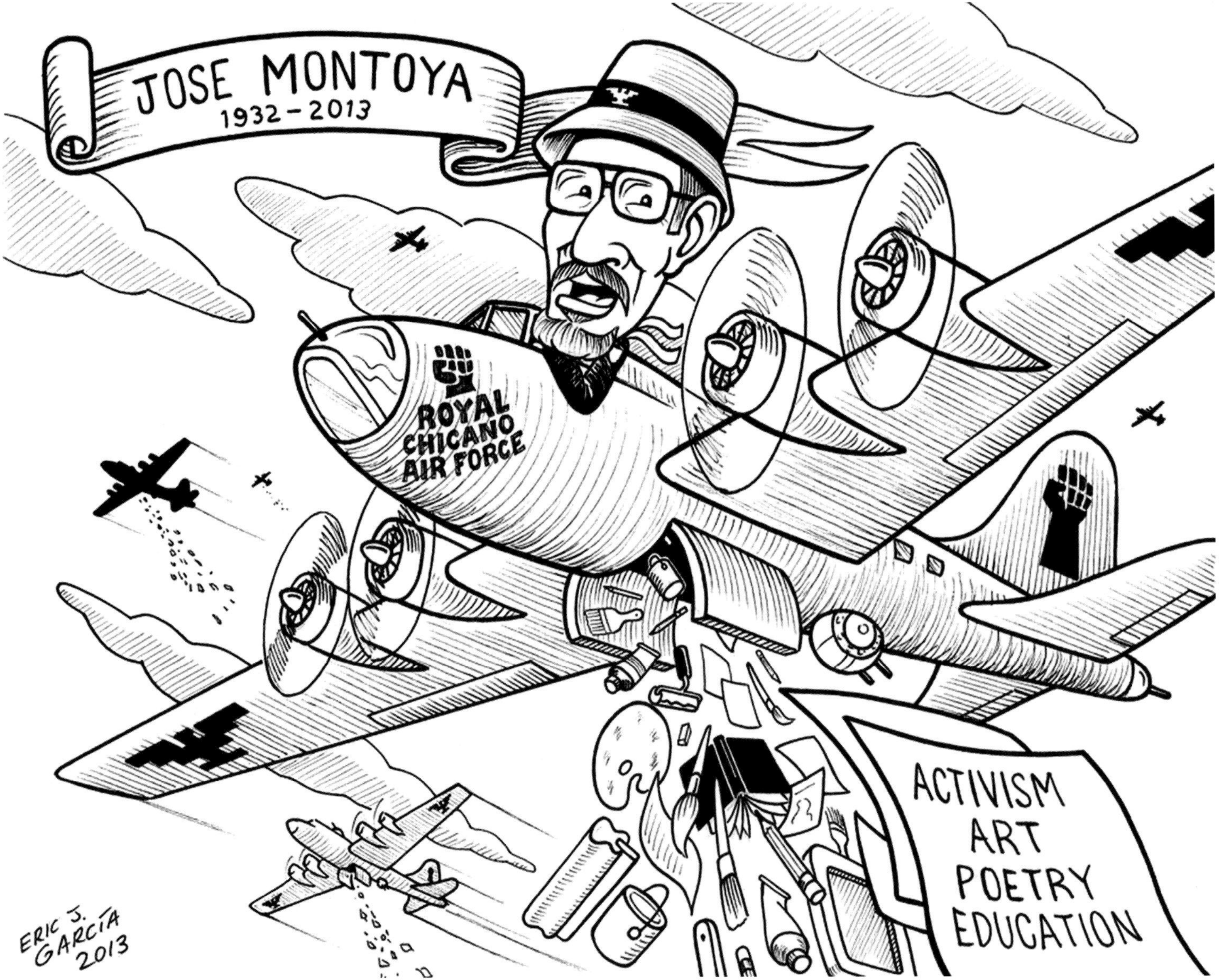
JOSE MONTOYA
1932 – 2013
ROYAL CHICANO AIR FORCE
ACTIVISM
ART
POETRY
EDUCATION
ERIC J. GARCIA 2013

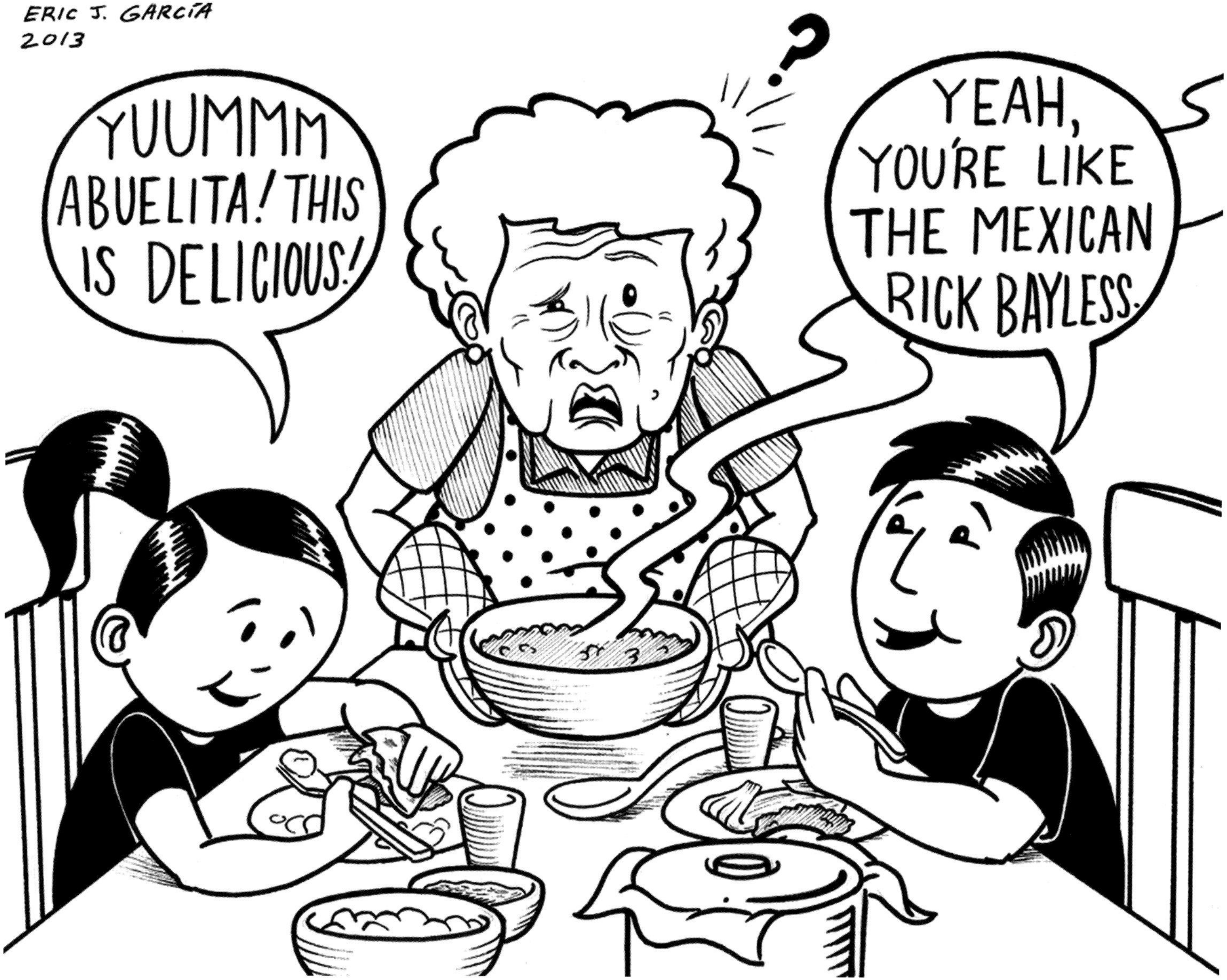
ERIC J. GARCÍA
2013
YUUMMM ABUELITA! THIS IS DELICIOUS!
?
YEAH, YOU'RE LIKE THE MEXICAN RICK BAYLESS.

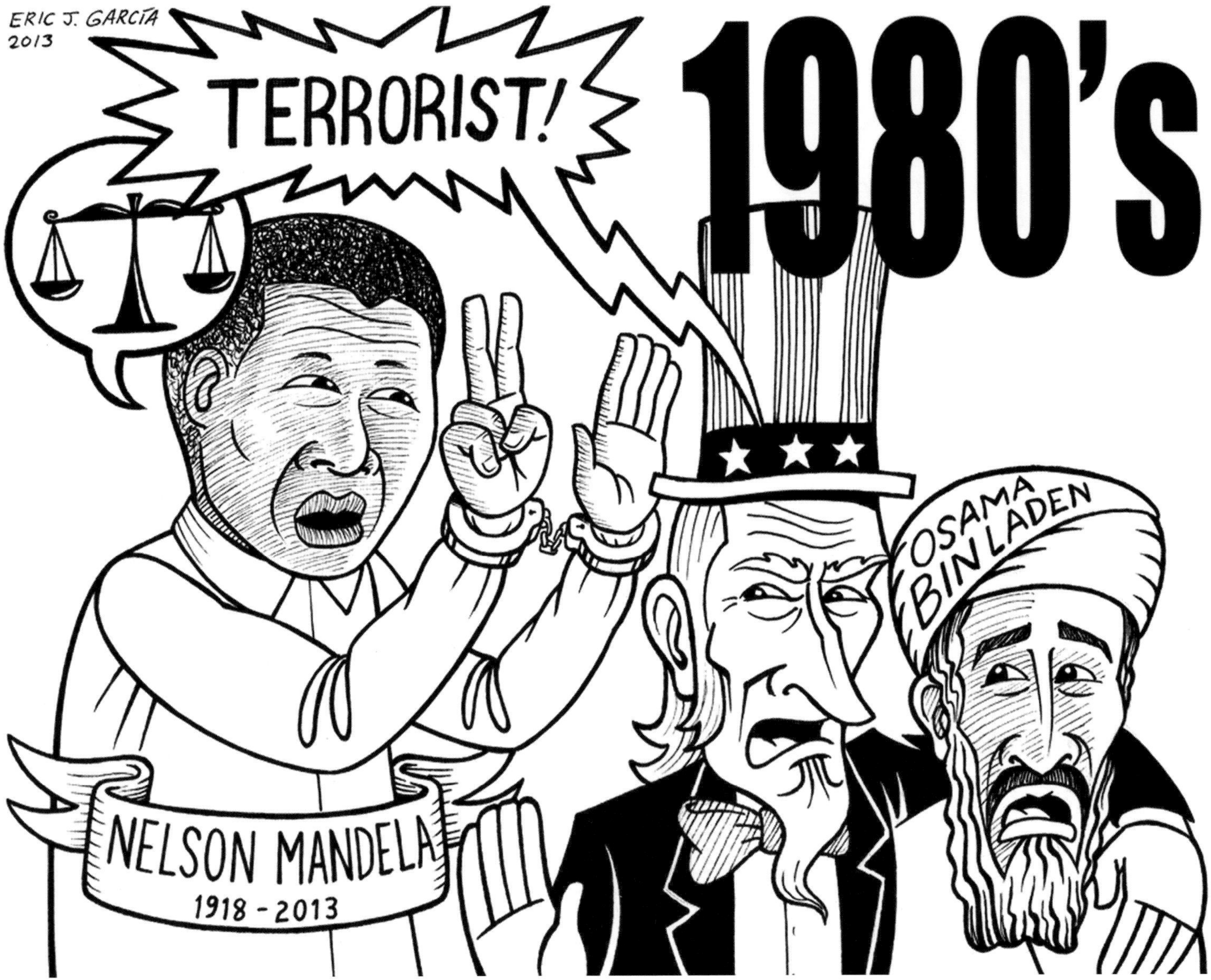
ERIC J. GARCÍA
2013
TERRORIST!
1980's
OSAMA BIN LADEN
NELSON MANDELA
1918 - 2013

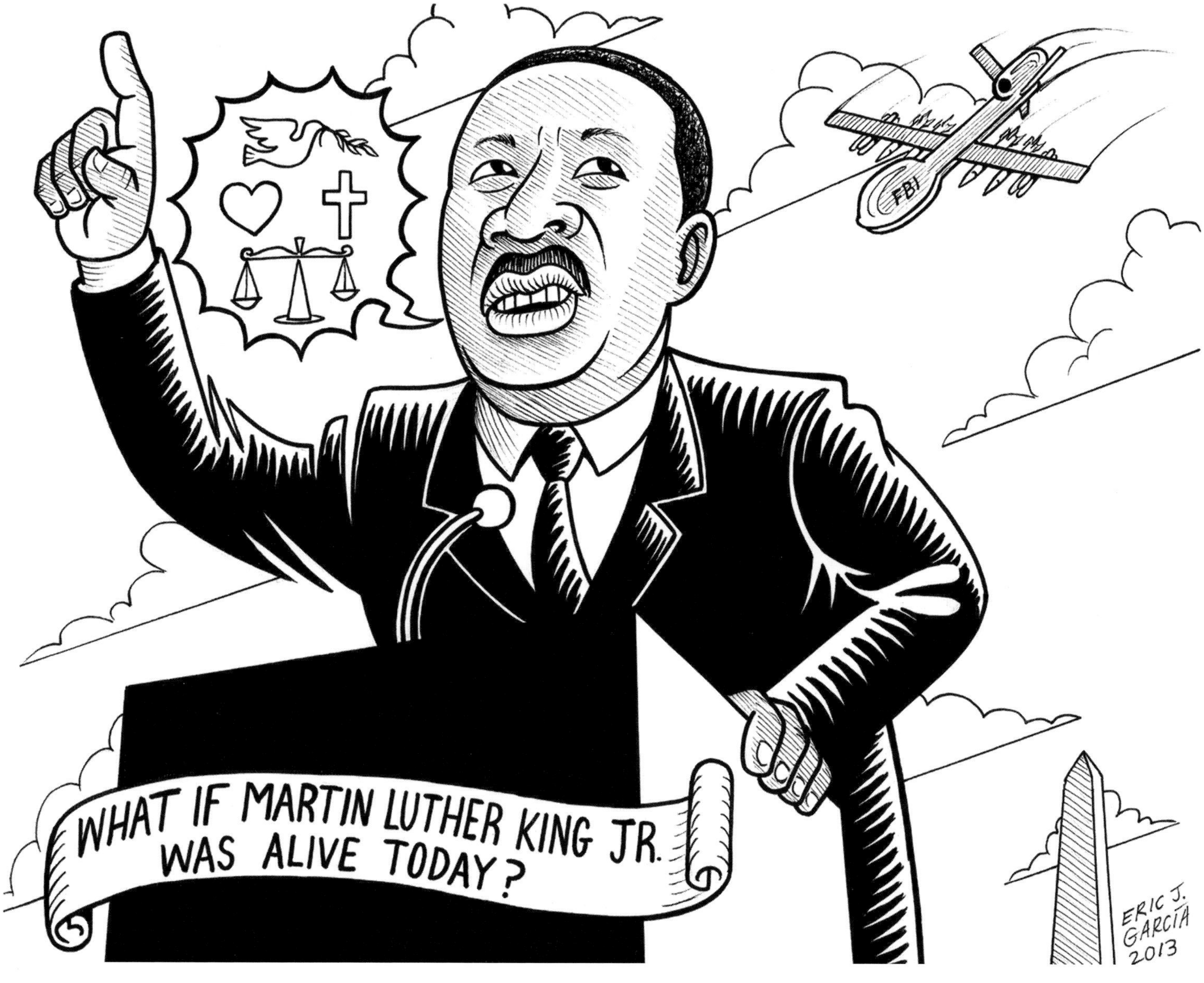
FBI
WHAT IF MARTIN LUTHER KING JR.
WAS ALIVE TODAY?
ERIC J.
GARCIA
2013

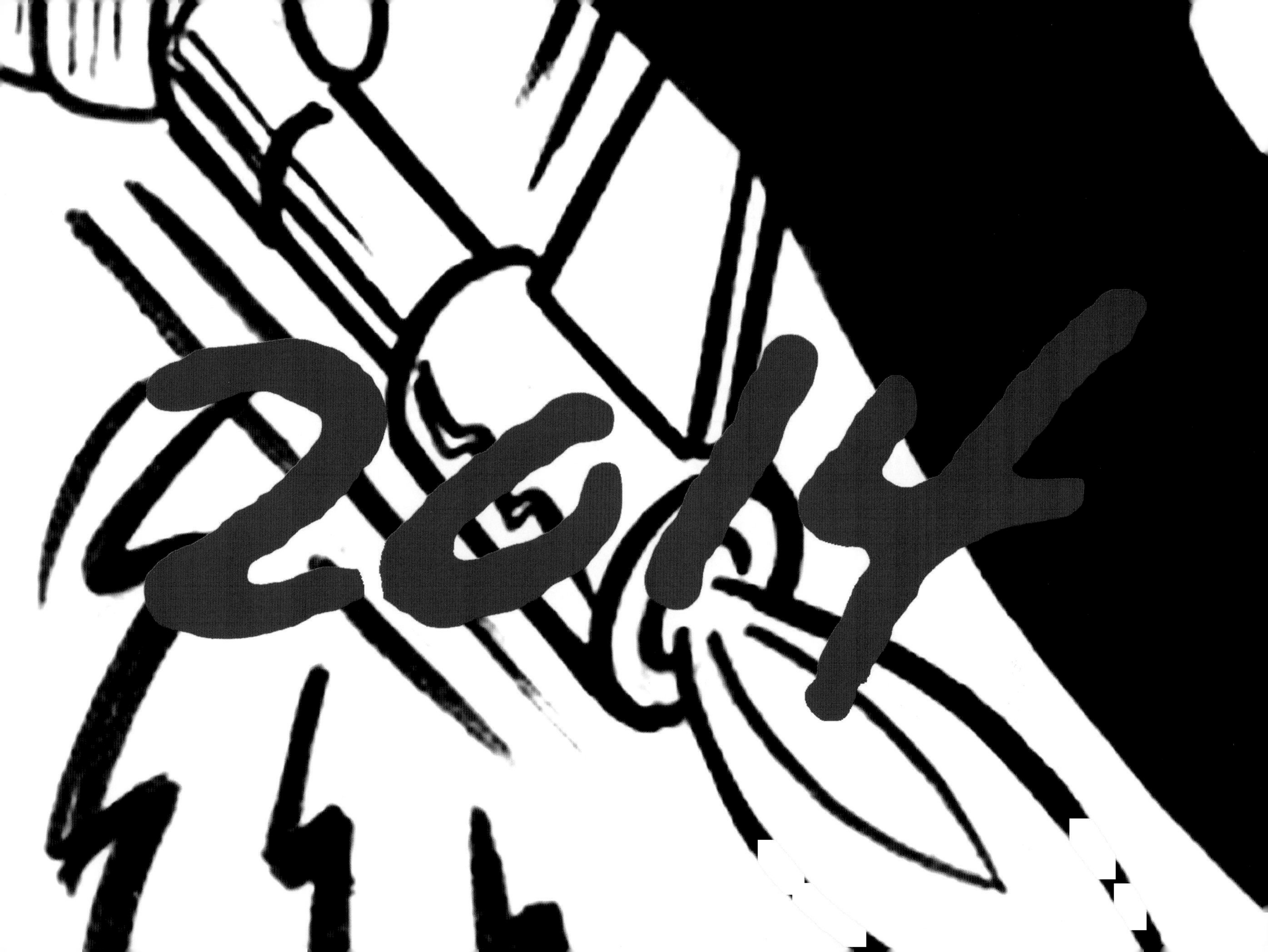
ZCHK

2014

Uncle Sam's Cold War foreign policy came back to haunt him as waves of Central American children fled their war torn, impoverished, puppet regimes of the United States. Another failed policy, the Merida Initiative in Mexico was supposed to help fight the Drug War but only made things worse. The killing of civilians was a common situation south and north of the border as police who were supposed to protect us were actually doing the opposite. As weapons and personnel came back home from the endless wars overseas, our domestic police forces became more militarized and looser with their triggers. "Protecting us" was the justification for the force-feeding of the GITMO detainees imprisoned for life without trial. It's good to know our tax dollars were put to good use in keeping us "safe" and distracted.

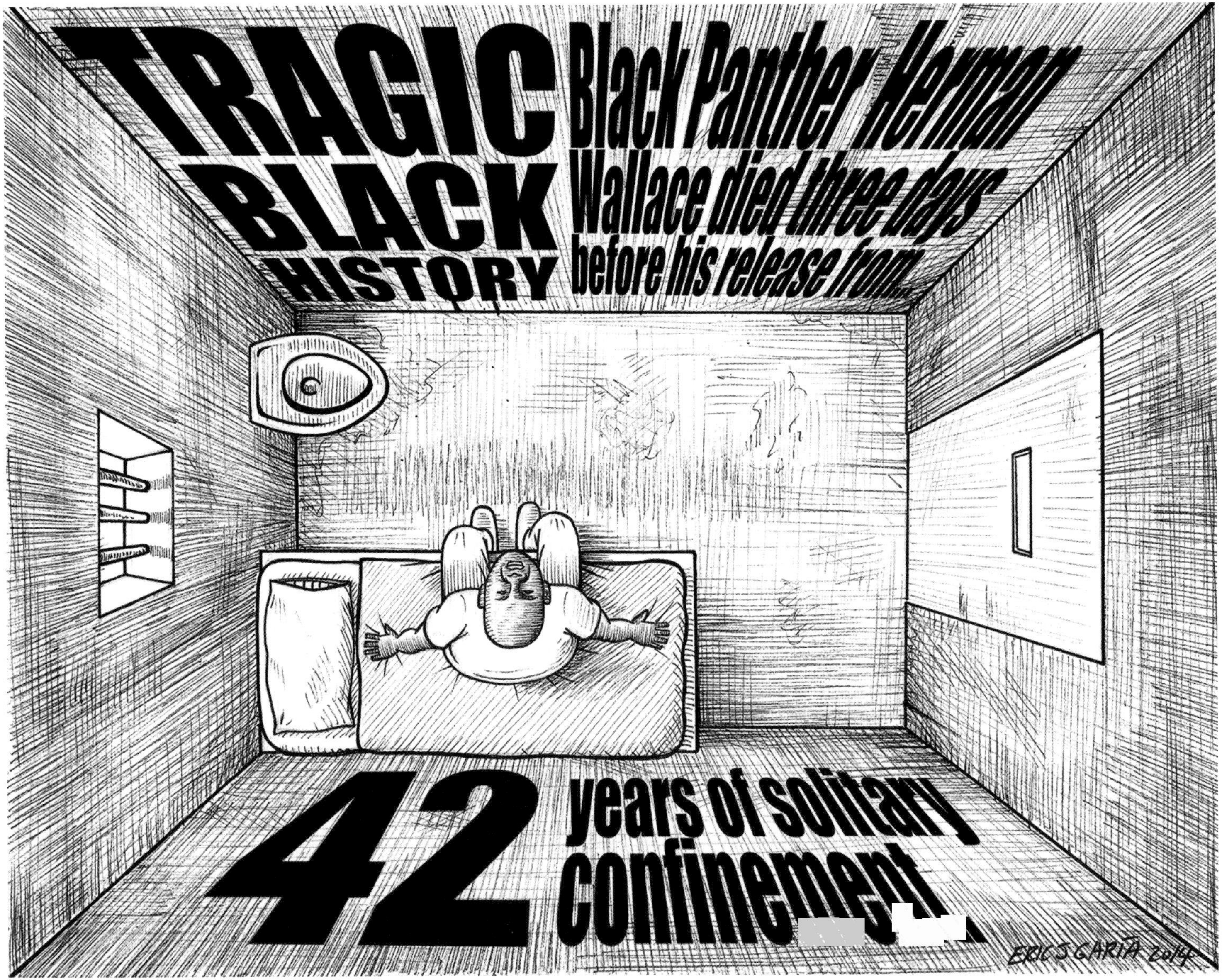
TRAGIC
BLACK
HISTORY
Black Panther Herman
Wallace died three days
before his release from
42
years of solitary
confinement
ERIC J. GARCIA 2014

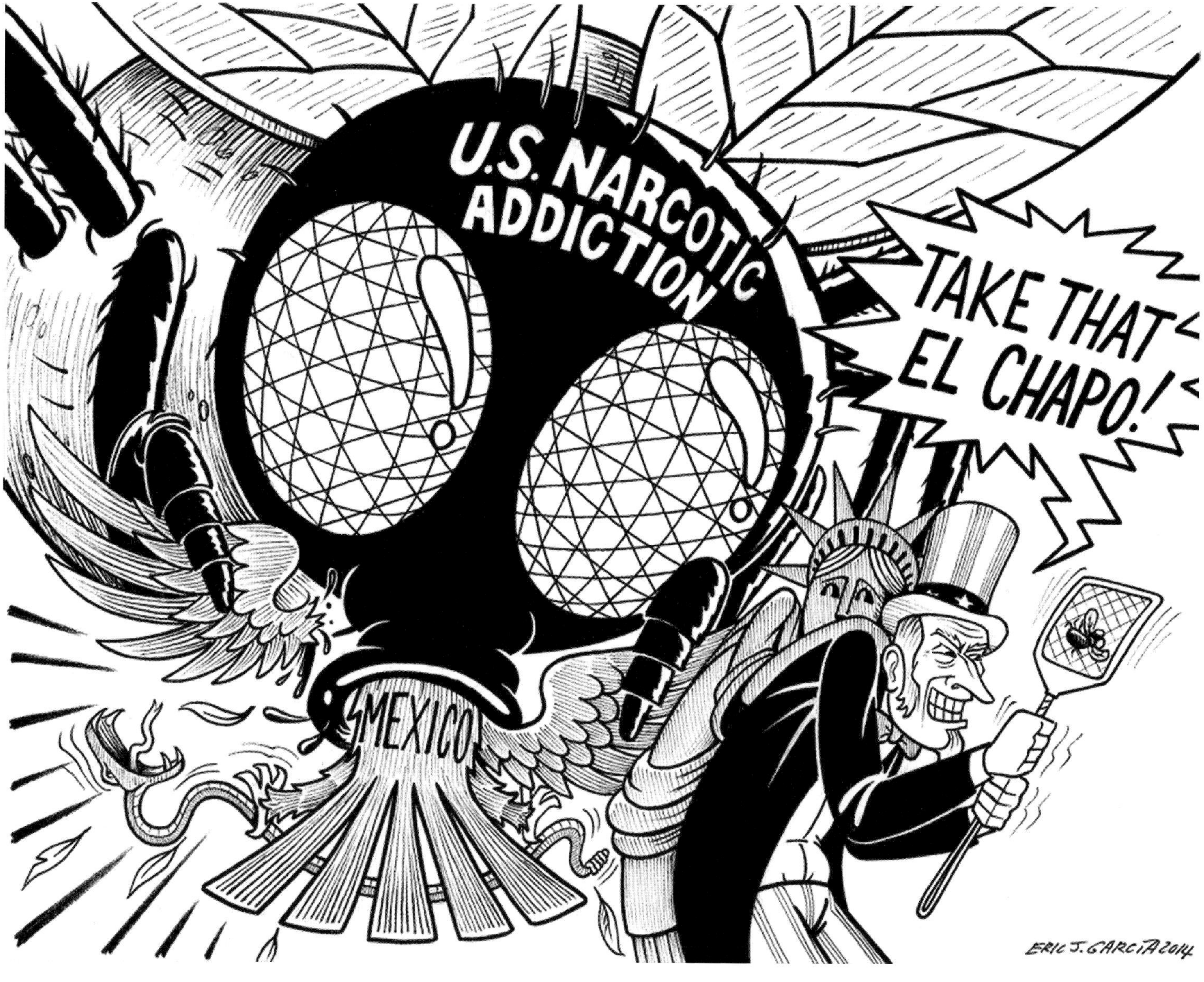
U.S. NARCOTIC ADDICTION
TAKE THAT EL CHAPO!
MEXICO
ERIC J. GARCIA 2014

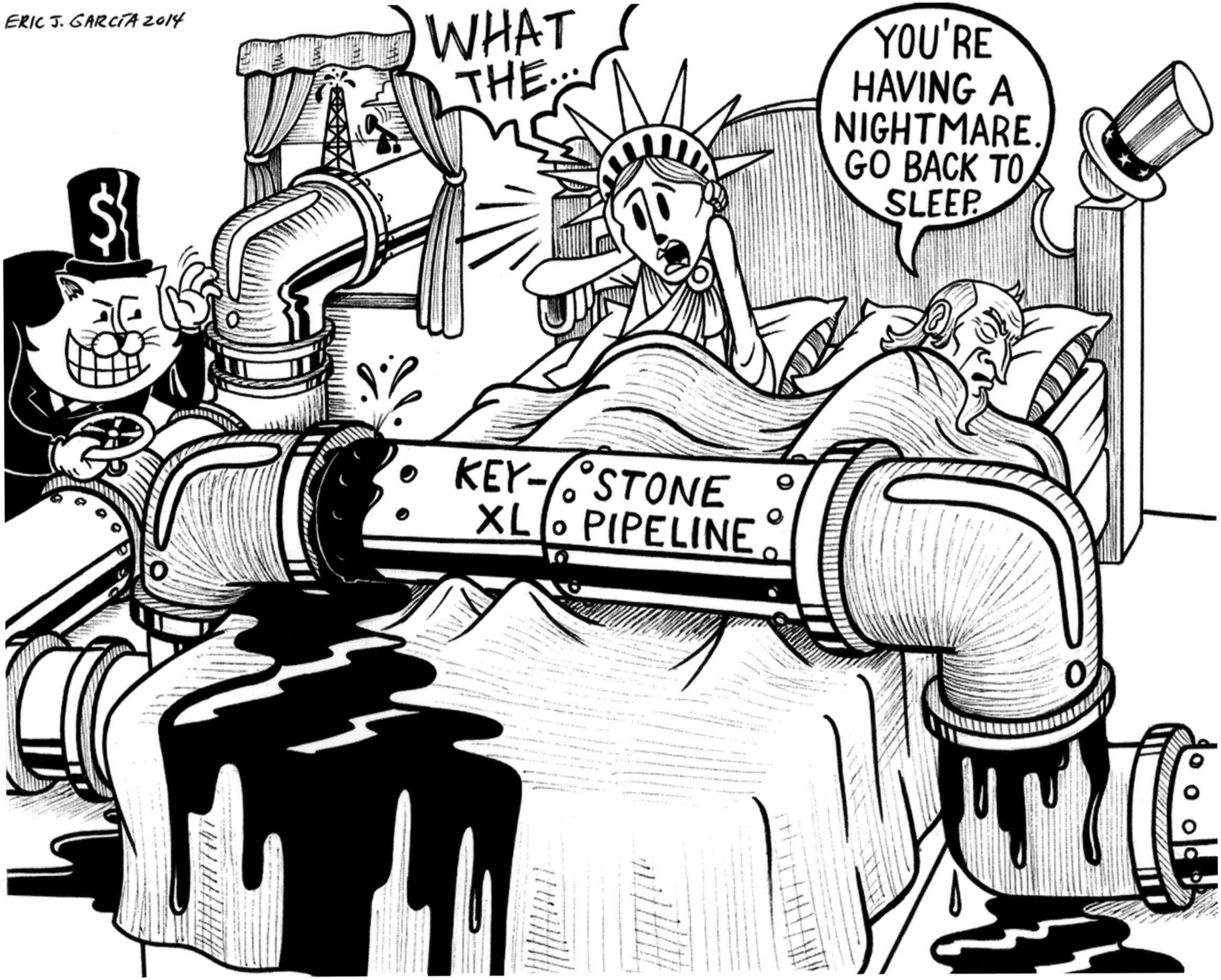
ERIC J. GARCIA 2014
WHAT THE...
YOU'RE HAVING A NIGHTMARE. GO BACK TO SLEEP.
$
KEY-STONE XL PIPELINE

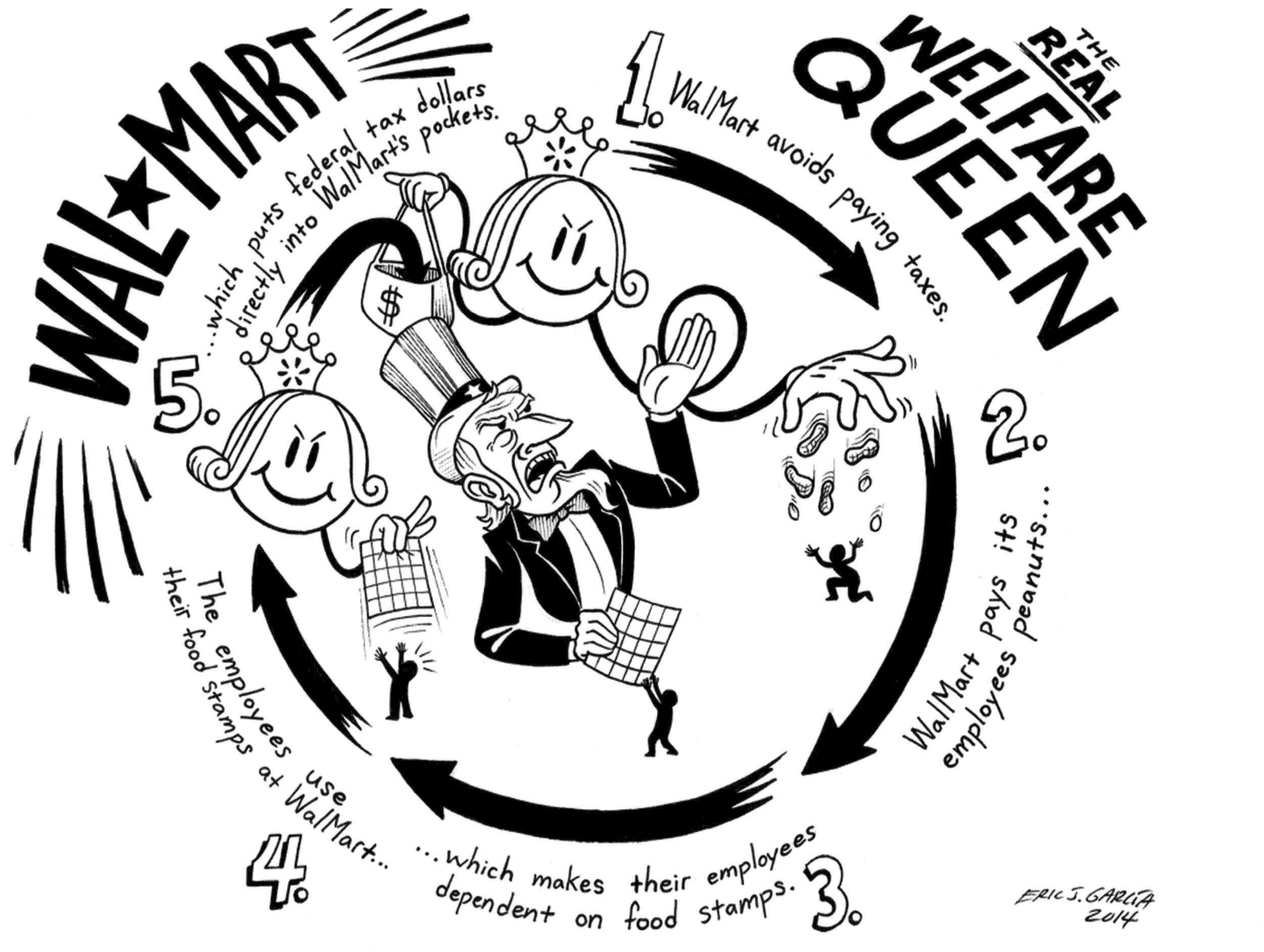
WAL★MART
THE REAL WELFARE QUEEN
1. WalMart avoids paying taxes.
2. WalMart pays its employees peanuts...
3. ...which makes their employees dependent on food stamps.
4. The employees use their food stamps at WalMart...
5. ...which puts federal tax dollars directly into WalMart's pockets.
$
ERIC J. GARCIA 2014

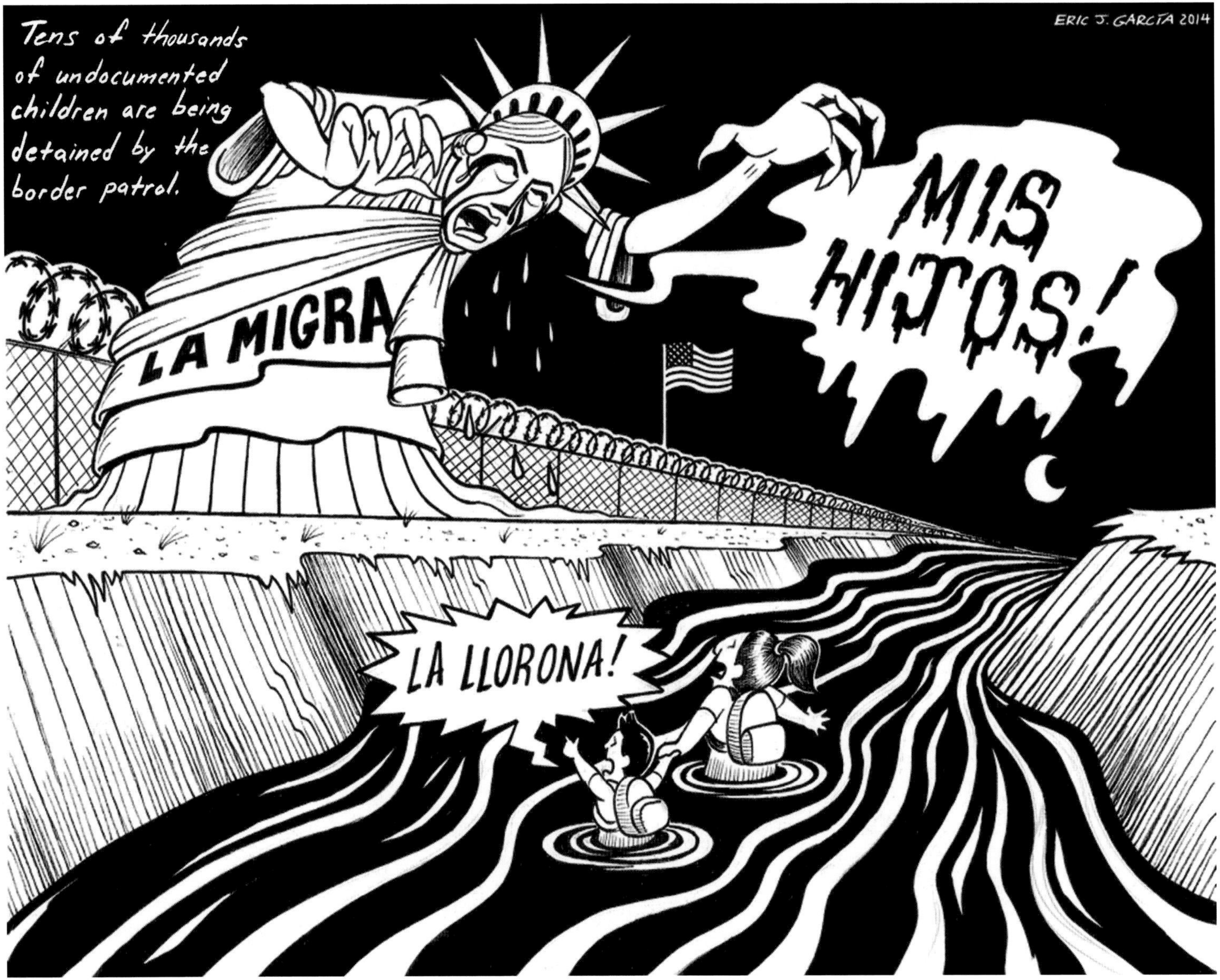
ERIC J. GARCIA 2014
Tens of thousands of undocumented children are being detained by the border patrol.
LA MIGRA
MIS HIJOS!
LA LLORONA!

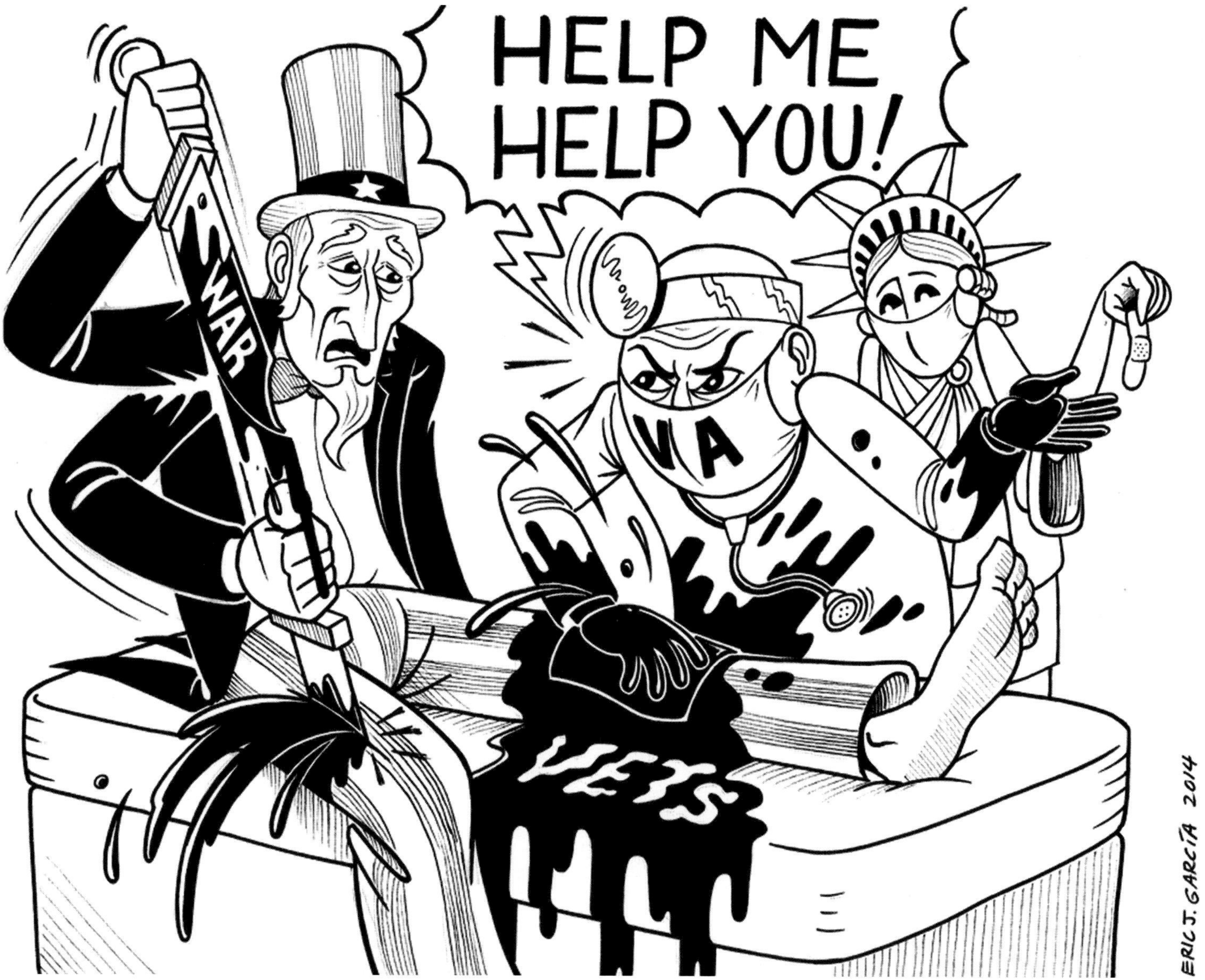
HELP ME
HELP YOU!
WAR
VA
VETS
ERIC J. GARCÍA 2014

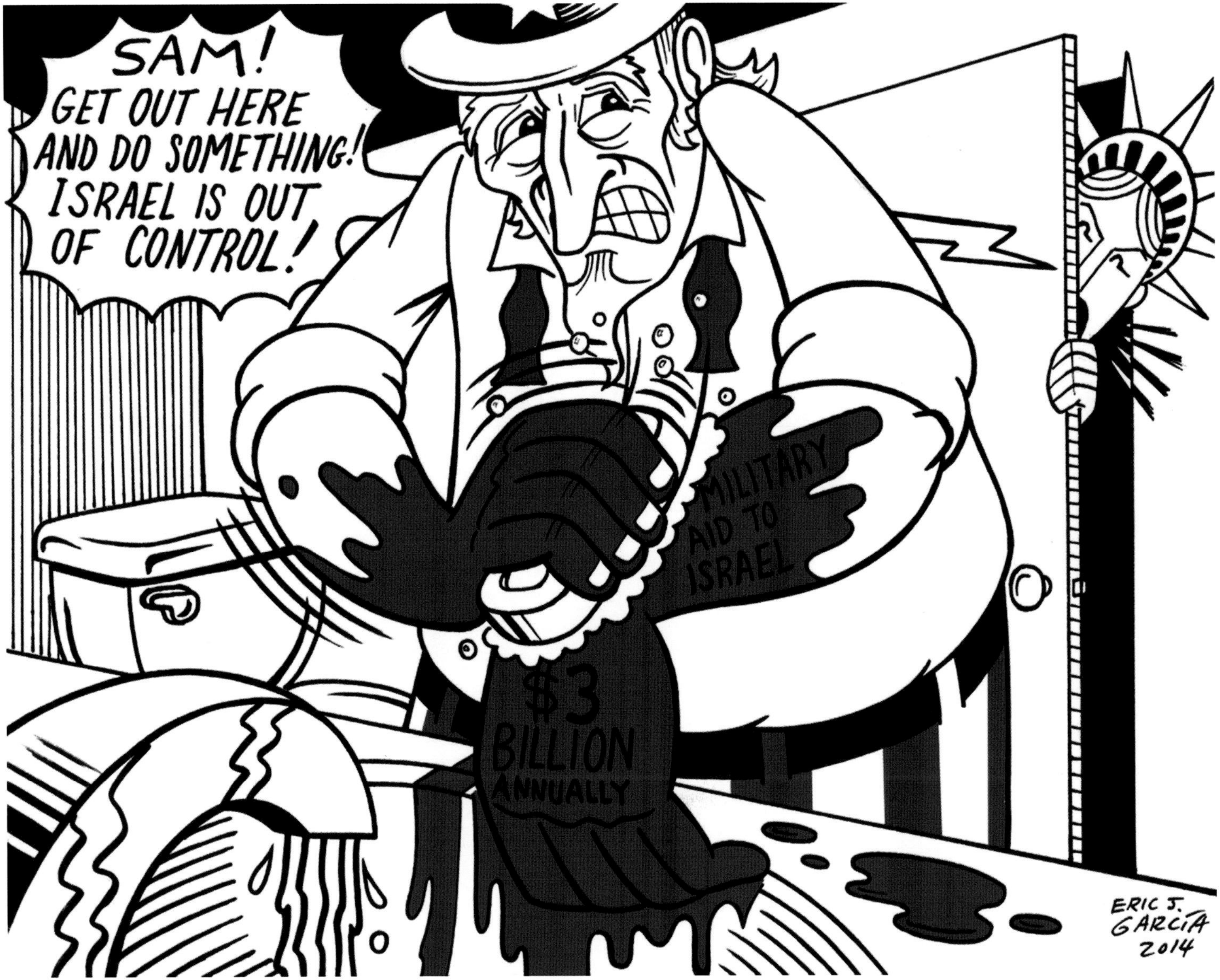
SAM! GET OUT HERE AND DO SOMETHING! ISRAEL IS OUT OF CONTROL!
MILITARY AID TO ISRAEL
$3 BILLION ANNUALLY
ERIC J. GARCIA 2014

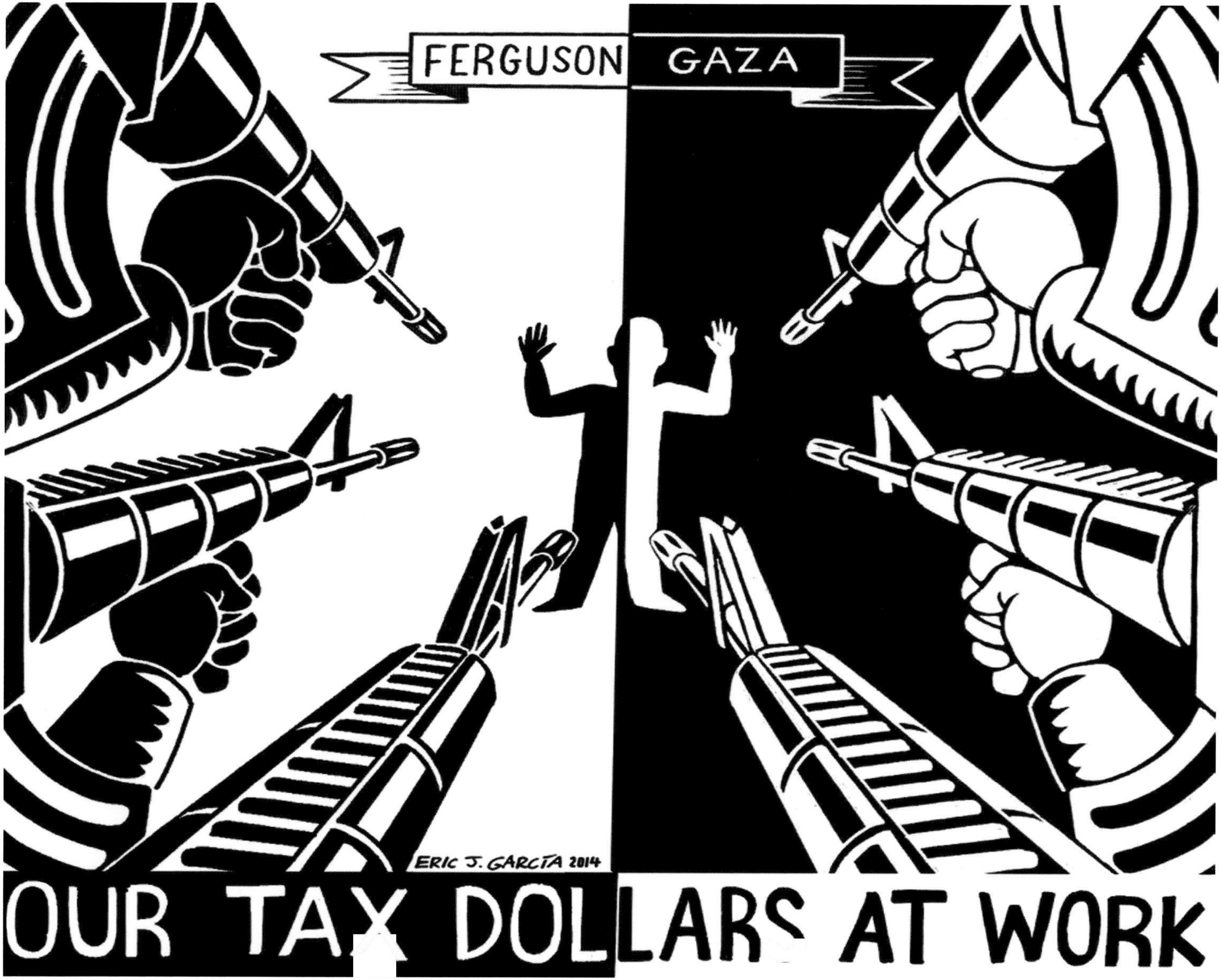
FERGUSON
GAZA
ERIC J. GARCIA 2014
OUR TAX DOLLARS AT WORK

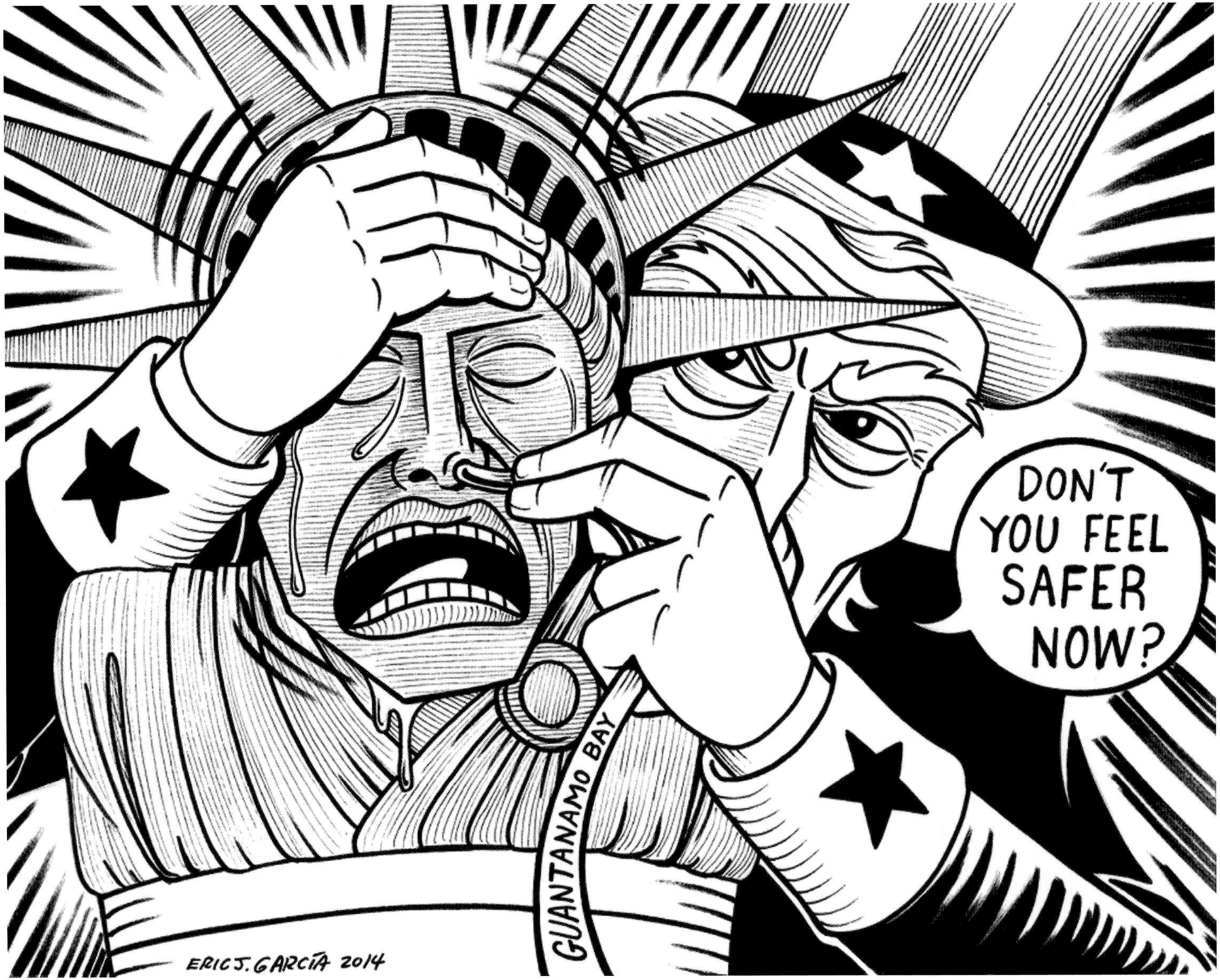
DON'T YOU FEEL SAFER NOW?
GUANTANAMO BAY
ERIC J. GARCÍA 2014

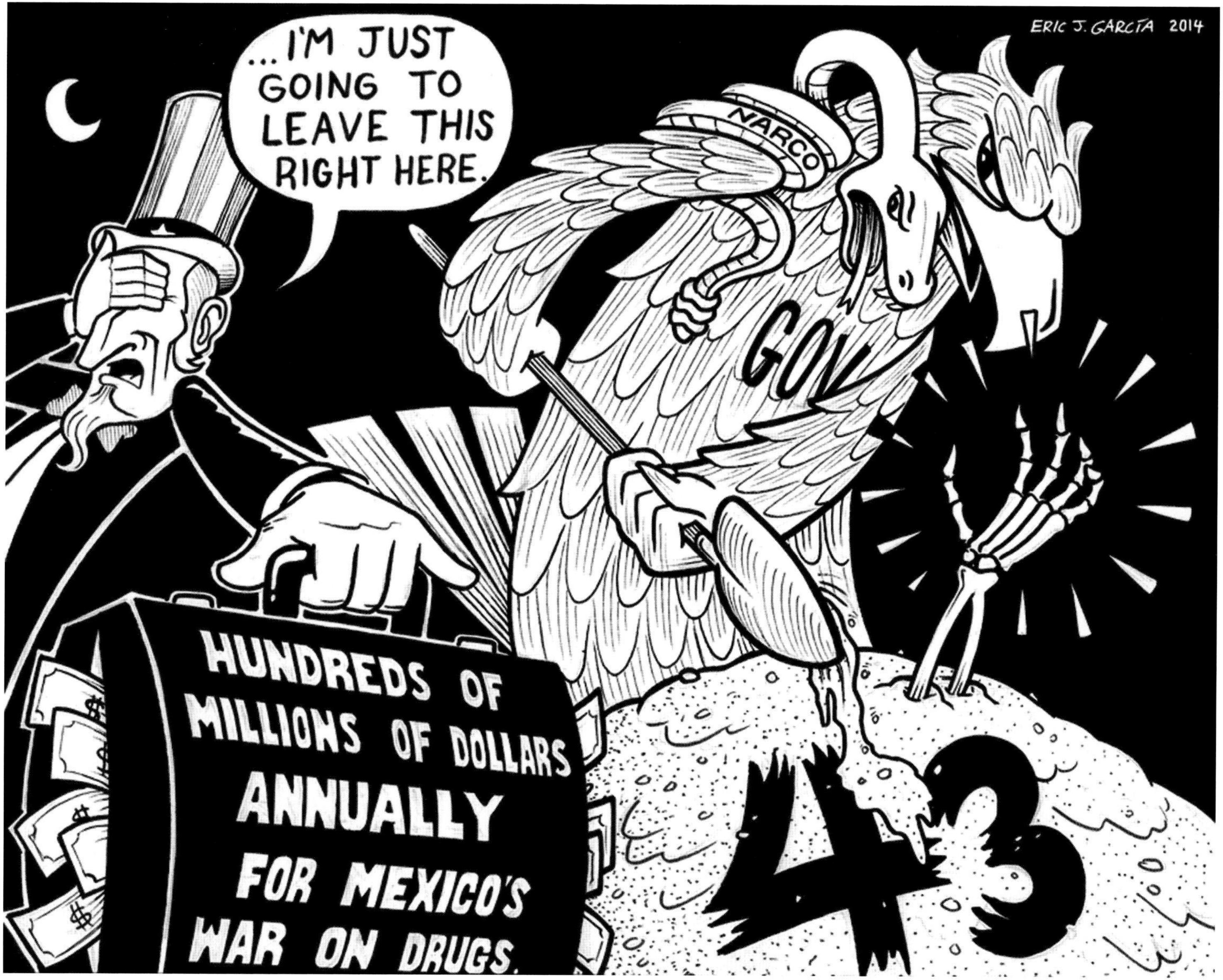
ERIC J. GARCIA 2014
...I'M JUST GOING TO LEAVE THIS RIGHT HERE.
NARCO
GOV
HUNDREDS OF MILLIONS OF DOLLARS ANNUALLY FOR MEXICO'S WAR ON DRUGS.
43

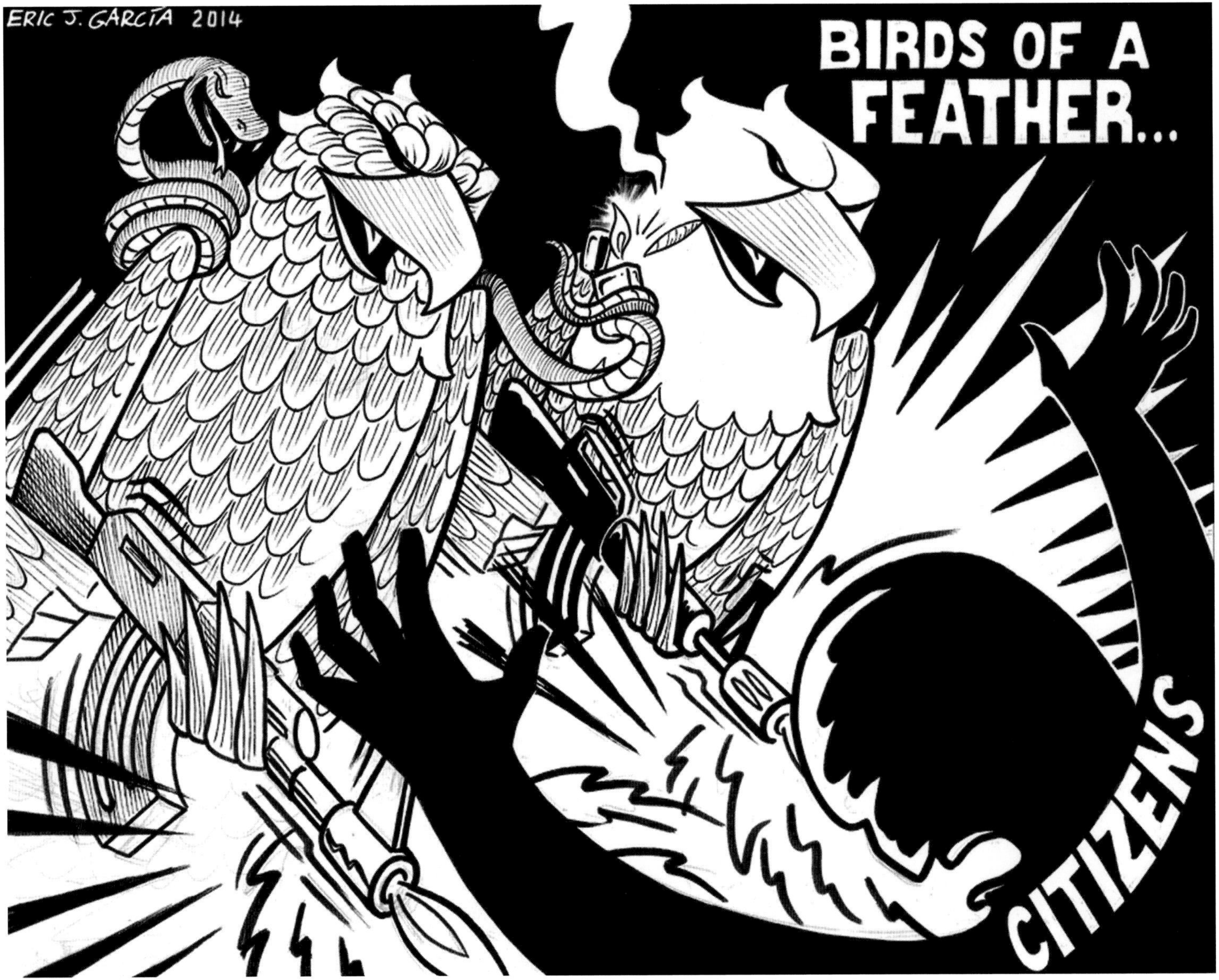
ERIC J. GARCIA 2014
BIRDS OF A FEATHER...
CITIZENS

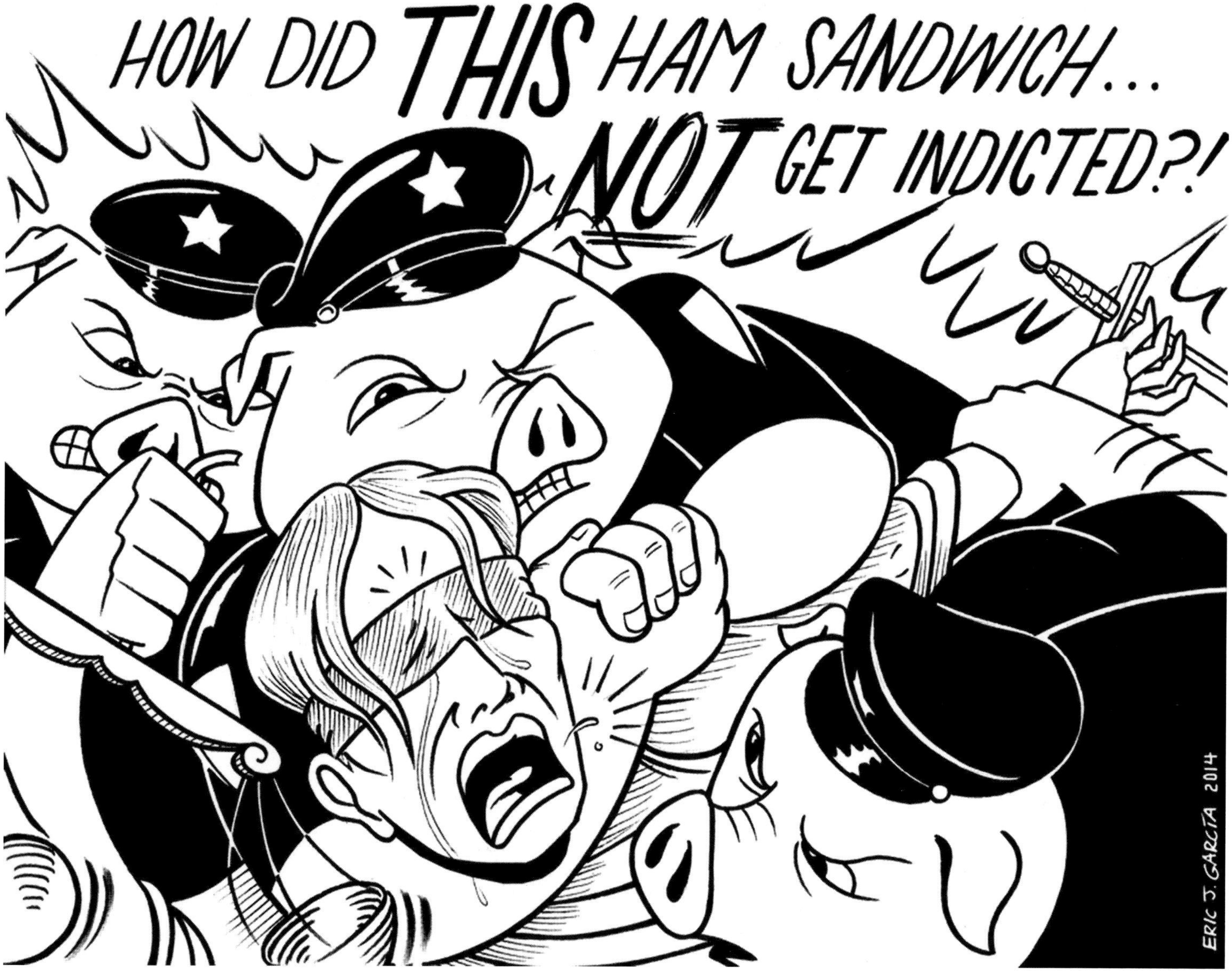
HOW DID THIS HAM SANDWICH...
NOT GET INDICTED?!
ERIC J. GARCIA 2014

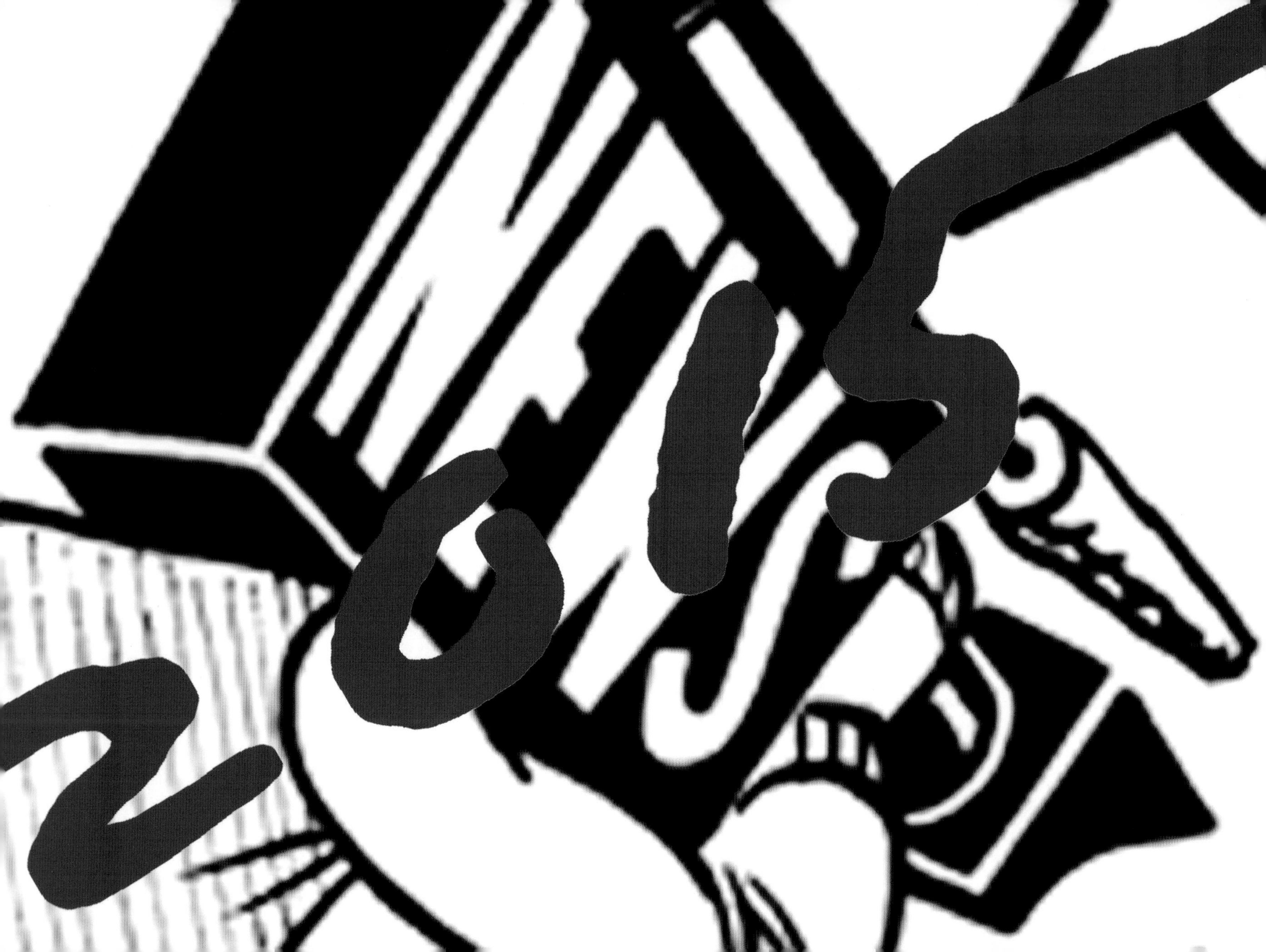
2015

2015

Yet another year of non-stop war, but I'm not talking about the war overseas. No, I'm talking about the one right here in our streets. Gangbangers trying to kill each other over territory, while innocent bystanders were caught in the crossfire. Over-militarized police playing judge, jury, and executioner left a trail of bodies across our nation. And don't forget the wackos, whose mass shootings terrorized the nation. Executions have become the norm, and according to President Obama, being blown up by a drone is way more humane than being beheaded. Why do we condone remote-controlled robot executions? Why do we never consider the arms dealers as accomplices, who flood our streets with tools of death while making a fortune doing it? We have plenty of tax dollars for war and weapons, but never any for schools and books. (Haven't I said this already?)

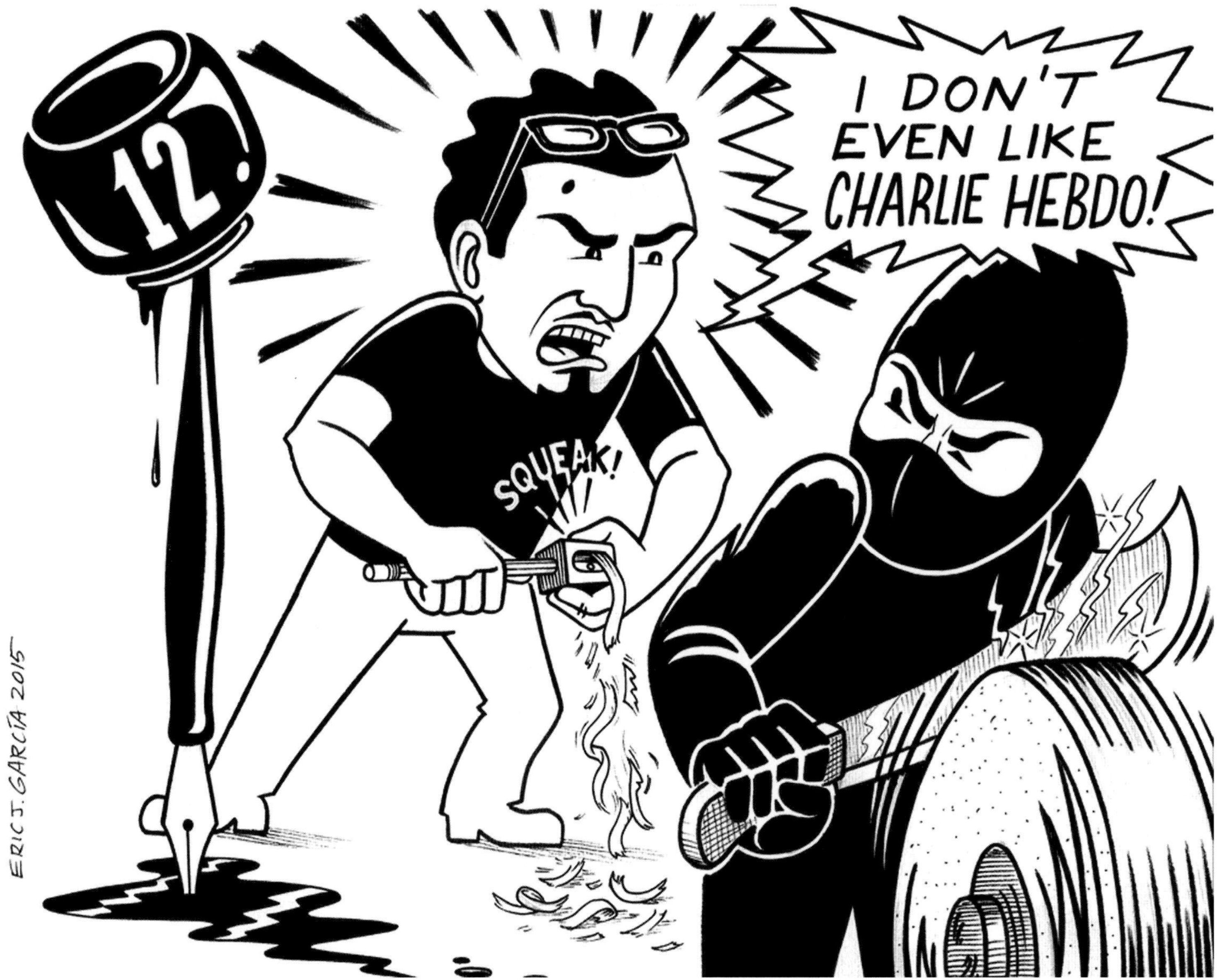
12.
I DON'T EVEN LIKE CHARLIE HEBDO!
SQUEAK!
ERIC J. GARCÍA 2015

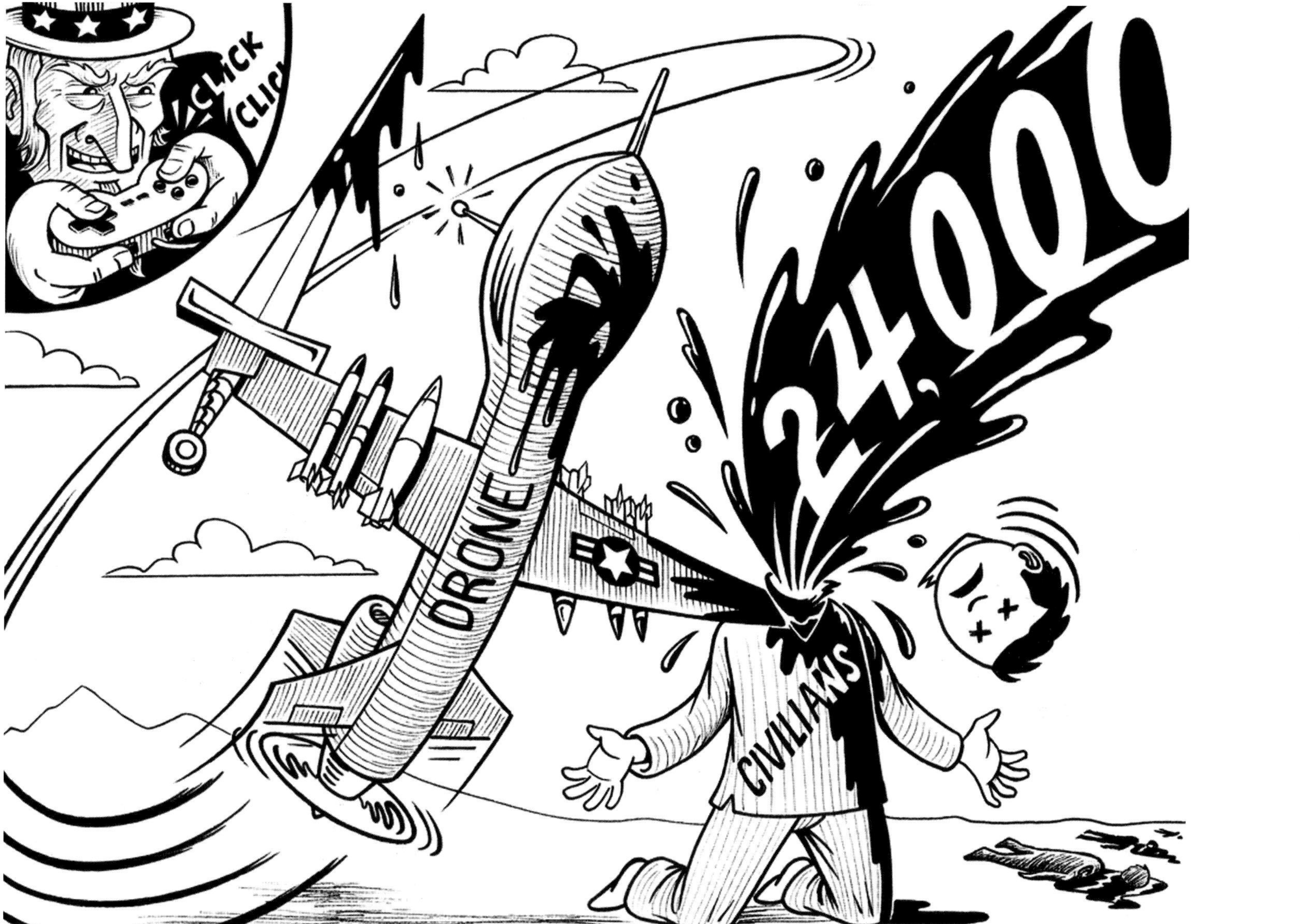
CLICK
CLICK
DRONE
24,000
CIVILIANS
ERIC J GARCIA 2015

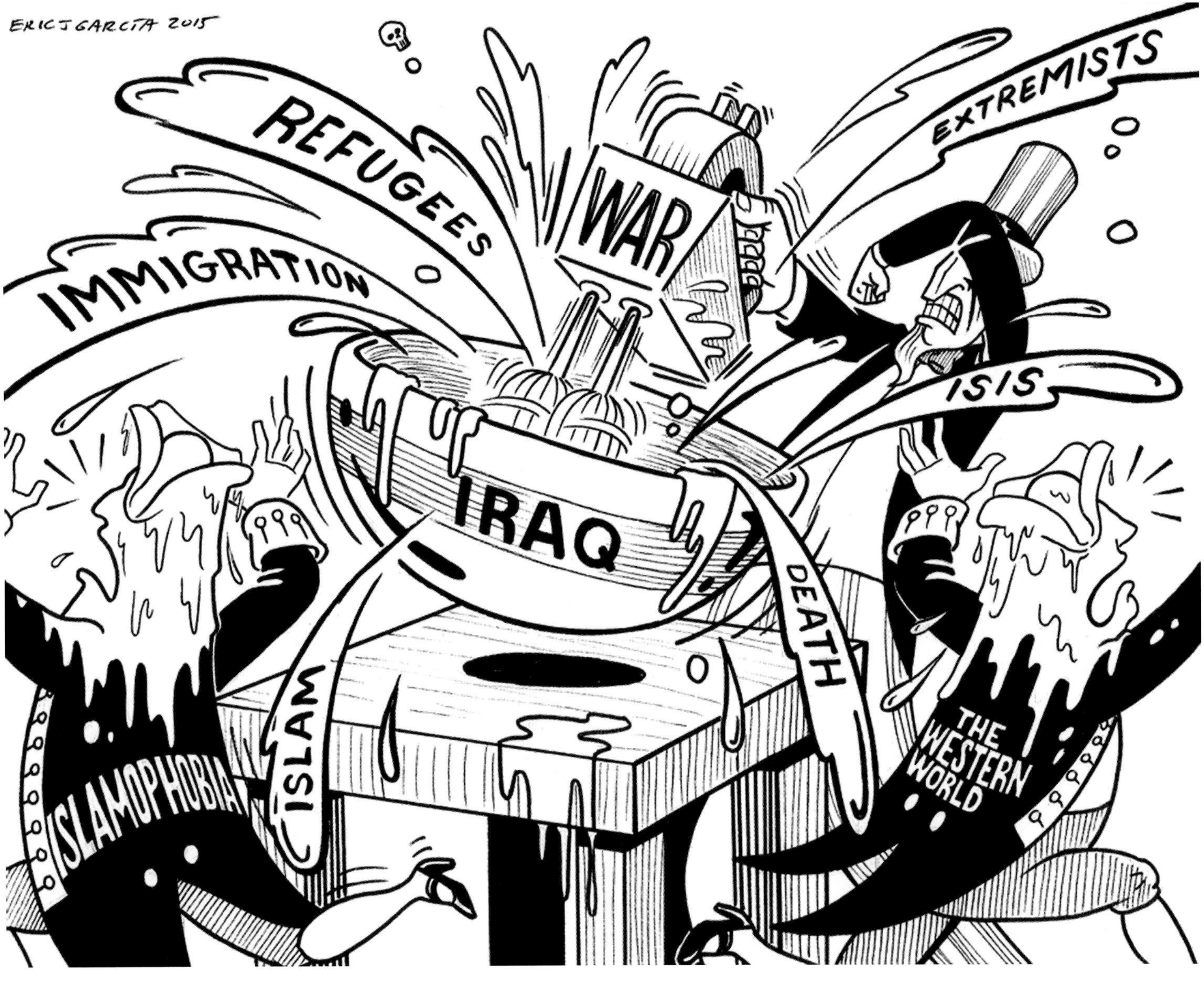
ERIC J GARCIA 2015
REFUGEES
IMMIGRATION
WAR
EXTREMISTS
ISIS
IRAQ
DEATH
ISLAM
ISLAMOPHOBIA
THE WESTERN WORLD

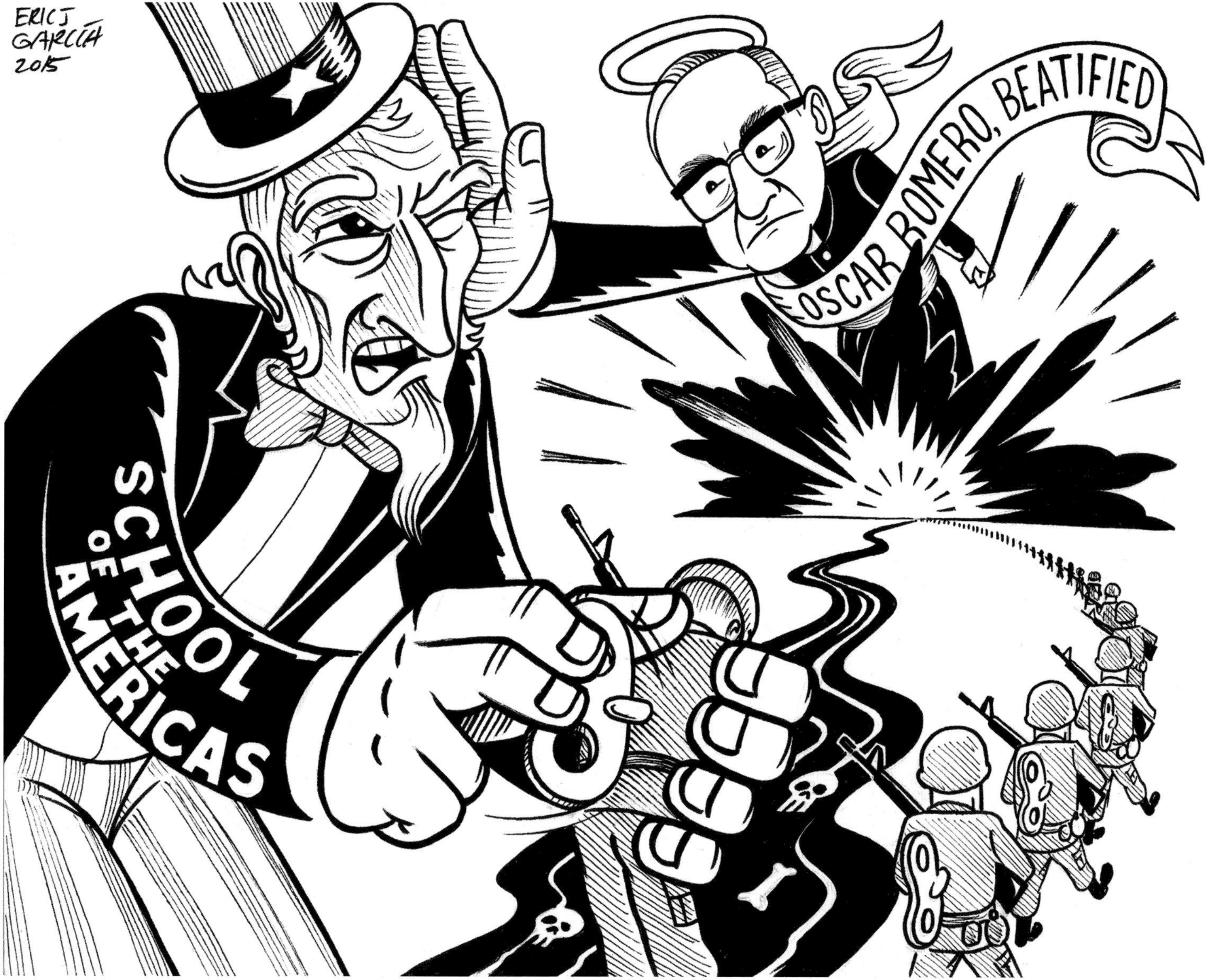
ERIC J GARCÍA 2015
OSCAR ROMERO, BEATIFIED
SCHOOL OF THE AMERICAS

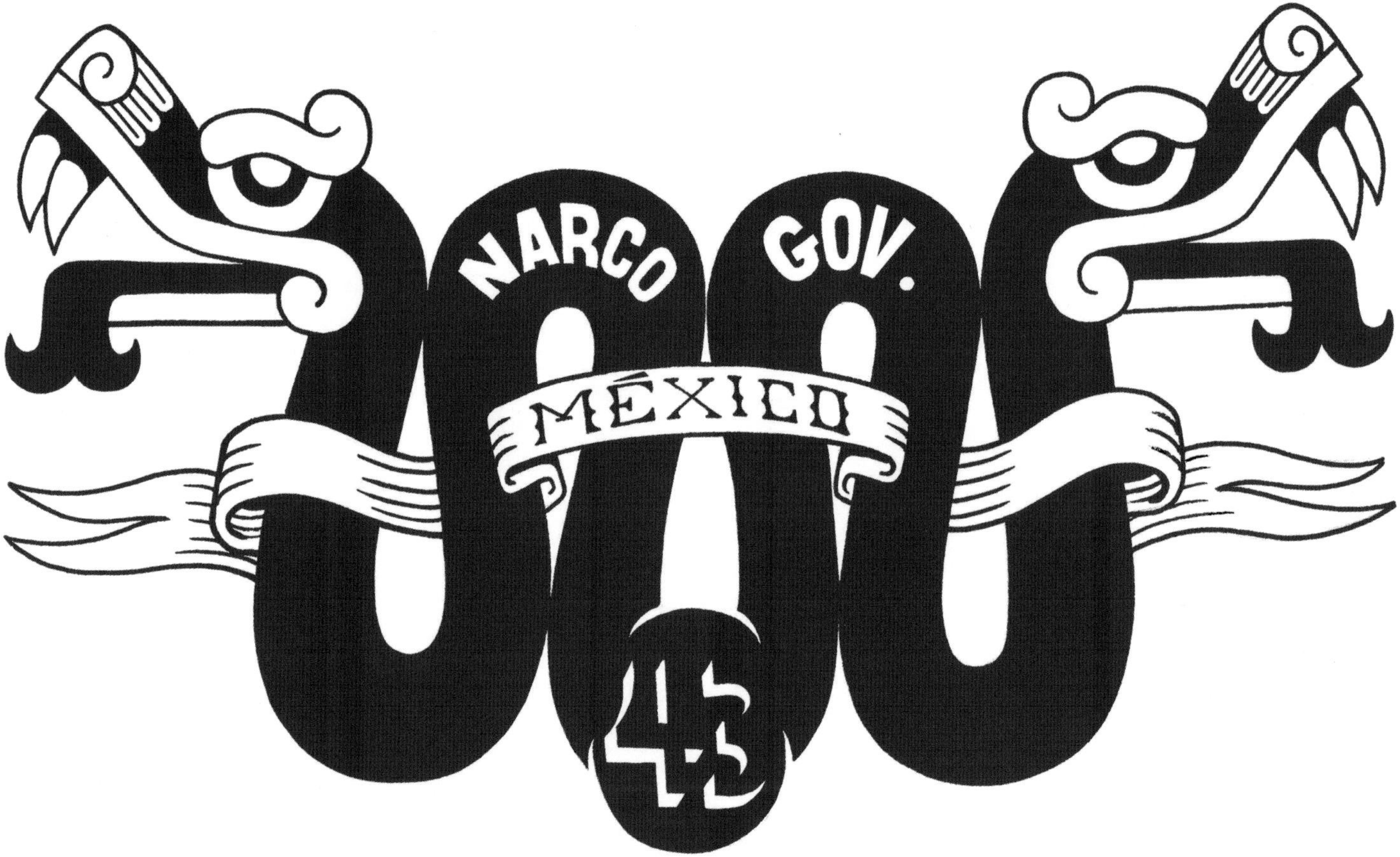
NARCO GOV.
MÉXICO
43

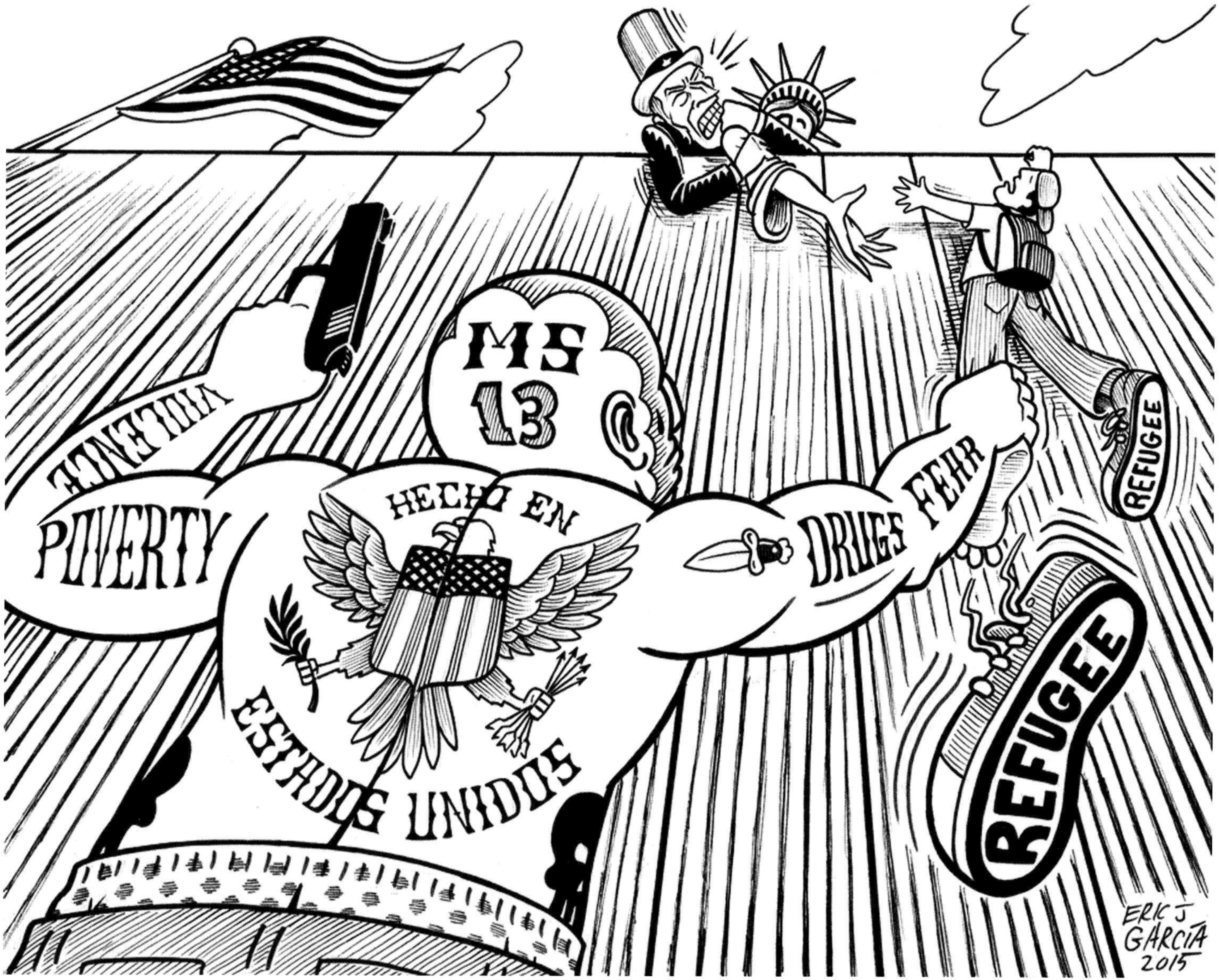
MS
13
VIOLENCE
POVERTY
HECHO EN
ESTADOS UNIDOS
DRUGS
FEAR
REFUGEE
REFUGEE
ERIC J GARCIA 2015

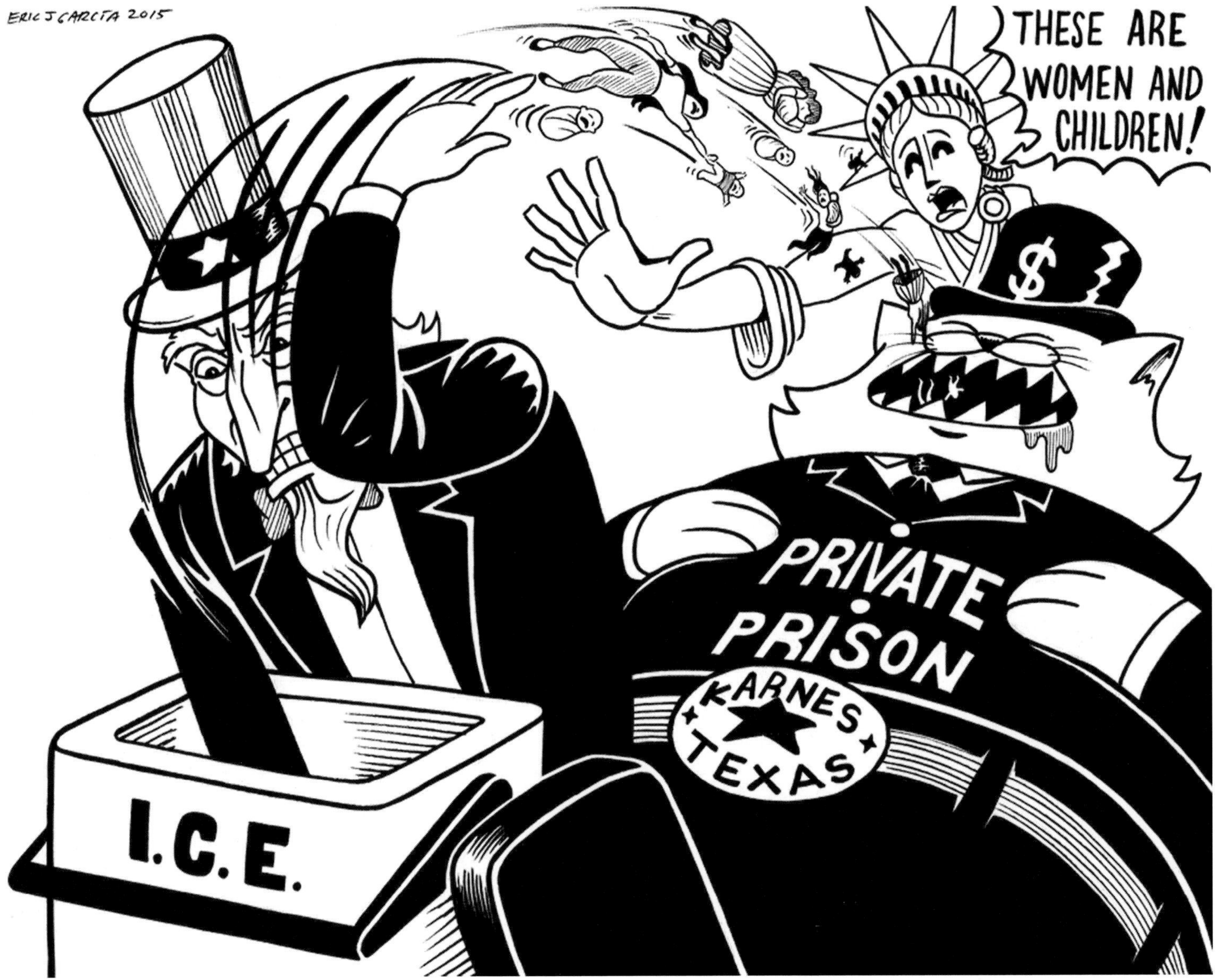
ERIC J GARCIA 2015
THESE ARE WOMEN AND CHILDREN!
$
PRIVATE PRISON
KARNES TEXAS
I.C.E.

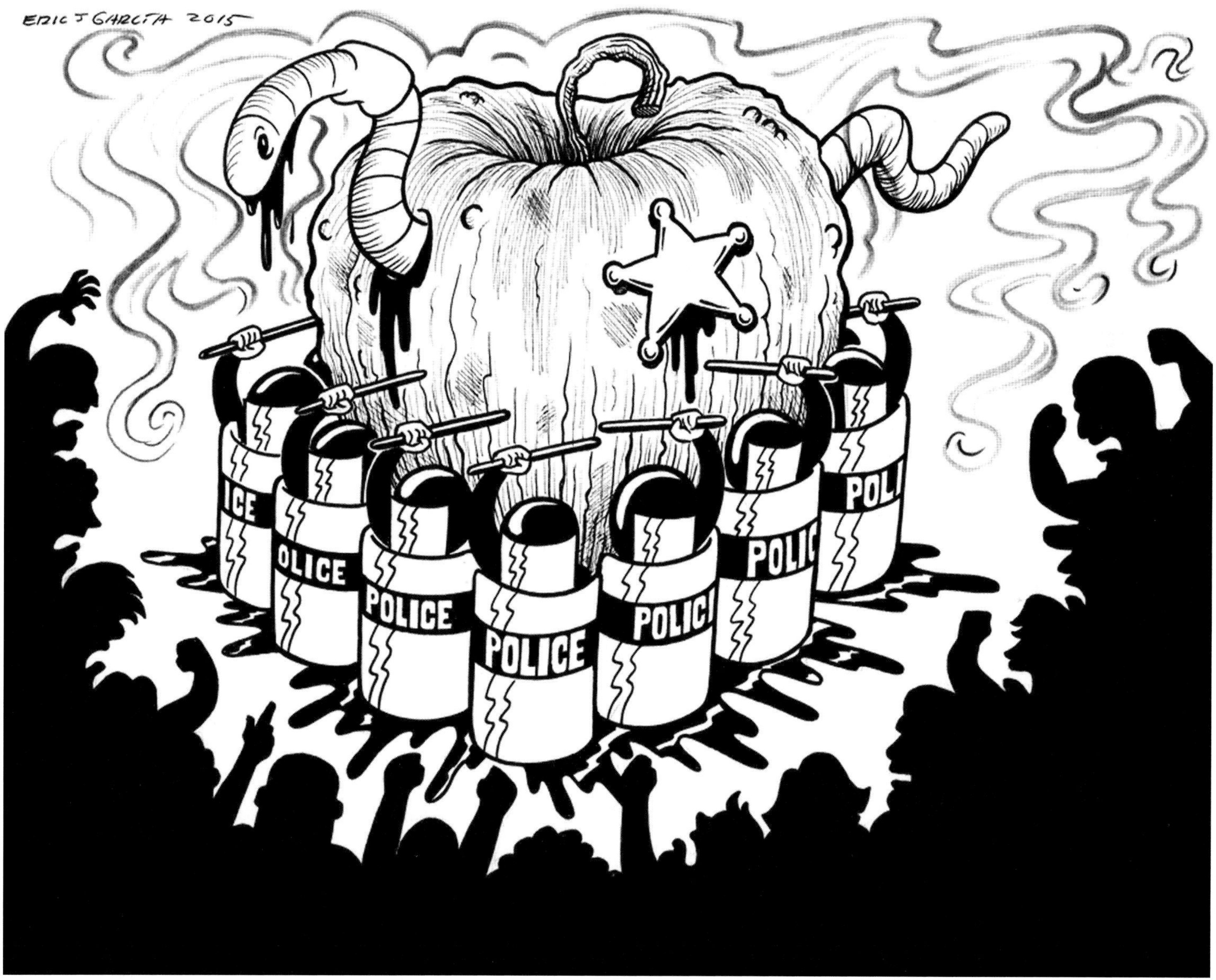
ERIC J GARCIA 2015
ICE
OLICE
POLICE
POLICE
POLICI
POLIC
POLI

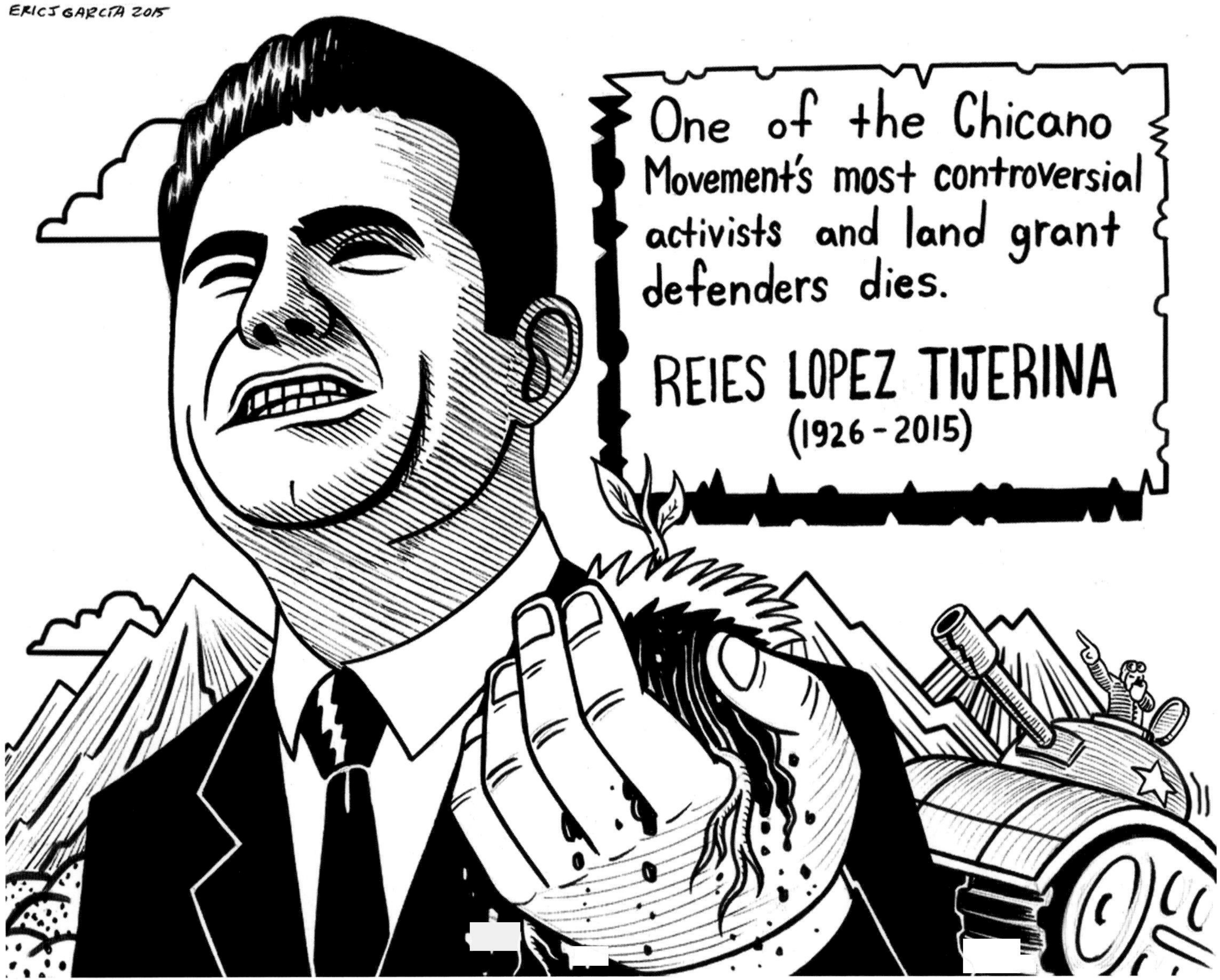
ERIC J GARCIA 2015
One of the Chicano Movement's most controversial activists and land grant defenders dies.
REIES LOPEZ TIJERINA
(1926 - 2015)

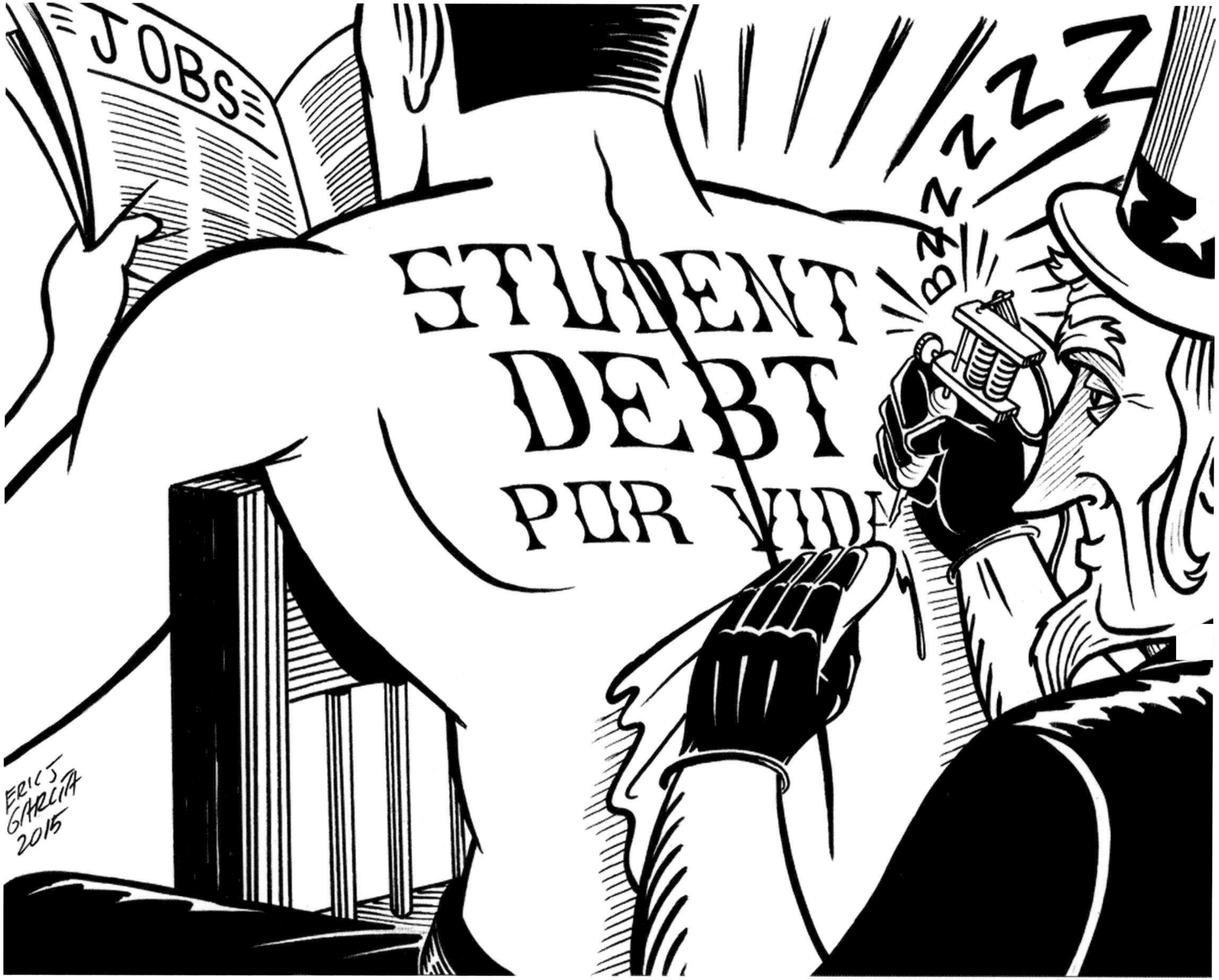
JOBS
STUDENT DEBT POR VIDA
BZZZZZZ
ERIC J. GARCIA 2015

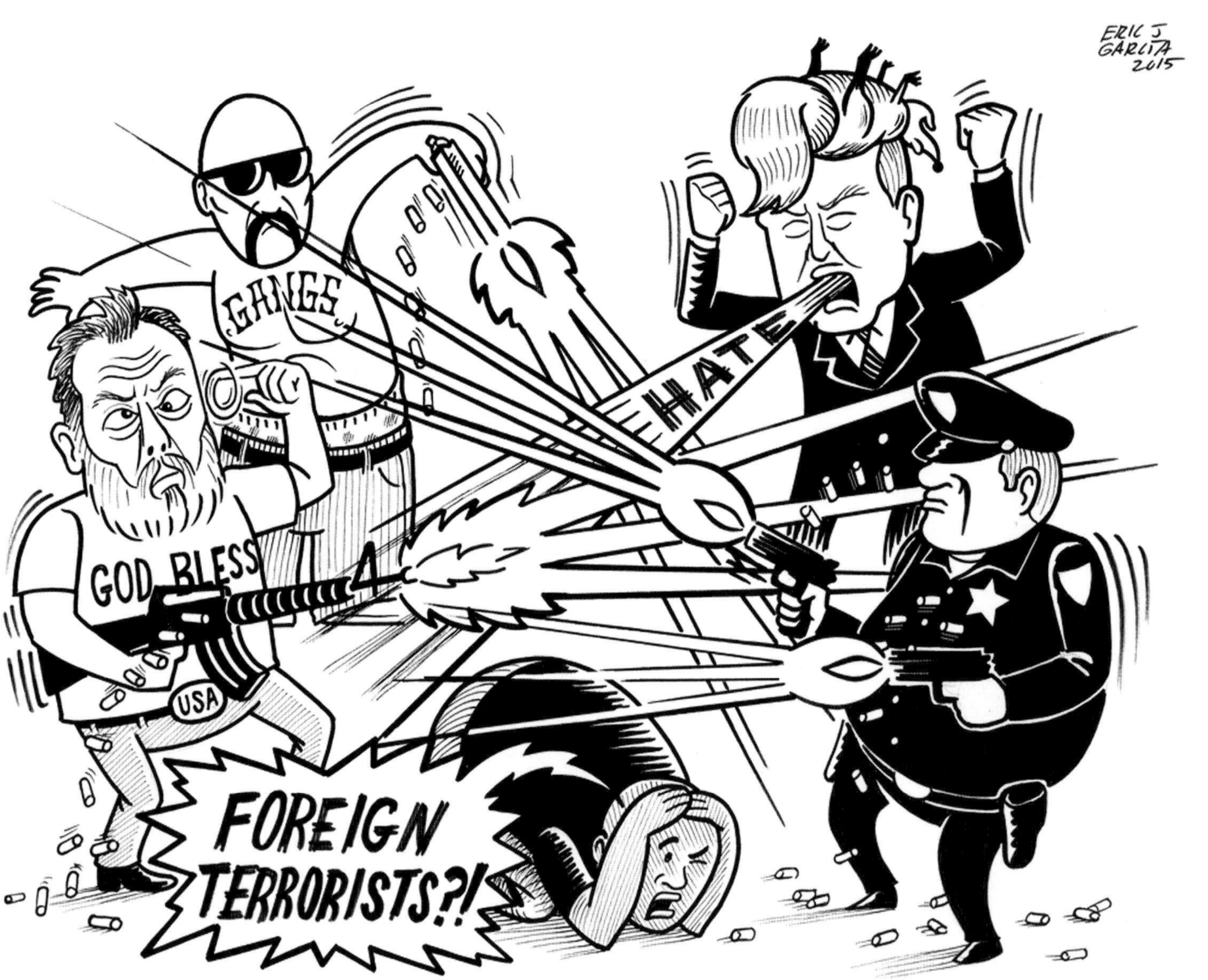
ERIC J
GARCIA
2015
GANGS
HATE
GOD BLESS
USA
FOREIGN
TERRORISTS?!

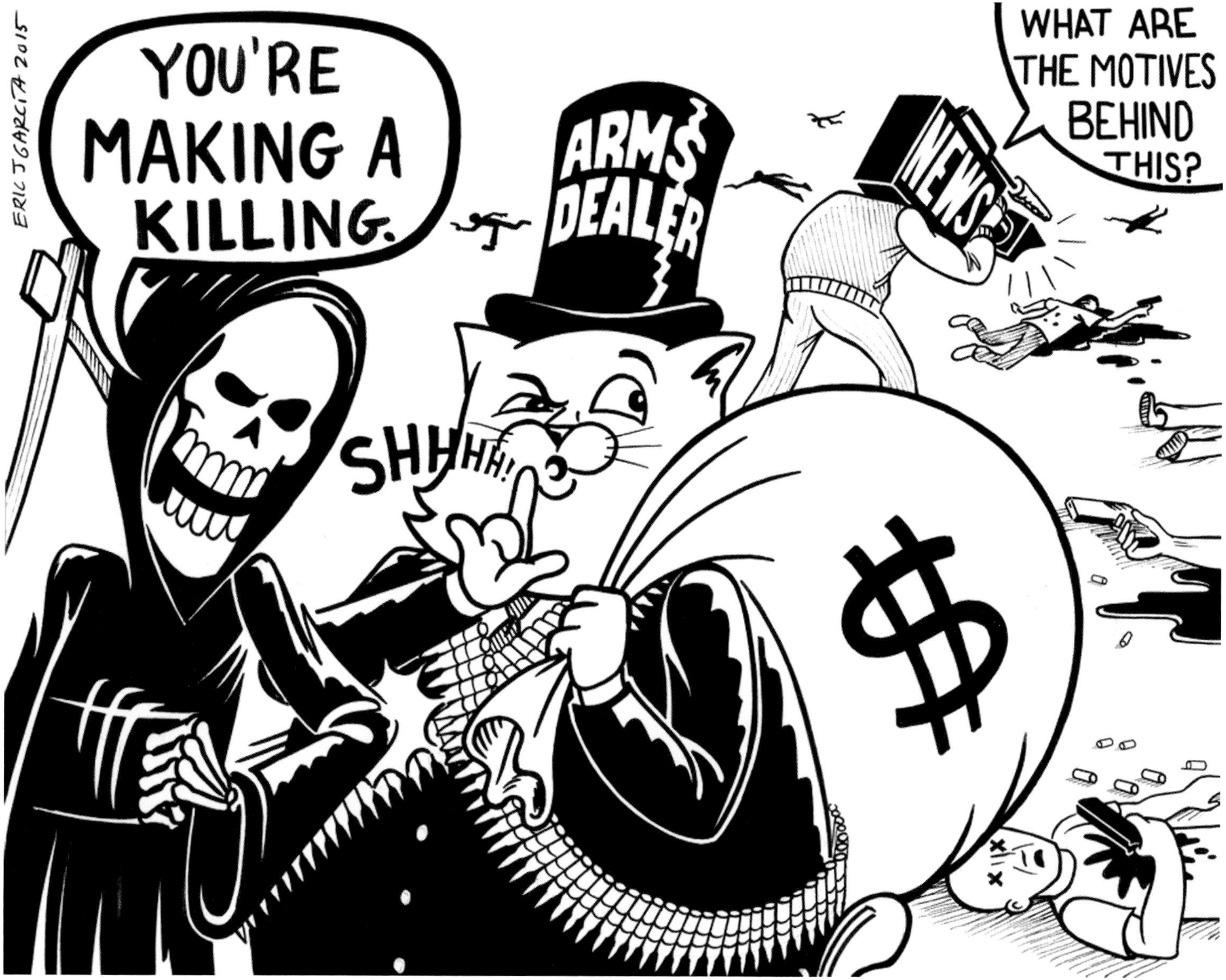
ERIC J GARCIA 2015
YOU'RE MAKING A KILLING.
ARMS DEALER
SHHHH!
NEWS
WHAT ARE THE MOTIVES BEHIND THIS?
$

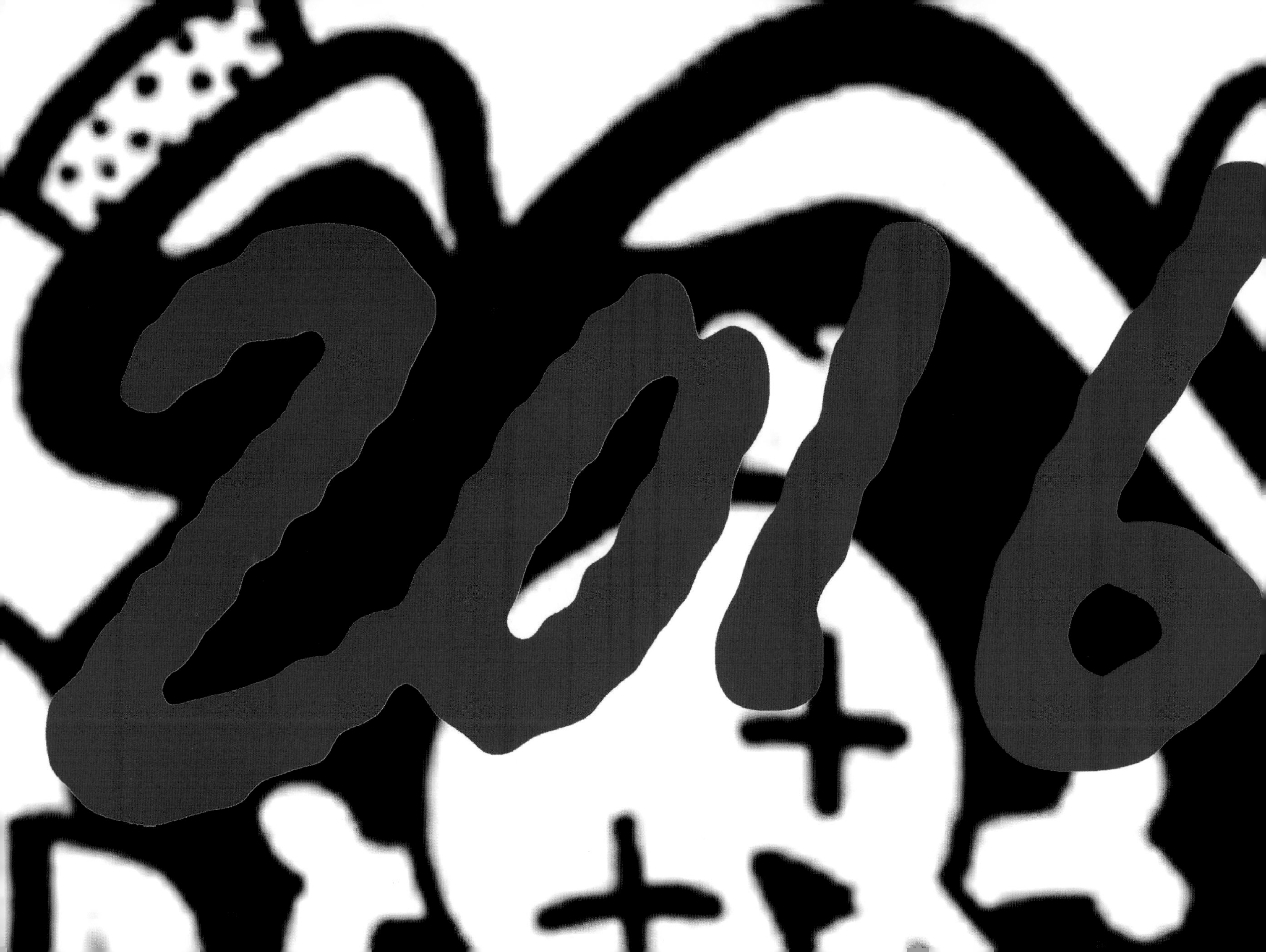
2016

2016

With the advent of the Rodent-Capped Celebrity about to take control of the most powerful position in the world, I began to work overtime. Meanwhile the Lame Duck President shed tears for the Sandy Hook elementary school massacre, but at the same time denied and deported thousands of Latin American children seeking refugee status. As the nation was distracted by the ultimate reality-TV show known as the presidential elections, I tried to plug in some real news. But Trump mobilized white supremacists and dominated mainstream media with open racism, overshadowing the true heroics of Colin Kaepernick and the late great Mohammad Ali. Thus, media coverage of this country's age-old tradition of abusing the indigenous people was slim to none. From Flint, Michigan, to Standing Rock, North Dakota, water supplies were being poisoned, and the public was not going to take it any more.

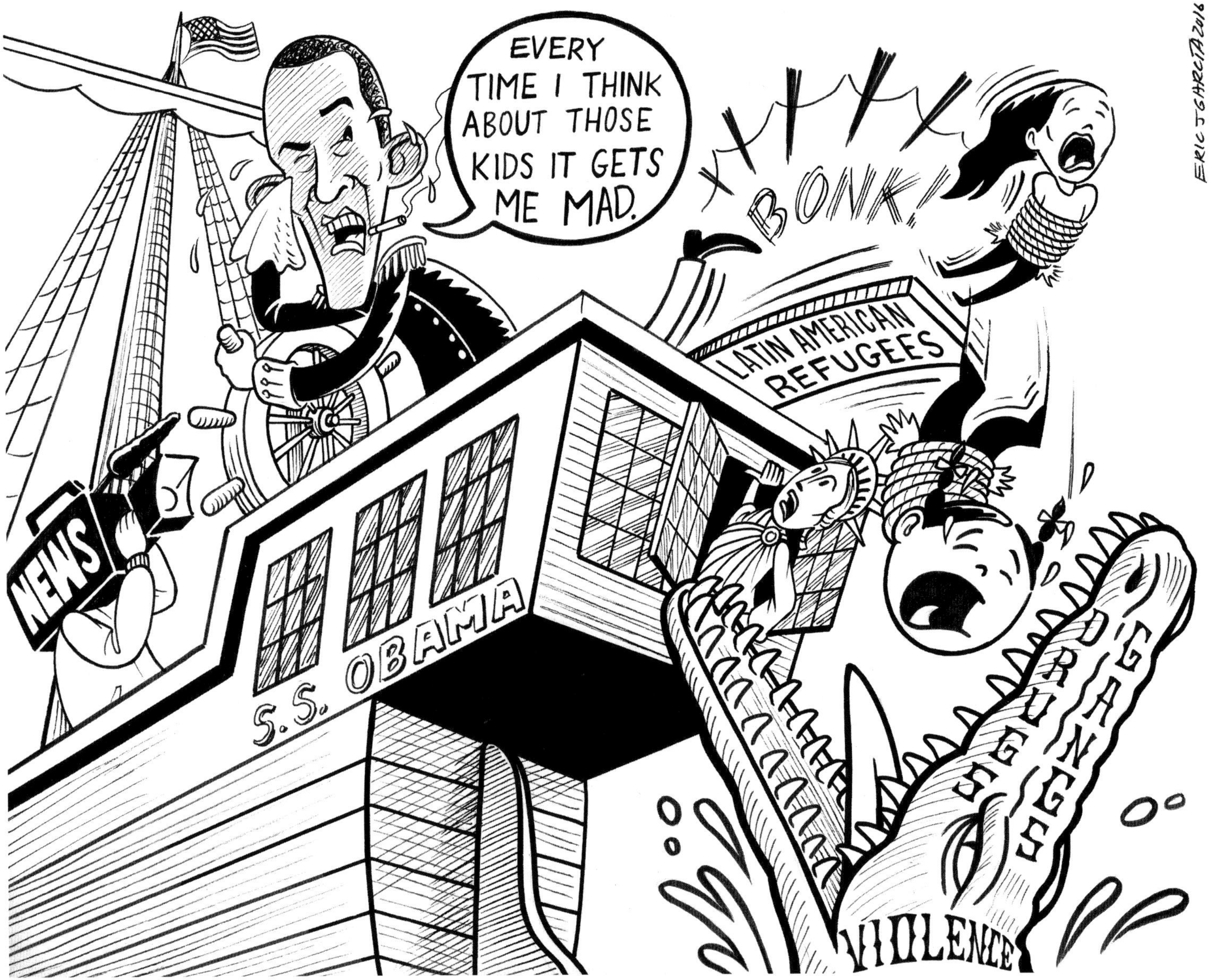
ERIC J GARCIA 2016
EVERY TIME I THINK ABOUT THOSE KIDS IT GETS ME MAD.
BONK!
LATIN AMERICAN REFUGEES
NEWS
S.S. OBAMA
DRUGS
GANGS
VIOLENCE

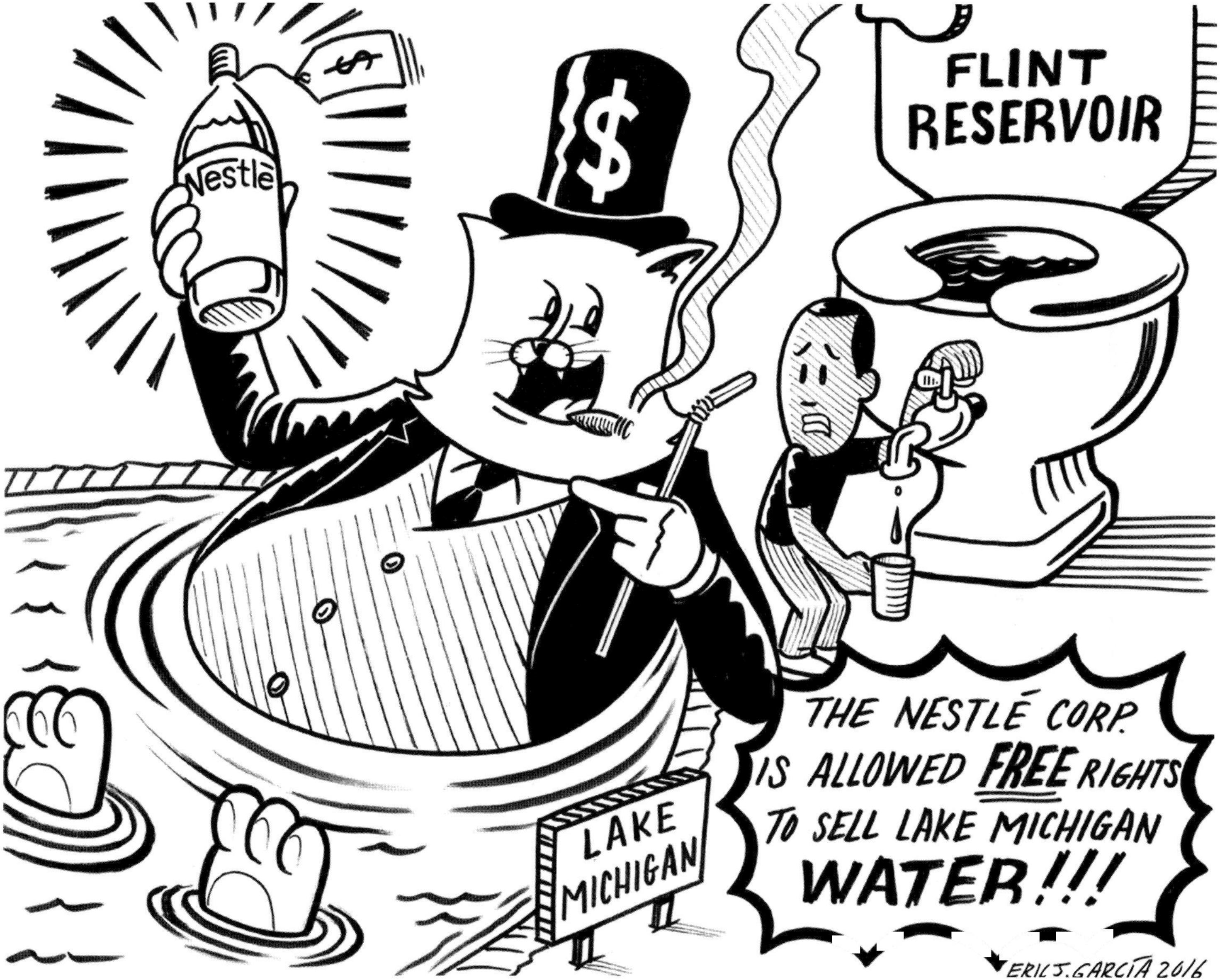
Nestlé
$
FLINT RESERVOIR
THE NESTLÉ CORP. IS ALLOWED FREE RIGHTS TO SELL LAKE MICHIGAN WATER!!!
LAKE MICHIGAN
ERIC J. GARCIA 2016

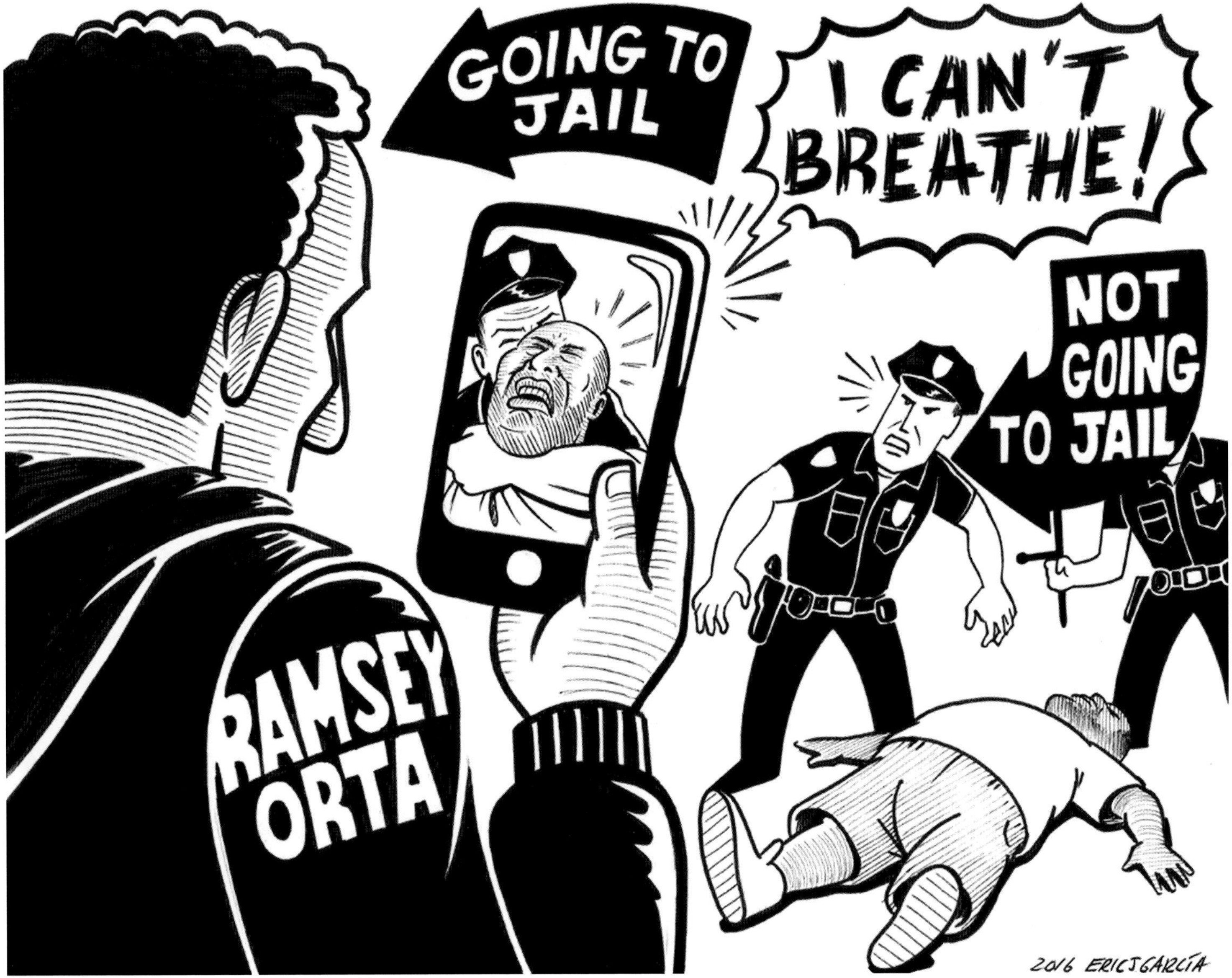
GOING TO JAIL
I CAN'T BREATHE!
NOT GOING TO JAIL
RAMSEY ORTA
2016 ERICJGARCÍA

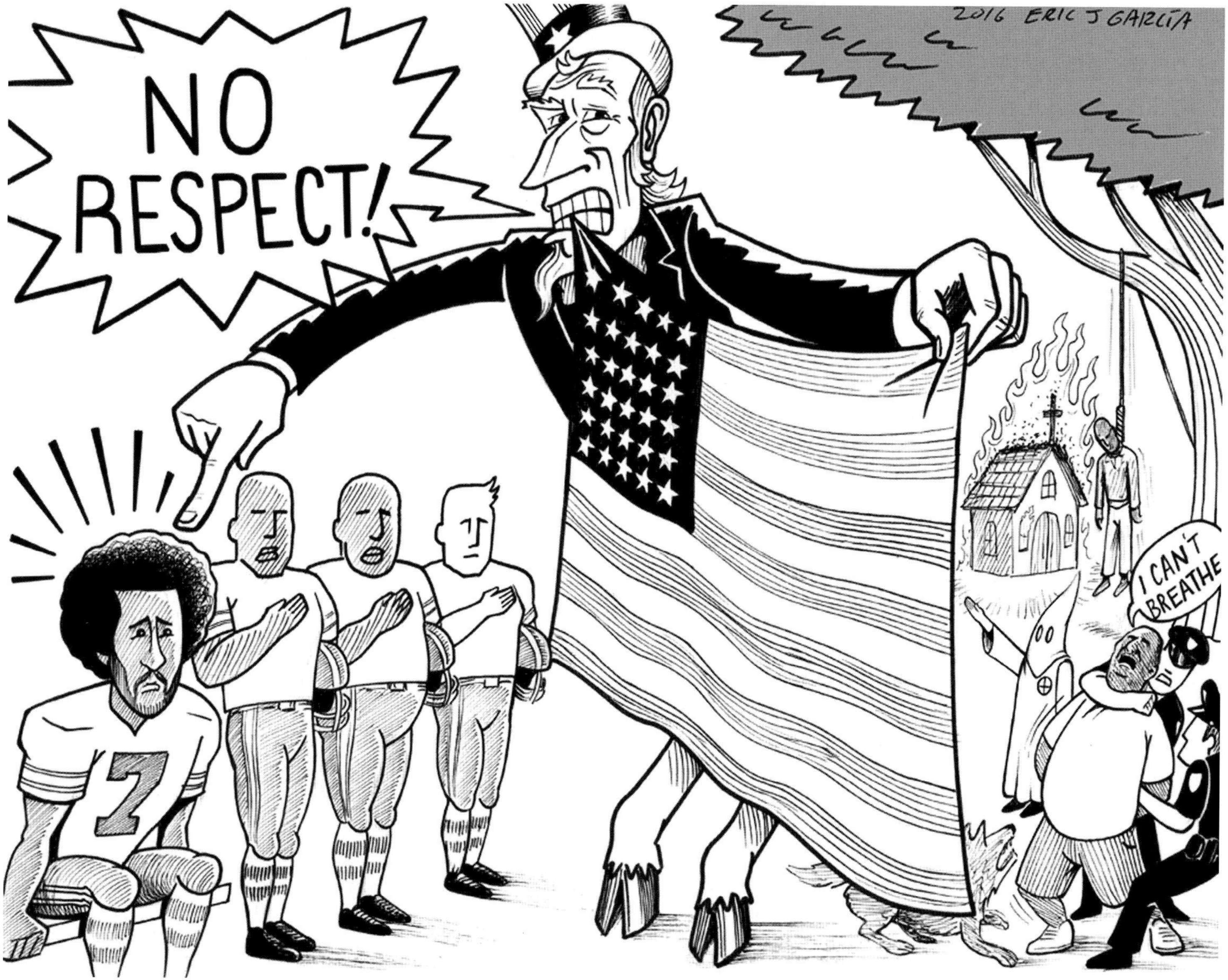
2016 ERIC J GARCÍA
NO RESPECT!
I CAN'T BREATHE

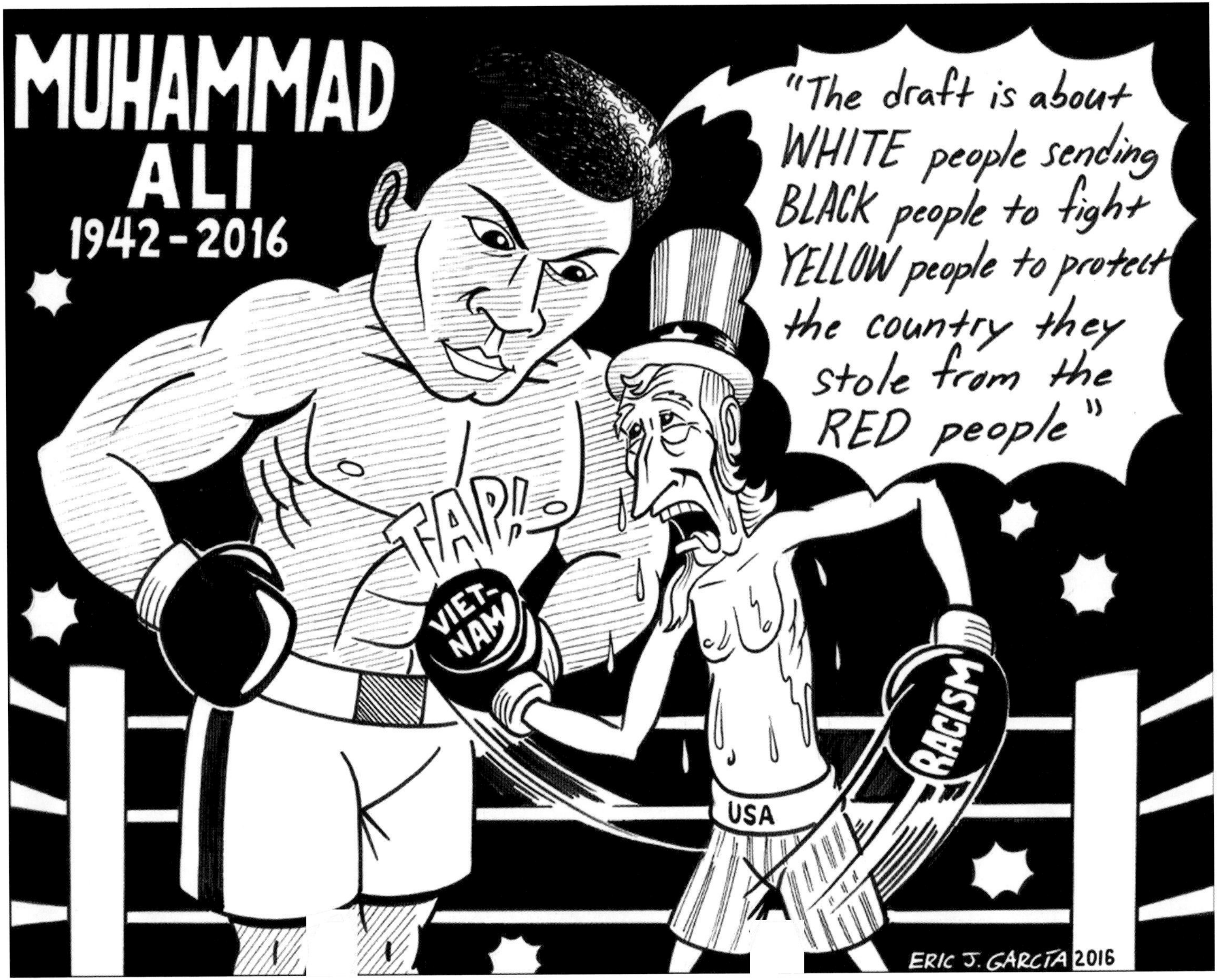
MUHAMMAD ALI
1942 - 2016
"The draft is about WHITE people sending BLACK people to fight YELLOW people to protect the country they stole from the RED people"
TAP!!
VIET-NAM
RACISM
USA
ERIC J. GARCIA 2016

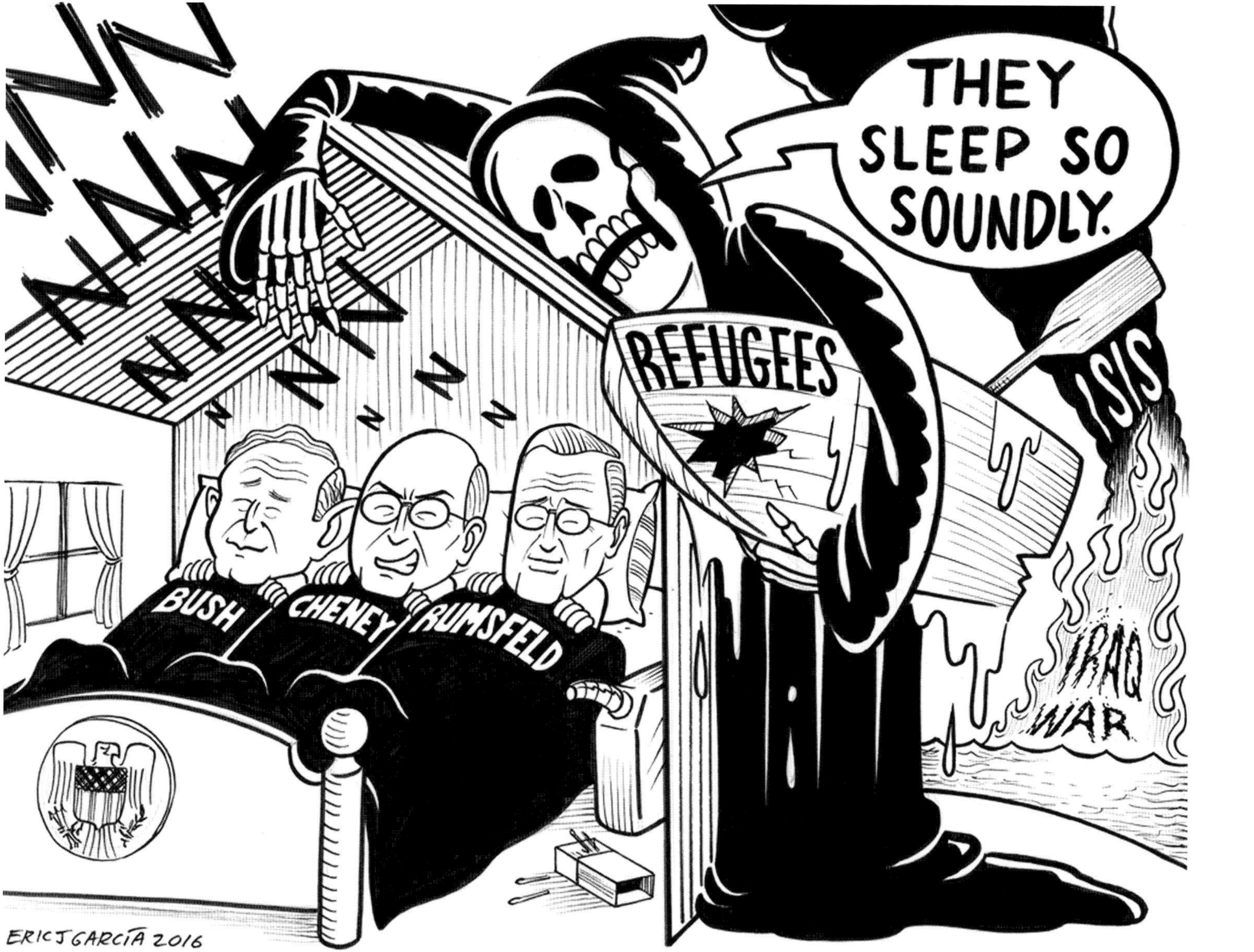
THEY SLEEP SO SOUNDLY.
REFUGEES
ISIS
BUSH
CHENEY
RUMSFELD
IRAQ WAR
ERIC J GARCIA 2016

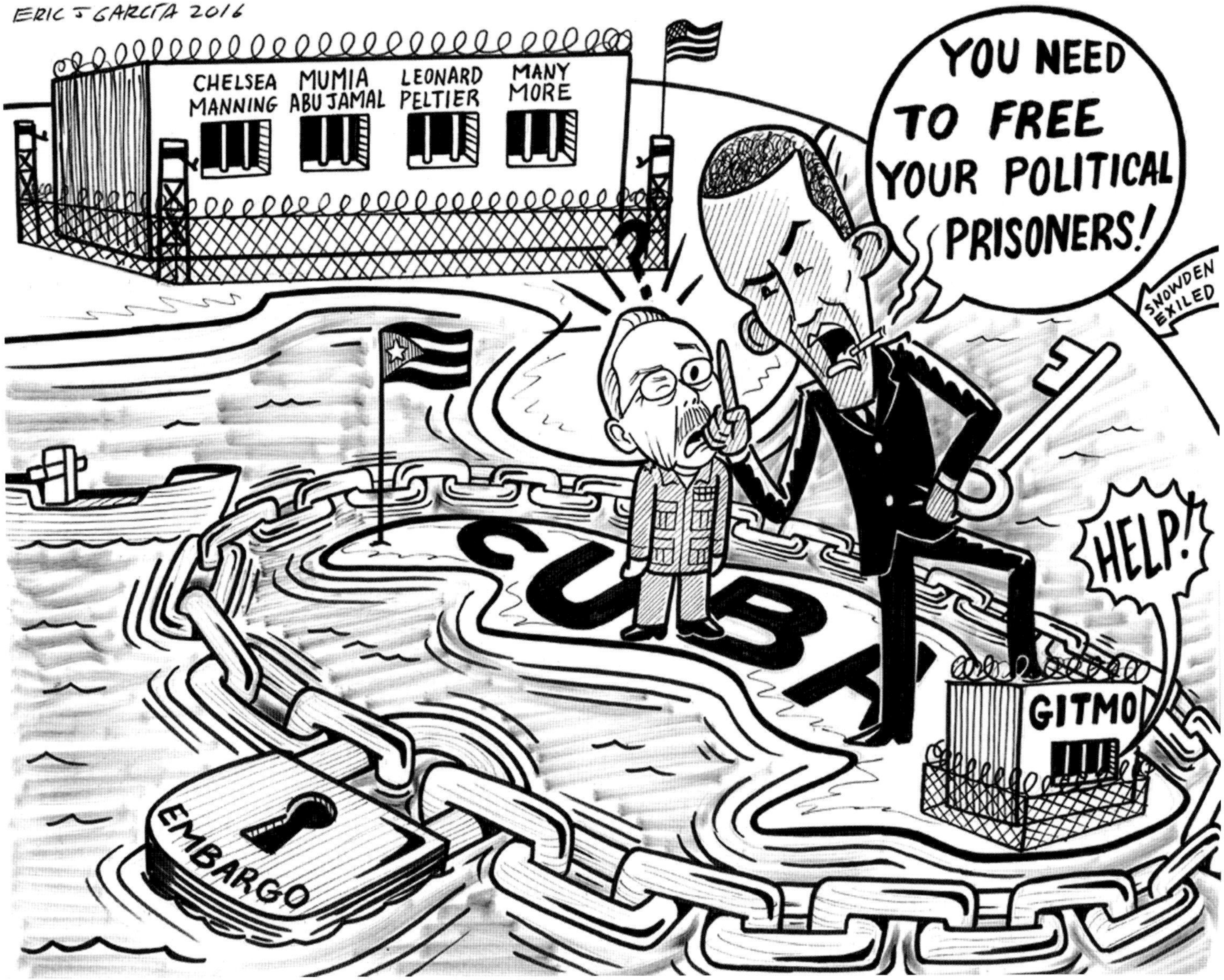
ERIC J GARCIA 2016
CHELSEA MANNING
MUMIA ABU JAMAL
LEONARD PELTIER
MANY MORE
YOU NEED TO FREE YOUR POLITICAL PRISONERS!
SNOWDEN EXILED
?
CUBA
HELP!
GITMO
EMBARGO

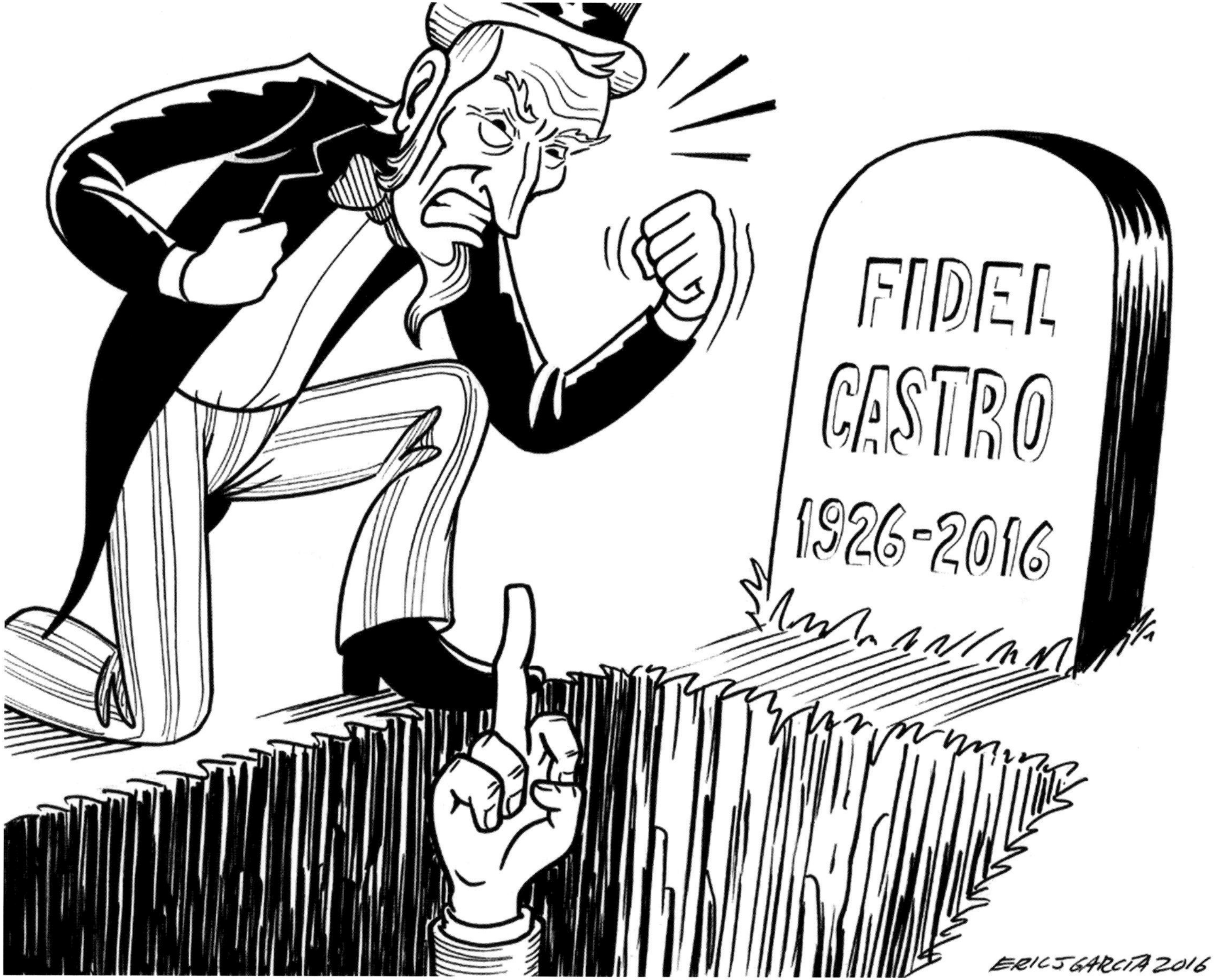
FIDEL
CASTRO
1926-2016
ERIC J GARCIA 2016

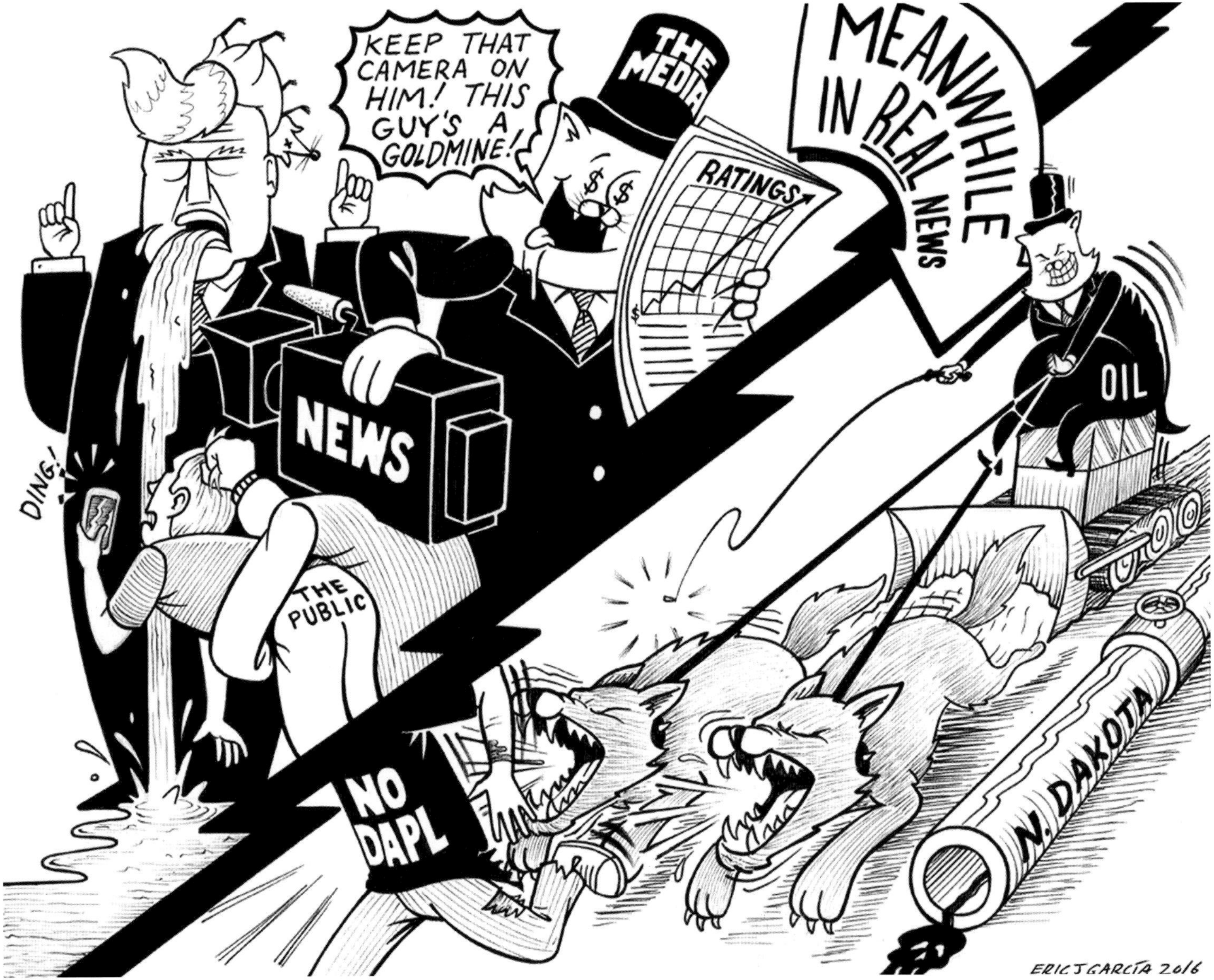
KEEP THAT CAMERA ON HIM! THIS GUY'S A GOLDMINE!
THE MEDIA
RATINGS
MEANWHILE IN REAL NEWS
NEWS
DING!
THE PUBLIC
OIL
NO DAPL
N. DAKOTA
ERIC J GARCÍA 2016

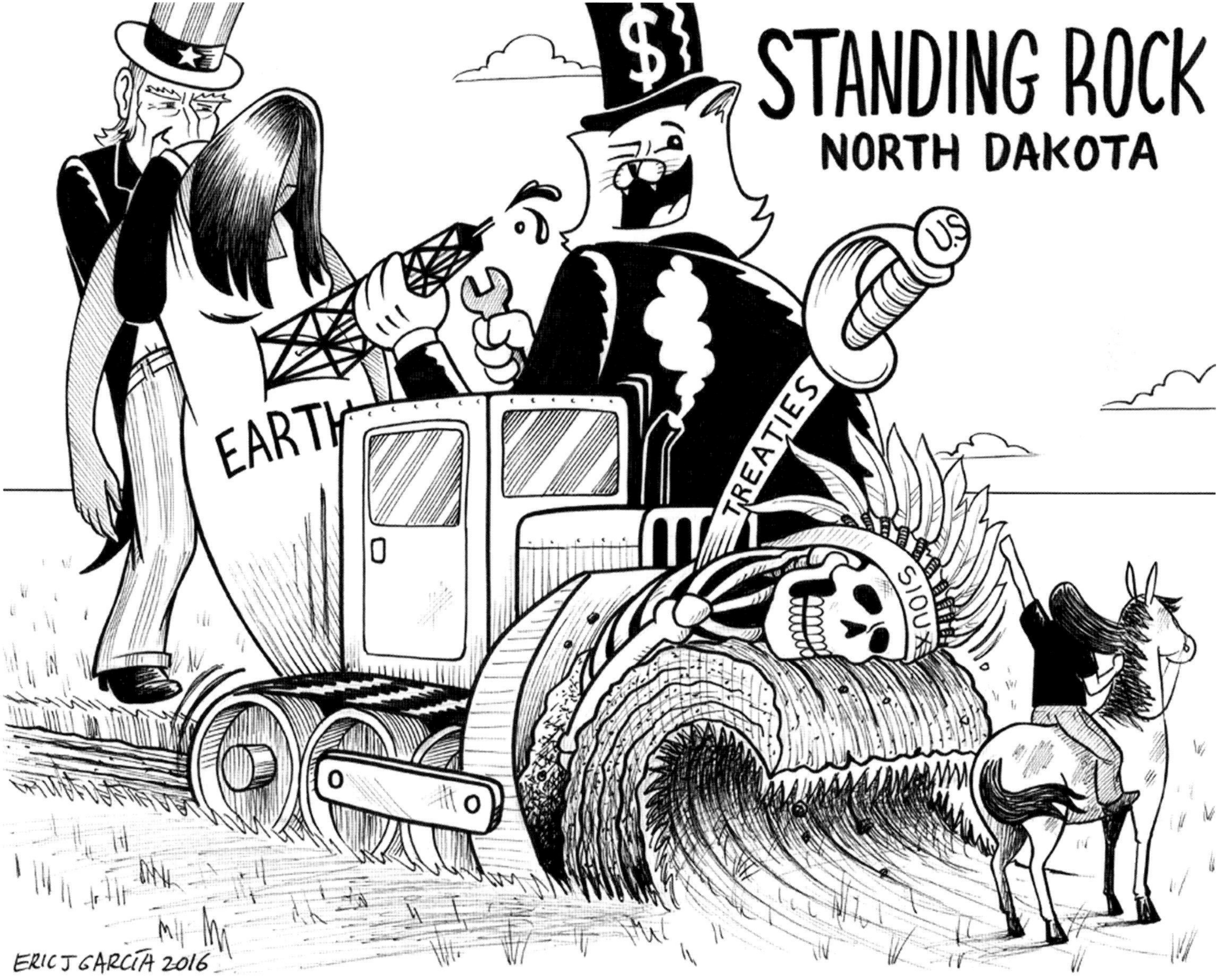
STANDING ROCK
NORTH DAKOTA
EARTH
U.S
TREATIES
SIOUX
ERIC J GARCIA 2016

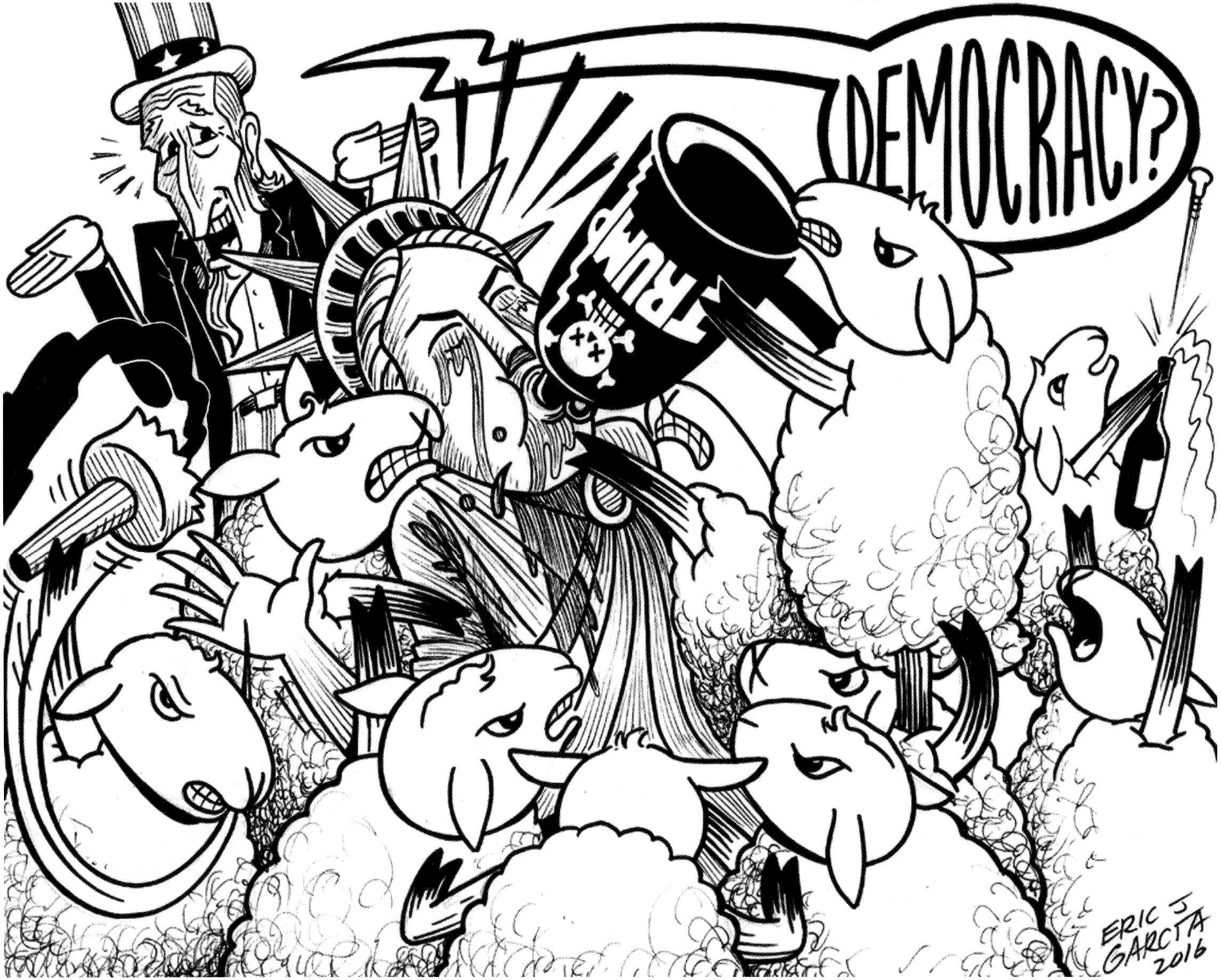
DEMOCRACY?
TRUMP
ERIC J GARCIA 2016

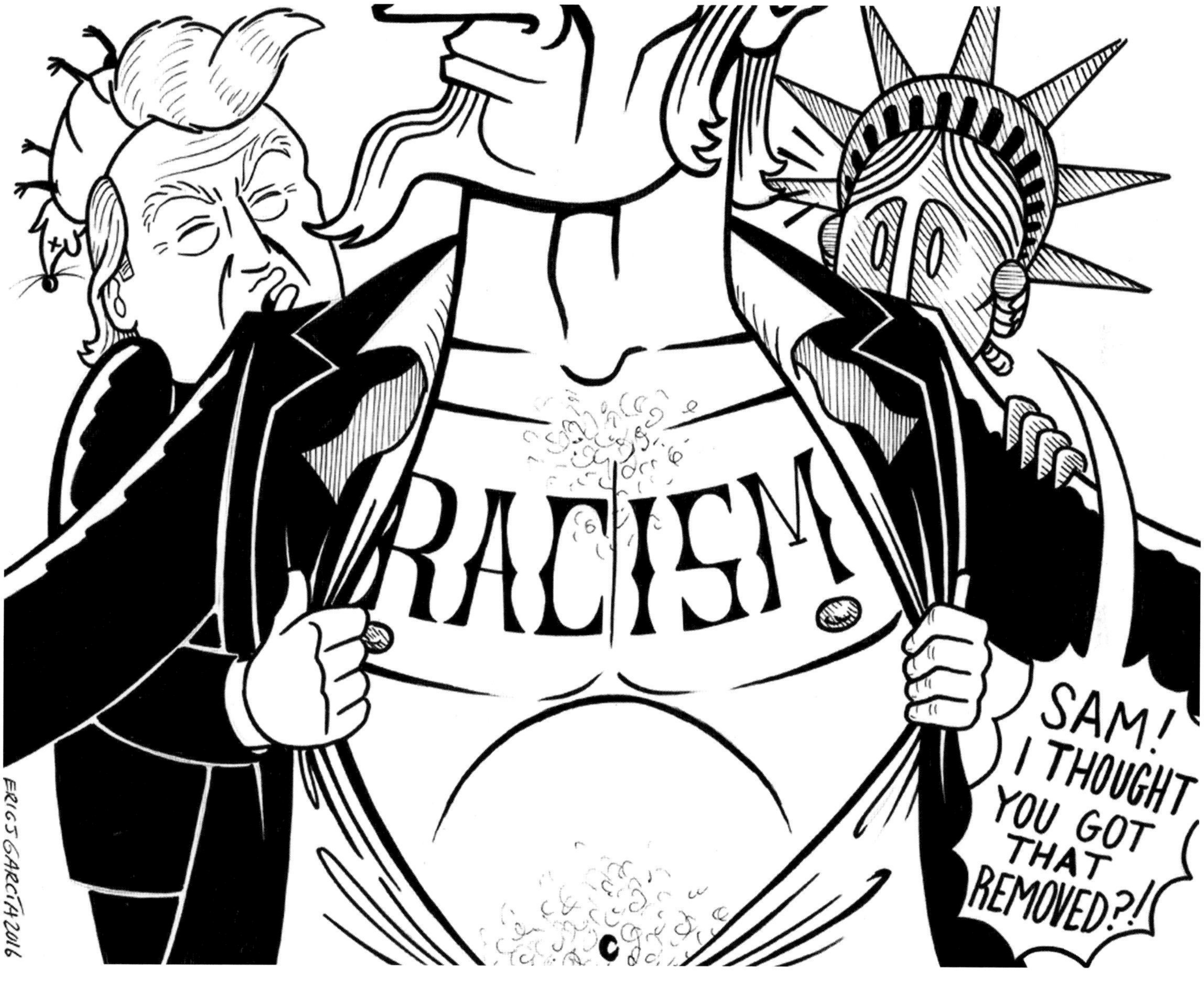
RACISM
SAM! I THOUGHT YOU GOT THAT REMOVED?!
ERIC J GARCÍA 2016

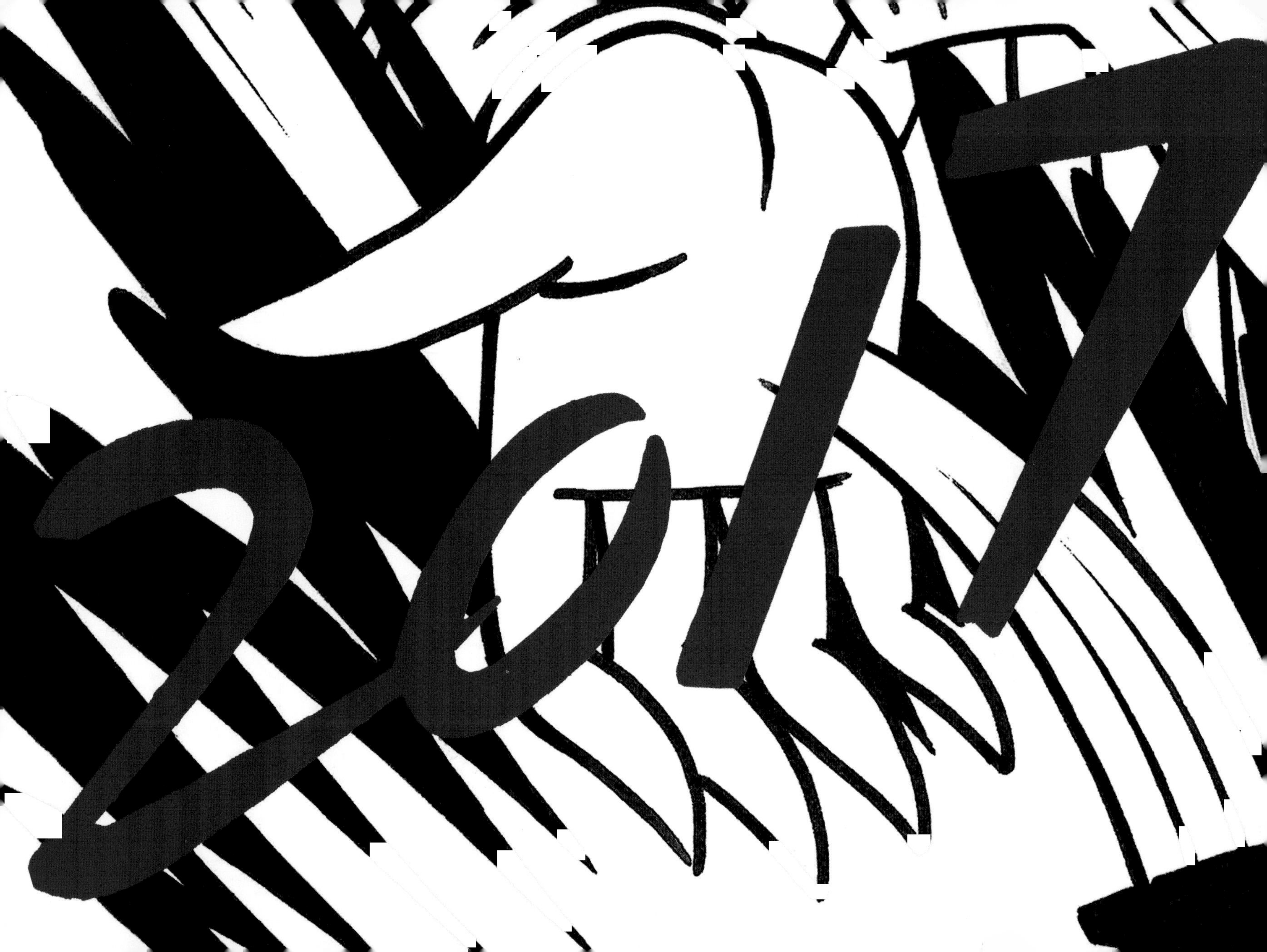
2017

2017

. . . and just when you thought it couldn't get any worse. In 2017 the very thin sheet that barely hid the festering racism of this country was not just unveiled but burned. Our Orange-Headed-Small-Handed leader left a trail of lies that no one could keep up with, much less hold him accountable for. That was just the start of a disastrous year, both man-made and natural. The Rodent-Capped Buffoon slashed environmental regulations, and Mother Earth struck back with cataclysmic disasters. Our fellow U.S. citizens in Puerto Rico, who have weathered colonialism, racism, and capitalism, struggled to survive the biggest hurricane to ever hit their island. Unfortunately the democratically elected Man-Child was more concerned with football players not standing for the national anthem than the lives of U.S. citizens. Why would a person stand for a flag that has waved over genocide, slavery, and war? Why would the president defend against the destruction of monuments to racist historical figures? Probably the same reason why the pouty-faced, ego-maniac used his executive power to halt Muslims from entering the country and backstab veterans returning from war. Unfortunately, I've been creating cartoons for 12 long years and have never run out of material. As long as chaos and hypocrisy lives, my pen won't run dry.

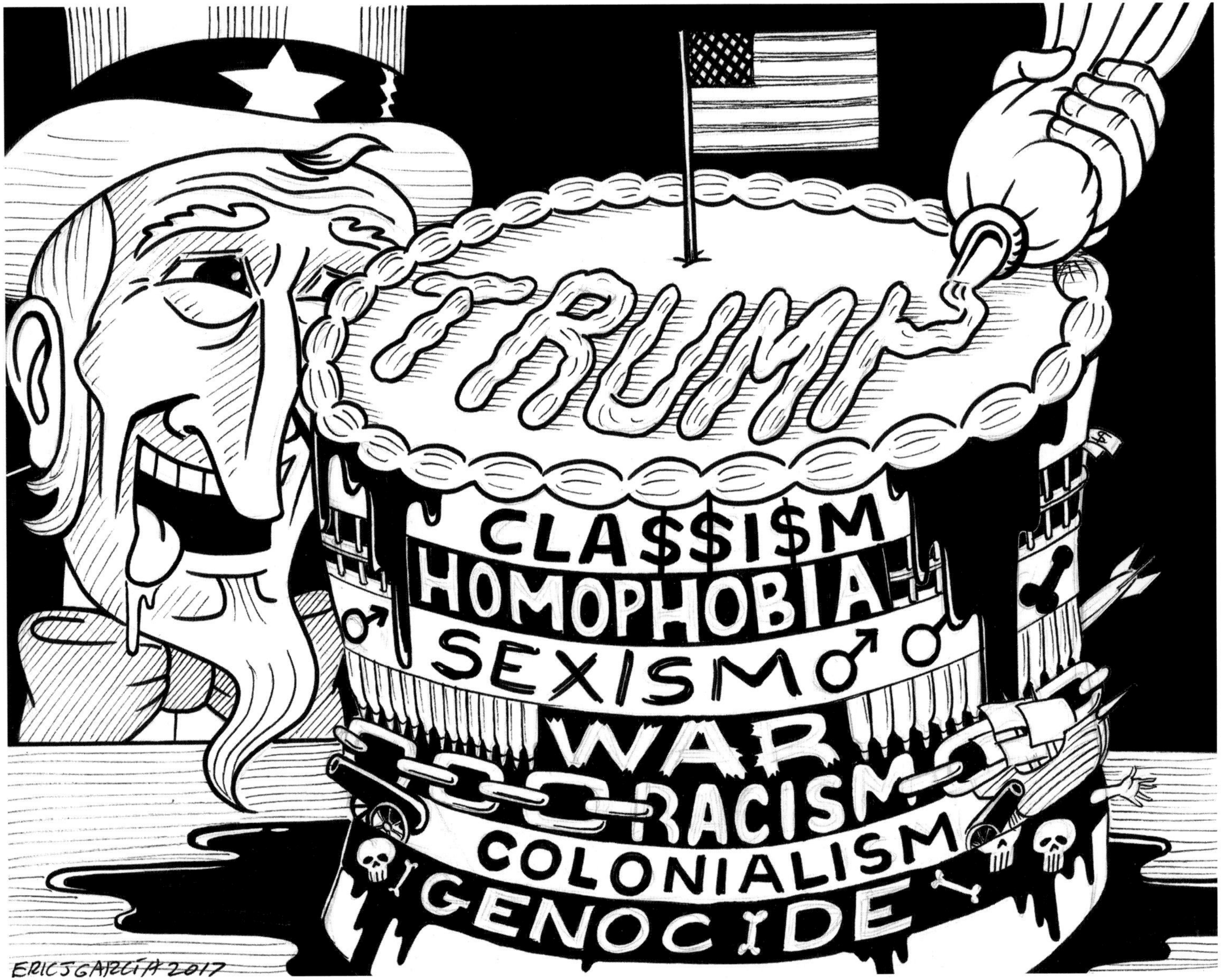
TRUMP
CLA$$I$M
HOMOPHOBIA
SEXISM
WAR
RACISM
COLONIALISM
GENOCIDE
ERICJGARCIA 2017

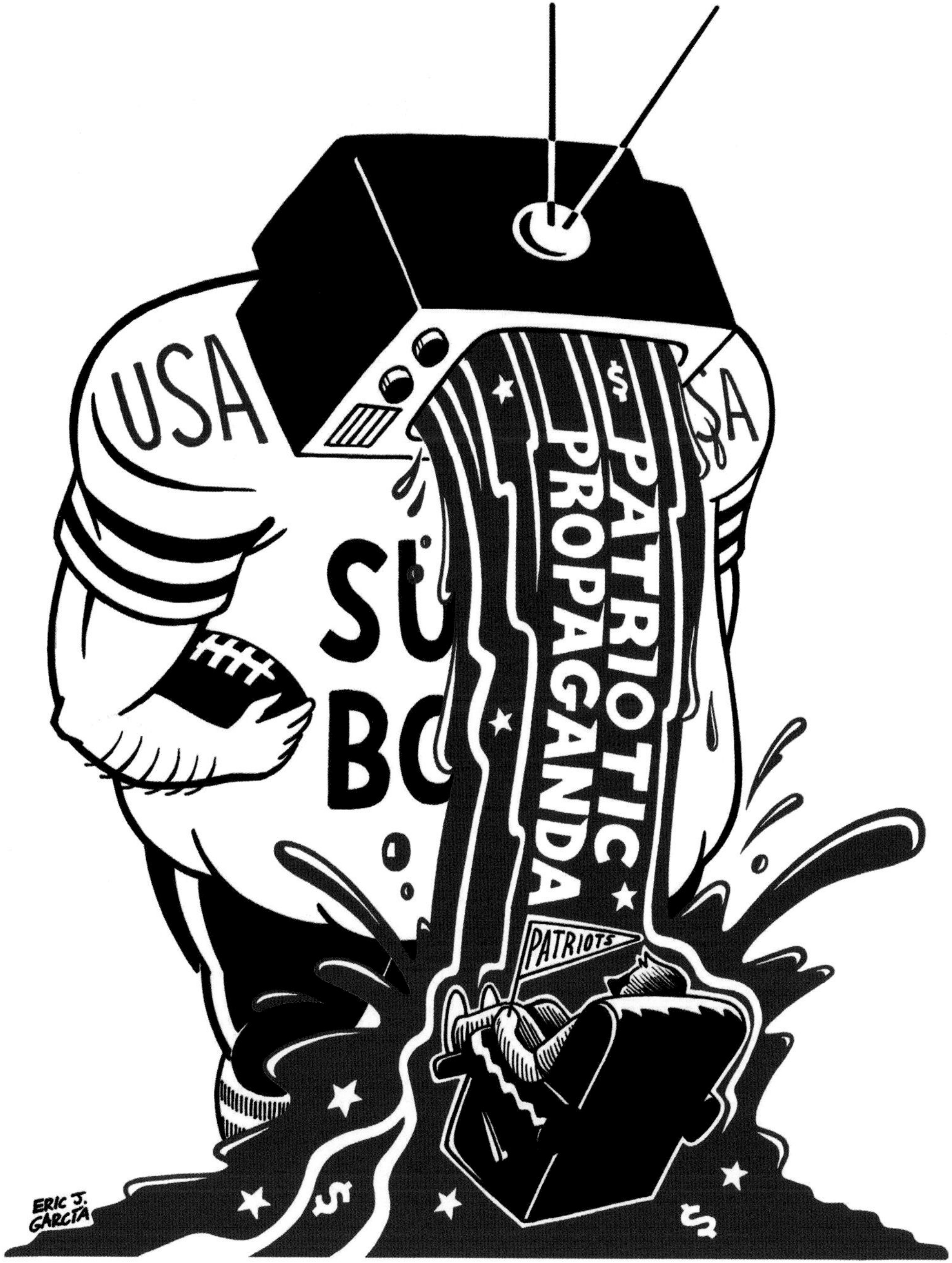
USA
SU
BO
PATRIOTIC
PROPAGANDA
PATRIOTS
ERIC J. GARCÍA

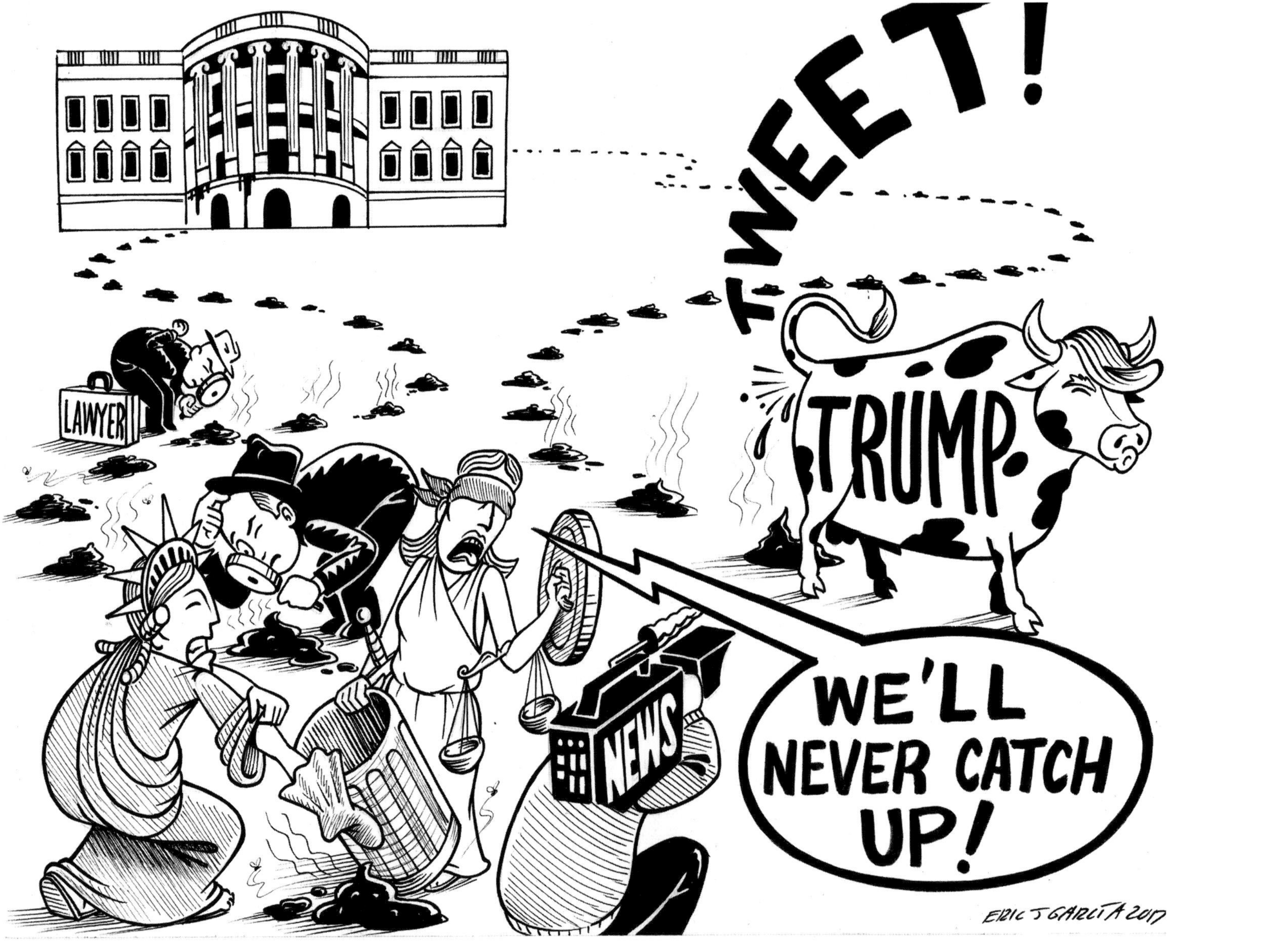
TWEET!
LAWYER
TRUMP
NEWS
WE'LL NEVER CATCH UP!
ERIC J GARCIA 2017

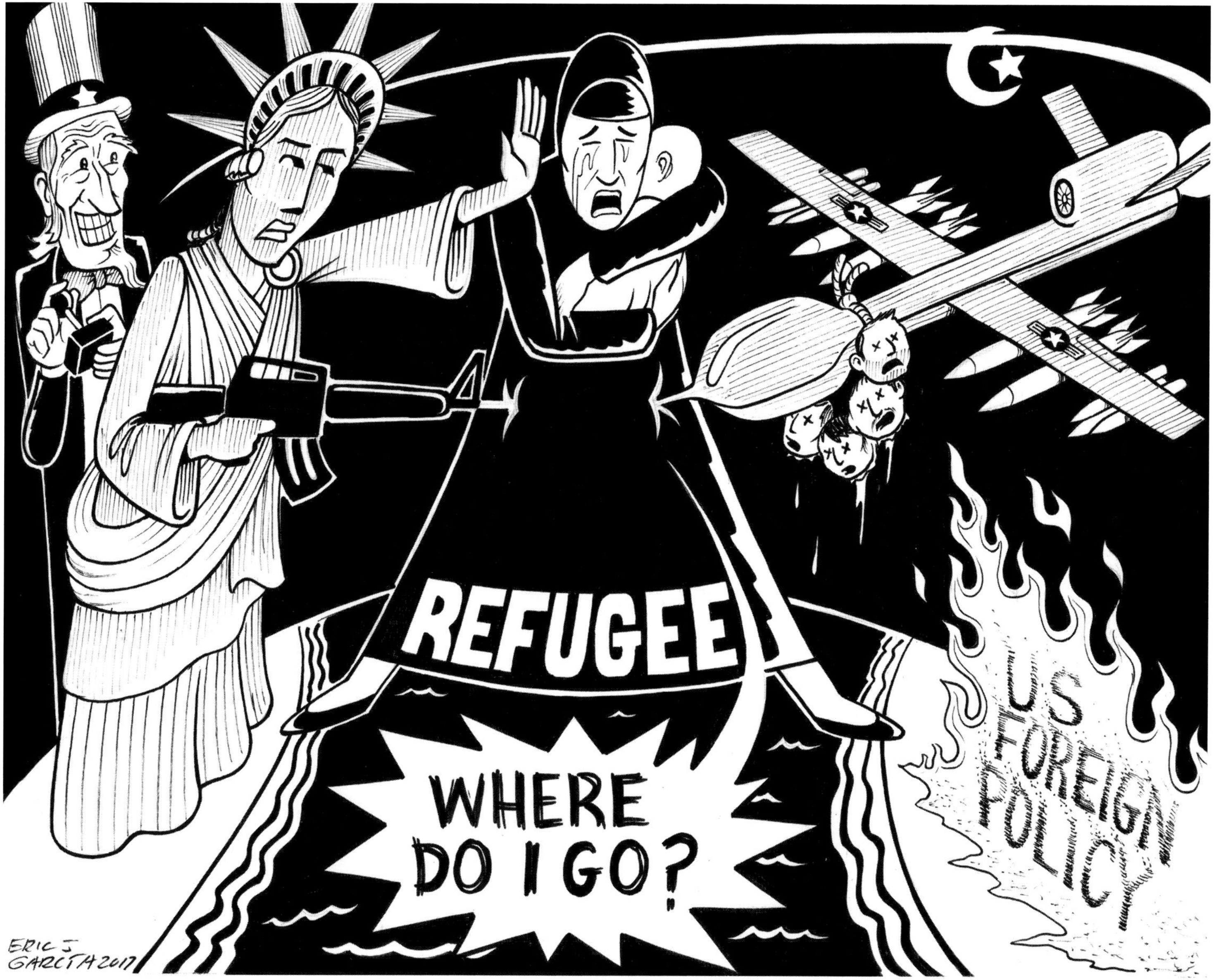
REFUGEE
WHERE DO I GO?
US FOREIGN POLICY
ERIC J GARCIA 2017

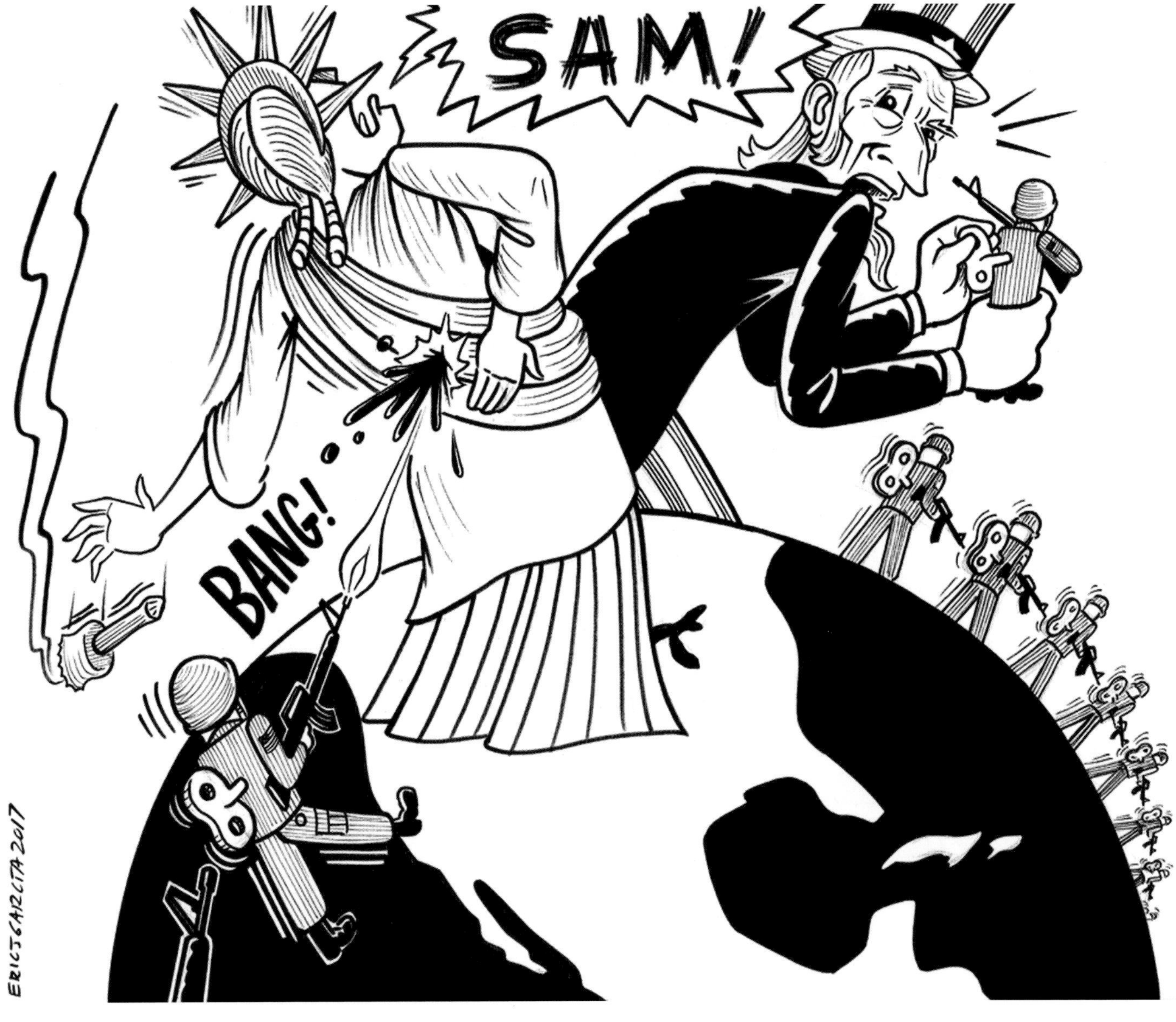
SAM!
BANG!
ERIC J GARCIA 2017

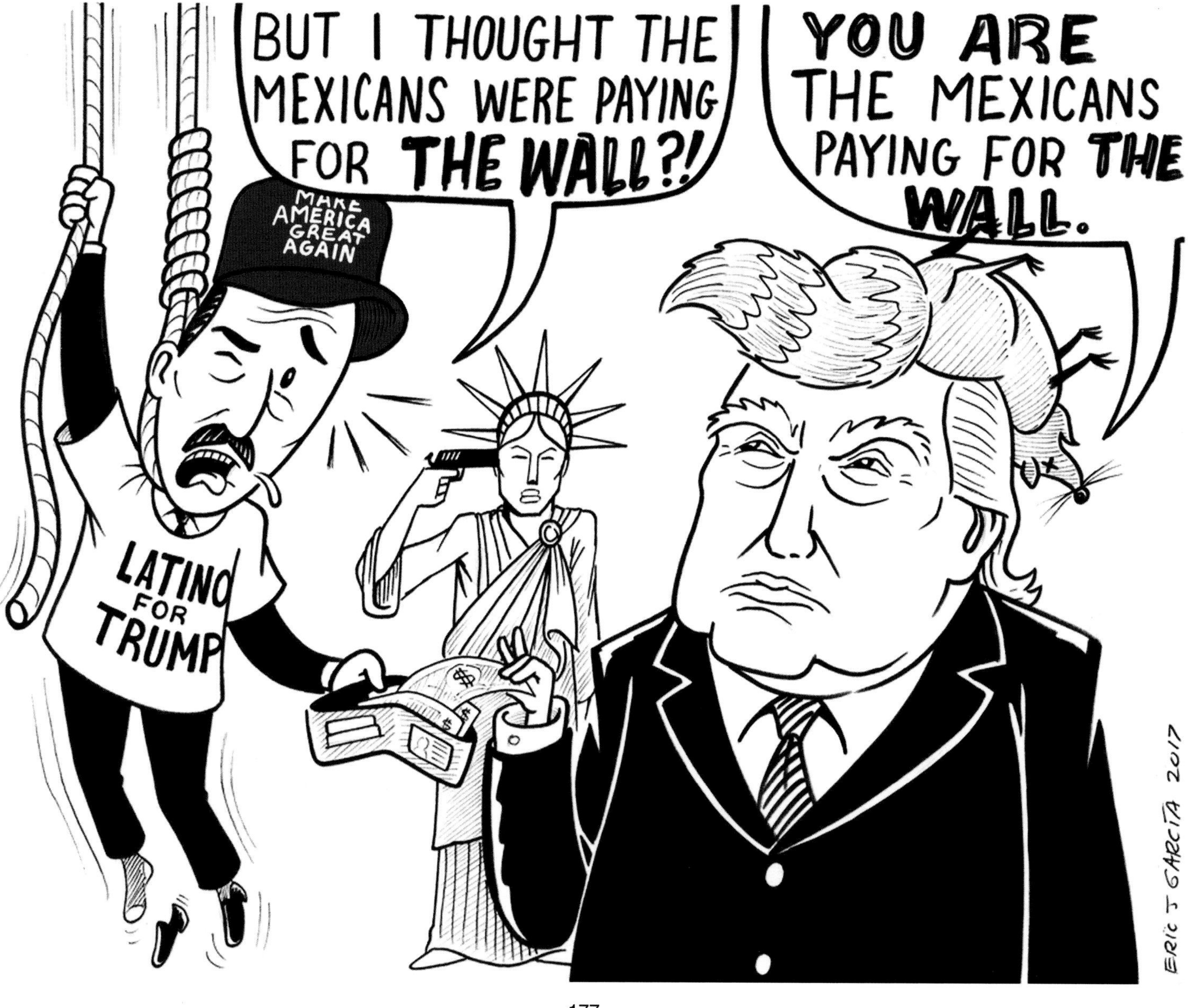
BUT I THOUGHT THE MEXICANS WERE PAYING FOR THE WALL?!
YOU ARE THE MEXICANS PAYING FOR THE WALL.
MAKE AMERICA GREAT AGAIN
LATINO FOR TRUMP
ERIC J GARCIA 2017

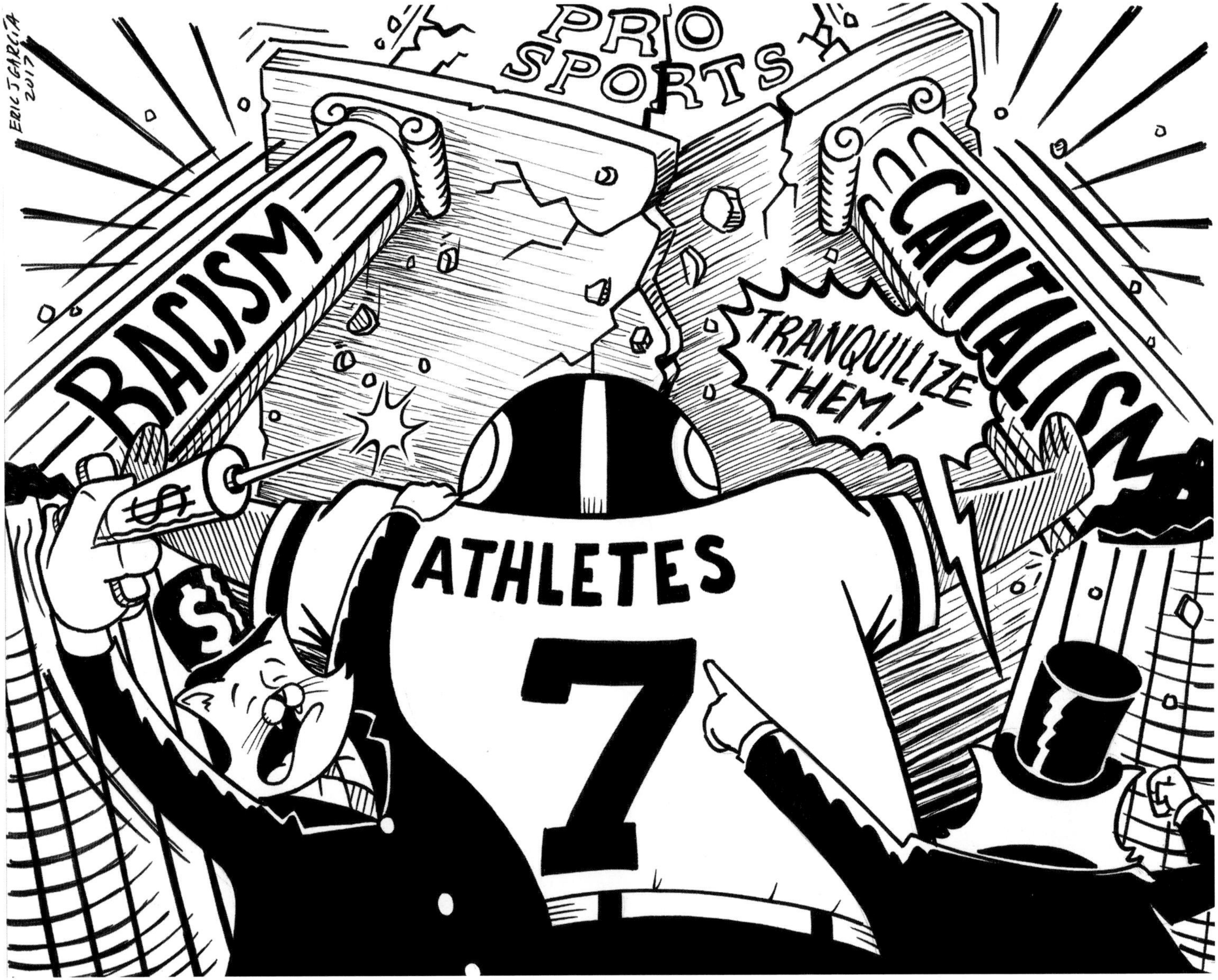
ERIC J GARCIA 2017
PRO SPORTS
RACISM
CAPITALISM
TRANQUILIZE THEM!
ATHLETES
7

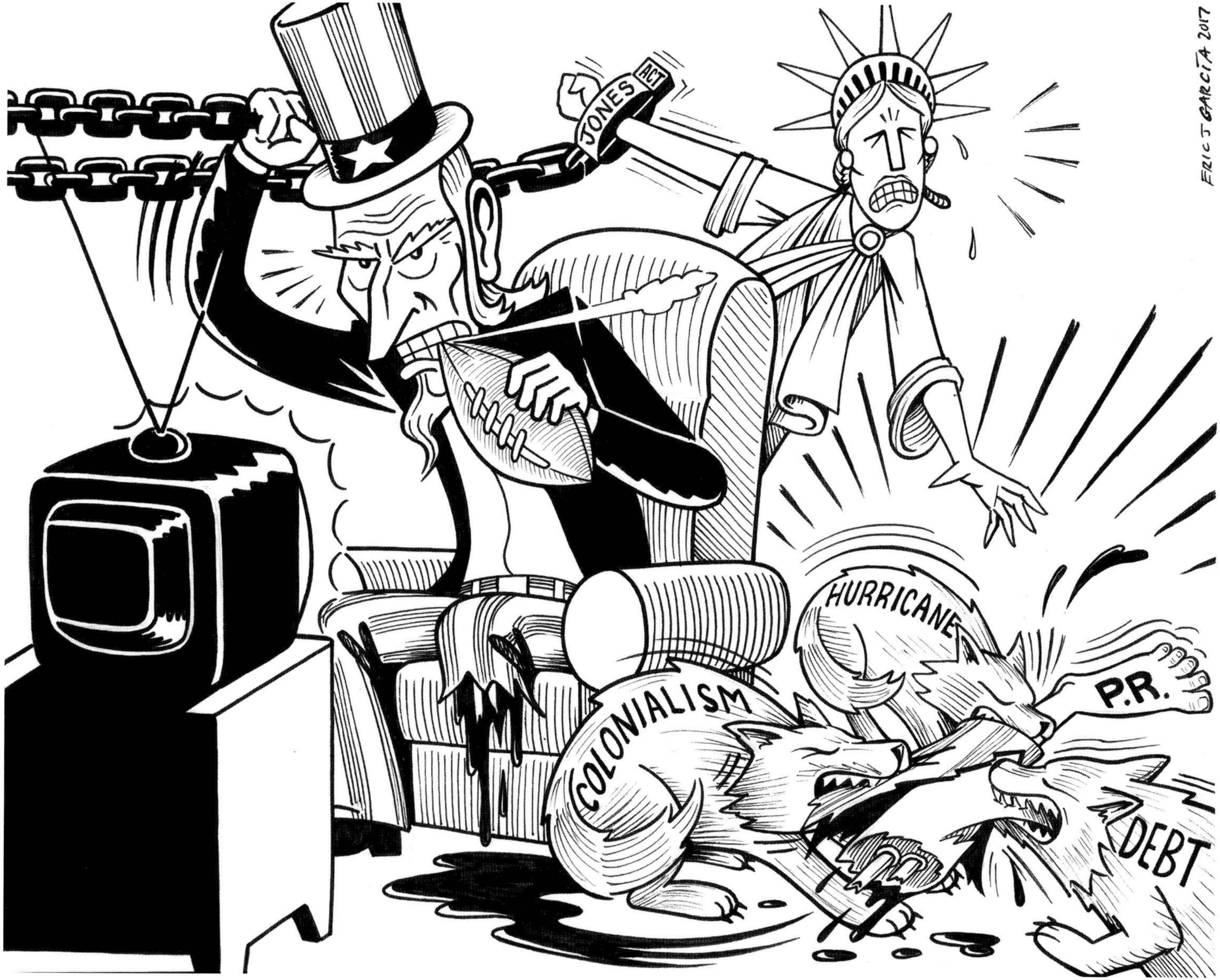
ERIC J GARCIA 2017
JONES ACT
HURRICANE
P.R.
COLONIALISM
DEBT

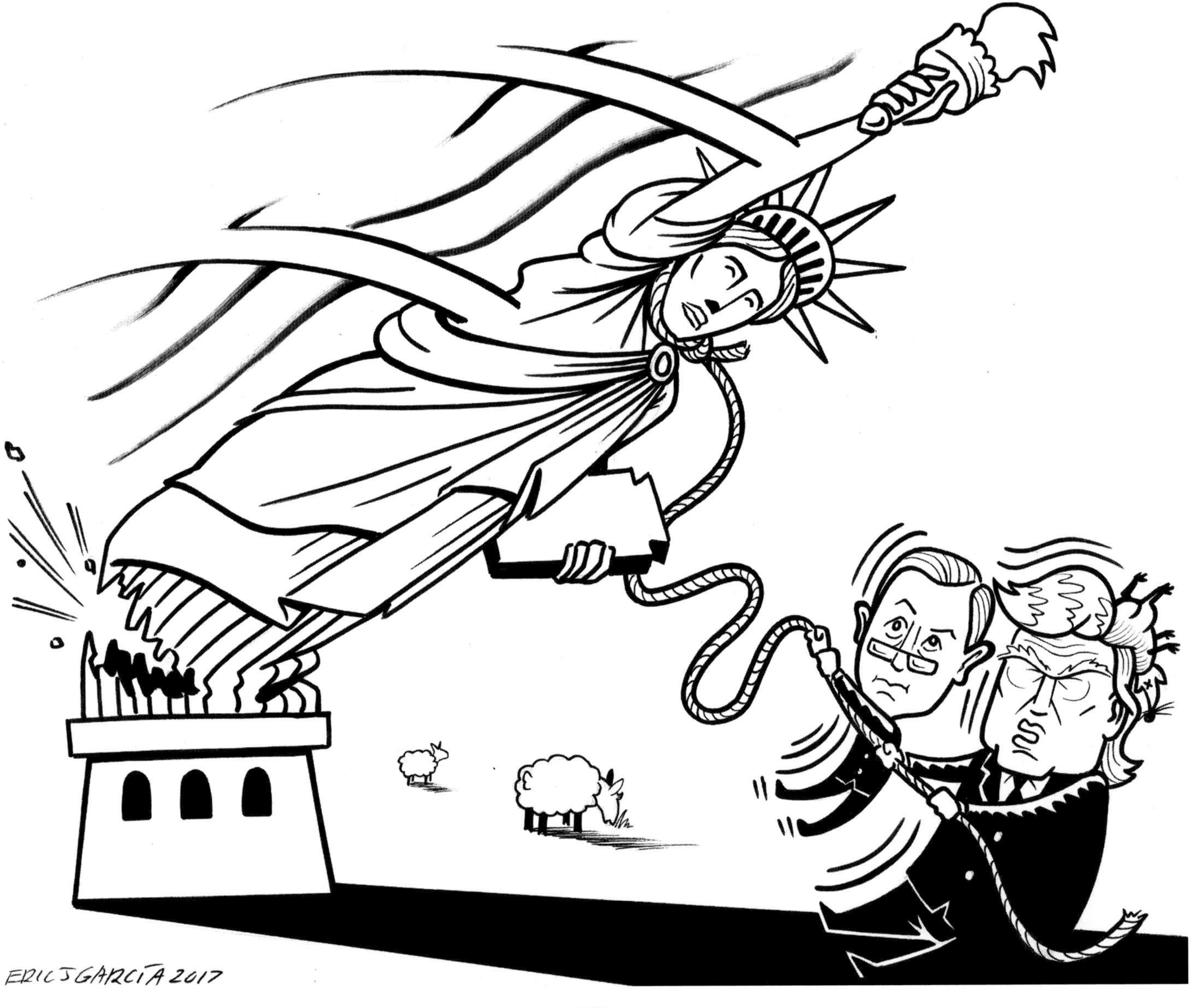
ERIC J GARCIA 2017

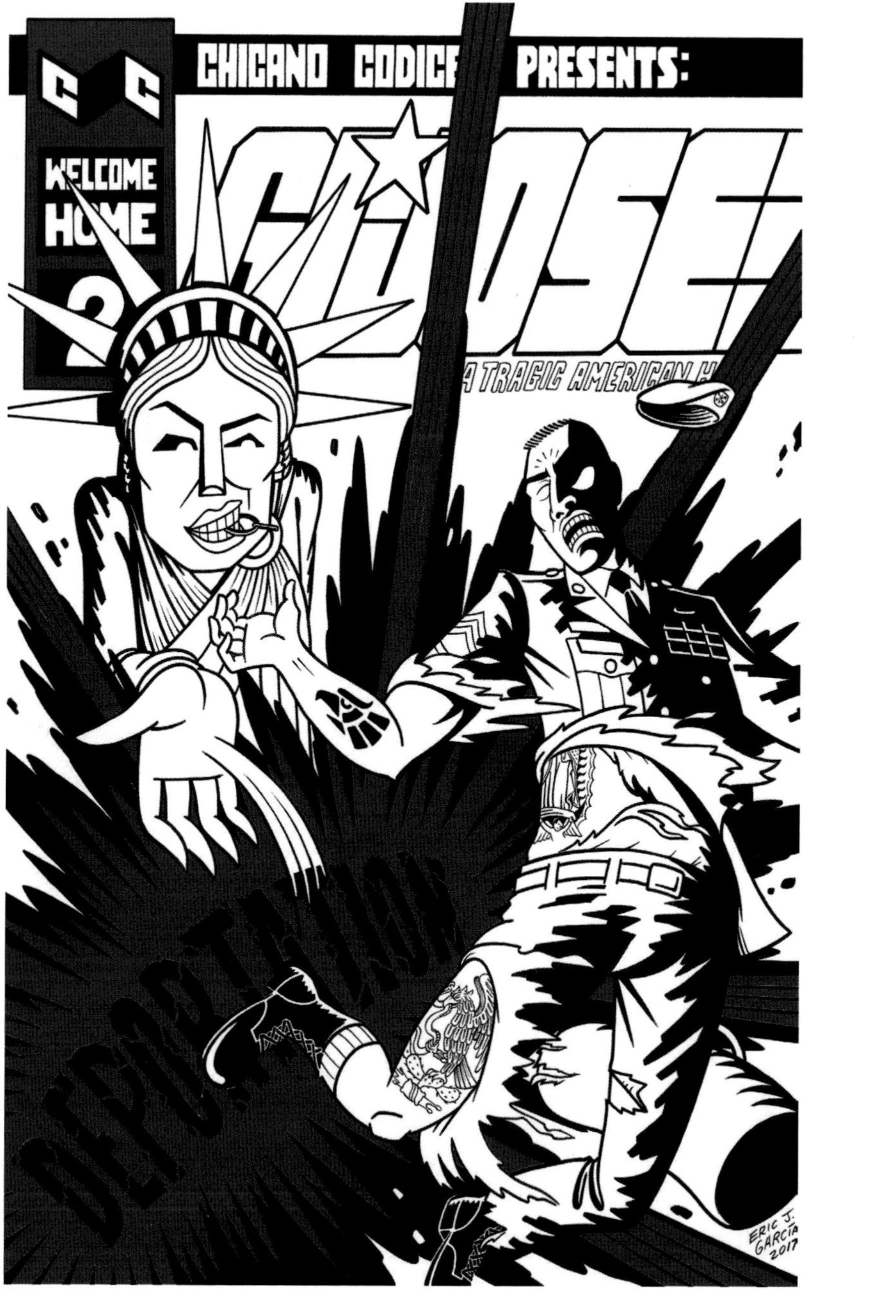

CHICANO CODICE PRESENTS:
WELCOME HOME
2
A TRAGIC AMERICAN
DEPORTATION
ERIC J. GARCIA 2017

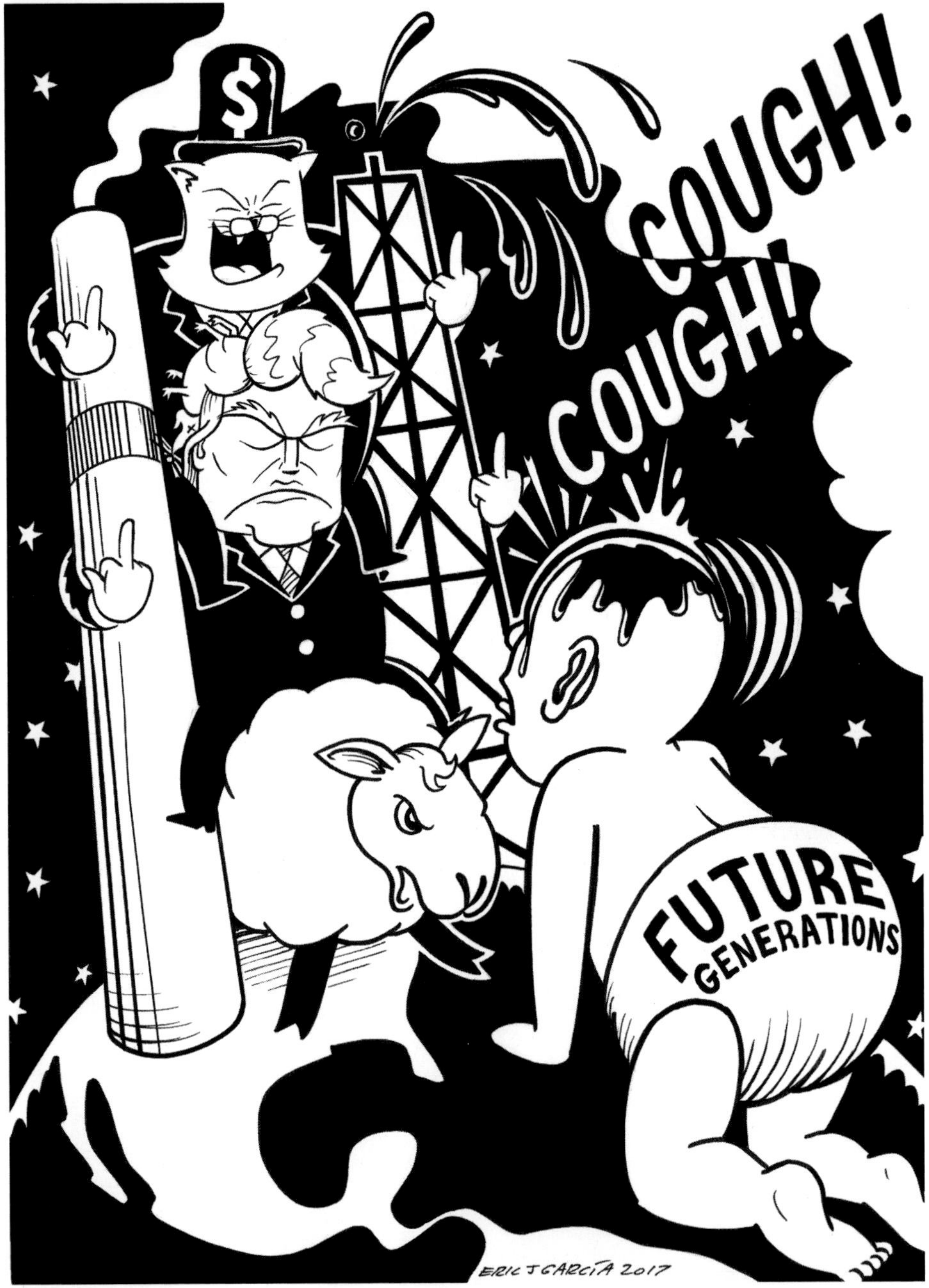
$
COUGH!
COUGH!
FUTURE GENERATIONS
ERIC J GARCÍA 2017

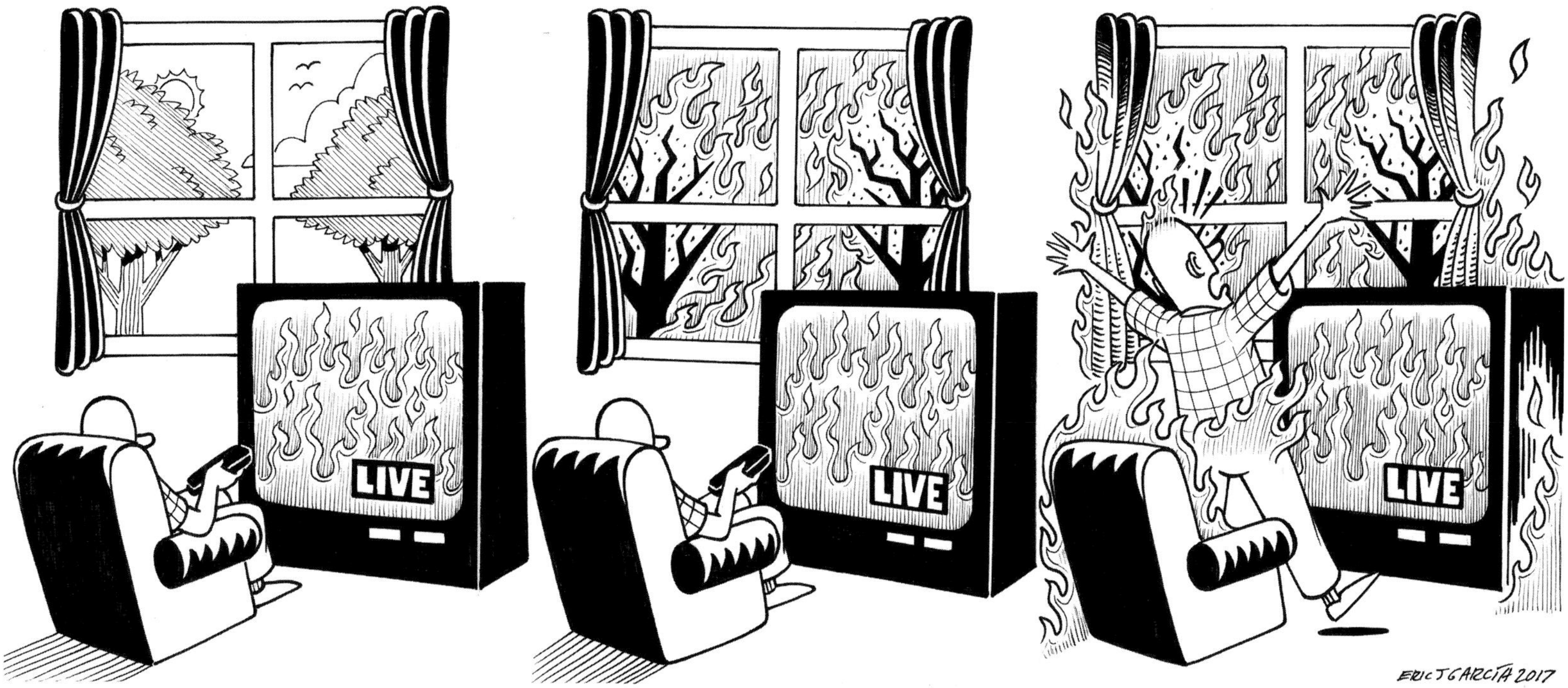
LIVE
LIVE
LIVE
ERIC J GARCÍA 2017

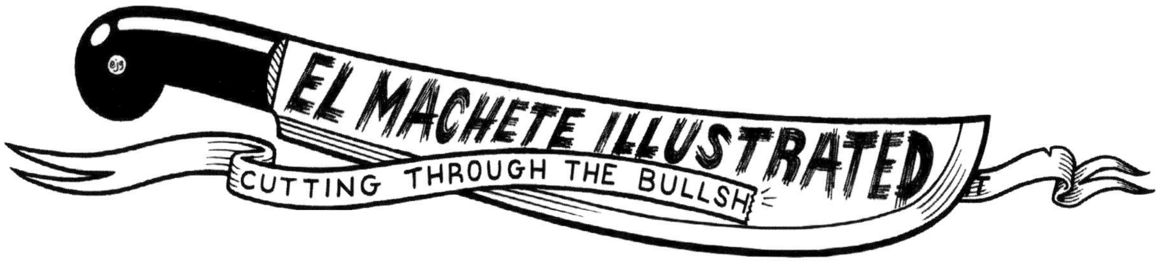
EL MACHETE ILLUSTRATED
CUTTING THROUGH THE BULLSH

Epilogue

by Dr. Theresa Avila
School of Transborder Studies, Arizona State University

Cutting through History: The Political Cartoons of Eric J. García

Our history typically describes the discovery and colonization of the Americas through the lens of European explorers, such as Christopher Columbus and Hernán Cortez, and omits the experience of the indigenous people of the continent. “Look What I’ve Discovered” (2004) presents an alternative perspective of the exploration and conquest of the Americas. In the image, the artist flips the roles of assumed relational power between discoverers and discovered or conquerors and conquered. This version or counter-memory revises, re-frames and re-focuses the dominant narrative of history by introducing the experience of those not typically acknowledged as active agents in history.

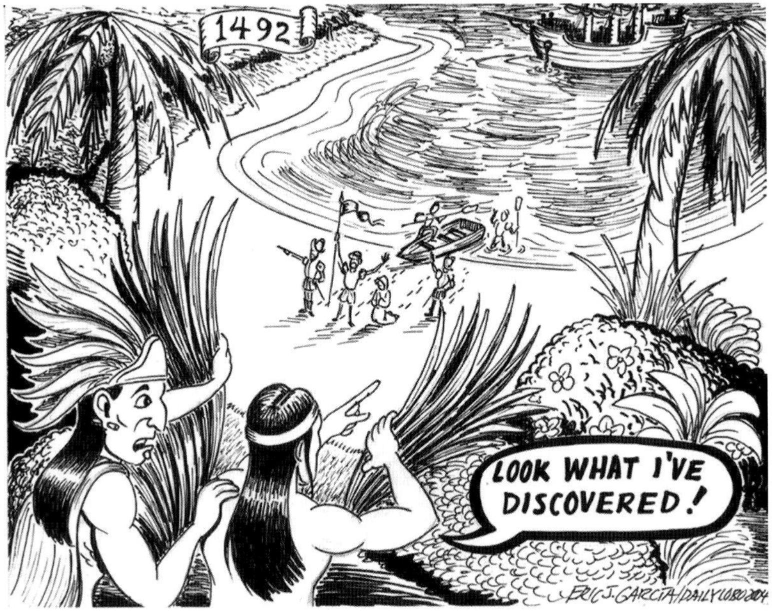
1492
LOOK WHAT I'VE DISCOVERED!
ERIC J. GARCIA/DAILY LOBO 2004

Cartoonists strip away the pretense of neutrality and reveal the biases often hidden in history and journalism. Through recognizable national symbols, figures, and story references, Eric García grounds his cartoons within the diversity of the United States. Mainstream media in the U.S. typically narrates current events for an audience who is assumed to be the “average” citizen or Anglo Saxon or white and conservative. Negotiating his own perspective and position, García (re)figures Latinos within U.S. history and freshens contemporary issues through a view distinct from what is typically found in U.S. mainstream media.

García's cartoons are disruptive and irreverent, lacing dark humor with satire to mock and lampoon his targets. García's visual language of resistance is anchored to a long history of print culture, satirical imagery, and a language of protest. The cartoons function as critical tools to advocate for social and political change that reaches back to include the graphic works by Honoré Daumier and Francisco Goya. To comprehend the significance of García's cartoons, it is important to remember the centrality of art, and print culture in particular, to counter-hegemonic social projects that oppose systems, institutions, and actions that oppress and disenfranchise. Particularly significant to García's approach to art is the work of Mexican modern artists and Chicano artists, such as Jose Guadalupe Posada, member artists of El Taller de Gráfica Popular, Enrique Chagoya, and Rey Martin Abeyta. How García and his artwork intersect with these artists is the focus of this essay.

Jose Guadalupe Posada (1852–1913) was a graphic artist prolific in the production of satirical caricatures. Posada generated material for popular consumption, which included news items, morality lessons, crime stories, tales of miracles, observations on news and politics, and corridos or songs. The artist is generally remembered for his humorous Calaveras, or satirical skeletal characters, that served as stand-ins for figural subjects in a vast amount of his work. The projection of current issues and problems onto skeleton figures permitted Posada greater latitude in making critical commentary on political figures and elite members of society.

JOSE GUADALUPE
POSADA
TIO SAM
GATO GORDO
MALVERDE
ACTIVISM
1852-1913

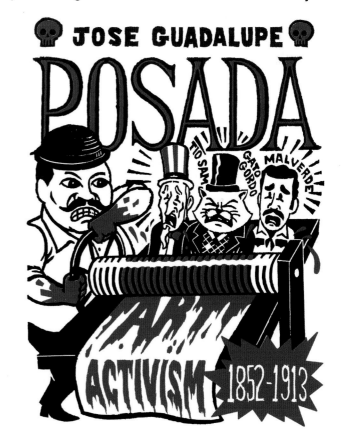

García has made a number of visual tributes to Posada, which indicate his admiration. However, it is a focus on current events and issues, a humorous approach, and an affinity for and appeal to the common man that connects both of these artists. In particular, caricatures of contemporary political figures are a common motif in the work of both artists. And although skeleton figures make their way into García's work, it is his treatment and repetitive application of Uncle Sam and the Statue of Liberty that I liken to Posada's calaveras. García portrays these two figures as a domestic couple. Uncle Sam represents U.S. right-wing conservatives. Lady Liberty represents the liberals, always questioning him. She is often disturbed and protests his antics but, nonetheless she remains always by his side. Much like the lives of calaveras in Posada's work who confront and are affected by the political wrongs and social ills of the day, so too do Uncle Sam and Lady Liberty confront the actions of the U.S. government and their resulting consequences. With mastery, both artists illustrate contemporary times, making us laugh and cry, while also calling us out on our complicity or actions.

The Taller de Gráfica Popular (Workshop for Popular Graphic Art) or TGP, a graphic art collective founded in Mexico City in 1937, also set precedent for García on many fronts. The member artists of the TGP operated as activist and educators who politicized the focus of their work. García also shares with the TGP's prints a common context of struggle where visual modes of resistance are deployed in the furthering of transformative social movements and actions. As activists, the artist members of the TGP promoted and lobbied for the improvement of social and political conditions in Mexico as they argued for human rights and civil liberties. In alignment with political protest, García's cartoons are important sites of articulation, contestation, negotiation, and agency. García's work echoes the cries of the TGP in his own denunciations of the corrupt and demands for the oppressed and victimized. Additionally, both the TGP and García adhere to artisanal modes of production through the physical labor they exert as they make by hand their prints and cartoons. Furthermore, each understands and is highly skilled in the production of readable and recognizable images that speak to the masses at every level of society. Additionally, many of the TGP member artists worked for and with the Ministry of Education of Mexico in its literacy campaign in rural areas, which served as a point of service, education, and connection. Similar interventions by García include his work with community and youth in various roles as artist, mentor, and teacher.

A more contemporary influence on García's cartoons is the work of Enrique Chagoya. Both artists address, critique, and navigate issues through a recognizable and understandable language. In his work Chagoya incorporates elements that refer to his own life experiences and through secular, popular, and religious symbols addresses the continued clashes between the United States, Latin America, and the world. Similarly, García too engages artistic, historic, and culturally specific iconography in his images to make connections to the past, traditions, and with a particular audience. The incorporation of a recognizable visual language resonates with pop culture as a mechanism to draw audiences in to examine and discuss complex issues. In this vein, both artists build on traditions found in Mexican art, which locates their work within a particular genealogy of resistance that extends back to the TGP and Posada. And, as is typical of satirical work, Chagoya too utilizes humor.

Like García, artist Ray Martin Abeyta was born and raised in New Mexico. As a result, these two artists share an affinity and heritage that is grounded within a unique backdrop specific to their home state. Abeyta's images reflect his New Mexican roots through a Spanish Colonial Baroque style, subject matter, and symbols. García's references to home are grounded in the visual, as well as in rebellion that extends to the Chicano Movement and the efforts by New Mexican Reies Lopez Tijerina, who led a struggle to restore New Mexican land grants to the descendants of their Spanish colonial and Mexican owners. Although both Abeyta and García have strong ties to their home state, they also both speak to a larger Latino context by addressing national and global issues and contemporary events and subjects. These two artists radicalize art as they incorporate their unique Nuevo Hispano perspectives, histories, and culture, and they challenge mainstream art and media to include them as Latino artists and historians. The efforts by these artists are crucial, because if history is knowable through images, then we need to make sure that all people, perspectives, and issues are represented.

García bombastically approaches the social and political situations that move him to put pen to paper, or rather his blade to the heart of the issues. Through his art, García is "Cutting through the Bullshit," which is how he literally frames his cartoons for his online venue.

Here, a large machete knife extends horizontally across the top of each drawing with the words "El Machete Illustrated" filling in the blade. A ribbon that runs across reads, "Cutting through the Bullsh." More than a trademark, this rallying cry motivates García's illustrations. Large cleaver-like knives are traditionally used for agrarian and utilitarian purposes throughout Latin America. Machetes also have a long history as popular weapons of the lower classes in rebellions, such as the Mexican Revolution when small landowners and agrarian laborers of the south of Mexico turned their daily attire and tools into their military uniforms and weapons. Therefore, the machete operates as a symbol that invokes rebellion and the common man's battle against oppressive forces. As a framing device both physically and contextually, the machete signifies the past and present communities, inequities, and revolutions.

García's weekly production of cartoons combined with their circulation multiplies the potential for impact. As T.V. Reed notes, political dissent and action are galvanized by repeated public displays of alternative political and cultural values.[1] Whereas once a political drawing would enjoy a short life span as an ephemeral object that would be seen once in a daily publication or flyer that would eventually end up thrown out with the trash, García expands the potency of his cartoons by expanding distribution through print in various publications and the internet, and now through this book. Within the internet, within an archive or database, and within this book, García makes his cartoons available indefinitely for contemplation and inspiration as a text that can be studied and contribute to ongoing discussion around the topics they address.

García's cartoons are historical text, and also operate as social witness and a call to arms. It is one thing to stand idly by and claim to not know or understand how things go wrong, but when you are confronted by a very clear picture by García that documents the culprits and victims of everyday injustices, corruption, and atrocities, it is hard to claim ignorance and turn a blind eye. In turn, to not act makes us complicit. The figures in García's cartoons often include nations and governments, systems and institutions, oppressors and violators, as well as those oppressed and violated. Most importantly the figures in García's cartoons are us . . . our country, our society, and our experience. His political cartoons are funny, until we realize that what he highlights, pokes fun

1. T.V. Reed, *The Art of Protest: Culture and Activism from the Civil Rights Movement to the Streets of Seattle* (Minneapolis: University of Minnesota Press, 2005): xiv.

at, and critiques is our reality. The raw sentiments in cartoons expose and critique problems and injustice, while they also demand viewers to confront their own roles and whether they are part of the problem or the solution. Through his cartoons, García cuts through the bullshit, and he asks us to do the same.

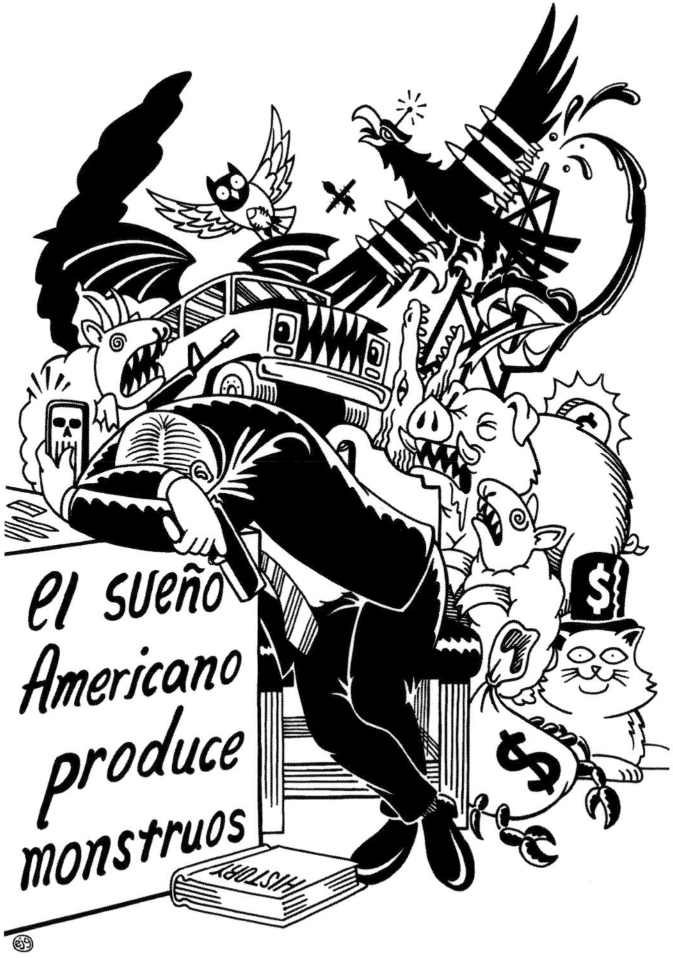
el sueño Americano produce monstruos
HISTORY
$
$

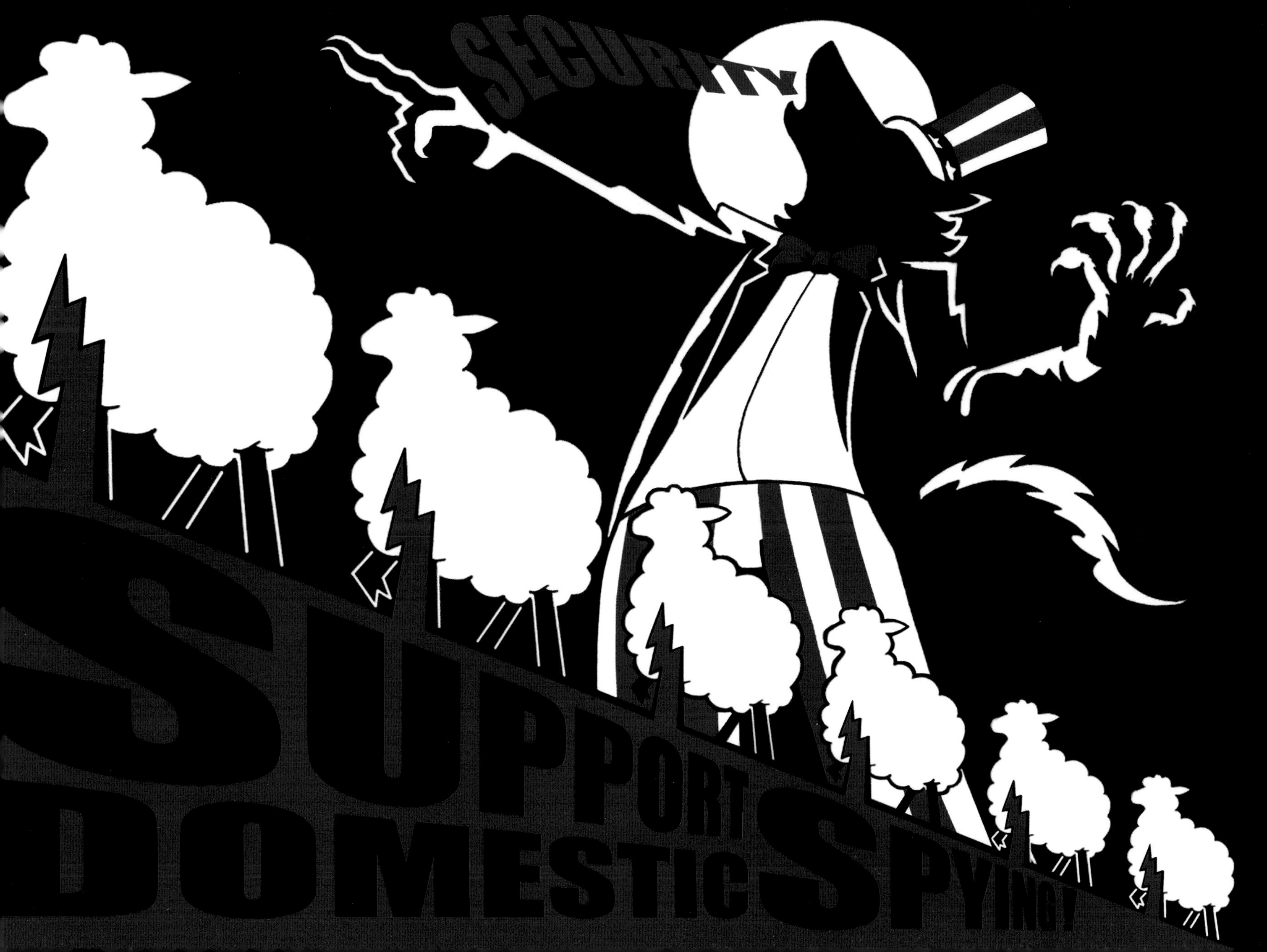
SECURITY
SUPPORT DOMESTIC SPYING!

LATINOGRAPHIX
Frederick Luis Aldama, Series Editor

This series showcases trade graphic and comic books—graphic novels, memoir, nonfiction, and more—by Latinx writers and artists. The series aims to be rich and complex, bringing on projects with any balance of text and visual narrative, from larger graphic narratives to collections of vignettes or serial comics, in color and black and white, both fiction and nonfiction. Projects in the series take up themes of all kinds, exploring topics from immigration to family, education to identity. The series provides a place for exploration and boundary pushing and celebrates hybridity, experimentation, and creativity. Projects are produced with quality and care and exemplify the full breadth of creative visual work being created by today's Latinx artists.

Drawing on Anger: Portraits of U.S. Hypocrisy
Eric J. García

Angelitos: A Graphic Novel
Ilan Stavans and Santiago Cohen

Diary of a Reluctant Dreamer: Undocumented Vignettes from a Pre-American Life
Alberto Ledesma